The Cambridge Footlights

RELATED TITLES

A Director's Guide to the Art of Stand-Up
Chris Head

Affair of the Heart: British Theatre from 1992 to 2020
Michael Billington

Alternative Comedy: 1979 and the Reinvention of British Stand-Up
Oliver Double

Dark Matter: Independent Filmmaking in the 21st Century
Michael Winterbottom

Off the Mic: The World's Best Stand-Up Comedians Get Serious About Comedy
Deborah Frances-White and Marsha Shandur

One Public: New York's Public Theater in the Era of Oskar Eustis
Kevin Landis

Questors, Jesters and Renegades: The Story of Britain's Amateur Theatre
Michael Coveney

The Cambridge Footlights

A Very British Comedy Institution

Robert Sellers

methuen | drama
LONDON · NEW YORK · OXFORD · NEW DELHI · SYDNEY

METHUEN DRAMA
Bloomsbury Publishing Plc, 50 Bedford Square, London, WC1B 3DP, UK
Bloomsbury Publishing Inc, 1359 Broadway, New York, NY 10018, USA
Bloomsbury Publishing Ireland, 29 Earlsfort Terrace, Dublin 2, D02 AY28, Ireland

BLOOMSBURY, METHUEN DRAMA and the Methuen Drama logo are trademarks of
Bloomsbury Publishing Plc

First published in Great Britain 2026

Copyright © Robert Sellers, 2026

Robert Sellers has asserted his right under the Copyright, Designs and Patents Act,
1988, to be identified as Author of this work.

For legal purposes the Acknowledgements on p. ix constitute an extension of this copyright page.

Cover design: Ben Anslow
Cover image Crayon lightbulb (© PRILL Mediendesign / Alamy)

All rights reserved. No part of this publication may be: i) reproduced or transmitted in any form, electronic or mechanical, including photocopying, recording or by means of any information storage or retrieval system without prior permission in writing from the publishers; or ii) used or reproduced in any way for the training, development or operation of artificial intelligence (AI) technologies, including generative AI technologies. The rights holders expressly reserve this publication from the text and data mining exception as per Article 4(3) of the Digital Single Market Directive (EU) 2019/790.

Bloomsbury Publishing Plc does not have any control over, or responsibility for, any third-party websites referred to or in this book. All internet addresses given in this book were correct at the time of going to press. The author and publisher regret any inconvenience caused if addresses have changed or sites have ceased to exist, but can accept no responsibility for any such changes.

Library of Congress Cataloging-in-Publication Data

Names: Sellers, Robert author
Title: The Cambridge Footlights : a very British comedy institution / Robert Sellers.
Description: London ; New York : Methuen Drama, 2026. | Includes bibliographical references and index.
| Summary: "In the first detailed history of the Cambridge Footlights in over 40 years, Robert Sellers chronicles the evolution of Britain's oldest student sketch comedy troupe, from its creation in the 1880s to the present. Its alumni have set the tone of cultural eras from the 1960s to today, via shows such as Beyond the Fringe, Monty Python, The Goodies, Not the Nine O'Clock News and, more recently, Peep Show, QI and The Great British Bake-Off. This amusing and diverting book includes first-hand interviews with former Footlights alumni and extracts from past Footlights productions"-- Provided by publisher.
Identifiers: LCCN 2025026548 | ISBN 9781350412187 hardback | ISBN 9781350412194 pdf |
ISBN 9781350412200 epub
Subjects: LCSH: Footlights Dramatic Club—History
Classification: LCC PN2599.5.T54 S45 2026
LC record available at https://lccn.loc.gov/

ISBN:	HB:	978-1-3504-1218-7
	ePDF:	978-1-3504-1219-4
	eBook:	978-1-3504-1220-0

Typeset by RefineCatch Limited, Bungay, Suffolk
Printed and bound in Great Britain

For product safety related questions contact productsafety@bloomsbury.com.

To find out more about our authors and books visit www.bloomsbury.com
and sign up for our newsletters.

CONTENTS

List of Illustrations vii
Acknowledgements ix

Introduction 1
1 Beyond the Fringe 3
2 Cheer-Oh Cambridge 7
3 Cabbages and Kings 21
4 The Last Laugh 31
5 I Thought I Saw It Move 37
6 A Clump of Plinths 45
7 Stuff What Dreams Are Made Of 51
8 Supernatural Gas 65
9 Norman Ruins 79
10 A Kick in the Stalls 91
11 The Cellar Tapes 101
12 Hawaiian Cheese Party 111
13 Another Fine Mess 125
14 Back and Beyond 141
15 Barracuda Jazz Option 155
16 Emotional Baggage 171

17 Far Too Happy 183

18 Devils 197

19 Are We There Yet? 213

20 Gone With the Clappers 231

Notes 235
Bibliography 269
Index 271

ILLUSTRATIONS

1.1	The cast of *Beyond the Fringe*	5
2.1	Norman Hartnell in drag in a variety of poses	12
2.2	Cambridge University Footlights with Victor Stiebel. The cast of the 1927 revue *Please Tell Others*	14
2.3	Members of the Cambridge Footlights at a dress rehearsal for the pantomime *Cinderella*. The undergraduate cast perform a cross-dressing number as a beauty chorus. 23 November 1932	15
6.1	The famous 1963 Footlights revue *A Clump Of Plinths*. 'Cambridge Circus' New Revue at the Lyric Theatre John Cleese (left), Bill Oddie (front sitting with trumpet) and Tim Brooke Taylor (glasses and hat)	46
7.1	The cast of the 1964 revue *Stuff What Dreams Are Made Of* at Cambridge University, 9 March 1964	54
7.2	Programme for the 1964 revue	54
8.1	Poster for the 1967 revue *Supernatural Gas*	68
8.2	Poster for the 1968 revue *Turns of the Century*	71
11.1	The cast of the 1981 revue, *The Cellar Tapes*. Actors (clockwise from back left) Stephen Fry, Tony Slattery, Paul Shearer, Hugh Laurie, Emma Thompson and Penny Dwyer in the BBC television show *The Cambridge Footlights Review*, 6 February 1982	107
12.1	The cast of the 1983 revue, *Hawaiian Cheese Party*, perform a spoof World Cup song	114
13.1	Poster for the 1986 revue, *Another Fine Mess*	133
15.1	Poster for the 1992 Footlights panto, *Peter Pan*	161
15.2	The Footlights writing cottage in Bacton, Norfolk. Left to right: Leila Hackett, Robert Webb, Beth Chalmers, Matthew Holness, Jonathan Dryden Taylor, Barunka O'Shaughnessy, James Bachman and David Mitchell	165
16.1	Jesus College May Ball, 1996. Left to right: Richard Ayoade, John Oliver, Lucy Montgomery and Neda Daneshzadeh	171
17.1	The 2005 Footlights tour performing at the Edinburgh Fringe	191
17.2	The 2005 pantomime, *Spartacus*	192

18.1	Visiting the ADC Theatre, Stephen Fry was introduced to the current Footlights president, Abi Tedder. 'He called me "Madam President" the whole time and I was delighted,' says Abi	199
19.1	Jade Franks and Adedamola Laoye (president after Jade) on stage in 2020 during the Covid-19 pandemic	222
19.2	The ADC Theatre, Cambridge, home of the Footlights	223

ACKNOWLEDGEMENTS

The author wishes to express his sincere thanks to the following people for sharing some of their Footlights memories. Mary Allen, Clive Anderson, Ben Ashenden, Pete Atkin, James Bachman, David Baddiel, Tom Bell, Martin Bergman, Pete Bradshaw, Katie Breathwick, Barry Brown, Spencer Brown, John Cameron, Angela Channell, Chris Stuart-Clark, Anna Cottis, Richard Crane, Helen Cripps, Sarah Dunant, Henry Eliot, Chris England, Mark Evans, John Finnemore, Peter Firth, Jade Franks, Michael Frayn, Robin French, Graeme Garden, Brian Gascoigne, Stefan Golaszewski, David Gooderson, Matt Green, Izzie H-P, Hasan Al-Habib, Nick Hancock, David Hare, Archie Henderson, Amy Hoggart, Matthew Holness, Emily Howes, Adam Al-janabi, Joel Jeske, Simon Jones, Chris Keightley, Naomi Kerbel, John Lloyd, Christopher Luscombe, Alex MacKeith, Andy Mayer, David Mitchell, Jordan Mitchell, Lucy Montgomery, Neil Mullarkey, Jimmy Mulville, Simon Munnery, Henry Naylor, Bill Oddie, Alexander Owen, Sue Heber-Percy, Ruth Pickett, Steve Punt, Frederic Raphael, Jan Ravens, Robert Rowe, Margaret Saunderson, Paul Shearer, Michael Marshall Smith, Geoffrey Strachan, William Sutcliffe, Abi Tedder, John Tothill, Nicola Walker, Ash Weir, Sophie Winkleman, Stephen Wyatt.

Every effort has been made to trace copyright holders and to obtain their permission for the use of copyright material. However, if any have been inadvertently overlooked, the publishers will be pleased, if notified of any omissions, to make the necessary arrangement at the first opportunity.

Introduction

If ever there was a candidate for a 'university' of comedy, the Cambridge Footlights can certainly lay claim to that title. For decades it has been a veritable conveyor belt of the best of British comic talent. Its graduates have shaped the landscape of comedy. Peter Cook was a member, as were three of the Monty Python team (John Cleese, Graham Chapman and Eric Idle), all The Goodies, most of The Mary Whitehouse Experience and two of The Inbetweeners. It's where Fry met Laurie, David Mitchell met Robert Webb, Mel met Sue and Armstrong met Miller. It also spawned the likes of Douglas Adams, David Baddiel, Richard Ayoade and Emma Thompson.

It started innocuously enough, back in 1882, when a group of Cambridge undergraduates organized a cricket match against a team made up of staff from a nearby psychiatric hospital. The following year the same undergraduate team returned, this time as part of a concert party putting on entertainments in surrounding villages, with an emphasis on comedy. Their success was such that it was decided to put these shows on a more permanent footing and the Footlights Dramatic Club was born.

During term, the club produce sketch shows, original comic plays and put on regular smokers, an event where members try out new material; there's even an annual pantomime. The famous Footlights revue is put on every summer, travelling to London and various UK venues, the Edinburgh Fringe, and in more recent years the USA.

The Footlights first came to prominence in 1960 when two of its recent graduates, Peter Cook and Jonathan Miller, joined forces with two recent Oxford graduates, Alan Bennett and Dudley Moore, to create *Beyond the Fringe*. This was a revolutionary stage revue that kick-started the British satire boom of the 1960s. It played the Edinburgh Fringe, the West End and Broadway.

This book covers the history of the Cambridge Footlights, from its origins right up to the present day. Over seventy past members have been interviewed by the author and share their, often amusing, insights, memories and stories of a time that for many was life changing. The book charts the changing tastes and volatile fortunes of the club, which has survived financial turmoil, two World Wars and the recent pandemic. The club has always faced accusations of elitism and privilege, that it has long been an enclave of public-school maleness so the book also charts the sometimes controversial role women have in the Footlights, who for the first eighty years weren't even allowed to become members, to how in recent years the club has moved to being more inclusive and welcoming to people from working class and diverse backgrounds.

1

Beyond the Fringe

What a great idea for a comedy sketch group, get two ex-graduates from Cambridge University and two from Oxford, light the touchpaper, stand back and see what happens. It was a notion borne out of necessity. By 1960, the Edinburgh Festival had grown to such importance it was attracting gate-crashers, theatre and revue groups performing 'unofficially' on the fringes. The festival organizer, Robert Ponsonby, set out to rival them with his own late night comedy show. It was his assistant, an Oxford graduate by the name of John Bassett, who arrived at the idea of a Cambridge/Oxford mix.

From Cambridge, Bassett sought out ex-Footlights star Jonathan Miller, then a junior doctor at University College Hospital in London. It was Miller who recommended fellow Footlights alumnus Peter Cook. On return visits to Cambridge, Miller had seen Cook perform and became fascinated at his approach to comedy, 'at right angles' to everything that had gone before. Bassett then approached Dudley Moore, who he knew from his days at Oxford. At the time, Moore was an accomplished pianist for hire in the burgeoning London jazz scene and hadn't given a career in comedy a moment's thought. Asked to recommend someone else from Oxford, Moore suggested Alan Bennett, whom he had used for one of his Oxford cabaret evenings.

The four met for the first time in an Italian restaurant to explore the possibilities of doing something. The atmosphere was quiet, apprehensive, each of them reluctant to tell a joke in case the other three didn't laugh. Moore eventually lightened the mood by doing an impersonation of Groucho Marx and following a pretty waitress in and out of the kitchen swing doors.

Despite reservations, the group agreed to press forward and were given carte blanche by Ponsonby to devise the show. Moore was to call Miller, 'a powerhouse of enthusiasm and curiosity,'[1] and after meeting Cook for the first time found him both urbane and sophisticated. Bennett was especially dazzled by the fact that Cook wore pointed shoes and had a tailor in Old Compton Street. Cook was already something of a theatrical success, providing sketches for hit West End comedy revues. He had an agent, too, who warned his client not to jeopardize his career by working with these three amateurs. While it's true to say that all four men brought something valuable and different to the show, the bulk of the writing was done by Cook, while Miller naturally gravitated to the role of director.

Beyond the Fringe opened at Edinburgh's Lyceum Theatre on 22 August 1960. Performances quickly sold out and it picked up glowing notices; *Daily Mail* reporter Peter Lewis wrote: 'If the show comes to London I doubt if revue will ever be the same again.' Offers to stage the show in the West End soon came in. Contracts were drawn up. For Miller the fee on offer was ten times what he earned as a junior doctor. For Bennett it was fifteen times what he would be getting as a medieval historian. However, there was some reluctance to accept. Cook and Moore were the most enthusiastic about going to London. Miller and Bennett struggled with their consciences about leaving their professions. In the end they agreed to take the plunge.

The plan was for a couple of try outs first, starting with a week's run at the Cambridge Arts Theatre in April 1961. The show was now very different to what it had been in Edinburgh, with much new material including Cook's now infamous satirical assassination of Prime Minister Harold Macmillan. Not surprisingly, the reception in Cambridge was enthusiastic. The next port of call was Brighton. Here audiences did not find favour with the show and it became a common sight to see people walk out in quiet disgust. During one sketch, 'Aftermyth of War', where Cook's military bigwig sends Miller's hapless young pilot on a suicide mission ('We need a futile gesture at this stage'), at least one audience member, an ex-soldier, did make his views plain. Shaking his fist at the stage the man roared, 'You young bounders don't know anything about it', before storming through the exit.[2] This skit continued to cause some controversy thanks to a misconception that it was ridiculing those who sacrificed their life during the war, whereas the real target was those stiff upper lip heroics so common in war films of the period.

Opening at the Fortune Theatre on 10 May, *Beyond the Fringe* was expected to last no more than six weeks. It ran for over a year. Even the Queen attended a performance. The reception was overwhelming. Both Kenneth Tynan and Bernard Levin, two of the most noted critics of the time, gave the show rave reviews, hailing it as a breakthrough in satire. 'It changed everything,' claims Michael Frayn, the playwright and novelist, who was in the audience on the second night. 'It was disrespectful. I had come out of national service and we all rebelled against the military discipline and we were all rather bolshie, and this sort of bolshie feeling then drifted on into civilian life.'[3]

Before *Beyond the Fringe*, West End revue had been light-hearted affairs, with nothing too controversial. As for the Footlight revues at Cambridge, they always contained an element of poking fun at the establishment, making merry about the masters, traditions and the university's way of life, but it was never too pointed. *Beyond the Fringe* was different. Its comedy had bite and tackled previously untouchable topics such as politics, religion, the monarchy and sex. 'There had been a feeling left over from the war that one should be respectful of authority,' says Frayn, 'and it was just beginning

FIGURE 1.1 *The cast of* Beyond the Fringe, *Archive PL/Alamy Stock Photo.*

to turn at that point.'[4] On the night Michael saw the show a young pair of Tories sat in the seats in front of him, laughing at everything until Cook's Macmillan lampoon. 'The man turned to the girl and said in an appalled whisper, "I say! This is supposed to be the Prime Minister," after which they sat in silence for the rest of the evening.'[5]

Beyond the Fringe had a profound influence on a whole slew of future comedians. Bill Oddie saw it with a group of friends. 'Those of us who were interested in performing comedy worshipped *Beyond the Fringe*.'[6] Eric Idle was still at school when he attended a performance. 'Like everybody else of my generation, I immediately bought the album and learned it all by heart – it really determined my career in comedy.'[7] Incidentally, the cast album was produced by Beatles producer George Martin, who later made use of the audience applause on the Sgt. Pepper LP.

While a new cast took over in London, the original foursome took the show to Broadway in October 1962 and played to packed houses. From a political point of view, they couldn't have timed their appearance any better, with the Cuban Missile Crisis in full swing. President John F. Kennedy came to one performance, with the special red telephone, from which he could order a nuclear attack, temporarily installed in the theatre's box office. Afterwards Kennedy congratulated the cast in their shabby dressing room.

It became especially noticeable during the Broadway run how much Cook and Moore appeared to enjoy working together, especially in moments of improvisation where they naturally sparked off each other, showing early signs of the double act they were soon to become. Inevitably, there was ad-libbing from everyone, along with efforts to make each other corpse on stage, which got worse the longer the run went on. Famously, Miller's wife, Rachel, gave birth in New York to their first child and during a sketch featuring Miller and Bennett, Cook walked onto the stage holding the infant, saying, 'Excuse me, sir, the wife has just delivered this. What should I do with it?' To which Miller replied, 'Just put it in the fridge would you.'[8]

Inevitably, there were tensions amongst the four performers after working and being together for so long. Slowly, the cast began to dissipate. After a year on Broadway, Miller was the first to go. He did not, however, return to medicine but went into television. He was soon followed by Bennett, then Cook, leaving Moore as the last of the original cast before he too departed.

By this time, another British revue had opened on Broadway, featuring wholly ex-graduates from Cambridge University, including John Cleese, Tim Brooke-Taylor, Graham Chapman and Bill Oddie. *Cambridge Circus* sprang from a Footlights revue and, like *Beyond the Fringe*, its success as a West End transfer also led to the chance to conquer America. Together these productions did much to change the landscape of British comedy, giving birth to Monty Python, Pete and Dud, and The Goodies. The Cambridge Footlights was changed by them, too; a club hitherto considered as merely a hobby, a bit of extracurricular fun, was now seen by incoming students as a passport into the world of entertainment. As Robert Webb commented on *Celebrity Mastermind*, when asked what a young aspiring comedian should do, replied, 'Go to Cambridge'. That philosophy really began in the early 1960s. Before that, it was a lark for its first eighty years.

2

Cheer-Oh Cambridge

The origins of the Footlights do not begin in some grand theatre setting, or the backroom of a pub or even in some church hall, but at a cricket match in the grounds of a psychiatric hospital. In 1882, a cricket match took place organized by Cambridge undergraduates against a team made up of staff from the nearby Fulbourn psychiatric hospital. Leading the university eleven was Morten Henry Cotton, a student at Christ's College.

The following February, Cotton and his team returned to Fulbourn as part of a concert party putting on entertainments in surrounding villages, with an emphasis on comedy. Such was their success, even coming to the attention of a local newspaper, that Cotton was encouraged to put these shows on a more permanent footing. In this he was helped by Henry Arthur Hickin of Corpus Christi College. Indeed, it was Hickin who came up with a suitable name: the Footlights Dramatic Club.

It was decided that the club's first production take place during May Week of 1883, which confusingly always happens in June. It marks the end of the academic year and so is a great cause for celebration as the students head off for their summer holidays. It is a week of boat racing, garden parties and May Balls. Cotton and Hickin decided to inaugurate their Footlights club with a 'one night only' performance of the burlesque tragic opera *Bombastes Furioso*, written in 1810 by William Barnes Rhodes, adding, however, a few topical songs and jokes of their own. It was presented at St Andrew's Hall in front of an enthusiastic audience; Cotton and Hickin took the lead roles. A critic from the *Cambridge Review*, a journal that focused on university life, wrote that Cotton, 'carried the house with him', with his singing and dancing and his amusing impersonation of the recently knighted actor, Henry Irving. The critic was less impressed by Hickin, 'he seemed hardly at his ease before so large an audience'. Overall, though, it was a good start for the club. 'And with plenty of material,' went the review, 'an evident intention of doing things in first rate style, and the experience that time alone can give, the "footlights" ought to take a high place among our permanent institutions.' Prophetic words indeed.

That November the club put on their second show, again at St Andrew's Hall, a production of H. J. Byron's 1861 burlesque *Aladdin*, with Cotton in the role of Widow Twankey. Again, there was the inclusion of topical songs and humour. This was to be the first of many Footlight pantomimes. Perhaps burned by the *Cambridge Review*'s dismissal of him, Hickin did not feature in the cast, but instead took the role of musical director and conductor.

By the time of the next production, 1884, both Cotton and Hickin had graduated, Cotton to become a solicitor, Hickin entered the clergy. The gap left was more than adequately filled by Lance Outram, who had played Abanazar in *Aladdin* and whose topical song in *Bombastes Furioso*, 'brought the house down', reported the *Cambridge Review*. Outram, the son of a clergyman, may be regarded as the Footlights first star. The *Cambridge Review* singled him out as, 'undoubtedly the finest actor that Cambridge has turned out in many years'.

Significantly, Outram was to write and star in the club's first original production in 1885. *Uncle Joe at Oxbridge*, a comic operetta in one act, told the tale of a layabout undergraduate who faces the dilemma of an important exam falling on the same day as his trial for the boat team. The solution is that his Uncle Joe takes the exam in his place. The scenario afforded ample opportunity to poke fun at the tenets and traditions of university life. Put on at the Theatre Royal during May Week, the *Cambridge Review* this time found the evening a disappointment, except for Outram's star turn as Uncle Joe, his acting, 'that of the true comedian'. It turned out to be Outram's final performance, he graduated that summer and like Hickin went into the church.

Putting on shows during May Week was now a fixed tradition, whether farces and burlesques, or original works. The club began to organize itself, too, electing a president, secretary, treasurer and a committee. They rented rooms at 62 Sidney Street which quickly became a social hub for members throughout term time. These rooms also became the home for smoking concerts, or as they were more commonly known, 'smokers'. Smoking concerts were all the rage in the Victorian era and were men-only affairs where live music was played, and much serious political talk went on. The Footlights adopted the smoking concert as a way of its members trying out material amongst themselves.

In the words of the student periodical *Granta*, the Footlights had established itself, 'among the permanent clubs at Cambridge', and was 'distinctly bohemian, but bohemian with a clean shirt'. It reported that its membership was in the region of fifty or sixty, which has pretty much remained the norm.

The 1892 show, *Alma Mater*, was another university-set comedy burlesque and proved so popular that it returned for two nights in November. The *Cambridge Review* urged its readers to go see it, if for nothing else, for the delight of seeing a certain Herbert Charles Pollitt. A dancer, cross-dresser and female impersonator, Pollitt was to become something of a Cambridge celebrity both on and off-stage. Close friends with Aubrey Beardsley, Pollitt also cultivated the friendship of Oscar Wilde by sending photographs of himself in a variety of costumes, including a transparent robe.

The son of a newspaper proprietor, Pollitt studied medicine at Trinity College and joined the Footlights in 1892, wowing audiences with his female impersonations. Pollitt was also the highlight of 1894's revue, *The Mixture Remixed*, an extravaganza of variety entertainments. Dancing in white silk, then in black and silver, Pollitt reminded one reviewer of, 'one of Rossetti's women brought to life'. That year at the London Photographic Salon, photographer Frederick Hollyer exhibited a photograph of Pollitt in drag as Diane de Rougy, his female alter ego.

Because no woman was allowed to be a member, female impersonation was a staple of the Footlights, but none were more celebrated than Pollitt. He graduated in 1896 but remained in residence in Cambridge and continued to hang around the university. Here he made the acquaintance of student Aleister Crowley and the pair became inseparable for months.

Pollitt also came to the rescue when the fledgling Footlights looked like being snuffed out. Since 1890 the club's treasurer and president had been Oscar Browning. The son of a wealthy merchant, Browning was educated at Eton and became a master there until his expulsion over a homosexual scandal. He arrived at King's College as a lecturer in history and soon became a prominent figure in the life of the university. Known to entertain widely, he was a most popular don at a time when there was a strict gulf between undergraduates and masters. At various times he was involved with hockey, swimming and music clubs and was treasurer of the Union Society. Known to have a broad sense of humour, Browning sometimes took part in smokers, however his treasurer-ship of the Footlights was clouded in accusations that he kept monies in his own bank account. This may have been why the club suffered a cash crisis in 1895, not helped by a dwindling membership, and why Browning pinned a notice on the door of the club's new rooms at 68 Bridge Street, declaring the Footlights were no more. Three irate members tore the notice down and looked to find the club a new home. One of the three was probably Pollitt, and in January 1896 he took over the presidency and henceforth it was agreed that treasurers and presidents be elected on an annual basis.

In March 1896 new rooms were acquired, on a nineteen-year lease, at 8 Corn Exchange Street. A small stage was erected, some chairs, writing desks and a bar put in. That year's May Week production featured Pollitt's now trademark serpentine dance, which in the words of the *Cambridge Review*, 'is beyond praise or criticism'. Described as, 'a musical farce', *The Sham Duke* opened at the New Theatre, an impressive auditorium recently built on the site of the old St Andrew's Hall. *The Sham Duke* was such a success, playing to packed houses over the by now customary three nights, that a charity performance was given at the Court Theatre (later the Royal Court), marking the club's London debut.

The following year's show was again described as, 'a musical farce', but this time its humour was sharpened by a political edge. Women had been allowed to study at Cambridge since 1869 and yet their years of hard graft were not rewarded with a degree. Fed up, they rallied themselves and managed to bring about a vote on the matter. Rather predictably, it lost to a thumping majority and the status quo continued until women finally won the right to a degree in 1948. *The New Dean* playfully looked at Cambridge in the year 2000 where women have taken over the top positions at the university. Only in the final act do all the women officials resign in order to marry, prompting this paean to female emancipation: 'Now feminine rule is ended, once more to men we bow, For guidance and light: and acknowledge their right to rule us as they know how.'

It was common practice for the club to hire professional artists to direct, write or contribute music to the revues. Paul Rubens was one and continued to provide material for the Footlights until 1907, by which time he had become a popular songwriter and librettist. He contributed to *The Freshman*, 1899's Footlights offering. Featured in the cast was Harold Monro, then club secretary, and later a noted poet and editor of *Poetry Review* magazine. He also founded the Poetry Bookshop, which in the years leading up to the First World War was an important meeting place for poets, including T. S. Eliot.

The Footlights was now flourishing, with a rich social calendar, too; there were dinners and balls in the Masonic Hall in Corn Exchange Street. The show for 1901, *The Oriental Trip*, starred Dave Burnaby, a law student. After failing his first exam, Burnaby left Cambridge and formed the Co-Optimists, a stage variety revue that was an early platform for Stanley Holloway. Burnaby also acted in films. As he approached middle age, he grew portlier in stature but was rarely seen without a monocle in his comic portrayals, a trademark that harked back to his Footlight days.

Memorably, 1908's show, *The Varsity BC*, had a prehistoric setting and included a couple of dinosaur props, one that flew in from above, while another, a large head and neck of a brontosaurus, arrived from the wings to devour a member of the cast. Alas, on the second night the pulley system went awry, resulting in the head, with the actor inside, breaking loose and collapsing onto the stage.

The Varsity BC was written by Henry Rottenburg, then a don at Cambridge. Rottenburg was an extraordinary man to say the least. Born in Glasgow, he was the son of a chemist and arrived at King's in 1895 to study engineering. He quickly involved himself with the Footlights, appearing in revues and later taking on the role of stage manager. On the sports field he excelled, especially at rugby, and he would go on to win five caps for Scotland. Graduating in 1900, Rottenburg was to return to Cambridge to become a lecturer in engineering. He also renewed his association with the Footlights, becoming president for a time and honorary treasurer from 1906 to 1922. His most significant contribution came with providing scripts for eight revues, performing in some of them. He also applied his engineering skills to inventing stage props; the dinosaur head was undoubtedly his creation. Later in life, Rottenburg applied his talent to sports equipment, inventing the modern starting blocks used by generations of sprinters, and which made their first appearance at the 1948 London Olympics.

By 1913, the taste of audiences had begun to change from musical comedies and burlesques to revue. Then all the rage in London, revues consisted typically of brief loosely connected skits, songs and dances. The Footlights new production, *Cheer-Oh Cambridge*, embraced this new trend, and the style of the show had much to do with a certain law undergraduate at Caius College called Jack Hulbert. The son of a doctor, Hulbert caught the showbusiness bug at an early age and his academic pursuits at Cambridge took something of a back seat to his love of performing and rowing. When his college tutor pointed out to him that, 'This is a university, not a drama school,' Hulbert replied, 'If I might be allowed to refute that statement, sir, I would say one of the best drama schools in the world.'[1]

Hulbert put together *Cheer-Oh Cambridge* almost single-handedly, writing the script and the music. He also took the main role of a laissez-faire Mayfair millionaire and performed the self-penned comedy song 'The Awfully Chap', which he went on to perform on his London professional debut. This came sooner than anyone expected. A charity performance of *Cheer-Oh Cambridge* in the West End was seen by producer Robert Courtneidge. Impressed with Hulbert, Courtneidge put him in his theatre company, quickly gaining not just another actor but a son-in-law when Hulbert fell in love with his daughter Cicely and they married. Hulbert was to become hugely popular on film and stage throughout the 1930s and his partnership with Cicely carried on until his death in 1978.

The outbreak of the First World War curtailed the activities of the Footlights. By 1915 there were no members at all and Rottenburg put everything in storage waiting until the university, and the world, returned to some sort of normalcy. By 1919, the prospects of the club's resurrection looked bleak when Rottenburg called a meeting and only six undergraduates bothered to turn up. Things perked up a bit at the second meeting when twenty were in attendance. Brynsley Nicholson, who like so many of his contemporaries saw his academic career interrupted by war service, was elected president. Rottenburg put together that year's revue and found new rooms for the club at 17 Corn Exchange Street. This was to be their home for the next twenty years. In rude health once again, the club began to look back nostalgically upon its past and decorated the walls of their new club room with photographs of old members and posters of previous productions.

Following in the footsteps of Jack Hulbert was his younger brother Claude, who was reading history at Caius. While Jack occasionally brought parties of friends from London to see the Footlights perform, including the likes of Beatrice Lillie and Gertrude Lawrence, Claude made his own mark in the 1920 revue, *His Little Trip*, playing a comic valet to a well-to-do household. Claude was to become a popular comic actor on stage, radio and cinema, specializing in silly ass roles, memorably on screen with Will Hay.

The dilemma facing the Footlights was always how to attract enough talented members, since many paid their subscription merely to use the club for social reasons. In January 1921, it was decided that all new members should be required to audition and prove that they could at least sing, dance or act a little. One of the first through the door under this new ruling was Eric Maschwitz, who spent £15 on a banjo and a tutor to teach him how to play it. 'After six weeks practice my rendering of Camptown Races was so enthusiastically inaccurate that when I went to give my audition the whole committee burst into roars of laughter, but nonetheless elected me.'[2] Maschwitz was later an entertainer, wrote and directed musicals for the West End and provided the lyrics for songs such as, 'These Foolish Things' and 'A Nightingale Sang in Berkeley Square'.

Another new member was Norman Hartnell, whom Maschwitz described as, 'A remarkable prima donna'.[3] A modern languages undergraduate at Magdalene College, Hartnell played the female lead in three revues (1921-3), designing all his own costumes. Like Pollitt before him, Hartnell was gay and a cross-dresser, and it was this aspect of his sexuality that was given full expression during his days with the Footlights. Born in Streatham, where his parents were publicans, Hartnell became interested in fashion as a young boy going to see West End musicals. A charity performance of the 1922 revue, *The Bedder's Opera*, given at Daly's Theatre, just off Leicester Square, featured several of Hartnell's designs and caught the eye of Minnie Hogg, who wrote a woman's page in the *Evening Standard* newspaper. 'Is the dress genius of the future now at Cambridge?' she wrote. Miss Hogg was

FIGURE 2.1 *Norman Hartnell in drag in a variety of poses. Chronicle/Alamy Stock Photo.*

instrumental in securing Hartnell a job at a London dressmaker when he dropped out of Cambridge, not bothering to finish his degree. Hartnell established himself as the favoured dress designer of debutantes, film stars and royalty. Famously, he designed both Princess Elizabeth's wedding dress and later her coronation gown.

Elizabeth, in all her coronation splendour, was captured for posterity through the lens of photographer Cecil Beaton, who followed Hartnell as another celebrated female impersonator at Cambridge. Beaton, the son of a prosperous merchant, acted in the university's drama clubs, the Amateur Dramatic Club (ADC) and the Marlowe Society, along with contributing costume and set designs. In his final term of 1925, Beaton opted for the frivolity of the Footlights, deciding to go down, 'in a flash of diamante'.[4] He went to see Harold Warrender, the club president, and was accepted. The new revue went by the title of *All the Vogue*, and during rehearsals Beaton voiced dissatisfaction with the club's relative unprofessionalism compared to the ADC and the Marlowe. He was further disappointed not to be included in any of the dance numbers, having practised his high kicks.

The third and final night of *All the Vogue* saw the attendance of Beaton's family, along with other dignitaries including H. G. Wells. In a variety of dresses, including a ballet skirt and black stockings, Beaton stole the show and at the end of the performance was inundated with bouquets of flowers. A critic for *Cambridge News* called Beaton, 'One of the best leading ladies the Footlights have had.'

Beaton left Cambridge without a degree, like Hartnell his studies had taken second place to his theatrical interests. Within a year he had taken up another of his passions, photography, earning a contract with *Vogue* magazine and later becoming court photographer to the royal family.

Female impersonation had been a popular element of Footlight shows for years but it was to fall foul of a prevailing conservativism. In October 1925, there was an editorial in the *Daily Sketch* newspaper labelling these performers as, 'The girl-men of Cambridge', and, 'Soft, effeminate, painted, be-rouged youths.' In 1934, the university paper *Granta* ran a poem that began, 'I am a Footlights fairy', alluding not only to the tradition of dragging up but the club's reputation for a large proportion of homosexual members.

Over the last few years, the Footlights had pitched themselves uneasily between revue and musical comedy, or a mash up of both, and while they remained popular with local audiences they met with critical indifference. Reviewing one such show, *Bumps*, in 1924, the *Cambridge Review* thought it might do on a music hall stage, 'but Cambridge expects more from the Footlights.' Things picked up with the 1926 revue, *May Fever*, which *Granta* termed, 'The biggest success that the Footlights have staged since the war.' Amongst the cast was Richard Murdoch, who didn't last very long at Cambridge, expelled for not doing enough work. He later become a comic actor, notably as straight man to Arthur Askey in the BBC radio show *Band Waggon*.

FIGURE 2.2 *Cambridge University Footlights with Victor Stiebel. The cast of the 1927 revue* Please Tell Others. *Chronicle/Alamy Stock Photo.*

Things went downhill again the following year with *Please Tell Others*, prompting the *Cambridge Review* to urge, 'We will be forgiven if we do not entirely accede to this request.' Now running across the whole week instead of just three nights, the 1928 and 1929 revues were also not a success. As a result, the club saw a decline in membership, and a paucity in talented performers. It had become instead a playground for rich undergraduates interested only in the social aspect of belonging to the Footlights and having fun. It became so bad that a professional director brought in to organize the 1930 revue complained about the lack of talent and that most of the cast was drunk at the dress rehearsal. That same year Ronald Hill was elected president, 'literally because there was no one else who would get down to putting a show on', he claimed.[5] Hill later quit Cambridge to become a singer-songwriter. In 1936 he was commissioned to write the theme song for a variety programme called, *Here's Looking at You*, intended for experimental broadcasts ahead of the launch of the BBC Television Service.

One drastic measure to solve the talent problem was for the inclusion of women in the May Week revue for the first time. This suggestion did not sit well with some members but at a general meeting the committee's proposal was carried. The result was 1932's *Laughing at Love*, a musical farce about

FIGURE 2.3 *Members of the Cambridge Footlights at a dress rehearsal for the pantomime* Cinderella. *The undergraduate cast perform a cross-dressing number as a beauty chorus. 23 November 1932. Photo by Fox Photos/Getty Images.*

a peer in love with a cabaret artiste. Two professional actresses were brought in, Naomi Waters, an Australian heiress who that same year was in the original cast of the Noël Coward revue, *Words and Music*, and Anna Lee, who relocated to Hollywood in the late 1930s and appeared in eight John Ford pictures including *How Green Was My Valley* (1941) and *Fort Apache* (1948). She was awarded an MBE in 1982 for her services to drama.

Critically, *Laughing at Love* hit the right note with *Granta*: 'The music was excellent. Mr Lowry's ukulele turn was particularly outstanding.' Mr Lowry was in fact Malcolm Lowry. A dab hand at the ukulele, it was a common sight to see him performing and singing at various pubs around the town. Lowry was to become a renowned poet and novelist, best known for his 1947 novel *Under the Volcano*.

Laughing at Love fared less well with the public. According to Albert Robinson, later Footlights president, 'The townspeople were disappointed because they liked seeing undergraduates dressed up as girls and playing feminine roles.'[6] So, next year it was back to the tradition of men in dresses. The title of the revue left no one in any doubt: *No More Women!* Indeed, this would be the case until 1957.

Having survived the one-off horror of participating women, the club was once again heavily in debt, due to the expense of putting on recent productions. These things didn't come cheap, with their large casts of almost thirty players, costumes and sets. Even relinquishing the lease on the club rooms and selling off its assets, such as the piano, was not enough. Henry Rottenburg, who had remained loyally aligned to the Footlights, confessed to the *Daily Telegraph*, 'Tragic as it may be, the famous club appears doomed.' The man who did much to restore its fortunes was Lord Killanin. A new member, Killanin had good connections and was literary editor of the student newspaper *Varsity*. The club made him business manager of the 1933 revue and later that same year elected him president. For the 1934 revue, Killanin brought in a BBC drama producer as director, along with a professional choreographer. Upon graduation in 1935, Killanin went straight to work at the *Daily Express*. In the war he participated in the D-Day landings as a brigade major with the 30th Armoured Brigade. After the war, he moved into film production and in the 1970s was president of the International Olympic Committee.

A recruitment drive to attract new members, instigated by Lord Killanin, helped to bolster numbers. Amongst the new intake was Hugh Latimer, an architecture and English undergraduate who discovered that he had a natural talent for making people laugh and went on to have a long career in the West End. Robert Hamer studied economics at Corpus Christi with the intention of a career in the Treasury, instead he made his name as a director at Ealing Studios, responsible for the classic *Kind Hearts and Coronets* (1949). There was Nigel Burgess, brother of the future spy Guy Burgess, a talented musician who became a leading member of the club, writing the lyrics and music for several productions. Terence Young appeared in the 1936 revue, *Turn Over a New Leaf*, performing a song dressed as a cowboy. In the audience one night was film director Brian Desmond Hurst, who encouraged Young's desire to work in movies. Young later became an international director, helming the early Bond films (*Dr No*, *From Russia with Love* and *Thunderball*).

Turn Over a New Leaf was another professionally mounted production, presented at the recently built Arts Theatre, beginning the Footlight's long association with the venue. The director was George Rylands, a respected theatrical scholar and lecturer in English literature. It was Rylands who brought in the principal dancer of Sadler's Wells Ballet to supervise the choreography – Robert Helpmann. During rehearsals, Rylands told Helpmann about two undergraduates that, 'We've got to put in somehow.' They were the son and nephew of the president of Panama. 'What can they do?' asked Helpmann. 'Well,' said Rylands, 'they say they want to present a new South American dance called the rumba.' Helpmann had never heard of it but for the sake of diplomatic relations inserted it into the show. It was the first time the rumba was performed in the UK.[7]

Helpmann found the Footlights, 'A fairly exclusive privileged group, very much the upper crust of Cambridge. It was elegant, but not decadent.'[8] He continued to choreograph the revues until 1939. One year he put on a comedy version of *Les Sylphides*, the ballet he had performed at Sadler's Wells, and chose the largest and hairiest specimens for his ballerinas, much to the amusement of the audience. The main ballerina was Peter Eade, later a theatrical agent, representing the likes of Kenneth Williams and Ronnie Barker.

By 1937, the club was in rude health, especially its finances, thanks to the formation of the Cambridge Arts Theatre Trust. This charity, which took over the running of the Arts Theatre, sought to put the university's amateur drama societies on a sounder footing by assuming direct financial responsibility over their productions. Any loss was borne by the trust, while any profits were shared equally. The Footlights could also call upon a healthier crop of talent and the 1937 revue, *Full Swing*, was a big success. Extracts of the show, which included pastiches of Hollywood musicals, Greek tragedies and Italian opera, appeared in a special forty-minute programme on BBC Radio.

A shadow hung over the May Week of 1939 as war with Germany appeared inevitable. The revue was put on all the same, in a mood of 'lightheartedness', according to one undergraduate, Ronald Millar, even if everyone knew they were supping the last of the summer wine, 'before once again the lights went out all over Europe'.[9] Dragged up as Millar's wife in one sketch was the future Lord Peter Rawlinson, Attorney General in Edward Heath's government. After a career as an actor and screenwriter Millar, too, became involved in politics as a speechwriter for both Heath and Margaret Thatcher. It was Millar's idea that Thatcher quote from the prayer of St Francis of Assisi as she stood outside No. 10 Downing Street on the day she became prime minister in 1979. He also provided the famous line, 'The lady's not for turning.' Millar was knighted in 1979.

According to Millar, the star turn of the 1939 revue, delivering a, 'remarkable tour de force', that 'brought the house down'[10] was Jimmy Edwards, a choral scholar at St John's College. Edwards played trombone in a local dance band and was prone to leaning out of the window of his digs and playing the instrument across the street. Invited to appear in the revue, Edwards played a music don in one sketch lecturing how to play the trombone. It ended with a stream of water gushing out of the instrument drenching those sat in the front row.

The start of the war changed everything, of course, not least the activities of the Footlights, which all but ended. With no revues planned, the club room was vacated. However, concert parties for the troops were given at nearby camps. 'Without much success,' wrote Jimmy Edwards. 'There were frequent shouts of "Join!" as we manfully ploughed our way through the opening chorus, dressed as folderol clowns.'[11] Ronald Millar chipped in, organizing a charity concert at the Arts Theatre when he heard the club needed money for a scenery van. Through his mother's theatre connections (she'd been an actress), John Gielgud and Peggy Ashcroft gave of their time to come and perform.

Millar joined the navy in 1940, while Jimmy Edwards served in the RAF. After the war, Edwards incorporated his Footlights trombone routine into a professional act, notably at London's Windmill Theatre. He gained wider exposure as a performer in the radio comedy *Take it from Here* and as the headmaster in the BBC sitcom *Whack-O!*

After the war, both the Footlights and the university took a while to return to normal life, although both would never really be the same again. Austerity gripped the country, somewhat dampening everyone's mood, so the return of the Footlights revue in 1947 gave cheer to many. One familiar name amongst the cast was Richard Baker, later a popular BBC newsreader. At Cambridge, Baker mostly concerned himself with producing plays for the Marlowe Society, but his talent on the piano led to his involvement in the Footlights.

The first post-war president was D'Arcy Orders who lived in a flat above his parent's hairdressers, and this became the club's temporary home. Smoking concerts were held at the Dorothy Café in Sidney Street, which had a large ballroom. The club held its first dinner in ten years here in February 1948, with Norman Hartnell and Jimmy Edwards as guests of honour.

Orders set about reviving the Footlights, appealing for students with an aptitude for theatrics to join. Those who did included Michael Westmore and Charles Parker, both of whom later worked at the BBC, and David Eady, son of Sir Wilfred Eady (who gave his name to the cinema tax, the Eady Levy), who became a film director. Orders also wrote to past members requesting funds and received a positive response. Understandably, the 1947 revue was rather hastily put together, but membership started to pick up and the 1948 revue was a much more professional affair. As with many previous revues, *La Vie Cambridgienne*, poked fun at university life. In a note of topicality, one of the songs referenced the fact that women, after many years of protests and petitions, had finally been granted degrees. A hearty success, one of the performances was recorded by BBC Radio and selections broadcast on the Light Programme, presented by ex-member Claude Hulbert.

La Vie Cambridgienne was directed by Stephen Joseph, an English literature student at Jesus College. The son of publisher Michael Joseph and actress Hermione Gingold, Joseph was a central figure in the Footlights and became a renowned stage director, establishing the country's first professional theatre-in-the-round and mentoring the young Alan Ayckbourn. On his death in 1967, at the age of only forty-six, Joseph was described by the *Times* as, 'The most successful missionary to work in the English theatre since the Second World War.'

One of the stars of *La Vie Cambridgienne* was Simon Phipps, who numbered amongst the many who had resumed academic life following military service; Phipps was in the Coldstream Guards where he won the Military Cross. Studying for the priesthood at Westcott House, an Anglican theological college, Phipps formed an unlikely creative partnership, writing comedy songs, with Trinity College's unorthodox chaplain, the chain-smoking and keen gin drinker Geoffrey Beaumont. One of their songs, 'Botticelli Angel', was sung at both the 1948 and 1949 revues, with Phipps wearing a halo, a long white nightshirt and carrying a harp.

One freshman who arrived at Trinity in the autumn of 1948 quickly fell into the orbit of Phipps and Beaumont, his name was Julian Slade, later the author of the hit musical *Salad Days*. Slade was encouraged in the songs he was beginning to write and invited to participate in the 1949 revue, *Always in June*. Produced by Phipps, then club president, *Always in June* featured an amusing parody of drawing room plays written by Peter Shaffer, later responsible for stage hits like *Equus* and *Amadeus*. Making his Footlight debut was future actor Peter Jeffrey.

Always in June had the advantage of a small orchestra, the first time one had been used since the war. The Footlights musical director at the time was Peter Tranchell of King's College. Following his studies, Tranchell returned to Cambridge to lecture in music. New Footlight members were often treated to a seminar given by him on lyric writing. Openly gay, Tranchell was noted for his wit and repartee. He had a number in one revue that opened with the lyric: 'It's Spring and we're feeling ourselves again.'

Phipps, too, returned to Cambridge, taking over as chaplain of Trinity College from Beaumont in 1953. Phipps was on friendly terms with Princess Margaret, who sometimes visited the college to take tea with him in his rooms, sometimes in the company of students. Frederic Raphael was a guest once. 'During the course of the afternoon with her she needed to go to the loo and we all listened to the Princess's tinkle.'[12]

3

Cabbages and Kings

The 1951 revue, *A Flash in the Cam*, used the Festival of Britain as the background to its series of sketches and songs, chosen from the best material of that year's smokers. Now running just under two weeks, *Varsity* wrote that the Footlights revue was, 'treated as the major event in the theatrical year from a popular point of view'. The club was even booked to present an hour-long version nightly at the Dorchester Hotel in London that summer. 'We lived it up,' recalls Peter Firth. 'It was just a rollicking time because there was nothing at stake. I don't think we thought about it as a big professional thing, so much as a very enjoyable fortnight.'[1] One of the highlights of the show was a song called 'Waterloo Road', where the cast dressed as Pearly Kings. 'And that was just the thing for London at that time and audiences loved it,' says Peter.[2] The Footlights also made their first appearance on television when the BBC presented a half-hour excerpt. The club was gradually making a name for itself beyond the ancient brickwork of the university, 'Getting their wings,' states Peter.[3]

Peter was studying history at Emmanuel College and recalls going to the Societies' Fair, which was always held on the first weekend of term and to which freshers were invited. 'All the clubs would be advertising themselves in this big room, they had a stall, manned by two or three aficionados of that subject. There was a stall for the Footlights, the football club, the literary lot, and you took a choice. It was a kind of market.'[4] Because he had acted at school, Peter preferred to join the ADC, 'The straight lot.'[5]

His introduction to the Footlights was an invitation to one of the smokers and it wasn't long before he began contributing sketches. 'I sang in those days as well so that was a help.'[6] Peter was swiftly installed as junior treasurer, 'which as far as I remember entailed absolutely nothing. I think the senior treasurer did all the work',[7] and took part in committee meetings. 'It was very much an informal but serious arrangement. It wasn't like being a paid official at some firm, where people sat on you if you didn't do the right thing, it was a much more friendly set up.'[8]

Inevitably, Peter's exertions at both the ADC and the Footlights impinged upon his studies. 'But in those days, one didn't really worry too much about that. There was a much more relaxed attitude towards what kind of degree you got, unless you were deadly serious. I remember when I said goodbye to the master of Emmanuel after the last term and he said, "If you hadn't done all this stuff with the Footlights, you would have a much better degree, but I'm rather glad that you didn't." '[9]

In 1953, Peter was elected president and saw his main duty as making sure the smokers were always supplied with talent and material. 'We'd try things out and if things went down well, we'd put it on the shelf and say, we'll take that out next June for the revue.'[10] By the 1950s, smokers had become something of a ritual and well organized. There were on average two a term and auditions for new members would be held on the same evening. Everyone was expected to wear a dinner jacket.

As president, Peter produced that year's revue, *Cabbages and Kings*, with an emphasis on making sure everyone enjoyed the process as well as taking it seriously. 'We treated it lightly. Apart from a few people, I didn't think of anybody as wanting to go on to being professional. It was all just great fun.'[11] Amongst the cast was a classics scholar at St John's, Frederic Raphael, who remembers Peter as, 'A very nice, un-showbizzy kind of person.'[12] However, confronted with the dress rehearsal of *Cabbages and Kings*, 'which was a bit ramshackle,'[13] Raphael predicted a disaster. 'It was very old-fashioned Footlights, which was, you just took a few numbers which had been in smokers and put them all together and hoped for the best. But it worked very well and was a great success.'[14] Modestly, Peter doesn't put this down to any kind of inherent excellence the show may have had. 'I think that however bad the revues were, they were always well received because it was the end of term, everybody had finished exams, and everyone was just out to have a good time. The audiences almost came to enjoy themselves rather than make judgements on the performance.'[15]

Frederic Raphael recalls one skit that he wrote, a parody of a news programme where he impersonated the MP Michael Foot. 'One line went, "We in the Labour Party will do everything in our power to get everything in our power." And I was astonished, and slightly horrified, by the amount of enthusiasm and applause that that particular line got. I realized that there really were young Conservatives, and a lot of them.'[16]

Cabbages and Kings got a write up in the *Daily Telegraph* and a London producer offered Peter a two-week run at the Phoenix Theatre in London. This would have been the first West End transfer for a Footlights revue. To the dismay of many in the cast, Peter turned the offer down. 'I nearly lost a few friends on that one.'[17] Exhausted after his exams and the rigours of putting on the show, Peter needed some rest. It was his girlfriend, later wife, who suggested going to a monastery where her uncle lived as a monk. 'I didn't have to go to any services, because I wasn't a practising Christian in those days. And I thought, this sounds very good, a week's rest in the country, so I arranged to go.'[18] That meant saying no to the West End offer. A decision that was to change his life. 'I went to this place, and I thought, what the hell am I doing here, because that was not the direction that my life seemed to be going. I wanted to be a teacher. Anyhow, from that very first day I began to take seriously what life's about. I went to see the head of St Stephen's House [an Anglican theological college] in Oxford. We walked round the cricket ground one afternoon and he said, "Well, term starts on Friday. I want to see you here." And that's how I began my clerical career. It was all very sudden.'[19] Peter was ordained in 1955, worked for many years for the Religious Broadcasting Unit at the BBC and was the last Bishop of Malmesbury.

Someone who did not take kindly to the missed opportunity of a West End run was a most ambitious young man by the name of Leslie Bricusse. He had arrived as a freshman at Caius College in October 1951 and wasted no time in presenting himself to the Footlights. Voted in, he celebrated by treating himself to the club's broad-striped, red, turquoise and purple tie. Bricusse was studying modern and medieval languages, but his real love was musical theatre, and he quickly found a keen collaborator in Robin Beaumont, an organ scholar at Clare College. Together, they were writing a musical comedy but Bricusse wanted someone to write the book. It was Peter who pointed him in the direction of Frederic Raphael, who had plans to be a novelist. At their meeting, Frederic told Bricusse that he hadn't dared to audition for the Footlights, 'Because of an awful realization I might be asked to sing. Bricusse said, "What absolute rubbish," and because he was the secretary, if I wanted to join I should consider myself a member.'[20]

Raphael didn't treat joining the Footlights with the same reverence as Bricusse by going out and buying the club tie, for example, which hardly anyone wore anyway. 'It was a bit of an honour to be elected, but I don't think anybody else gave a damn. We didn't think we were an elite. The ADC gave itself those airs. I think the ADC was far more self-important. They thought they were very grand, and Peter Hall moved very promptly into the command position there, rather as Leslie did at the Footlights. The ADC thought we were rather silly and flippant.'[21]

Bricusse thought it would be a good idea if Raphael joined the committee. A meeting was held, after which Bricusse had the uncomfortable duty to inform Raphael that three members had blocked him, because he was Jewish. This was nothing personal, because Raphael was well liked. 'It was, God help us, a principle.'[22] Raphael had experienced this kind of antisemitism before, but Bricusse was livid and promised to expel the culprits and get his friend on the committee. This Bricusse did the following year when he was elected president.

Raphael quickly warmed to Bricusse. Here was a professionally-minded individual. Peter Firth had sensed the same thing. 'Apart from being a charming man, he was deadly serious, you knew where he was going.'[23] Raphael noticed that Bricusse had an address book with Paris, London and New York written into it. When asked if he knew a lot of people in Paris, Bricusse replied that he did not, but was going to. 'Leslie had a simple ambition,' observes Raphael, 'a bit like Noël Coward who said he wanted to travel first class through life, and Leslie had something in common with that.'[24]

To his surprise, Raphael found it easy and enjoyable writing comedy sketches for the Footlights. One of his friends in Cambridge was Tony Beecher, later a professor of education. 'And he had a great facility for rhyme and wrote rather good lyrics,' says Raphael.[25] At the time, Lord Montagu of Beaulieu had been imprisoned for homosexual acts and Beecher wrote and performed a song at one smoker that he entitled: 'Lord Mount-a-few of Beaulieu'. No malice was intended. It was this kind of gentle ribbing that was indicative of Footlight humour then. 'We thought we were being very naughty,' argues Raphael. 'In fact, being naughty was really what the game was. It was a strange mixture of sophistication and childishness.'[26]

The Footlights had always poked gentle fun at university life, its traditions and institutions, and it was much the same at this time, a desire to not actually damage any sacred cows or any individual. There had been an odd bit of social comment during the mid-1930s on the rise of Hitler, in one sketch the proctors were turned into Nazis, and another that made fun of Britain's Imperial past. But this was rare. By the mid-1950s there was some social satire but nothing political. This was also the case in the revues of the West End. Satire, or as Raphael calls it, 'jeering at our betters', had not yet bared its teeth with *Beyond the Fringe*. 'The strange thing about Britain was that it was fun to knock because it had a very solid door. Now the door is very flimsy and almost anyone can get in.'[27]

In 1955, the *Cambridge Review* criticized this kind of attitude, that here was, 'A distrust for any reforming zeal, a disinclination towards any change or radical modification of current standards.' Remember, this was all before the Suez crisis, Britain's botched military response to the nationalization of the Suez Canal by Egyptian President Nasser. Britain had lived with an Iron Curtain across Europe for ten years. There was a Cold War, but the situation politically was stable. 'We lived in a Cambridge which seemed to be in continuity with pre-war Cambridge,' says Raphael. 'Suez altered everything because England lost its vanity. Something cracked, in particular respect for the older generation.'[28]

Raphael looked forward to the next revue, which Bricusse was going to produce. It was called *Out of the Blue* and Bricusse brought a degree of professionalism to proceedings. 'It was quite seriously rehearsed,' confirms Raphael, who personally approached the whole thing, 'as a bit of fun'.[29] Some of his sketches got in, including one he performed that sent up the literary pretensions of Graham Greene and Evelyn Waugh. One line went: 'We were nearly subjected to rape/By the man from Jonathan Cape/Victor Gollancz? No thanks!' This exchange reached the ears of the publisher and, far from mortified, Gollancz asked for tickets to the show. Afterwards, he took Raphael out to dinner. 'And when he asked me what I was going to do in life I said I wanted to be a writer and he said, "That's a very bad idea."'[30] Besides a distinguished career as a novelist, Raphael became a screenwriter, winning an Oscar for *Darling* (1965) and collaborating with Stanley Kubrick on the screenplay of *Eyes Wide Shut* (1999).

In the words of Bricusse *Out of the Blue* contained, 'smart, relevant, highly topical and downright funny material, interspersed with sharp satirical songs'.[31] It also had a secret weapon in the shape of a nineteen-year-old medical student by the name of Jonathan Miller. Fellow student John Drummond was to call Miller, 'The great original humourist of my time. There was a mad surrealism about his ideas, and something extraordinary about the way he used his body, like a tipsy giraffe. None of us had his originality, and few of us his intelligence.'[32] Miller's reputation as a performer in his college revues preceded him, as did a beguiling quirkiness. Playwright Michael Frayn has a clear memory of Miller, 'walking round the streets of the town in bare feet'.[33] Bricusse certainly knew talent when he saw it and snatched Miller up, employing him wisely, dragged up at one point as Elizabeth I, with dark glasses and bouncing the royal orb like a basketball. This skit referenced the second Elizabeth's coronation and Britain's new Elizabethan age.

Two offers came to stage *Out of the Blue* in London and Bricusse accepted a three-week run at the Phoenix Theatre that July, thus presiding over the first Footlights revue to transfer to the West End. Dropping some of the stuff that didn't work, Bricusse shoehorned in a few 'best of' items from the previous two revues. The package worked. The critic of the *Spectator* thought it, 'greatly superior both in wit and verve to any revue that I have seen this year in the West End'. This he put down to the writing having more bite and freshness in the hands of amateurs than the more jaded professional. 'Perhaps the trouble is that they write down to their audience, whereas the authors of *Out of the Blue* took it for granted (quite rightly) that they were dealing with reasonably intelligent people.'

The cast became the talk of the town, and there were appearances on television panel shows and on radio, along with invitations to posh house parties from the theatre critic Kenneth Tynan amongst others. Most critics agreed that Jonathan Miller was the star of the show. The *Spectator* called his debut that, 'of a very considerable artist'. *Beyond the Fringe* was six years away. 'The success of *Out of the Blue* did owe a good deal to Jonathan Miller,' argues Frederic Raphael. 'He didn't really want to be in the company, he just wanted to shine, which he undoubtedly did.'[34] Miller was even caricatured by the cartoonist Ronald Searle for the theatre review column of *Punch*.

Offers of work came flooding in for Miller, and while he accepted some of it, he seemed cooly determined not to be sidetracked from a career in medicine. 'Jonathan always felt he should be a doctor because his father wanted him to be,' states Frederic.[35] It was Bricusse who benefitted the most. The popular actress and singer Beatrice Lillie attended the first night and invited Bricusse to write material for her and to be the leading man in her new show. Catapulted into the world of the West End, Bricusse never looked back, going on to become a successful composer and lyricist of stage musicals such as *Stop the World – I Want to Get Off* (1961) and the film musicals *Doctor Dolittle* (1967) and *Willy Wonka and the Chocolate Factory* (1971).

Taking over from Bricusse as club president was Brian Marber, who came from a rich North London Jewish family. He could sing and dance reasonably well and was quite funny. 'But Leslie never thought that he should be president of the Footlights,' recalls Frederic Raphael. 'Not because he was Jewish, because he wasn't good looking enough.'[36] Marber produced the 1955 revue, *Between the Lines*, which again starred Jonathan Miller, alongside the likes of Peter Woodthorpe and Rory McEwen, who performed calypso-like songs. Woodthorpe was finishing his second year reading biochemistry at Magdalene College. A month later he was playing Estragon in the first British production of *Waiting for Godot* at the Arts Theatre in London. 'Peter Hall more or less wrenched him out of Cambridge before he had graduated and put him into *Godot*,' says Frederic. 'And I think Peter regretted not going on to finish his degree.'[37]

Rory McEwen came from a wealthy Scottish family and was Miller's close friend at Cambridge. When *Between the Lines* transferred to the West End for a three-week run, Princess Magaret attended a performance and arranged an after-show party for the cast at Clarence House. Miller and McEwen left early as they were performing late night cabaret at the Royal Court Theatre's upstairs dining club. The Princess organized chauffeured cars to take everyone at the party to go and watch them.

In just a couple of years, McEwen was to become one of the leading lights in the post-war British folksong revival, inspiring the likes of Van Morrison and Billy Connolly. McEwen was also one of the best botanical artists that Britain ever produced, and by the mid-1960s was devoting himself entirely to the art. Tragically in 1982, McEwen was diagnosed with terminal cancer and took his own life at the age of fifty.

Once again Jonathan Miller was singled out for praise by the critics when *Between the Lines* came to London. Bernard Levin called him, 'a genius', others compared him to Danny Kaye, then appearing at the London Palladium; the American comic thought Miller very funny. What was so fascinating about Miller was an obvious and powerful intellect combined with a natural clownishness. Frederic Raphael thinks Miller's Jewish heritage was important, too. 'The thing which a great many Jews have done is to avert hostility by being amusing, and I think Jonathan discovered that he was very good at making people laugh and it's a rare piece of good fortune and he took advantage.'[38]

One of Miller's comic monologues in *Between the Lines* caused a minor stir in the conservative press. 'Our Island Heritage' took a pot shot at national heroes like Nelson and a doddery Churchill, all impersonated by Miller. It poked fun at establishment figures in a way that anticipated *Beyond the Fringe*.

Such was the esteem in which Miller was held that when Geoffrey Strachan came up to St Catharine's College in autumn 1955, to study modern languages, it was his advice that he sought about how to get into the Footlights. Geoffrey, later a distinguished author and publisher, had always loved comedy theatre, be it pantomime, variety, Shaw or Sheridan. He had seen his first West End revue in 1951 at the age of sixteen and was immediately hooked. The next revue he saw was *Out of the Blue* at the Phoenix Theatre. 'I, and some of my fellow national servicemen, were so totally enthralled that we decided to write and perform a "Footlights-type" revue of our own in a rented small theatre in London.'[39]

Miller's advice to Geoffrey was to join his college revue club first. Most of the colleges put on shows or had their own revue clubs. St Catharine's was called the Midnight Howlers, 'which was on the go in the 1920s, when my father was at the college', recalls Geoffrey. 'They were planning a revue that term. I started writing songs and sketches and began submitting them. Several were accepted and I was offered a part in the revue.'[40]

The proliferation of college revue clubs in those years was highly significant. Geoffrey recalls watching lively and accomplished revues at Queens', Christ's, Trinity Hall and St John's. 'They certainly acted as a training ground for revue performers and successful songs and sketches from college revues would find their way into the Footlights May Week revue.'[41] Some of Geoffrey's material from the Midnight Howlers ended up in both the 1956 and 1958 Footlight revues.

There was huge enthusiasm for all kinds of theatre at Cambridge: classic and modern plays, revue and cabaret. 'People threw themselves into it with little restriction,' reports Geoffrey. 'I used to visit Oxford friends frequently, with whom I had made our Footlights-inspired revue, and I got the impression that the scope for amateur theatre among students was more limited, more restricted by university authorities in Oxford than in Cambridge.'[42]

The most striking example of a college revue of high quality during this period was *Share My Lettuce*, staged at Magdalene College. This was written and directed by an English literature student called Bamber Gascoigne, later the host of the television quiz show *University Challenge*. It was seen by the producer Michael Codron and put on in the West End starring Maggie Smith and Kenneth Williams.

The previous year, Gascoigne had contributed one sketch to the 1956 Footlight revue. *Anything May* was unusual in that it had a theme running through the whole piece: man's journey from birth to death; it closed with the cast dressed as devils. Again, it was rewarded with a London transfer, this time to the Lyric, Hammersmith. In the cast was Daniel Massey, whose father, the actor Raymond Massey, brought along with him a group of notable theatricals and threw a grand first night party.

The 1957 Footlights offering, however, was even more radical. A recent revue called *Cranks* had proved something of a sensation in the West End and a touring version played in Cambridge. Amongst those who went to see it was a philosophy student at Emmanuel College, Michael Frayn. 'It was very abstract and offbeat, quite ahead of its time. I was very taken by it.'[43]

Michael had spent his National Service with the Joint Services School for Linguists learning Russian, which included a spell at Cambridge. 'We couldn't take part in university life when we were in the army, but we were observing the university from almost the inside and I knew exactly what I wanted to do, I wanted to write for *Varsity* and I wanted to write for the Footlights.'[44] In his first term, Michael won a writing competition sponsored by the *Observer* newspaper. Half of the £100 prize money he spent on a dinner jacket, so he could join the Footlights. 'It was a very hermetic society,' claims Michael. 'It was very much old public schoolboys in their dinner jackets. But there were a lot of clubs in Cambridge where people wore dinner jackets and had dinner together and too much to drink, and the Footlights was just one of those.'[45]

Very quickly, Michael forged a reputation, writing material for *Varsity* and *Granta*, as well as providing sketches for the *Anything May* revue. He was then given carte blanche to devise 1957's revue, which he wrote with his friend John Edwards, who had also seen and been inspired by *Cranks*. 'We were devoted to a new aesthetic,' says Michael. 'Traditionally, the Footlights had been very much about local Cambridge events, and we decided that we wanted to get away from that. There wouldn't be any references to Cambridge or local traditions. So, we absolutely ditched that and had this completely abstract show.'[46]

Everyone in the cast was on board with Michael's ideas and, 'reasonably positive', about what he was trying to do. 'Except one of them, a delightful man called Bob Wellings, and he had a lot of really thick upper-class friends in Trinity, and they came and mocked him for doing the show. And he was far too nice to take it out on me or refuse to do the thing, but he was obviously very upset by this.'[47] In the 1970s, Wellings became a popular television presenter working on the BBC's *Nationwide* current affairs programme and the consumer show *That's Life!*

Michael cast another interesting performer, Joe Melia, after seeing him in a revue at Downing College. 'He was very funny and hadn't been a member of the Footlights up to then. I think there was some resistance to my having him, but he was a real talent, and he went on to become a professional actor.'[48]

One welcome addition was the inclusion of women in the cast for the first time since 1932. 'I remember there was quite a lot of arguments about that,' Michael confirms. 'A lot of resistance. But I made it a condition of being involved that we had women playing women's roles.'[49] Michael cast Dorothy Mulcahy, an undergraduate at Girton, an all-female college, who had been in other revues. And there was Ann Jones. 'She was not a graduate,' confirms Michael, 'but was the girlfriend of someone in Trinity. She had been a Tiller Girl, so she knew how to dance. They were both terrific.'[50]

Zounds was directed by Graeme MacDonald, Footlight's vice president and subsequently Controller of BBC 2. By Michael's own admission, it was not a success. 'Some of the numbers were quite smart, but it simply didn't work. That's the trouble with comedy, with anything else you can say, if the audience isn't responding, it's because they're thinking about it or they're so moved they can't speak, but if it's comedy you need them to laugh.'[51] *Zounds* also ended the run of Footlight revues transferring to a London theatre. 'It was a big disappointment, and I felt that I'd let everybody down with the script.'[52] Such was Michael's sense of failure that it completely soured any theatrical ambitions he may have had. 'When I started writing a column for the *Guardian*, I devoted a lot of them to mocking the theatre, and saying how awful plays were and that one was just waiting to be embarrassed by actors dropping their props or forgetting their lines. And I see with hindsight that I suppose I was working up to writing my play *Noises Off*.'[53] Michael was to enjoy a successful career as both a dramatist and novelist.

The following year's revue, *Springs to Mind*, reverted to the tried and tested formula of songs and sketches. And no women in the cast. It's also interesting to note that the large casts of previous revues had also been dispensed with over the past few years. Geoffrey Strachan contributed material, including a hybrid parody of *Under Milk Wood* that went down very well. 'It was crammed with allusions to a score of recently staged plays, from *Waiting for Godot* to *A Streetcar Named Desire*, as well as jokes about Kenneth Tynan and the Lord Chamberlain.'[54] Before 1968 and the abolition of theatre censorship, the script for all plays and revues, even those performed at university, had to be sent to the Lord Chamberlain's office in London for approval.

Geoffrey found there to be little appetite inside the Footlights for anything political or for heavy satire. He had written some stinging lyrics to a song about South African apartheid and intended to perform it at a smoker. 'I was told, a few days in advance, that it was to be omitted. I went round to see the organizer and he confessed that members of the Pitt Club had heard that it was to be in the programme and had let it be known that if the song were performed, they would "break up" the smoker.'[55] Not wishing to cause a scene, Geoffrey accepted the situation. He did perform the song later at a Midnight Howlers' smoker. Certainly, it would not have got into *Springs to Mind*.

What Geoffrey recalls most from that revue was the singular presence of Joe Melia, who did wonderful sketches miming to gramophone records, with exaggerated mouth and physical gestures. All the cast wore boiler suits. 'Melia did a wonderful act of "blowing up" a guy called Bill Wallis until he was like an inflated Michelin man, and then puncturing him,' recalls Geoffrey.[56] Wallis went on to be a character actor on film and television. Not in the cast but providing material was David Nobbs, later a celebrated television comedy scriptwriter, responsible for the sitcom *The Fall and Rise of Reginald Perrin*.

Springs to Mind was certainly amusing, if unoriginal. The *Cambridge Review* found it, 'predictable, unexceptional, amiable'. Harold Hobson, the drama critic of the *Sunday Times*, praised the poetic diction as well as the comedy.

But things were about to be dramatically shaken up, and the Footlights would never be the same again.

4

The Last Laugh

Peter Cook arrived at Pembroke College in October 1957, reading French and German in preparation for a life in the diplomatic service, like his father. He had written and performed comedy at boarding school. Like a lot of comedians, Cook used humour and the art of making people laugh to stop much bigger kids from picking on him. It was a self defence mechanism that grew out of a desperately unhappy and lonely childhood where his parents were absent most of the time.

As a freshman, Cook consciously avoided the Footlights, considering them, 'A tremendously elite club. I was too bashful to even consider applying for it.'[1] It wasn't until his second year that Cook plucked up the courage to present himself at the rooms of then president Adrian Slade with a script called 'Polar Bores', a gentle knocking of an Arctic explorer's stiff upper lip reminiscences. Slade liked it so much he suggested the pair of them do it together at the next smoker. Slade then asked if he had written anymore. 'Yes,' answered Cook, 'quite a few.'

At that smoker Cook also donned a dirty mac and rumpled hat to perform an early prototype of what became his famous E. L. Wisty character. It went down a storm. 'From that moment Cambridge cabaret and revue never looked back,' stated Slade. 'A new genre of Footlight writing was born.'[2]

Cook numbered amongst a new intake of undergraduates raised on the surreal radio humour of The Goons. While to some extent the early plays of Beckett and Ionesco brought in a wave of nonsense humour to undergraduate comedy, for the most part the Footlights revue followed a safe, traditional path. Cook was new and very different and his dominance at smokers prompted John Bird to go and see what all the fuss was about. A Nottingham grammar school boy who had won a scholarship to study English at King's, Bird was seen as one of the most talented theatrical undergraduates, prone to wearing black and smoking Gauloises. Impressed by Cook, Bird invited himself to tea at his chambers and came away from the experience with the belief he had just met, 'The funniest man in England.' Word was even spreading beyond the environs of Cambridge. Donald Langdon, a young theatrical agent, caught Cook's act in a Footlights smoker and agreed to represent him.

At another Footlights smoker Cook performed with an eager new undergraduate by the name of David Frost. They also began to do cabaret together. The grammar school son of a Norfolk Methodist minister, Frost was desperate to join the Footlights after being captured by the comic skills of Cook. Frost was already the founder of a gourmet club and had begun to write articles for *Varsity* and *Granta*, for which he was eventually made editor. Soon it was difficult not to notice Frost, he had an admirable sort of dreadnought confidence. He made it his business to get to know the right people, the people who mattered.

Predictably, Frost auditioned for the Footlights in his first term. The smokers, which to Frost seemed, 'impossibly grand'[3] still took place in the ballroom of the Dorothy Café. For the occasion Frost bought his very first tuxedo. When elected it was, he said, 'The greatest thrill for me of that first term.'[4] The subscription was two guineas, plus ten and sixpence election fee, paid to the club's junior treasurer, at the time David Howell, later a Tory Minister in the Heath, Thatcher and Cameron administrations.

Frost was not especially liked by his fellow Footlights. 'He provoked mixed reactions in people,' recalls member David Gooderson. 'He was always very nice to me, and I liked him, not everyone did. He was a big personality.'[5] Cook, too, found him quite amiable, although he was unimpressed by his comedy acting. Despite that, they continued to perform together. For one smoker, Frost wrote a sketch where Cook narrated a passage from a novel that Frost acted out with increasingly convoluted and painful actions. Another skit lampooned a NATO meeting, in which delegates were referred to by their country's name: 'Take off your earphones, Holland!' Cook played a French delegate. Frost's real forte was monologues, and one regular persona was a television announcer spoofing BBC religious epilogues.

John Bird had been asked to direct the 1959 revue, *The Last Laugh*, and intended to break with tradition by offering for the first time a political satire. The theme of the show was nuclear destruction, with the whole thing taking place in an underground bunker. Atomic weapons were a political hot potato at the time, with the Cold War in full stride and the formation of the Campaign for Nuclear Disarmament (CND).

Frost was disappointed not to make the cast, or for any of his sketch material to be selected. Cook did appear, in this his first revue. Other cast members included Adrian Slade, future film and television composer Patrick Gowers, Geoffrey Pattie, later a minister in Margaret Thatcher's government, and Timothy Birdsall, a talented cartoonist. After Cambridge, Birdsall drew political cartoons for *Private Eye* and was resident cartoonist drawing live on the BBC's *That Was the Week That Was*. Tragically, he died of leukaemia in 1963 at the age of twenty-seven.

Then there was Peter Bellwood, a law student at St Catharine's College. Performing comical songs with the Midnight Howlers, he was spotted by Adrian Slade and invited to join the Footlights. Cook and Bellwood bonded almost immediately and became friends for the rest of their lives. Visiting Cook in his rooms one day Bellwood was standing in the doorway on one leg scratching an irritant blister and became the inspiration for the classic 'One Leg Too Few' sketch. According to Bellwood, Cook started improvising lines on the spot. 'Now, Mr Spiggott, you are auditioning, are you not, for the role of Tarzan.' This became one of Cook's most famous sketches, and a personal favourite.

The cast of *The Last Laugh* was completed by the inclusion of Eleanor Bron, who had seen *Zounds* and, smitten by Joe Melia, arrived at Cambridge determined to be in a Footlights revue. Attending Newnham College, Eleanor was not the first female student in a Footlights revue, but she was the first to perform in a Footlights smoker, a claim to fame she owed to Bamber Gascoigne who didn't know the rule about no women in smokers and wrote a part for her into one sketch.

The Last Laugh featured some sharp, satirical swipes at fox hunting and class warfare, a pastiche of Scott of the Antarctic and prime minister's question time done as a quiz show. Even the usual Cambridge-centric humour was given a new twist in a parody of *West Side Story* with two warring gangs representing posh students and those subsisting on grants. Instead of the usual orchestra, Bird brought in a ten-piece jazz band.

The opening night, however, was a disaster. Some of the effects and back projections didn't work and it went on so long that the manager of the Arts Theatre ordered the curtain be brought down lest the show go over midnight. For the first time in the history of the Footlights, the revue was booed. On the second night things ran much better with the technical issues sorted out and heavy cuts made.

Peter Cook emerged very much as the star. Along with Bird, he was responsible for much of the sketch material, certainly the ones that most of the audience found the funniest. A highlight took place in a train carriage where Cook informs his fellow passenger, played by Timothy Birdsall, that the cardboard box on his lap contained a viper, most definitely a viper, and not an asp. 'If anything, the viper is more voracious than the asp. My viper eats like a horse.'

In the audience that second night was Alistair Cooke, the celebrated British/American broadcaster. He had brought some American friends with him to give them a taste of a typical Footlights revue. *The Last Laugh* wasn't typical, but Cooke admired it greatly, writing in the Manchester *Guardian*. 'If the West End does not soon hear of John Bird, Patrick Gowers, Geoff Pattie and Peter Cook, the West End is an ass.'

Cook's agent managed to persuade two London producers to see the show. William Donaldson, who later co-produced *Beyond the Fringe* and found posterity with his fictional letter-writer Henry Root, preferred the humour of John Bird and got him to direct an ill-fated West End version of the revue. Cook found better fortune with the other producer, Michael Codron, who was looking for material for a new show starring Kenneth

Williams. Cook's humour, he thought, especially the viper sketch, seemed to suit Williams's style and delivery and he put the two together. Cook was to spend that summer largely writing what became *Pieces of Eight* and returned for his third term at Cambridge lauded as the author of a West End hit. It was no surprise to anyone when Cook was elected president for 1960.

By this time, Cook had already made his television debut. He had been asked to devise a comedy festive edition for Anglia's weekly series, *Town and Gown*, that focused on happenings in and around Cambridge. Cook wrote the show and brought in David Frost and Timothy Birdsall. Frost was, by now, living well in chambers, running up bills in wine houses and indulging in breakfast in bed, sometimes hiring a taxi to bring him the Sunday papers. The *Town and Gown* experience was the first time Frost had stepped inside a television studio and he felt at home immediately. His father watched at home, expecting a religious broadcast, having misheard that his son was on Anglican television.

The producers of *Town and Gown* were not alone in seeking out talent from the university. Both the BBC and ITV's various regional companies were sending out scouts to see the various revues being performed. Frost was spotted by scouts from Rediffusion and offered a trainee job after he graduated. This kind of thing went on for years, adding greatly to the importance of being in the Footlights, and led Bill Oddie to call it, 'A portal to fame.'[6] At that time there wasn't the comedy circuit as there is today, so these scouts relied almost totally on going to Cambridge, Oxford and other universities to find new talent.

The rise of Peter Cook and David Frost coincided with the Footlights acquiring a new club room, their first permanent home since 1939. The idea of new club rooms had been discussed many times over the years, and now with the Arts Theatre Trust handling the club's revue finances the money was available to do something about it. In May 1960, the lease was signed on premises in Falcon Yard, situated in the centre of the town just off Petty Cury and only a short distance from the Arts Theatre. This was to be the home of the Footlights for the next twelve years.

The area around Falcon Yard was pretty much condemned, earmarked by the council for future re-development. The club room was down an alleyway and situated on the first floor. It had recently been vacated by the university's Labour Club. It was a long room, not particularly wide. The windows on both sides had Victorian coloured stained glass. A stage was at the far end with a curtain that could be drawn across. 'It was very primitive and crude,' recalls later club member Pete Atkin.[7] There was a piano and a few rigged up lights. The stage had no deep wings, so those waiting to go on could be seen sitting on a wooden bench at the side. Because the room was above the back of Mac Fisheries, a fishmonger's shop, it had, shall we say, an odour and atmosphere all of its own.

At the other end of the room was a small bar, where members ran up bar bills, and dotted around was furniture all very tatty and second hand. The room was open to members and guests for lunch from 12.30 until 2.30 on weekdays and in the evening until quite late, becoming the perfect place to go after the pubs closed. The room quickly became a place to hang out socially or for script sessions and rehearsals. Smokers were also held there, along with private parties. Some evenings there would be live music.

As president, Peter Cook took on the responsibilities for that year's revue, entitled *Pop Goes Mrs Jessop*. In fact, he took it over, writing sixteen of the twenty-nine sketches, including another classic Cook character, the bore on the park bench full of 'interesting facts'. His 'One Leg Too Few' sketch also made its Footlight revue debut. Eleanor Bron once again made the cast, but was often relegated to the role of a secretary; so often a role women ended up playing in sketch comedy at that time. David Frost contributed some material and performed two monologues, one as the head of commercial TV's Adulterated Rediffusion extolling the virtues of imported American pap. While not as politically motivated as the previous year, *Pop Goes Mrs Jessop* still retained a satirical kick with Cook daringly taking aim at left wing politics and CND.

Cook left Cambridge in 1960 with the triumphant success of *Pop Goes Mrs Jessop* resounding in his ears; waiting for him was *Beyond the Fringe* and a career that was to lead to many, including Stephen Fry, to call him the funniest man who ever lived. A contemporary of Cook's at Cambridge, Christopher Booker, the future co-founder and first editor of *Private Eye*, had this to say about him: 'It is quite impossible now to recreate just how Peter managed so unfailingly to inspire laughter. That is why those who did not know him in those early days will never know just why he seemed to tower over everybody else.'[8]

5

I Thought I Saw It Move

No sooner had one comedy legend left the Footlights, than another replaced him. John Cleese arrived at Cambridge to study law in October 1960. He was offered a place at Downing College, although his first choice had been Pembroke. Not to be outdone, Cleese spent so much time in and around the Pembroke cloisters that most of the masters thought he was a student there anyway. 'John pretended to be at Pembroke, if anybody asked him,' remembers Bill Oddie, who was legitimately at the college, reading English literature. 'Because he hated where he was, John used to come and eat with us.'[1]

Like so many of his generation, Cleese was influenced by The Goons, and performed comedy skits at Clifton College, the boarding school he attended in Bristol. So accomplished was Cleese that when news of his acceptance into Cambridge arrived his teachers automatically assumed he would be joining the Footlights. At the Societies' Fair, held at the Corn Exchange on the first weekend of term, Cleese wandered around the numerous stalls and tables manned by eager undergraduates trying to sell their own club or society. When he saw it, Cleese made a beeline for the Footlights stall and enquired about how one might join. He was given a leaflet and asked if he could sing or dance. Wondering what this had to do with comedy Cleese said that he could do neither. 'So . . . what do you do?' slightly embarrassed and confused, Cleese said that he tried to make people laugh, before turning around and bolting.

Cleese tucked the whole ghastly episode away. For him, it wasn't the end of the world, having never considered a career in comedy anyway, he was going to be a lawyer. As it happened, Cleese's friend Alan Hutchison knew someone on the Footlights committee and took Cleese with him to the new club room one evening. Both men decided to audition at the next smoker. Hutchison performed a mock TV news broadcast while Cleese did two sketches, a scientific lecture in the gobbledegook manner of Stanley Unwin, and a spoof of police thrillers in which he played the detective engaging in fisticuffs with the murderer while at the same time explaining his deductions. The three pieces went down well and both Cleese and Hutchison were accepted as members. Christopher Stuart-Clark was at that smoker. 'And it was very funny. Cleese was very good company. He would deliberately provoke on occasion because he enjoyed the to and fro, which would have made him a brilliant advocate. He enjoyed getting into arguments.'[2]

Cleese was to spend a lot of time at Falcon Yard. 'It was relaxed and comfortable. But what really excited us was that it was plumb in the middle of Cambridge – the perfect place to pass time between lectures and to grab a quick and incredibly cheap lunch.'[3] Bill Oddie, who arrived at Cambridge at the same time as Cleese, is convinced that having their own club room was instrumental to the burst of activity and creativity during those years. 'A lot of us virtually lived in the Footlights club room. I used to go there all the time. One of the great things about it was, if you had an idea you'd go in, let's say it was lunch or something like that, and you might start talking about this idea you had, or maybe a song, and you'd ask, any piano players in, can we work on this. You got a chance to do the work on the spot.'[4] For member Andy Mayer the club room was the heart of the Footlights. 'There was a good mix there. It was a weirdly shabby place with broken sofas. You could sleep on the floor there if you wanted. It's hard for me to remember the Footlights without the club room because it was so much part of it.'[5]

Cleese always found the atmosphere there, 'friendly, funny and good natured',[6] largely because Footlight members came from such a diverse mix of academic subjects, 'bright without being show-offs'.[7] This was in direct contrast, Cleese found, to the occasional group of drama students who were let in and sat together at a corner table discussing acting theory in an intense and serious manner. All of them were intent on an acting career, whereas Cleese and most of his Footlight colleagues were just doing it as a laugh, with a view on eventually becoming doctors, lawyers et al. As Clive James was to say, many Footlights were, 'just passing through an amateur dramatics phase on the way to the real world'.[8]

As preparation began for 1961's revue, letters were sent out to members inviting them to audition. Cleese duly turned up at the Arts Theatre but once on stage was requested to sing a song and do a brief dance. Utter humiliation followed. As he trudged off someone in the queue waiting to go on offered a few words of consolation. Afterwards the two met up again and shared a coffee and a chat. The man introduced himself as Graham Chapman, a medical student studying at Emmanuel College. They shared a few laughs, finished off their coffee and agreed to stay in touch. It was the start of a writing partnership and a lifelong friendship.

The course of Graham Chapman's life had changed when at the age of fourteen he caught a clip of the revue *Between the Lines* on television one evening, impressed especially by Jonathan Miller. Noting that the troupe came from Cambridge, it just so happened that Chapman's elder brother was studying medicine there, so why couldn't he as well. 'Attending Footlights was the sole reason I wanted to go to Cambridge,' Chapman said. 'Medicine was just the excuse.'[9]

At the Societies' Fair, Chapman hunted down the Footlights stall. Manning it was David Frost who pointed out that one couldn't just join, you had to be elected or asked to audition. Chapman asked what was the point of the booth. Someone else rather keen to get into the Footlights was Tony Branch, who told Chapman that the way to do it was to hold your own smoker, invite some of the committee along and ply them with free food and drink. This they both did. Frost attended, as did Peter Bellwood, who had succeeded Peter Cook as president. Amongst the highlights were Chapman's impersonations of a carrot and a man with iron fingertips being pulled off stage by a large magnet. Sufficiently impressed, Chapman was asked to audition and got in.

Chapman was well liked. 'I do remember one time in the club room,' recalls Christopher Stuart-Clark, 'when somebody was taken ill and Graham Chapman, based on being a medical student, leapt in to see what he could do. He was a lovely man. Quite one-off, really. And one could see why he and John Cleese clicked. Both had fairly zany approaches to humour.'[10] Indeed, it didn't take Cleese and Chapman long to start playing around with sketch ideas, inspired by Cook, whom both admired greatly. It was obvious to anyone that they made a perfect team. Cleese gave structure and put in the hours and hard graft to hone the material while Chapman took their ideas to absurd levels.

While neither Cleese nor Chapman were cast in the forthcoming revue, *I Thought I Saw It Move*, a Cleese sketch did feature. 'Mine Disaster' was a parody of local TV news covering a rescue attempt by a Cornish family of their collie dog trapped on a ledge, 120 feet down a disused tin mine. Already several family members had fallen to their deaths, some within barking distance of the dog. Cleese went to see the show and was delighted the piece went down well with the audience. The whole revue, he thought, was expertly done. A professional choreographer had been brought in to whip the mostly rhythmically challenged cast into shape for the musical numbers.

Amongst the cast was John Wood, who would become better known later as John Fortune. He was reading English at King's and the previous year had been chosen by Peter Cook to direct *Pop Goes Mrs Jessop*, despite being just a freshman and having never directed anything before in his life. It was in the Footlights that Fortune was to meet fellow grammar school boy John Bird, thus beginning a lifelong comedy partnership. Fortune stood out from most of his fellow players, but for Cleese the main personality in *I Thought I Saw It Move*, was David Frost. Cleese had seen Frost around the club room and, despite his vaunted reputation around the university, seemed always to be friendly to the minnows.

Frost was to graduate that year and went to work in London for Associated Rediffusion. He didn't get much opportunity to shine there but continued to perform a few cabaret dates. He was spotted by BBC producer Ned Sherrin and asked to front a new topical comedy television programme called *That Was the Week That Was*. Looking for material, Frost got contributions from ex-Footlights Peter Cook and Michael Frayn and returned often to the university to catch smokers and lift ideas and jokes, sometimes with the consent of the students, sometimes not. Nevertheless, everyone would cram round the newly installed television set every Saturday night at Falcon Yard to watch, hoping to hear one of their bits on the show. 'That was the big event of the week,' recalls Graeme Garden.[11] Cleese's 'Mine Disaster' sketch, for instance, was performed by Frost one evening.

That Was the Week That Was began in 1962 and was at the forefront of the satire boom in Britain that was to last for several years. Like *Beyond the Fringe*, it had no respect for traditional figures of authority. It debunked religion, politics, royalty and sex to a national audience and turned Frost into a celebrity, a success that wasn't altogether celebrated by his satirist contemporaries.

Suddenly satire was everywhere. There was a new satirical magazine, *Private Eye*, and Peter Cook opened a comedy venue called the Establishment Club in Soho along with Footlight colleague Nicholas Luard, who was junior treasurer when Cook was president. It was during his final year at Cambridge that Cook was seized by the idea of opening his own satirical venue that would be run as a private club to escape the clutches of the Lord Chamberlain's censorship laws. He found the perfect place in the premises of a former strip joint at 18 Greek Street. Cook's wife, Wendy, recalled first stepping foot inside. 'It was the seediest of beer-sodden atmospheres. There were discarded G-strings, used condoms, plastic chandeliers – all the tawdry remnants of a former strip club.'[12]

The main stage featured former Footlights alumni John Bird, John Fortune and Eleanor Bron performing a 'fringe'-style satirical revue, while the basement stage featured Dudley Moore and his jazz trio. Roger Law, later co-creator of *Spitting Image*, was the club's artist-in-residence. Celebrities and would-be celebrities alike crowded into the club to be part of the scene. In his role as impresario, Cook booked the controversial American comedian Lenny Bruce and a young Australian comic not long arrived in London, Barry Humphries. Audiences, by now expecting something shocking, were baffled by Humphries' appearance as Melbourne housewife Edna Everage discussing her domestic troubles. The act was impolitely reviewed and his engagement cut short.

With Cook so much in demand, he never could spend as much time at the club as he would have wanted and after three years it ran into financial trouble and folded. And yet such was the sensation it created that even today it is regarded as one of the most iconic comedy venues ever.

When John Cleese returned to Cambridge for the start of the new academic year in autumn 1961 one of the first things that he did was head over to the Footlights club room. There he saw a group of people huddled over the notice board. On it was a list of names of those who had been appointed to the committee and to his amazement Cleese was amongst them. It helped that so many seniors had left that summer and new blood was required. Indeed, that summer's revue featured only one survivor from the previous year's production, Humphrey Barclay, a Classics scholar at

Trinity. Barclay, who after Cambridge worked for BBC radio and was later head of comedy at London Weekend Television, was encouraged to join the Footlights by his cousin, Julian Slade. At first Barclay doubted his ability to get in and so initially joined the ADC. It was here that he first encountered Trevor Nunn, who was reading English at Downing College. Almost from the word go, Nunn was involved in several ADC productions and meeting other likeminded students Derek Jacobi and Ian McKellen. In his third year it seemed an excellent idea to bring in Nunn to direct the 1962 Footlights revue, *Double Take*, although he was doing his finals at the same time, as well as directing a Marlowe Society production. The fact he was awarded a 2:2 in his exams, Nunn took as a minor miracle.

Like its predecessor, *Double Take* was put together very much in the shadow of *Beyond the Fringe* and Peter Cook. As Cleese said, 'Cook's influence was so thick in the air for two or three years you could cut it with a knife. I remember Trevor Nunn used to sit around and convulse us merely by recounting sketches Peter had done.'[13] When Eric Idle arrived at Pembroke College, he found that, 'Cook's spirit lurked everywhere in the funny voices he had left behind.'[14]

The only way to combat this was to avoid comparison at all costs. Out went the satire and in came an element of silliness and surrealism that later found its way into Monty Python and The Goodies; not surprising given that the cast featured John Cleese, Graham Chapman and Tim Brooke-Taylor, with sketch material from Bill Oddie. Brooke-Taylor was to refer to the show as, 'A complete rejection of the satire movement.'[15] The revue also contained smatterings of music hall, given the current Footlights president Robert Atkins's nostalgia for that sentimental art form, so it was an odd mix.

Growing up loving the radio comedy of Tony Hancock and Kenneth Horne, joining the Footlights was for Tim Brooke-Taylor a happy case of serendipity. At his interview with the committee considering his grant application, he was asked what he intended to do at Cambridge, besides studying. He couldn't exactly tell the truth, that he was going to drink and generally have a good time. Footlights suddenly popped into his head as an answer, recalling that his brother had spoken about them. 'I wouldn't have had the nerve to join if I hadn't promised the grant committee! In fact, it was so important to me that I had several sleepless nights before my Footlights audition.'[16]

In his first year at Pembroke, where he read law (his was a family of lawyers), Brooke-Taylor became a fan of Peter Cook, going to the opening and closing night of *Beyond the Fringe* in the West End. He also began to hang out with Cleese and Chapman. Soon he was to make an even more significant friendship. Bill Oddie can't recall how the two of them first met but is reasonably certain that it was Tim Brooke-Taylor who advised him to audition for the Pembroke smoker rather than the Footlights because it was less intimidating. 'The Footlights scared the life out of me at first,' admits Bill. 'I didn't know who these people were. I thought, this is too posh for me.'[17]

Bill Oddie hailed from Rochdale and had been raised by his father and a disagreeable grandmother; his mother was diagnosed with schizophrenia and spent much of Bill's youth in a hospital. 'So, there wasn't a lot of laughs at home. And that's what got me going out a lot.'[18] He would bicycle into the countryside, developing a love of nature and birdwatching. 'It was an escape.'[19] His father encouraged his interests. Bill had always been academically inclined and when the family moved to Birmingham he got into King Edward's, an independent boys' school that had an excellent reputation. One year Bill performed in a school revue, written by one of the older pupils. He found he enjoyed it and when that pupil left, Bill took charge of the next one, writing all the sketches and songs.

Passing the interview and entrance exam, Bill won a scholarship to Cambridge and arrived at Pembroke. He found that Tim Brooke-Taylor was right about the Pembroke smoker, and he gained a place in the college revue. Bill's forte was writing funny songs, something that had interested him since he was a child. It was this talent that got him into the Footlights, with the help of Cleese and Taylor, because no one else at the time was writing comedy songs with a pop sensibility. 'I thought, there's nobody actually using modern music, it still sounds like *Cheer-Oh Cambridge!* stuff.'[20] Bill wrote an Elvis Presley parody and an amusing pastiche of Adam Faith that featured in *Double Take* and was later performed on *That Was the Week That Was*. 'I got a double kick out of doing those songs because if I got laughs that was great, but I liked singing them as well.'[21]

Bill didn't bother to audition for *Double Take*, which was cast with a brilliant eye by Trevor Nunn. With Humphrey Barclay, Nunn also wrote the opening and closing numbers, as well as some material for the only woman in the cast, Miriam Margolyes. 'The rest of us were hopeless at this,' admitted Cleese, 'as we had literally never written for a woman.'[22] Miriam was in her second year at the all-female Newnham College and very much in demand as an actress, doing many plays because there simply weren't enough good women actors to go round. She could play comedy, too. 'I remember seeing Miriam at smokers and things being very funny,' recalls Sue Heber-Percy, a student at Girton College. 'She was exactly like she is now. She hardly changed.'[23] *Double Take* was to be her first appearance with the Footlights, and it was not a happy experience. As she was later to write in her memoirs, she felt excluded and ignored by the rest of the cast, and the fact that she was funny and got good reviews was resented. Women still only sporadically appeared in Footlight revues, and then in minimal numbers, usually just one. They were certainly not allowed to be members. Miriam came to the view that this attitude towards the female sex stemmed from the minor public schools many of the Footlights members had attended. 'During the entire run of the 1962 revue they treated me as if I were invisible and did not speak to me at all. I was nineteen and it was painful. I used to go back to my room and weep.'[24] Miriam wasn't even invited to the after-show cast party.

Another cast member was Tony Hendra. At boarding school in St Albans, where his classmate was Stephen Hawking, Hendra was intent on becoming a monk until one of his teachers advised him to accept the scholarship he had been offered to go to Cambridge. On a whim one night he went to see *Beyond the Fringe* and immediately set out to join the Footlights, having hitherto never heard of them. 'They took over my life completely.'[25] After graduating, Hendra partnered with fellow Footlight alumnus Nick Ullett to perform comedy on the club circuit, including dates at the Establishment Club. In the mid-1960s they went to live and work in America. By the 1970s Hendra focused more on comedy writing, becoming the managing editor of a new satirical US magazine called *National Lampoon*. Hendra is perhaps best known for the 1984 comedy *This Is Spinal Tap*, playing the band's long-suffering manager.

Double Take was well received and featured several Cleese/Chapman sketches. Cleese resurrected one of his audition pieces, the police detective sketch, along with a parody of television presenters and their scientific statistics. Talking about a new star, Cleese held up an orange for the audience: 'If you imagine this is the size of the dome of St Paul's Cathedral, then Regalla is 3.2 trillion times the size of the Isle of Wight.' Chapman also performed his now infamous impersonation of a carrot and a sketch where a wrestler fights himself. This routine would later feature in many of Monty Python's live shows and can be seen in *Monty Python Live at the Hollywood Bowl* (1982).

Cleese loved taking part in *Double Take*, despite a feeling that it was rather on the conventional side; the whole experience was an invaluable learning curve. It also gave him his first encounter with fame when a family recognized him walking out of the theatre, pointed and waved. 'I can still remember the sudden feeling of warmth around my heart that swelled and lifted my spirits.'[26]

Double Take had the distinction of being the first Cambridge revue to appear at the Edinburgh Fringe. While at the festival, Cleese and Chapman performed for the first time as a double act in a few shows at a local coffee house. For Chapman, this was his last involvement with the Footlights. He'd already graduated and after Edinburgh was off to St Bartholomew's Hospital in London to continue his medical studies. He still had a hankering to perform but felt that doing medicine was the right thing to do. Even so, he agreed to stay in touch with Cleese, who had another year to do, which turned out to be a momentous one.

6

A Clump of Plinths

Few revues in the history of the Footlights had quite the impact as 1963's *A Clump of Plinths*. It might not have had the catchiest of titles, but it was an enormous hit, playing in the West End and on Broadway and touring the world.

The title was a little abstract. Tim Brooke-Taylor, who was elected president that year, wanted it to be called, 'You Can't Call a Show Cornflakes'. At another meeting John Cleese suggested, 'Owl Stretching Time', later a potential title for the Monty Python TV series. 'We ended up with the show being called *A Clump of Plinths*,' says Bill Oddie, 'which was almost as bad, but it did at least describe the set.'[1] The set was a clever minimalist design made up of a series of interlocking wooden boxes.

As president, Brooke-Taylor oversaw the production and chose Humphrey Barclay as director. When Barclay asked why, Brooke-Taylor said it was because there was nobody else. Barclay had been head boy at Harrow so carried with him just the right air of authority. 'Humphrey was an inspired choice because he was just the best director,' recalls David Gooderson, who unsuccessfully auditioned for *A Clump of Plinths*. 'He was a Footlights man down to his toenails. He'd been in the club since his first year. He had this organizational quality. And although it was a group of incredibly talented people, with very good material, Humphrey drilled them and was very disciplined with them and he got an excellent show, smooth running, which wasn't always the case.'[2]

A Clump of Plinths was very much an ensemble. There was no dominating figure as there had been in the past with people like Peter Cook. 'We'd had the big names, Miller, Cook and then Frost, who may not have been the greatest talent, but he was certainly a big personality,' affirms David Gooderson. 'But the thing about *A Clump of Plinths* was, it was a true ensemble. Overall, it was excellent.'[3] Cleese, however, was to single out Tim Brooke-Taylor as the best out of the whole company, able to play everything, from drag to upper class twits, and he was a brilliant physical comedian. In one sketch, Taylor played a robot hospital visitor that keeps breaking down, speeding up, slowing down etc. In a court sketch, written by Cleese, Brooke-Taylor was a decrepit old court usher who takes an age to bring on and set up an exhibit. 'Do you recognize this object,' asks Cleese's lawyer. 'No,' says

FIGURE 6.1 *The famous 1963 Footlights revue* A Clump of Plinths. *'Cambridge Circus' New Revue at the Lyric Theatre: John Cleese (left), Bill Oddie (front sitting with trumpet) and Tim Brooke-Taylor (glasses and hat). Phillip Jackson/ANL/Shutterstock.*

the witness. 'No further questions,' says Cleese. Brooke-Taylor totters back on and takes an age to dismantle said object and totter off again. 'He managed to spin that bit out for five minutes some nights!' recalls Bill Oddie.[4]

The idea for the court sketch was for something that could feature the entire cast. Cleese agreed to write it but each time he was asked how it was going he'd say that he hadn't got round to it yet. 'And we waited and waited and waited until quite close to when we were due to do the show,' recalls Bill, 'and then one day he said, "There's some good news, I've finished the court scene."'[5] After that it was worked on and improved by the cast during rehearsals. 'It's a great piece of writing,' declares Bill, 'but he took so long to write the fucking thing. We used to tease him about it, "Well, it should be good, you took long enough." But it was wonderful. It was a sort of classic thing we could build on all the time. It was always growing.'[6]

David Gooderson recalls that sketch being performed for the first time at a smoker. He played a dwarf who comes on at the end as a witness, a role Bill Oddie played in the revue. 'And watching from the wings I was in hysterics, barely able to go on to do my bit because it was so funny. And watching John, this big man on that tiny stage. He was brilliantly funny.'[7]

A Clump of Plinths was a very visual show, with a lot of silliness and physical comedy, deliberately so; again, it was a reaction against the satire of *Beyond the Fringe* and *That Was the Week That Was*. The feeling was that satire was now a bit passe and the public had had enough of it. 'I know a lot of the reviews when we came into London almost accused us of not being satirical,' says cast member Christopher Stuart-Clark.[8]

Bill Oddie co-wrote an amusing sketch with Cleese, a BBC news broadcast set in biblical times, with the weather man warning of things like a plague of locusts moving in from the west. 'It was just the sort of thing David Frost could steal.'[9] But his main contribution were several catchy songs. One of them, about Green Line buses, featured a group of London businessmen in bowler hats discussing bus routes in the style of an American minstrel song. Oddie had been slightly reserved around the Footlights clubroom in the beginning, not making much of an impression. However, his contribution to *A Clump of Plinths* deservedly caught the attention of the critic of the *Guardian* who described him as, 'A real discovery,' and 'A dazzling comic who should go far.'

The token woman this time was Jo Kendall, up against six lads. She was not a student, instead she taught English and drama at a Cambridge secondary school, while acting in some ADC productions. Barclay spotted her and cast her as, 'The obvious choice as the female component.'[10] Jo, it appears, did not encounter the same troubles Miriam Margolyes had the previous year. 'We all got on very well,' recalls Christopher Stuart-Clark. 'Jo was lovely.'[11] In one sketch she appeared with Cleese as an English couple in the tropics in a Somerset Maugham take-off who in-between anguished pauses swat various deadly creatures like a snake or poisonous spider. Jo went on to have a prolific career on radio and television; she uttered the very first line of dialogue in the TV soap *Emmerdale Farm*.

Rounding off the cast was David Hatch, later a BBC radio producer, and Anthony Buffery, a psychology postgraduate student. Cleese thought he, 'couldn't act for toffee'[12] but was extremely intelligent and brought a certain eccentricity to the cast. He did one mime in the show as a spear thrower at an ancient battle who takes an age to lob his weapon then has nothing else to contribute. Finally, there was Christopher Stuart-Clark, whose Footlights audition had been overseen by David Frost and John Fortune, so no pressure at all. Reading English and Classics, Christopher was at Pembroke with Tim Brooke-Taylor and they became very close friends. 'Tim was a naturally funny guy. We wrote scripts together and, on the whole, laughed at each other's contribution.'[13] David Gooderson had a lot of time for Tim Brooke-Taylor, too.

'He was such a lovely man. Just a charming guy. And a very self-deprecating man in a sense, all the ego you need for performing, but not any extra.'[14]

Once the cast was announced everyone came back a week before term specifically to compile the revue out of the best sketches of the year, along with some new material. 'We were all sworn not to do any work towards our degrees for that week, but just to write and put together the revue,' recalls Christopher. 'I did catch Cleese doing some law on the side once.'[15] Highlights included a send up of BBC sports commentators and a spoof Oscar Wilde play in which Tim Brooke-Taylor played a Lady Bracknell-type, an early version of his Lady Constance de Coverlet character, who graced many episodes of the long running *I'm Sorry, I'll Read That Again*. 'That was one of his high moments,' affirms Graeme Garden. 'He also tended to play the little man against John Cleese as the overbearing superior.'[16] One sketch included the line: What is the difference between an egg, a carpet and a bit of crumpet? You can beat an egg, you can beat a carpet but you can't beat a bit of crumpet. 'This was rejected by the Lord Chamberlain,' recalls Christopher Stuart-Clark. 'When we replaced "crumpet" with "crackling" it passed.'[17]

The opening night of *A Clump of Plinths* was an unqualified success. Brooke-Taylor and Oddie got the best ovations, 'They were outstandingly the stars of the show,' said Cleese.[18] Graham Chapman came up from London to see it. Following the experience of the previous revue, Cleese was surging with a confidence that allowed him to be more inventive and adventurous in his comedy acting, developing many of the traits and characteristics that was to inform his later comedy persona. After one performance he was approached in the club room by a couple of BBC employees inviting him to work as a trainee producer-writer in their radio light entertainment department. Cleese had never really considered taking this route before, but following this chat concluded that after Cambridge he should ditch law and accept the BBC's offer. First, *A Clump of Plinths* was to have an extraordinary second, third and even fourth life.

In the audience one night was an aspiring impresario named Michael White. He happened to be in Cambridge over a weekend and was told that the current Footlights revue was on but that all the major London managements had seen it and passed, saying it was inferior to *Beyond the Fringe*. White caught the final matinee, 'and felt that I saw pure comic genius at work'.[19] Undergoing a change of name to *Cambridge Circus*, White brought the show to the West End, minus one cast member. Anthony Buffery had jumped ship, deciding to continue with his studies to become a neuropsychologist. He was greatly missed. 'Tony was a very funny guy,' recalls Richard Crane. 'But he decided not to go pro. He was a great supporter. He was the only one who made me feel at home the first time I did the Footlights audition.'[20] For his replacement Cleese suggested Graham Chapman and Chapman ended up performing in the evenings having done his ward rounds at the hospital during the day.

Cambridge Circus opened at the Lyric Theatre that July. As a publicity stunt the cast enacted the Oscar Wilde sketch in full costume on the actual Cambridge Circus, a partly pedestrianized intersection where Shaftesbury Avenue crosses Charing Cross Road in London. 'It stopped a lot of traffic,' recalls Christopher Stuart-Clark, 'and eventually a policeman moved us on, "for wearing fancy dress within three miles of Charing Cross," not a law we were familiar with. A photo of us with the constable was posted outside the theatre (and on the sleeve of the LP of the show) much to the amusement of his fellow officers.'[21]

The show met with some positive notices: 'You cannot expect every Footlight revue to start a new wave or spew up a vast amount of talent,' said the *Observer*. 'But of course you do, and of course they don't. *Cambridge Circus* . . . does the expected rather well.' Others weren't convinced. Bernard Levin found the material, 'pretty thin'. During its run of 100 performances, audiences began to dwindle, something that Michael White noticed the cast was not all that bothered about. 'Most of them were ready for the show to end so that they could get on with their true careers.'[22] Rabid ambition to use the Footlights as a vehicle to enter showbiz was then not all that prevalent, as Christopher Stuart-Clark notes, 'There were plenty of members of the Footlights who perhaps had no particular ambition to take it any further.'[23]

Next, White organized a six-week tour to New Zealand in May 1964. This time Christopher Stuart-Clark pulled out, having already accepted a teaching post. 'It had never occurred to me to go into the entertainment profession,' he says. 'I knew it was pretty risky. But the whole revue was an extraordinary experience.'[24] His place was taken by Footlights member Jonathan Lynn, who was the drummer in the band. 'Jonathan was an amazing jazz drummer,' claims Christopher. 'And he knew the revue like the back of his hand because he'd been in the orchestra pit for the whole West End run.'[25] Jonathan Lynn went on to become a film director and writer, famous as the co-creator of *Yes Minister*.

Then an offer arrived to play Broadway that October, the only time for any Footlights revue. Opening at the Plymouth Theatre, the cast was in the fortunate position of following on the heels of the successful *Beyond the Fringe* and were asked to appear on the top-rated Ed Sullivan show on CBS. 'I don't think we knew how prestigious that was,' recalls Bill Oddie, 'except that the American journalists would say things like, my God, you boys are doing well.'[26] Waiting to go on, Bill opened a window in his dressing room to get some air and noticed a group of girls outside cheering and clapping. 'I thought, what's that all about. It can't be for me. And The Animals were on the same show and at that stage in life I bore a slight resemblance at a distance to their singer Eric Burdon. So, I think I was mistaken for Eric Burdon, because I was small and British.'[27]

Despite such exposure and positive reviews, it was a short-lived run. Bill had a theory why it failed. The American impresario who put it on, Sol Hurok, tended to specialize in spectacular shows, like operas, ballets and circuses. 'I was convinced he thought it was a real circus. He had no sense of humour. He was like Lew Grade at his worst with this big cigar.'[28] Did Hurok bother to check out the show before bringing it over? Did he assume that since Moscow had a circus, so did Cambridge? The cast met Hurok just the once, at a rehearsal. He wished everyone good luck and they never saw him again. 'We thought it was like 'Springtime for Hitler',' says Bill, 'Mel Brooks' *The Producers*. We thought it was the same thing, that he'd taken us on as a tax loss. But unfortunately for Sol we got rave reviews. We were tipped as that year's hit. I got compared to Mickey Rooney. I didn't know if that was a compliment or not. And then they said, well, we're closing down now. We'd only been there three weeks or something.'[29]

Luckily, the cast was taken on by another pair of producers who transferred the show to a smaller club theatre in the hippy and arty Greenwich Village, and it ran successfully there for three months. 'We thought, this is actually a better place to be,' recalls Bill.[30] During its run, Terry Gilliam, then working for the satire magazine *Help*, met Cleese for the first time and asked him to do some work for the magazine.

But *Cambridge Circus* wasn't quite finished. The BBC wanted to commission a radio sketch show, to be recorded in front of a live audience, with the *Cambridge Circus* cast. This turned out to be the prototype for *I'm Sorry, I'll Read That Again*. The title derived from something that BBC announcers tended to say when they made an error on air, something that always made Cleese and Tim Brooke-Taylor laugh. It was produced by Humphrey Barclay, who had been recruited by the BBC and was proving helpful in launching Footlights comedians on their way to success. David Frost did likewise, notably in starting John Cleese's television career with the comedy show *The Frost Report* in 1966, which also introduced the British public to Ronnie Barker and Ronnie Corbett.

As the brilliance of *Beyond the Fringe* cast its shadow over the next generation, so too did *Cambridge Circus* and talents like John Cleese. Its success did much to inform and influence the way comedy was performed in the Footlights for many years to come. Eric Idle called the revue the funniest thing he had seen since *Beyond the Fringe*. Fast forward to 1983, there was even a *Cambridge Circus* reunion. Humphrey Barclay organized a charity show one Sunday evening at the Drury Lane Theatre and brought back the original cast to re-enact Cleese's court room sketch. Only Anthony Buffery was absent. His place was taken by a young Rowan Atkinson.

7

Stuff What Dreams Are Made Of

When Graeme Garden first arrived at Emmanuel College to study medicine, he found the Footlights rather too daunting a society to get into straight away. 'But I did join the Light Entertainment Society, CULES as it was called, which was a sort of second cousin to the Footlights. We used to go round to hospitals and old folks' homes to do concerts and I met several people from the Footlights in that who said why don't you come along and audition.'[1]

By the end of his first year, Graeme plucked up enough courage to give it a go. Still, it was quite daunting to face the committee all sitting there, luckily not stony faced. Amongst them was the current president, Tim Brooke-Taylor. Graeme had met and seen Brooke-Taylor around, 'but this was the first serious Footlights encounter I had with him'.[2] Graeme knew that everyone else was writing terribly witty sketches for their audition. At school he hadn't done much acting but was interested in art and drawing. 'I've always been a great fan of cartoons. I suppose when we did *The Goodies* eventually that was like an animated cartoon.'[3] Deciding that the best way to make an impression was by doing something totally different, Graeme's audition was drawing a series of cartoons. 'I had a big easel with a load of paper on it and I think the first one I did was the various types of students, the nerdy ones in specs, the brash ones in little pork pie hats, and which pubs they went to and things like that.'[4] He got in.

Graeme didn't have much time to strike up any kind of friendship with Tim Brooke-Taylor, who graduated that year. As did Bill Oddie, though Graeme got to know him a little bit better, first meeting him in the club room. They both liked art and drew, and when Graeme became art editor of *PA* magazine at the university, he asked Oddie to contribute some cartoons. It's amusing to think that all three future Goodies were in the Footlights at the same time, although they never appeared together on stage.

Graeme's first taste of action, certainly his first exposure to a paying audience, was when Humphrey Barclay put together a B-team to perform *A Clump of Plinths* in Edinburgh while the original cast was in the West End. 'It was very exciting and quite nerve wracking. I don't think it was make or break career time for any of us, so we were quite gung-ho about the whole thing. And having done it for the first time and got away with it, as it were, it was a great buzz. It's a huge rush the first time you get that audience reaction.'[5]

Another member of that B-team was Eric Idle, who arrived at Pembroke on a scholarship. He was spotted by Barclay performing in his college smoker and introduced to John Cleese. Both men encouraged him to audition for the Footlights. But it was Bill Oddie and Tim Brooke-Taylor who Idle was always to feel beholden to, as they were on the panel that oversaw his audition, as Bill recalls. 'Eric came in with two other guys; he was the quiet one. And one of the other guys was full of himself and he just kept giggling at whatever he did, and we said, "Is there any chance you can stop laughing at yourself and actually do the sketch." And whoever it was said, "I'm sorry, but we only wrote it this morning and we still find it terribly funny." And Eric was going, oh fuck. And we said afterwards, we want the quiet one. I didn't know who those two guys were, but I didn't want to see or listen to them again.'[6]

Also in the cast was Richard Eyre and David Gooderson. 'We had a big success with the show in Edinburgh,' David recalls. 'And I had the fun of performing in a lot of that extremely good material.'[7] Harold Hobson of the *Sunday Times* said of the revue, 'They attract admiration as effortlessly as the sun attracts the flowers.'

Richard Eyre, later a renowned theatre and film director, was not a Footlights man, he had been roped into the revue because he was appearing concurrently in an ADC production of *The Tempest*. 'And he was very good in our show,' states David.[8] The revue cast went in the other direction, too, and had small roles in *The Tempest*. 'And we all had these terrible false beards,' recalls Graeme. 'In one performance, David, playing the king, his beard started falling off. Eventually he pulled it off completely and that allowed the other courtiers to pull off our beards as well, him being the king.'[9]

Graeme, along with Idle and Gooderson, also featured together in the Footlights cabaret team that was often hired to perform at private parties and functions. Because it was a professional engagement, each of them got paid. 'It was a nice little earner,' declares David. 'A lot of us paid off our bar bills that way.'[10]

David Gooderson knew all about Cambridge, his father was a don at St Catharine's College, and even though he had been at boarding school he knew all about Jonathan Miller and the Footlights and caught a performance of *Pop Goes Mrs Jessop*. 'It was a very slick and funny revue.'[11] Still, when he came up to Queens' College to study law and English, he didn't gravitate towards the Footlights. Having caught the acting bug at school he joined the ADC; on his first day David sat next to another new arrival in Trevor Nunn. 'But I found the ADC not particularly to my liking. It was rather competitive and took up too much time.'[12] Instead, David began appearing in smokers at his college, finding he was rather good at sketches. 'I've always been a character actor, so I love playing different characters and that's why I fitted into revue.'[13] It was at one of these smokers that David was spotted and asked to join the Footlights. His recollection is that he wasn't required to audition. 'I think they had scouts or people went round Cambridge looking for talent.'[14]

David felt very much at home in the Footlights, 'where people enjoyed themselves and had many different interests'.[15] He recalls, for instance, a long conversation with John Cleese in the club room about law and teaching, nothing at all to do with comedy. 'I wouldn't have put John down as a man who was going to do anything but what we were talking about, either be a lawyer or a teacher.'[16] David went into teaching, only to later go back into acting. 'The Footlights was what I would call amateur in the best sense. It was relaxed. There were rarely dramas or battles. It was a great place to be.'[17] And as far as David was concerned that feeling carried over into the revues themselves. 'But in a very disciplined way, particularly with someone like Humphrey Barclay in charge.'[18]

This relaxed atmosphere was something that Bill Oddie picked up on, not least the fact that because no one was afraid to try something different or take risks, it was an aid to creativity. There's nothing worse than a comedian dying on stage. At the Footlights audiences were on your side. 'I always worked on the theory, or the comforting belief, that if you're going to get up on stage and try and get the audience to like you, then you'd better like them first.'[19] Indeed, nothing much had changed since the late 1890s when *Granta* reported that members at smokers, 'form themselves into a mutual admiration society, and in turn loudly applaud the histrionic, musical or dramatic efforts of their friends'.

Smokers were still held twice a term. 'They were really to try out new material,' says Graeme Garden, 'and the best material from the various smoking concerts would be earmarked and would form the basis of the revue'.[20] They took place at the club room in Falcon Yard. 'And that was a very nice social place,' recalls David Gooderson, 'where jokes were flowing, people were funny and witty, but it wasn't pressurised.'[21] Graeme Garden spent a lot of time there, too. 'It was a place where you could go and just drop in and see people at lunch, or in the evening have a drink and a chat. It was like a gentleman's club, and it was a gentleman's club in those days.'[22] Christopher Stuart-Clark also fondly recalls the warm atmosphere there. 'It was fun because they were a very entertaining, good friendly group. I almost remember the lunches in the club house as much as I do the smoking concerts. It was a very happy time.'[23]

The 1964 revue went by the name of *Stuff What Dreams Are Made Of* and included amongst the cast were John Cameron, Graeme Garden, Jonathan Lynn and David Gooderson. Graeme performed some of his own material, notably a mime with a ticking alarm clock. 'Jonathan Lynn was also the drummer in the band, and he was in the wings with a couple of drumsticks doing the ticks. And as time went on the ticks got louder and louder and I was trying to sleep, and then they started doing rhythms.'[24]

FIGURE 7.1 *The cast of the 1964 revue* Stuff What Dreams Are Made Of *at Cambridge University, 9 March 1964. Photo by John Bulmer/Popperfoto via Getty Images.*

FIGURE 7.2 *Programme for the 1964 revue. Reproduced with the permission of Sue Heber-Percy.*

After several attempts to silence the clock, Graeme finally stamps on it. 'The clock stopped ticking. And I walk back to the bed and with each footstep it ticked.'[25] This sketch was always well received. Brian Gascoigne was the musical director. 'That mime by Graeme provided one of only two occasions when I couldn't help laughing every night.'[26]

Graeme was always an excellent physical comedian. A fan of Buster Keaton, many of the sketches he wrote and performed in revues and smokers were visual in nature. One was called: 'Pets Corner'. 'It was lots of little silly props and jokes about vampire bats and things. It's been a great standby.'[27] Graeme was still performing it as late as the 1990s on tour in Australia.

Despite *A Clump of Plinths* being a huge success, Graeme and the rest of the cast felt no pressure following on from it. 'We didn't think we would go to Broadway. We just enjoyed doing the show.'[28] Like most, Graeme was merely content to be funny rather than using the revue as a stepping stone. He had, though, been made president that year, but saw little work to be done. 'It was pretty-well self-governing by then. You knew who the best people were. For example, you'd appoint someone to put on a smoking concert and it would be their responsibility to get people involved and produce a show.'[29] As president, Graeme was obliged to attend all the smokers, dressed in the president's jacket. 'It was a velvet smoking jacket which was beginning to fall apart I have to say.'[30]

David Gooderson was also asked to serve on the committee, as vice president. 'It was a well-run club. There were five or six of us on the committee.'[31] One of these was Harry Porter, who had been a member in the 1950s and was back at the university lecturing in history. 'He was a lovely, very jokey sort of gentleman,' David recalls. 'He wore his learning very lightly and was very good fun and people loved him.'[32] Harry Porter was to be a presence around the club for many years as senior treasurer and later its archivist.

David appeared in *Stuff What Dreams Are Made Of* but thought in general it was a step down from *Plinths*, despite a capable cast. The sketches were reasonable, it was quite anarchic, but his recollection is that the group almost lost confidence in the show. 'We cut some of it or pruned it right at the very last minute, rather than going with it and making it work, and looking back I think that was a failure of nerve in a sense.'[33] And there wasn't quite the same steady hand on the tiller as there had been under Humphrey Barclay. Saying that, *Plinths* was difficult to top. Musically it was sound, thanks to John Cameron who took over the Bill Oddie mantle of providing contemporary songs rather than the traditional Footlight ditties.

John Cameron arrived in Cambridge to read history but had a strong music interest and regularly played in jazz bands around the town. He had been writing songs, many of them satirical, for quite some time, and performed one for his successful Footlights audition. Quite soon he was writing material with Eric Idle, who he found, 'Quite charismatic even then. He stood out as somebody that was going to go somewhere.'[34] This is a view shared by Andy Mayer, a student at Jesus College. 'Eric was a very good performer and very professional. He was much more ambitious than a lot of us. He got an agent before anybody else.'[35]

One of the songs John wrote with Eric Idle, a Beatles pastiche called, 'I Wanna Hold Your Handel', was used in the revue. It was also put into the Broadway production of *Cambridge Circus* when new material was needed. 'Suddenly Eric and I got little blue envelopes every month on the mantlepiece at Falcon Yard which was our royalty, and which kept us in the manner that we'd like to be accustomed to. Although it did cost us a lot of drinks in the bar.'[36]

Graeme Garden featured in the Beatles sketch. 'Graeme was a lovely guy,' John recalls. 'Very friendly and a great collaborator.'[37] On piano was the regular pianist in CULES and the Footlights, law student Jim Beach. 'Jim was probably not the finest piano player in the world,' admits John, 'but ended up being one of the greatest rock managers in the world with Queen.'[38]

The Beatles song, along with some of the others John wrote, he terms as, 'softly satirical.'[39] That included another parody, this time of Frank Sinatra. 'It was a fond satire; it wasn't a chew you out satire. That's how *Cambridge Circus* affected us, we were looking for things that held people to account but didn't tread on them. *Cambridge Circus* was nice because it slightly broke the mould. It wasn't heavy satire but silly sketches and songs. I think by then the public had got a little bit tired of satirists just chewing everybody out.'[40]

Not one but two women featured in *Stuff What Dreams Are Made Of*, Sue Heber-Percy and Felicity Hough. Both Sue and Felicity were reading English at Girton College and had appeared in a few college revues and some amateur theatrics. 'We had great times together and always laughed a lot,' Sue recalls fondly. 'We would write our essays together at the last minute up to about three o'clock in the morning. Felicity was very pretty. She was very stylish. She was very funny. And she was a good friend.'[41]

Sue has never forgotten her first glimpse of Cambridge. She had left boarding school at her own request, a grim place in Escrick, near York, but still wanted to go to university. Her mother found a cram school near Cambridge so they both went down to look at it, taking a walk through the university town. 'It was evening, and the sky was a kind of purple. We came round the corner from Trinity Street into King's Parade and I saw this amazing stretch of buildings, white against this purple, and it was so beautiful I said, I have to come here. I have to get to Cambridge. I just fell in love with the place.'[42]

According to Sue, the Footlights liked to have some girls around for the revue, 'But it was still very male in those days.'[43] However, both she and Felicity encountered a very different atmosphere to the one Miriam Margolyes complained about. 'They were all very sweet to us. And I kept up with several of them for decades since. I had fun. I loved it. It was a bit of a boys' club, but the whole university was like that.'[44] In the show, Sue did a skit on Ibsen plays, 'It was fashionable at the time to love Chekhov and decry Ibsen,'[45] and performed a solo song about Christine Keeler, which she thinks Eric Idle wrote. Idle had not been asked to be in the revue, much to his disappointment, but he did write a lot of material and was at rehearsals. 'I can remember him coming up with one gag after another,' says Sue, 'most of which were terrible and we all groaned, and then he'd come up with a really good one. But he had just endless inventiveness.'[46]

For Graeme, the revue did rather interfere with his final exams. 'I had a couple of exams which actually coincided with matinees, and I managed to get there for the second half, so they were able to re-jig the running order to accommodate me.'[47] This was always a problem for students, balancing studies with their extracurricular activities. Although something like the Footlights was often a positive. 'The workload was fairly heavy, so it was a great relief to be able to spend an evening larking about and being silly,' says Graeme. 'It was a very good balance.'[48]

Following graduation, Graeme continued his medical studies at King's College Hospital in London. When Graham Chapman opted out of the chance to be in, *I'm Sorry, I'll Read That Again*, Humphrey Barclay asked Graeme if he would do it. 'So, I joined the team and that's really when I started working properly with Tim and Bill.'[49] Oddly enough, it was after Graeme qualified as a doctor that he got an offer to do his first television, a BBC sketch show called *Twice a Fortnight* with Bill Oddie, Jonathan Lynn, Terry Jones and Michael Palin. It lasted one series. 'After that finished, I was sharing a flat with Eric Idle and he suggested that Tim and I did something together because Tim was slightly at a loose end, as I was. So, Tim and I devised a TV show which was *Broaden Your Mind*, and that's when Tim and I really started working together. And looking back I think Tim and I worked together every year for the rest of his life.'[50]

Returning to *Stuff What Dreams Are Made Of*, Graeme had taken part in a short tour to Oxford, Bury St Edmunds and Newark. 'It was fun to go out on the road. That seemed very grown up. We were looked after by the locals and stayed in their homes. We were treated rather like pets.'[51] In Bury St Edmunds, John Cameron remembers the cast being put up in a house in the middle of nowhere. After asking when the bus into town was, they were told Thursday. This raised the question of how they were going to get to the theatre every night. The homeowner said they could borrow his Land Rover, only the starter motor was gone so it had to be parked on a hill and given a push start. 'So, everywhere we went we had to find somewhere to park where there was a bit of a hill so it could either be pushed forward or backwards to start the damn thing.'[52] The entire cast managed to fit in. 'Totally illegal, I'm sure,' thinks John.[53]

Sue and Felicity joined the boys on tour. Sue had written and performed a sketch of her own and Felicity wrote lyrics for two of the songs. There was no resistance or stuffiness regarding the two women providing material. 'There was never any sense of superiority,' states David Gooderson. 'We were glad to have them, and their talent.'[54] It was a case of, if the material was good enough it was chosen. The success of Sue and Felicity in the show,

'They were terrifically good,' remembers Graeme,[55] raised the issue of women being allowed to join the Footlights. 'I was the president at the time,' says Graeme, 'and the committee felt it was time that the female students who had appeared in Footlight revues ought to be members as well. It seemed silly not to. And so, we suggested that we made Sue and Felicity full members of the club. And Harry Porter said he would resign if we appointed women members, which left us in a bit of a quandary.'[56] Both Sue and Felicity had begun to kick up a fuss about it. And so, a compromise was reached to offer them associate membership for the duration of the revue. 'They did that as a sort of sop to us,' claims Sue.[57]

This situation only served to emphasize how stuck in the past the Footlights were. 'At the time it was beginning to be a puzzle why the club was not open to women, who by then were appearing on the comedy scene,' says Graeme.[58] Most people, it appeared, just accepted it as the way it had always been. It was tradition. 'The club carried on much as before,' declares David. 'It seems funny that now it's such an obvious thing that it was not really considered. It wasn't that we were thinking, keep them out or even carry on tradition. I think it was rather more focusing on performing and running a successful club than changing anything very fundamental about it.'[59]

It was very much the same situation in the university itself. At that time the ratio was something like eight men to one woman in Cambridge, which meant that women felt they had to be eight times as forceful as a man if they wanted to get anywhere. 'And there were no women in men's colleges either,' says Footlights member Richard Crane. 'Everything was very separate. It was just a continuation of public school.'[60] But society was beginning to change by the mid-1960s. People were beginning to query things and asking the question: Why?' 'It was very old fashioned,' recalls Bill Oddie. 'The Footlights still had this thing about women, that they shouldn't really be here because they're not funny. I always felt that not allowing women to be part of it was just iniquitous, and you didn't have to be a feminist as a woman to want to say, why the fucking hell aren't we allowed in this. I think unfortunately there was a lurking kind of early chauvinism where unless the woman was pretty, they really didn't want to know.'[61]

The change came about quicker than most people might have anticipated. When the new term got underway in 1964 and Eric Idle took over from Graeme as president, he made it a point of his presidency to allow women to become members, writing to the senior treasurer, 'I think it is degrading and fantastically backward looking that women should not have the same opportunities at university as men.'[62] Despite some resistance, and calling Harry Porter's bluff, Idle got his way and in October the first women were elected members of the Footlights after successfully passing an audition, although they were still not allowed on the committee for another year. The women in question were Hilary Walston, Sheila Buhr and Germaine Greer.

As vice president John Cameron was 100 per cent behind Idle's decision. 'I'm rather proud of the fact that we did that. I felt it was a natural progression. It was inevitable. We had all known about Miriam Margolyes who should have been a member and railed against the fact that she wasn't able to have the same status as men. You just thought, this has got to happen.'[63] This was especially true when the club was faced with a personality like Germaine Greer. 'My feeling was,' says John, 'when somebody like Germaine comes along, and the force of her charisma and her personality was so much, you thought, she's got to be a member. Sometimes it's somebody like that that crashes the ceiling and Germaine did.'[64]

From the first moment she arrived in Cambridge, Germaine Greer was a force of nature. She was a mature student from the universities of Melbourne and Sydney, and turned up for her Footlights audition at Falcon Yard with fellow Australian Clive James, who was kitted out in the required dress of a dinner jacket which he had to hire. The audition was a Noël Coward pastiche, with James as Noël Coward and Germaine as Gertrude Lawrence. James confessed he was dreadful, but Germaine was so good she got them both in. James also got the impression that the decision to allow women to become members was not wholeheartedly embraced. 'Most of the dons who congregated around the club's small but thriving bar made it piercingly clear that they had preferred the era of good, straightforward transvestitism, with properly shaved legs and no nonsense about it.'[65]

Clive James's influence and importance within the Footlights over the next few years was to be considerable, but he didn't get into the 1965 revue. Germaine did and stole the show. Called, *My Girl Herbert*, it transferred to the West End for a three-week run at the Lyric Theatre. It didn't exactly play to full houses and matinees were deathly, 'during which the cast ran some of the sketches backwards to see whether the old age pensioners would notice,' recalled Clive James, who provided some sketch material.[66]

Germaine shone, however, leading one critic to refer to her as a cross between Eleanor Bron and Joyce Grenfell. 'She was a very strong performer,' recalls Andy Mayer, who in 1968, when he was at Granada, gave Germaine her first break presenting on television. 'She was good in sketches. She could do monologues. She could sing. And she looked amazing. She was a big asset.'[67] And ballsy. In your face. Germaine did a stripping nun act that became her tour de force, people would always ask her to do it at smokers. It began with her walking onto the stage dressed as a nun in a wimple and then slowly she began to strip down to, well not a lot. 'That was a knockout,' confirms Andy. 'She used to do that in cabaret a lot. She also did a blinding rendition of "Land of Hope and Glory" in the style of Dame Clara Butt.'[68]

In one sketch in *My Girl Herbert*, a send up of the Three Musketeers, Germaine appeared as the Queen of France in a stunning black and white long frock. The line went, 'Lo, 'tis the Queen of France, dressed in the colours of Tottenham Hotspur.' John Cameron considered Germaine, 'A commanding personality every time she came on stage.'[69] Off-stage, too. 'She was the force in our lives,' claims John. 'We had no idea about feminist ideas until Germaine crashed into the place.'[70]

John was musical director on the show and brought in his jazz pals to form the band. 'We were trying to get the music content back a little bit to what it had been in the old days, when there was quite a lot of music content.'[71] With an explosion of music in the mid-1960s, with the emergence of bands like The Beatles, that certainly made sense. John Cleese and Graham Chapman had been eager to try to cut back on the musical element of revues. There was one story of a Saturday matinee of a revue on tour. A typical *Salad Days*-type ditty was closing the first act with the singer at the front of the stage and everyone else behind singing along. As the number began Cleese emerged from the back of the stage with a custard pie. 'The first person in the chorus saw him and corpsed, then the next,' recalls John Cameron. 'And of course the audience saw him. The one person who didn't see him was the guy singing, until he got the full force of the custard pie in the face.'[72]

Both John and Eric Idle left Cambridge in 1965. In their very last smoker, they wrote a pastiche of the old revue called *Cheer-Oh Cambridge!* The idea was to send it up rotten – cheerio, we'll miss you – that kind of thing, and that they couldn't wait to leave and get out into the real world. 'And we found about half-way through the numbers we both had tears in our eyes,' recalls John, 'as had most of the audience.'[73]

The Footlights had been an extraordinary home for John during those three years; he virtually lived at Falcon's Yard. 'I used to eventually walk home over Silver Street Bridge about three in the morning. Get back to the rooms in Newnham House, put John Coltrane on and finish a history essay. My neighbours wanted to kill me.'[74] He recalls the conversations that one had in the club room, where people expressed a desire to write for television, to act, or whatever. 'And almost everybody did. There was a can-do kind of attitude to things. It was a powerhouse there and a hotbed of ideas.'[75]

After Cambridge, John and Eric did a bit of cabaret together and even wrote a musical before going their separate ways; Idle into comedy and John into a career as a film and theatre composer, arranger and musician. 'And it was probably the Footlights that gave me the balls and the confidence to go out into the world and say, I'm a composer!'[76]

Germaine Greer also appeared in the 1966 revue, called *This Way Out*, and again turned out to be the star. Unusually, three women were in the cast, precisely due to the presence of Germaine. 'We thought two girls against Germaine was more of a balance than one girl vying to be like Germaine,' says Richard Syms, who directed the production.[77] Fully aware that a lot of people joined the Footlights merely to have fun, and for the social element, Richard was careful to cast those who would bring professionalism to the revue and take it seriously.

Richard was in his final year at Cambridge having arrived in 1963, 'and in that first year we were all under the spell of Cleese, Brooke-Taylor and Oddie.'[78] Richard knew Eric Idle, too, and recalls going on a Footlights tour with him and ending up in Southampton where the cast was given a list of addresses where they were to be staying. Everyone bundled into a car and were deposited one by one at their digs until there was just Idle and Richard left. 'The next address belonged to somebody called Mrs Bloodworthy, so we tossed a coin and decided that whoever lost the toss would get Mrs Bloodworthy and whoever won the toss would manage to escape and go on to the last one on the list. I lost the toss. We got to Mrs Bloodworthy's house and Eric watched as I walked up the path. I knocked at the door and this gorgeous girl in a negligee-type thing came out. I said, "Mrs B, B, Bloodworthy?" She said, "That's right, do come in." And I looked back, and Eric's face out of the back of the car as it drove away was a picture.'[79]

Richard also appeared in *This Way Out*, and in one sketch dragged up as the MP Barbara Castle. Even though women now regularly featured in the cast some of the men still put on a dress for comic effect. 'As the first backseat driver to become Minister of Transport,' was his opening line. Mrs Castle didn't drive. The sketch poked fun at government transport policy. Another line went, 'Any car travelling less than fifteen miles per hour will be considered parked and therefore fined occasionally.' Richard didn't consider himself much of a writer, but did have one of his sketches included, called 'Inner Circle'. 'It was basically a row between husband and wife that just went round and round and then came back to the beginning and we were saying the same things we had said before, only it was the other partner saying it. We stopped the sketch when the audience suddenly clocked it.'[80]

The tone of *This Way Out* very much followed recent revues. It was general poking. It was whimsical. 'If there were targets, they were literary targets like a D. H. Lawrence sketch that Clive James wrote,' says Richard.[81] While not in the cast, Clive James was behind some of the material and stage manager. Another Clive James sketch was about Tarzan, only Jane turns out to be the tough one. Someone else who contributed greatly to the show was Richard Crane, who arrived at Jesus College with ambitions to be an actor. Before coming to Cambridge, he taught at a school near Stratford-upon-Avon and every weekend hitchhiked into town to go to the Shakespeare Memorial Theatre. One Saturday he'd just seen *Julius Caesar* and was hitching a ride back. A car pulled up and he got in. He and the driver started chatting and when Richard said he hadn't thought much of the production, the driver replied, 'Well, I just played Julius Caesar.' It was the actor, Roy Dotrice. 'Anyway, we carried on talking,' adds Richard. 'And I said I wanted to be an actor, but I was going to Cambridge, and what was the view on drama schools these days. And he said, "Cambridge is actually the best drama school. And there are two things you must join, the Marlowe Society or the Footlights. These are the hot-houses for talent." So, I went to Cambridge, and I treated it like a drama school.'[82]

In his first term, Richard tried out for the Footlights. 'It was very frightening because you had to write the sketch yourself, nobody else was going to write it for you.'[83] The process after that was fairly rigorous. Each smoker was chaired and organized by two members of the committee and each candidate was required to audition for them first to see if they were worth putting forward. If it was deemed good enough, they would be given the date of the next smoker and told to turn up on the night. Most of the membership would be crammed in the club room. There was a running order, so you waited, nervously, to go on. Then after the smoker the committee had a meeting and decided whether to offer a membership. As Richard recalls he was the only one auditioning at that particular smoker. 'I did it and I think they laughed a bit, but I wasn't elected.'[84] He decided to join the Marlowe Society instead.

At Jesus, Richard Crane was good friends with Andy Mayer, who was reading English. Andy had seen a performance of *A Clump of Plinths* without really knowing much about the Footlights. 'I loved it and thought, that's what I want to do when I start being a graduate.'[85] At the Societies' Fair he came across the Footlights stall, which was manned by Eric Idle and Graeme Garden. 'I asked them how to join, and they said, "Well, you don't really. You do an audition and if you make us laugh then we might invite you to join."'[86] Andy found out when the next smoker was but didn't have any material. Generally, it was the rule that you had to write your own material. In some instances, newcomers were given other people's proven good monologues, and so Andy was obligingly fixed up with an old one. It wasn't very good but Andy diligently learnt it and performed it at the smoker. 'It was pretty intimidating. I did this monologue to total silence. Not a sound. After the smoker finished people were drinking at the bar. Nobody wanted to talk to me, so I went off back to my room and thought, fuck this, either give up or do another one. So, I went back and asked Graeme, how about the next smoker.'[87] This time Andy wrote it himself, a funny piece about an actor reading a children's story on the radio who loses it when he goes 'live' and makes a complete mess of things. It went down a storm and Andy was in.

Andy's tale encouraged Richard Crane to try again and this time he was successful. And while it was something of a baptism of fire, the Footlights was everything he hoped it would be in that it turned out to be the best training he could have had. 'It's not like going to a drama school to learn how to act, you're actually thrown in front of an audience immediately and you sink or swim.'[88]

Richard wrote several sketches for *This Way Out* and was in the cast. There was a spoof of Enid Blyton's Famous Five. 'It was a bit like what eventually the Comic Strip did. It was a bit childish, but it got laughs.'[89] He performed a monologue as Scrooge, the concept being that in Dickens' time London's air quality was so bad the character probably had acute asthma. 'Every time I wheezed, I got a laugh. And I wasn't expecting that. It was one of those times when suddenly you got that connection with an audience.'[90] He incorporated a multitude of characters from all the Brontë novels and ended in a song with the Brontë sisters morphing into the Beverley Sisters, 'and one by one they cough themselves to death till only Germaine as

Charlotte is left.'[91] And there was a Shakespeare skit that raced through the Bard's canon in something like five minutes. All the characters had the name of diseases, but when the script was sent to the Lord Chamberlain's office, which still vetted all theatrical productions, they took umbrage to one of them being called Syphilis (but spelt 'Cyphilus') and it was removed.

This Way Out went down well with audiences. 'It had music and dancing as well as comedy,' says Andy, 'so it was a revue in the more old-fashioned sense. It was all-round entertainment. It was an attempt to put on a show that *we* would like to see.'[92] The tour played Oxford, where the Footlights always got a good reception, and packed out at the Playhouse, York and Bury St Edmunds. Here the cast got a little bored and decided to play a game of murder through the entire week they were there. The murderer could say to somebody, you're dead, and that person had to 'die' and everyone else had to guess the identity of the murderer. 'One night at the curtain call,' recalls Richard Syms, 'we bowed, and one of the girls in the cast, Chris, just flopped down in the middle of the stage and we all rushed over. "What's the matter," we asked. "I'm dead, you fools." The murderer had given her a poison that was going to work at the curtain call that night.'[93] It was things like that, according to Andy, that really bonded them as a group. Performing and going out on tour does tend to bond a group fast. As future Footlights member Nick Hancock confirms, 'Because it's a risky thing and you have to trust each other. It's a bit like being a sports team because you need the other person to carry you through.'[94]

Something else that bonded members was the cabaret group. To help the coffers a bit, the Footlights had been doing cabaret performances since 1958 when the first 'master of cabaret' was John Drummond, later director of the Edinburgh Festival and controller of BBC Radio 3. These were usually held at May Balls, dinner dances or private parties, for which half the fee went to the club, the other half divided between the performers. 'It was a thing you tended to do more for the money than anything else,' confesses Andy. 'It could be good, depending on where you were doing the cabaret. Some colleges it would be fine. Sometimes if you were doing some kind of rugby club do it could be fucking awful because they'd all be pissed and not listening.'[95]

It was not unusual for the team to find themselves with only blank faces staring back at them. 'It's always a strange interaction with the public if you're in the wrong place,' declares John Cameron. 'I remember doing Butlin's and thinking, what are we doing here?'[96] At least each one of them could feel like they were being treated as professionals, in that they got paid, and sometimes the gig was a good one. 'I recall coming down to Brighton for the opening of the Pussycat Club,' says Richard Crane. 'We were on stage with The Kinks.'[97]

Sadly, *This Way Out* did not follow its recent predecessors and transfer to London. Impresario Michael White came to see it but didn't think it would work in the West End. 'We were in the wake of *Cambridge Circus*,' claims Richard Syms, 'and our group tried to get to the state that they had.'[98] It wasn't to be.

Richard Syms left that year. Studying English and then theology, he went into the priesthood before turning to acting and enjoyed a long career in television and film. Andy Mayer and Richard Crane graduated, too. For all three of them *This Way Out* represented their sole revue appearance, although Andy had contributed material to the previous two revues. As president in his final year, Andy was totally engrossed with the club, often to the detriment of his academic work. 'My director of studies was very understanding about it.'[99] Both Andy and Richard Crane studied English under the novelist and critic Raymond Williams. 'And often instead of writing an essay, we'd write a sketch,' says Richard. 'Raymond didn't seem to mind.'[100]

Andy returned the following year to see the revue and the one after that, before realizing that he didn't know anyone anymore. They were all new people. The Footlights wasn't a club in the same way a club in say London is, where you are a member all your life and there are always the same old faces. There is that three-year turnaround, the life span of a student. What stays are the friendships made and the overall experience, and Andy credits the Footlights as a big influence on his life. Working first at Granada, writing and producing, it was at LWT that he created *The London Weekend Show*, a current affairs programme aimed at young adults that launched the career of Janet Street-Porter. Richard Crane, who became a playwright, also has a lot to be grateful for. 'It became my club. It's where I went pretty well every night. Because that's where your friends were. That's where the banter was. It was like home.'[101]

8

Supernatural Gas

The arrival of Germaine Greer and Clive James did much to change the Footlights. 'I was in my second year when Clive and Germaine arrived,' Richard Syms remembers, 'and they sort of took the place by storm.'[1] Richard Crane agrees. 'The Australians did change the whole tone of the Footlights very strongly. It was no longer a bunch of little Englanders; these people were coming from somewhere else in the world. They were older as well. Clive and Germaine were postgraduates. We were still school boys, really.'[2] It wasn't always harmonious, however. 'They were fierce rivals, Clive and Germaine,' claims club member Barry Brown. 'Both seemed to have a bit of a chip on their shoulders. And they were both muscular humourists, in that they came at you full-bore.'[3]

Clive James zeroed in on the Footlights fairly swiftly and once in began to take it over. Richard Syms found him, 'formidable, but generous,'[4] and they became friends thanks to a shared love of opera. He left an impression on others, too. 'Clive was this weird mixture of being very sophisticated and not at the same time,' says Andy Mayer. 'He was keen to establish his credentials as an intellectual. He was a very nice guy. He was a very limited performer when it came to sketches. But he could do monologues.'[5] During his time in the Footlights, James was seen as much more of a writer than a performer. 'Though he did like performing,' says Richard Syms. 'And certainly, during my last year, he was saying, "All I want is that velvet jacket. I want to be president of the Footlights."'[6] This he achieved in 1967.

Clive James took the position of president extremely seriously, involving himself in administration and delegating tasks. One of the more interesting things he had to contend with was the arrival of Prince Charles at Trinity College. James assumed, probably rightly, that unless instructed not to, every revue and smoker would include wall-to-wall Prince Charles jokes. James issued an embargo on royal knockabout with a prominent notice on the club room wall.

Prince Charles was at Cambridge until 1970 and did take part in a Trinity revue, but deliberately kept clear of the Footlights. Perhaps had he joined he would have opened himself up to even more attention. Footlight member Adrian Edwards was a contemporary of Charles's at Trinity and was surprised how relaxed everything was around him. 'I think he had one private detective who was discreetly hanging around. And a friend of mine thought, oh, I'll go and see if he wants to be involved in some production. He just went along and saw him. Just as you can in those colleges, you just go round and knock on people's doors. That's part of being an undergraduate, casually dropping in on each other.'[7]

While Charles did not perform with the Footlights, he did attend a few smokers. At one of them, Adrian was in the middle of preparing some props when Harry Porter approached him and said, 'Adrian, I want you to meet the Prince of Wales.' Adrian was president at the time. 'We exchanged a few pleasantries. He said, "I seem to know your face," and I resisted the temptation to say the obvious, "Yours rings a bell." '[8]

As president, Clive James directed the 1967 revue, *Supernatural Gas*. Amongst those involved were two friends, Pete Atkin and Barry Brown. A self-confessed 'townie', Pete Atkin was born in Cambridge, although growing up he didn't know much about the university. 'I knew it was there, because it had such a presence. But no one in my family had ever been to university. And when I went up, I only knew in the vaguest possible way about the Footlights very existence.'[9] Pete had no real artistic ambitions, although he was musically inclined, performing in local bands, and he got involved with revues at his college, St John's. There he met Barry Brown, who had arrived from a minor public school in Wimbledon to study architecture, a course that ran five years. By this time people had identified the Footlights as a stepping stone into the entertainment world. As Eric Idle joked, 'Certainly in your last year you were nobody if you didn't have at least three agents coming to look at you in a smoker.'[10] Barry, on the other hand, had never performed in his life, although he did enjoy comic writing. Still, he was keen to join the Footlights, despite a warning from his tutors that he simply wouldn't have the time. 'And, of course, they were right because my architecture suffered a bit. But the Footlights was a very good release from the pressure cooker world of architecture.'[11]

At these St John's revues, it was clear to both Pete and Barry that they needed a girl to perform in some of the sketches and to sing a selection of the songs that Pete was beginning to write. Barry's girlfriend was at Homerton, then a female teacher training college, and suggested that some of the students doing drama might be interested. Barry and Pete put up a notice in the college, something like 'We will make you famous', and several of the students showed up to audition. Amongst them was a young Julie Covington. 'I don't think Pete could believe his ears,' says Barry. 'There was something very special about Julie. Not only could she sing with real passion and rage, but she was also a really good actress.'[12] Julie was chosen, along with Maggie Scott, another excellent singer.

It was Pete who suggested they all try for the Footlights. Barry admits being absolutely terrified at the prospect. Pete performed a song he had written called, 'Ballad of an Upstairs Window'. It was an exercise in how to write the most boring song ever and was about a young man waiting for his date to show up, only she never does. All of them passed the audition.

Attending that smoker was Clive James. 'And it's only half of a joke to say that when Clive heard me sing "The Ballad of an Upstairs Window", it was then he realized that I needed somebody else to write the words for me.'[13] Both men began to collaborate and Falcon Yard played an important role. It was available to them twenty-four hours a day. Because both were on the Footlights committee they had keys to the building, 'and so you could go in any time you damn well liked,' recalls Pete.[14] Most of the other university societies didn't have the luxury of their own space. 'Having that club room was absolutely central to the way it all worked,' says Pete.[15] Usually nursing a pint, Pete and Clive worked on their songs at the club's old upright piano that had been autographed by Dudley Moore. 'He came round to the club once after hours and played the piano,' Pete recalls, 'and someone persuaded him to scratch his autograph: D Moore was here.'[16]

By the time Pete met him, Clive James was already a huge influence on the club. 'Mainly because he was personally extraordinarily funny. He was clearly immensely talented. His gift for words and jokes was beyond what most of the rest of us could aspire to.'[17] And like most naturally funny people, Clive James loved an audience. 'Even if it was just one person,' says Pete, 'if there was anyone in the room, he would make them laugh.'[18] Often when Barry went to Falcon Yard at lunchtimes James would be holding court there. 'And whatever opinion you might tentatively offer he'd already done it or discarded it.'[19] Being a mature student, James couldn't help but seem incredibly worldly and grown up to everybody else. 'He was an iconic figure that we kind of looked up to,' observes Adrian Edwards. 'Just as he did later in his career he could hold forth and you kind of hung on his words and you just got the feeling that this was the most intelligent person you'd ever met.'[20] He certainly knew more about the history of the club than almost anybody else. 'He came to Cambridge knowing about the Footlights and wanting to be a part of it,' says Pete, 'and wanting to use it as a way of working.'[21]

As he admitted later, when Clive James began to put *Supernatural Gas* together, he was sensible enough not to include himself in the cast, everyone else was a lot funnier. Again, he wrote material, including a parody of a BBC sports commentator he called Alexander Palace. It was performed by Jonathan James-Moore, later a BBC radio producer and Head of Light Entertainment. James-Moore was a well-known figure within the Footlights and a fine comic performer, unmistakable with his shock of russet hair and largely unkempt beard. He suffered from very poor eyesight. When *Supernatural Gas* played Edinburgh, the stage manager was required to help James-Moore off the stage after blackouts. One evening he forgot, and James-Moore was forced to make his own way, but fell off the stage, landing in the front row. Instead of staying there in a heap, he asked a couple to push up and make room for him on the chair. The audience thought it was all part of the show.

Supernatural Gas had an unusually large cast, with three girls, including Julie Covington. This was a deliberate choice. 'Partly because Clive wanted

FIGURE 8.1 *Poster for the 1967 revue* Supernatural Gas. *Reproduced with the permission of Pete Atkin.*

to give an outlet to a lot of the people who were quite good performers,' confirms Pete.[22] But the whole thing looked at times too cumbersome. 'There were one or two big cast numbers that were not actually very good,' admits Pete.[23] Clive James's talent did not extend to directing, he also avoided politics and satire. 'I think it's true to say that all of us who were members at that time didn't feel that satire was what we wanted to do,' says Pete. 'We didn't feel either able or desirous of attacking anything contemporary.'[24]

Supernatural Gas sold out its two-week run at the Arts Theatre, as the Footlight revues tended to do. A slimmed down version went out on tour and played Edinburgh with some success. However, there was no West End transfer. Pete wasn't surprised. 'Revues were out of fashion. Perhaps it was felt by producers that satire was the kind of thing they still wanted and came to see us and saw something rather old fashioned.'[25] In any case, Pete didn't feel necessarily in competition with past successes like *Cambridge Circus*. 'We were always aware of the history, but we didn't know what it was, we'd never seen any of those shows. We just knew that a lot of cast members had gone on in the business and they were something, somehow, in the most vague and general way to be lived up to. In a way the history was, not oppressive, because that gives it too much weight, it was something we were aware of, but it didn't affect what we did.'[26]

One good thing to come out of *Supernatural Gas* was that Pete and Clive began to write songs for Julie Covington. When Pete discovered it was possible to get LPs pressed privately, he put together an album. The songs were recorded on the Footlights piano, 'which was terrible,' admits Pete,[27] and 160 copies were made and sold in the club room. These represented Julie's first recordings.

By this time Julie had begun to have an impact around the university. David Hare was on the periphery of the Footlights; he performed in a student revue at Edinburgh in 1966, directed by Clive James, 'but the Footlights was not really my beat.'[28] However, during his time at Cambridge, the standout performer for him was Julie Covington, 'who became by far and away the greatest British singer in musicals that I ever heard. The moment you saw her, you knew she was truly great – like Sinatra, a great voice, but an incredible way with the lyrics.'[29]

Julie also appeared in the following year's revue, *Turns of the Century*. This was Barry Brown's revue debut, having only provided material to *Supernatural Gas*. It took Barry a while to find his niche in the Footlights, 'Even though it was a nice mix of people there.'[30] Unlike much of the university, where a good portion of the intake still came from public schools, the Footlights was as classless as it got. 'They were an enormously mixed bunch,' recalls Pete. 'I don't remember class being a factor in the Footlights at all.'[31] Competition was, however. While some members displayed the energy and ambition of wanting to get far in the business, and others were content just to have fun and enjoy themselves, there remained quite an intense rivalry. 'And you had to fight to keep your own voice in a way,' claims Barry.[32]

As Barry began to get more involved, a style of comedy emerged that he labelled, 'sub-Peter Cook'. Barry had been brought up on *The Goon Show* and the theatre of the absurd, which also influenced Cook. At first Barry had not been confident performing his own material and so decided to start out in his own college revues. 'Here you learn very quickly what gets a laugh and what doesn't. And my stuff was not massively rib tickling. It was more character driven. I developed a character who made the stuff work. And that was out of sheer terror.'[33] Barry became known as a monologue specialist. Monologues were very popular in the Footlights and were usually done in character. There was hardly any stand-up at all. 'The stand-up tradition we thought was quite old fashioned at that time,' argues Adrian Edwards. 'Then it was revived in the 1980s with people like Ben Elton.'[34]

As his confidence grew, Barry decided to audition for the revue. 'There was such competition to get into the May Week show. That was the big deal.'[35] Barry got into *Turns of the Century*, 'and I enjoyed every minute. That first night in a proper theatre, 700-seater, and having a real audience in front of you, it wasn't just a club audience. When you get a laugh in that situation, that's the most intoxicating thing there is.'[36] Barry wrote some sketches and lyrics, and designed the look of the show, which had an Edwardian feel. Also featured were several Pete Atkin and Clive James compositions sung by Maggie Scott and Julie Covington. Pete always enjoyed performing in the revues. 'It wasn't a riotous audience. They were ready to be entertained. And the Arts was a compact and well-designed theatre. The audience felt close to you.'[37]

By this time, Pete was on the Footlights committee, indeed had been vice president. Each year committee members would leave and new ones invited to join, based on how much they contributed to the club. 'It was an honorary thing, really,' claims Pete,[38] who can't recall them meeting up very often. Pete also involved himself with the cabaret team, which usually consisted of four people, one of whom it was desirable to own their own car. 'You never knew what the venue was going to be like, what the facilities were or even if there was a stage. We did our best, but it was different every time, because audiences were different every time.'[39] It could be a May Ball, a student dance, anything. 'In my day the cabaret wasn't a terribly successful thing,' reveals Adrian Edwards, 'partly because we didn't have that stand-up tradition. When you're trying to do a parody of Chekhov in front of 300 drunks it was very hard work.'[40] For many, these cabarets were something to endure. You almost had to do them to find out how horrible they were.

Pete recalls one cabaret that fell dismally flat in front of the Farmer's Association of Needham Market. Afterwards, the team congregated ashen faced in the foyer, when one of the farming committee members approached them asking, 'Do you get paid for this sort of thing?' Great gigs were few and far between. One special evening took place at Goldsmiths College summer ball in London. A ticket got you a dance band, John Mayall and the Bluesbreakers, and headlining was Cream, 'with the biggest loudspeakers I had ever seen up to that point,' says Pete.'[41] The Footlights were the third cabaret act on the bill. 'The top cabaret was the Bonzo Dog Doo-Dah Band in their full glory,' Pete recalls. 'And the number two cabaret was John Cleese doing a stand-up. So, we were feeling somewhat intimidated.'[42]

The year 1968 was Pete's last at Cambridge and he pursued a successful career as a singer/songwriter. He kept in touch with Clive James; indeed, they shared a house in London for a time and collaborated on several albums during the 1970s. It was a lifelong friendship. The partnership resumed after the turn of the millennium when they took a two-man show to Edinburgh and on UK tours. 'For both of us,' wrote Clive James, 'being on the road was like being back in our first days in the Footlights when we sat up late in the ratty old club room and wrote song after song.'[43]

FIGURE 8.2 *Cover for the 1968 revue* Turns of the Century. *Reproduced with the permission of Pete Atkin.*

A new year, and a new president, Barry Brown. The appointment came as somewhat of a surprise, although he had been perhaps the biggest contributor to *Turns of the Century*. Amongst his tasks was to organize the Footlights annual dinner that took place in the club room. The president always had to invite a starry guest. When Clive James was president, he arranged for Joyce Grenfell to be guest of honour. 'Most of the rest of us didn't really know very much about who Joyce Grenfell was,' admits Pete Atkin.[44] Clive James was a huge admirer. For his dinner, Barry approached comedy writers Frank Muir and Denis Norden, who politely turned him down. Galton and Simpson did likewise. In the end actress Fenella Fielding stepped into the breach.

Barry has never forgotten the steward who attended on such evenings. 'He was an extraordinary bloke. At the dinner he would go round with a bottle of white and a bottle of red and he would ask, "Do you want red, white or rose?" And he would literally construct the latter.'[45] Each time Barry went into the club room the steward used to ask him, 'Can we help you. Are you a member?' This when Barry was president. 'The place was full of characters. The club felt very companionable.'[46]

Barry oversaw 1969's revue, *Fools Rush In*, which was directed by Clive James. 'Clive was a very good choice, but he was a hopeless director,' Barry admits.[47] Barry performed a couple of his monologues, including one about science fiction where he wore a space suit. There was also a send up of *Gone with the Wind* that had just been re-released into cinemas. Again, Barry designed the show along with the poster. 'The poster was the figure of a fool, and I thought, we've got to personalize this in some way so I put Clive's face on it.'[48] Being so well known around the campus by then, Clive James's fear was that the poster would be defaced. It wasn't.

Amongst the cast was Robert Buckman, who Barry remembers as, 'A very energetic performer. He wasn't really a writer, but he was certainly funny.'[49] Buckman was a medical student at St John's and went on to become both a doctor and a television personality. Then there was Russell Davies, a keen jazz trombonist who played in local bands. A good and quite experienced performer, Davies ended up in many sketches. So many in fact that he started oversleeping in the morning and Clive James took to sending a taxi to wake him up and bring him to rehearsals. Even then he often fell asleep in his chair and had to be shaken awake when his presence was required. Later in Edinburgh, playing a Cossack dancer in one sketch, he performed with such vigour every night that after a week he complained that his feet were hurting, took off his boot in the dressing room and blood poured out.

For Adrian Edwards, in his second year at St John's studying engineering, *Fools Rush In* was his first tase of performing in a revue. Adrian had enjoyed amateur dramatics at school, but the Footlights wasn't necessarily the reason why he went to Cambridge, 'Although it was a kind of plus.'[50] After joining he found it a very welcoming environment. 'It was slightly competitive, but it was also reasonably welcoming and collegiate.'[51] The club house still sported photographs of Jack Hulbert and Cicely Courtneidge on the wall. 'We were made aware of the history,' confirms Adrian. 'Harry Porter was very good at that, his knowledge of the history. Harry was a wonderful, sweet, funny man who was a great guide to us all, really. A great person to know and a very generous individual.'[52]

Adrian found himself gravitating towards a history undergraduate at Trinity called Bill Gutteridge. Discovering they worked quite well together Adrian and Gutteridge formed a double act. 'I was tall and could put on an upper-class manner, comically. Bill was quite small and naturally funny and tended to be the butt of my arrogance in the comedy. Of course, the irony is I was a grammar school boy and Bill went to a very good public school.'[53]

One of their first hit sketches was a pseudo-Samuel Beckett piece set on a desert island. 'I'm sitting arrogantly in my deck chair,' recalls Adrian, 'and Bill swims up and joins me on the beach. And it's clear that although we are the only human beings on the island, I don't really want to talk to him because I think he's a 'little oink'. The line is, "Are we the only human beings on this island? – Yes, I am." And that always used to get the thing going.'[54] Looking back, Adrian admits to squirming occasionally at what must have sometimes seemed juvenile or tasteless material; surely, he isn't the only one. 'Although I suppose it's always OK to poke fun at the Germans. We did a thing called the "tickle spiel." I know Clive James loved it. It was a kind of fighting contest where you tickled each other and tried not to laugh.'[55]

Fools Rush In went on tour to the Oxford Playhouse, the Nuffield Theatre at the University of Southampton, and Bristol, finishing off in Edinburgh. 'I was blown away by Edinburgh,' recalls Adrian. 'When you've been born and brought up in Slough, as in *The Office*, your visions of the world can be a bit limited. I had never seen anything so magnificent or known such an exciting environment as the Edinburgh Festival. You fell in love with it.'[56] The Footlights were obliged to appear in an ADC production that went on early in the evening, a Brecht or Shakespeare or a straight play. 'Then at 11 o'clock at night we'd get into our glad rags and do a one-hour late revue.'[57]

In 1970, Adrian became club president and Bill Gutteridge was his vice president. They also appeared in that's year's revue, *The Footlights Comic Annual*. Although he had graduated, Barry Brown came up with the title, which allowed him to design a poster that featured a host of characters from the *Beano*. *Comic Annual* followed on very much from recent revues in being quite traditional with quite a lot of music and musical parody. 'That was the strength we played to that year really,' says Adrian. 'But there was always some cheesy opener and a closing song. It was rather like the opening of *It Ain't Half Hot Mum* – Meet the gang 'cause the boys are here, the boys to entertain you. In some ways those revues followed ancient practice.'[58]

Bill Gutteridge graduated that year and trained as a doctor at Barts Hospital in London. 'He was studying history,' says his friend Mark Wing-Davey, 'and then decided that it had no social relevance for him and decided he wanted to become a doctor.'[59] Mark also enjoyed a writing partnership with Bill Gutteridge in the Footlights, although Mark was more interested in becoming an actor than a comic; his mother, Anna Wing, was an actress, best known as Lou Beale in BBC's *EastEnders*. Before Cambridge he worked as an assistant stage manager at the Citizens Theatre, Glasgow, along with bits of acting work, so in the insular world of university he had more experience than most and began to play lead roles with the Marlowe Society. Playing a comedic role in one production, Mark was approached by Jonathan James-Moore who suggested he audition for the Footlights.

Comic Annual turned out to be Mark's only Footlight revue. He didn't have any ambitions to be president or the funniest member. 'I wasn't entirely buying what they were selling. But I felt lucky to be part of it, and still do.'[60] After a successful acting career (he was Zaphod Beeblebrox in *The Hitchhiker's Guide to the Galaxy*), Mark turned to directing and teaching where the discussions around staging a revue proved extremely useful. 'Things like, what would be the best order of putting those sketches, how would that then work, discussing effectively the kind of techniques of how you might put something together.'[61]

Mark involved himself, too, in the cabaret team and performed at smokers. Writing songs, at one smoker he got a friend he knew vaguely to play the guitar for him. It was Fred Frith, now a celebrated avant-garde guitarist and composer. 'I remember being at another smoker and someone was performing and there was a low sound in the audience going, "Steal. Steal." Because you had to perform original material, and it was someone saying, I know that sketch. Certainly, I think a lot of the members had a kind of encyclopaedic knowledge of sketches going back forever.'[62] Clive James was to speak about a strong Footlights oral tradition by which fragments of sketches are passed down from one intake to the next.

Mark stood out from most of his contemporaries, with his long hair and flamboyant dress sense, certainly in the world of the Footlights. 'I was a kaftan kid.'[63] For Mark, the Footlights, 'had a vague public school feel to it.'[64] The late 1960s, with its heady politics, drugs, hippies and free festivals hadn't permeated the club at all. 'There wasn't anyone in my time, certainly I wasn't one, with a kind of distinctive, harsh political voice that it could kind of bounce off. It wasn't there.'[65] A song about the Vietnam War did appear in the *Turns of the Century* revue, but that was about it.

Things were slightly different on campus. For Simon Jones, who arrived at Cambridge in 1969, 'There was quite a lot of radicalism going on, even in the gilded halls. We all wanted Barclays Bank to divest themselves from South Africa, that was going on at the time.'[66] In February 1970, a dinner to promote Greek tourism at the city's Garden House Hotel was disrupted by a student demonstration against the country's ruling military junta. The protest turned violent, the hotel was damaged, and police and students engaged in running battles. Eight students were jailed. 'There was a kind of anarchist movement,' says Mark, 'which I wasn't part of but kind of understood, of people standing up and saying exams are shit and tearing up their papers. It very much was the sense of the boundaries being broken. But Footlights was not a boundary breaker as such.'[67]

According to Simon Jones, 'We just wanted to make people laugh. I don't remember any political jokes at all, except a few light-hearted side swipes at the government.'[68] At a committee meeting, when this subject was brought up, somebody made the point, 'You can't say Biafra on stage and expect people to laugh.'[69] Maybe the Footlights resistance to embrace political humour at a time of huge social change and political unrest went back to its heavy association with the satire movement of the early 1960s. 'It wasn't because we were particularly respectful of the establishment,' offers Simon, 'but it had rather been done and was going on, too, in the mainstream by then.'[70]

Simon got into the Footlights when he and a couple of fellow Trinity Hall students performed at their own smoker. By then, Simon had decided to be an actor and the Footlights seemed like a good place to start, and being a member, 'gave one a certain amount of pride.'[71] Even though by now the club room had seen better days. 'Falcon Yard looked like something out of Dickens,' admits Simon.[72] The area had been allowed to run down till all the properties had been sold and then the developers would move in. The place had that air about it. 'The club room was situated in a back alley, and you went up these rather rickety stairs,' recalls Simon. 'Inside the stage curtain didn't work and there were holes in the carpet.'[73] The stage lights were a bit ropey, too, according to Barry Brown. 'They were very badly earthed. You could get a shock off it if you weren't careful.'[74]

Still, the place was an important social anchor for members, a home from home, not just because of the smokers, but it was somewhere to go for a drink instead of the pub. 'You might meet up with someone you hadn't seen for a little while and have a chat or a gossip,' Mark Wing-Davey remembers, 'or you'd buy the album that Pete Atkin had made with Julie Covington, all that kind of stuff. So, it was quite a cosy and at the time, who knew, I didn't, privileged environment.'[75] Because it stayed open late, you could also get a drink there after a show had finished. Whenever a play was on at the Arts Theatre there was always a notice put in the actor's dressing rooms announcing if they would like a drink after their show was over to come along to the Footlights club and sign on as temporary members.

Simon wasn't in the cast of the 1971 revue, *Gone with the Clappers*, but enjoyed doing the smokers. He recalls an English literature student at Magdalene always turning up with sketches that he had written with a couple of friends. His name was Julian Fellowes, later the creator of *Downton Abbey*. While an active member, Fellowes never did a revue show. 'And I don't think he wanted to be in one particularly,' claims Simon. 'It was odd.'[76]

Simon went on to do the Christmas pantomime, *Aladdin*, playing Abanazar. 'I had a fabulous time on that. It was a wonderful script. It was very well done. And it was a great success.'[77] The panto tradition had been revived by the Footlights, in conjunction with the ADC, and very quickly became as eagerly anticipated as the summer revue. While the panto was always professionally put together, it lacked the competitive edge of the revue. It was more fun, and the cast was encouraged to interact with the audience. It was more democratic, too, with a lot more club members able to take part. In many ways they were like a gang show.

Robert Rowe recalls playing an ugly sister in *Cinderella* one year and enjoying it immensely. 'What you learnt doing the panto was that you must pitch these things for an adult audience and for small children. The writing was quite clever, and we improvised a great deal. Every night we used to change it.'[78] After one matinee, Robert and his fellow Ugly Sister had removed their makeup and costumes and were about to leave when the stage manager came to their dressing room. 'There's two young kids from the audience who would like to meet the Ugly Sisters,' he said. 'Are they available?' The stage manager was asked to tell the children that the Ugly Sisters would be out in five minutes. 'We put all the make-up back on and the costumes, the wigs, the whole thing,' Robert explains, 'and invited these two kids, who must have been about seven. And we behaved in the persona of the Ugly Sisters. 'Are you really the Ugly Sisters?' they asked. 'Well, of course we are! What a cheek!' We just carried on with the improvisation. To them they'd actually met the ugly sisters.'[79]

Robert also appeared in *Gone with the Clappers*. Having earlier read modern languages, Robert was now a postgraduate doing modern Greek. He was urged to join the Footlights by his friend Stephen Wyatt, as they shared a similar sense of humour. 'I went along and just as an audience member looking at it, I thought, this would be great fun.'[80] As indeed it was, much to the detriment of the academic work he was supposed to be engaged in at the time, 'A thesis on a Byzantine Greek statesman and writer of stultifying dullness who just couldn't match the stage for glitter somehow.'[81]

For the first time since the War, the club called in an 'outside' director to oversee the revue. Bert Parnaby, a former BBC producer, was working as a school's inspector. His appointment was not altogether a success as Simon Jones got to hear. 'Bert Parnaby was rather exacting. He had taught an awful lot of people drama at Manchester Grammar School, including Nicholas Hytner. He was rather revered. But he was a bit of a martinet when it came to directing. A terribly nice man when not directing. But he got a bit fierce and had exacting standards. I don't think the cast enjoyed it very much.'[82] There was some decent stuff in the show. 'But it somehow didn't quite click,' argues cast member Adrian Edwards. 'It was not a particularly happy show.'[83] There was one amusing sketch, about Dracula preying on a young woman who lives in a Coronation Street-type terrace house. 'It's all very well you going off with this tall dark stranger,' says her mother. 'But do you realize that it means giving up your chance of going to training college.'

Parnaby brought in his own musical director for the show, and this is where Robert Rowe thinks the revue may have suffered, from having too much outside material and influence. It was also very music-heavy; Robert performed a Maurice Chevalier take-off. Another musical item was a chorus kick line with the male members of the cast as Scotsmen in kilts. 'We were directed to do it right at the front of the stage near the footlights,' recalls

Robert, 'so, of course, everybody was looking to see if we were wearing anything underneath. We all protested a great deal about having to do this, it was cheap and nasty, but Bert Parnaby insisted on it. When we took the show to Edinburgh, probably to avoid being lynched, we left that particular number out.'[84]

Amongst the main contributors to *Gone with the Clappers* were Steve Thorn and Paul Wolfson, who often wrote together. Steve Thorn did an amusing impersonation of the then Prime Minister Edward Heath, accentuating the way the politician laughed, which involved his shoulders going up and down. Heath happened to be in Edinburgh for the Festival and read in the newspaper that there was a send up of him in the Footlights revue. 'And he came in to watch that bit of the show,' Robert recalls. 'We all stood in the wings and watched. Steve was standing on the stage doing this very accurate impression of Heath and Heath was standing at the back laughing, and you could compare the two.'[85]

If he gave a certain expression, Steve Thorn was also a dead ringer for Peter O'Toole in distress during *Lawrence of Arabia*. 'He could turn into Peter O'Toole within a flash, and it was very funny,' recalls Sarah Dunant who was in the cast of *Clappers*.[86] Sarah had fallen into the orbit of both Thorn and Wolfson. 'I would sit in their room and listen to The Who Live at Leeds album and smoke a joint and we started to write together and that gave me some in.'[87] As far as Sarah could make out, the role of women in the Footlights revues was to sing and dance and be an adjunct to the men in the sketches. 'And I think the only way you broke out of that was to start writing your own stuff.'[88]

As a child, Sarah had grown up with comedy on the radio, listening to The Goons and *Round the Horne*. She was a big devotee of *I'm Sorry, I'll Read That Again*, and then Monty Python. 'So, without realizing it I grew up in a school of humour that was partly marinated or soaked in the Cambridge style of humour.'[89] And Footlights comedy still retained that absurdist element that Peter Cook brought to it and that was enhanced by revues like *Clump of Plinths*. 'They took a kind of Goons absurdity and placed it within a mad intellectual framework,' observes Sarah.[90]

Sarah's involvement in a writing capacity with Steve Thorn and Paul Wolfson was important given the paucity of women in the Footlights and within the university itself. It was still at least ten men to every woman on campus. Men still found it easier than women to get onto courses because there were more places. Much to the annoyance of some of the women, men were also accorded more licence in pursuing extracurricular activities, such as the Footlights or rowing or whatever. Women were very much encouraged to take themselves and their studies very seriously. You could have outside pursuits, but you did the work. Sarah recalls at the start of her third year, when she was going to be doing the final part of history tripos, hearing from many friends within the Footlights and other theatre clubs that male colleagues went at some point to their director of studies to say, for example:

Look, I'm really keen on English but it's my intention to go on and become an actor, so I don't think I'm probably going to get a great degree. 'And, without exception, what I heard was the equivalent of, let's have a glass of sherry and I'll look forward to one of your performances. So, I march up to my director of studies in Newnham College and give virtually the same spiel and she does not bring up sherry, she says, "An extraordinary number of women worked very hard to get your place in this university and if you don't get a 2:1 I will be extremely disappointed and want to know the reason why." And that tells you something about the difference in the culture right there.'[91]

9

Norman Ruins

As a member of the Footlights committee, Simon Jones was sometimes put in charge of smokers, and if someone was auditioning that evening, to act as gatekeeper, as it were. 'Because some people just wrote dreadful stuff. There had to be a selective process.'[1]

Simon had never met Douglas Adams until he arrived at one smoker to audition with two friends, Will Adams and Martin Smith. 'They did this particularly silly sketch in which Douglas was a human water pump.' recalls Simon. 'Either Smith or Adams gave him a glass of water, he retained it in his mouth, and the other one pumped his arm, and he spat it out into the face of the person who'd given him the glass of water. For some reason or other this made me laugh uproariously. It was such a change from all these intellectual sketches, which weren't really funny. And I said, put him in. I think I may have had a little bit of a discussion with the rest of the committee, but they didn't have a leg to stand on because I was in charge.'[2]

Douglas Adams was born in Cambridge and arrived at St John's to study English literature and with an ambition to join the Footlights. He had been an avid fan of *The Frost Report*, especially John Cleese, and made up his mind to write and perform comedy as a career. Discovering that he couldn't merely join the Footlights, rather he had to ingratiate himself with the right people or audition, initially put Adams off, and he found those associated with the club, 'rather grand and aloof, rather cold and unencouraging.'[3] Instead, he joined the university's less snooty Light Entertainment Society, or CULES for short. Then came his mime that so impressed Simon Jones. Adams was extremely appreciative when he came to learn that Simon had gone to bat for him with the doubters on the rest of the committee and, in Simon's estimation, more than repaid him a few years later with Arthur Dent and *The Hitchhiker's Guide to the Galaxy*.

Adams is remembered as an ambitious and enthusiastic member of the club, although not entirely successful at what he was trying to achieve in terms of the comedy material he was producing. 'He was very good company,' recalls Simon. 'I had no idea that, and who would, and nor did he, that he would go on to find immortality with *Hitchhiker's Guide* because it hadn't even crossed his mind.'[4] Barry Brown was of a similar opinion. 'I had absolutely no inkling that he would go on to greater things. There was nothing that he'd done or written that suggested he was going to.'[5]

As a physical specimen, Adams certainly stood out being extremely tall, 'and he would say,' adds Simon, 'with a large nose under which small creatures could find shade on hot days.'[6] It was self-evidently clear early on that Adam's talent lay as a writer, and not as a performer, and during his time in the Footlights he was never involved in any of the revues. 'It was a cause of annoyance to him that he didn't make any of the casts,' confirms Simon.[7]

Barry Brown was the director of the 1972 revue, *Norman Ruins*, and wanted Adams to participate. 'Douglas was a perfectly nice chap. He was unnecessarily tall. I got on fine with him. But a terrible performer. But I thought he was worth a go, but the committee didn't want him, and I was steered away from him.'[8]

Barry had already graduated and was back in Cambridge working for an architectural firm when he was asked to return and direct the revue. 'One was trying to recreate the feeling one had when one was in it – and it isn't the same, it never is the same.'[9] Some faces he did recognize, but most of them he didn't, and so Barry was required to familiarize himself with new people along with a whole bunch of material he didn't know. The concept he came up with for the show was that of an old music hall performer and an evening of his theatrical reminiscences. 'And it did work.'[10] Barry wrote some songs and a couple of new sketches.

There were other performers, along with Douglas Adams, who Barry had wanted to put in the show and felt sorry that they had missed out. His solution was to write a short film that was screened during the interval and featured a cast that included Adams and Simon Jones. 'And Doug was very good in it,' confirms Barry.[11] It was a send up of things like Ken Russell and those provincial adverts you used to get in your local cinema. 'It meant that you could use all sorts of filmic gags that you couldn't do live on stage,' says Barry.[12]

It so happened that Barry's brother, Richard, who was at St John's, wanted to be a filmmaker and so borrowed a camera, raised a bit of money, and directed it. The location was the Cherry Hinton chalk pits outside Cambridge. 'That was fun,' recalls Simon, 'except all our costumes got covered in white clay.'[13] Sadly, the film has since vanished, but it always went down well with audiences. 'It didn't matter that it was a bit amateurish,' argues Barry. 'That was part of the joke in a way.'[14] The *Cambridge Evening News* called it, 'Undoubtedly the funniest thing in the show.'

Norman Ruins was seen as a modest success. Sarah Dunant featured, her second revue appearance. She was also a member of the cabaret team, something she found for the most part unappealing. 'They were dreadful. I hated them. You didn't want to do them; it was sort of well-paid prostitution really because by the time you got on stage, they were all absolutely pissed in the audience. I don't think that played to our sense of self-importance.'[15]

By now, Sarah had begun contributing material, as did Sue Limb, the other woman in the cast who was seen as very much a comedy writer. Sarah recalls one sketch she and Paul Wolfson performed together in *Norman Ruins*. It was a man and woman alone in an apartment. 'It was Paul saying, "Will you have another drink, darling?" And me going, "Gosh, I think I've had enough, but alright, just a little one." And him saying, "Well, I'm going to have another one." We did this in the dark and you heard the two voices. And then you heard us going upstairs. And then you heard the beginnings of grunts. And then you heard Paul saying, "Oh god, darling, I'm sorry, I think I must have drunk a bit too much." And that was a wonderful sketch because it had an unexpected punchline, it was a bit naughty, and if you like it played against the sexism.'[16]

The tour went well, including a by now customary visit to the Robin Hood Theatre in Newark, which stood in the shade of the gigantic cooling towers of a nearby power station. 'Newark was such a bizarre place to go,' recalls Simon Jones. 'And this lovely little theatre which obviously had been built as an extravagant whim by some local landlord. The audiences were fun. And you certainly learnt what was funny and what wasn't, because they weren't genned up like the Cambridge or Oxford audience.'[17] It was good practice for when they arrived at the festival, which was always the culmination of the tour. 'Edinburgh allowed you to step back from the material that had been a real rush to get onto the stage at the end of May Week,' says Sarah, 'when almost everybody was doing exams at the same time, and you were juggling a million different things. It allowed you to take time out and come back to the material a bit more relaxed.'[18]

Simon Jones is of a similar mind to Sarah, that their best work was the late-night revues in Edinburgh. 'They were quite good because they were a distillation. Those summer revues were a terrible obligation, and they became more and more cumbersome. They were hard work. But by the time we went to Edinburgh we could distil the whole thing into a much shorter programme.'[19] Simon recalls the opening number was about child molesters. One of the lyrics went: 'Never take sweets from strangers, you don't know where they've been./Never take sweets from strangers, they might do something obscene'. 'It set the tone.'[20]

There was a London transfer, of sorts, when *Norman Ruins* was put on in the unusual environs of the Roundhouse, then better known as a music venue. 'We did OK there,' Sarah recalls. 'We certainly got audiences. I remember that Prince Charles came to see it. He would have only graduated a couple of years before so he would have had a relationship with Cambridge still.'[21]

However, the production of *Norman Ruins* was put on under the cloud of the Footlights losing their cherished club room. For years the area around Falcon Yard had been earmarked for redevelopment. The Footlights committee even went so far as to make the developer an honorary member to stave off the inevitable. Sadly, on 19 June 1972, just a few days after

Norman Ruins closed at the Arts Theatre, Falcon Yard was demolished. There was a farewell drinks party in the club room a few days before. Thirty-seven people turned up, about half the membership, to say goodbye to the old place. There was genuine sadness it was going. 'I left Cambridge thinking, well that's the end of that,' remembers Simon Jones. 'They'll have to perform in somebody's sitting room.'[22]

Simon paid the club room a visit the day before the bulldozers went in. 'And the place was devastated, there was nothing left. I don't know where it had all gone. There wasn't much of any value except for a portrait of Lord George Germain, a reproduction etching, which, as legend it had, was presented to the club by Germaine Greer. He was a figure in the American Revolutionary War. I saved him because he was about to be thrown into the garbage, and I still have him to this day.'[23]

Following the loss of Falcon Yard, the Footlights considered moving into a warehouse next door to the ADC Theatre in Park Street, but the cost of converting it proved too prohibitive. The possibility of acquiring a room in the arts centre that was projected to be part of the redevelopment of the area around Falcon Yard also came to nothing. Without a club room the allure of the Footlights was greatly reduced, and membership began to suffer. For a while, smokers took place in a little theatre in Trinity College, committee meetings happened wherever, in various rooms, and in the spring of 1974 the club took a room above a pub for two nights a week, but this didn't last for long.

Despite all this the 1973 revue, *Every Packet Carries a Government Health Warning*, carried on as normal, directed by Stephen Wyatt, a research student. As an undergraduate Stephen had appeared in the 1968 revue, *Turns of the Century*, despite being, as he says it, 'very much the new boy. One sketch – a spoof Greek tragedy – was written by me but otherwise I felt I was a bit there to make up the numbers. But it was a very jolly show and basically a friendly company.'[24] Appearing in the 1970 revue, *The Footlights Comic Annual*, was not a happy experience. 'The talents involved didn't really gel. There was one sketch, a Chekhov spoof – in which I played the servant deliberately causing mayhem. It made me realize I didn't have the talent or chutzpah to be a comedian.'[25]

By the time of his involvement with *Every Packet*, Stephen was better known for directing college productions than as a performer. Even so, directing the Footlights revue was a strange job. 'On the one hand, you're script editor pulling the material already available into shape and generating group sketches specifically for the show during rehearsals. On the other hand, you have constantly to keep in mind the visual aspect of the show and how it will look and play on a main stage. Perhaps the trickiest part of all is the running order. You need to open and close with items you believe are rock solid, you must give space to contrasting work by the writers, balance songs against speech and make sure nobody gets left with an impossible costume change.'[26]

Stephen saw the show as very much in the mould of *Turns of the Century*, with sketches and numerous musical numbers, which was very much to his taste. 'But for some was already somewhat outdated. However, the show was very well received.'[27] Simon Jones saw it and recalls one sketch. 'It was about a man who is sitting in a chair, and nothing happens for quite a while, and then he suddenly realizes he's dead. But he only finds out he's dead by doing all the various tests you do to find out whether anyone's dead, like sticking a mirror under his nose, and sticking a pin in his hand and finding there was no pain.'[28]

Stephen put together a very talented company but felt it lacked a strong extrovert comic presence. 'Footlights president Robert Benton suggested Griff Rhys Jones, who at that point wasn't a member. I auditioned him and then at the next smoker he performed and became a member so he could appear in the show. He fitted in well and the company worked well together.'[29]

Also making his revue debut was law student, Jon Canter, who was already keen on writing comedy. 'When I was thirteen, I used to go to the Ace holiday schools, which were in Worthing. It was Jewish kids from London and Manchester, and they did talent contests, and I can remember aping Peter Cook doing a sketch about taking rice out of a ramekin and counting each grain and being amusingly boring.'[30] Jon was a big Cook admirer and a fan of Monty Python. 'So, I really wanted to go to Cambridge and be part of that.'[31]

Jon found the prospect of writing and performing his own audition sketch, 'quite scary. And the lord and master, the overseer at that point was Clive James. He was still there and very much a presiding spirit.'[32] Jon did a mime about getting into a bath that was too hot and got accepted. 'Then I went to a smoker, and I did a monologue which accidentally became famous, not because of me. It was a monologue about a northern football manager being very pissed off about everything, and the opening line was: Life! Don't talk to me about life. And Douglas Adams took that line and made it Marvin the Paranoid Android's catchphrase in *Hitchhiker's*.'[33]

Memorably, on the first morning of rehearsals, Stephen Wyatt announced, 'Normally the first three days of rehearsing these shows we debate what the title is. The title is *Every Packet Carries a Government Health Warning*, and that's saved us three days of rehearsals, let's go.' As already mentioned, it was a very traditional revue. 'We were still doing a lot of song and dance,' says Jon, 'which was a curious thing. We were still in the *Cheer-Oh Cambridge!* 1930s version of the Footlights.'[34] But it had some very funny moments. 'I did a very simple visual sketch,' recalls Jon. 'Somebody gave me a tie for my birthday. It was a very long tie, and it was just nicely widely spaced at the bottom, it came over your crotch, and I came up with this sketch. A man goes into a restaurant beautifully dressed and asks for a table for two, and the maître d' says, I'm sorry, you're not wearing a tie, so he leaves. Second man comes on, not wearing a tie, would you leave. I come on stage naked but for this tie. I've never heard laughter like it since, I should have retired then. And here you are at Cambridge, you're supposed to be part of a cerebral intellectual elite.'[35]

The average Footlights revue now tended to have between five and six men and two women. In *Every Packet* the women were Mary Allen and Pam Scobie. Mary had been a member of the Footlights since arriving in Cambridge in 1970. 'I'd done a lot of acting at school, my mother had been an actor, acting was something that I was desperately interested in.'[36] Mary was principally a performer rather than someone who contributed material. 'There were very clear writers.'[37] And most, if not all of them, were men. Not because of any sexism, Mary stresses, that's just the way things were, most comedy writers in the business were men. 'If a woman had written a good sketch, I'm sure it would have been welcomed.'[38] Jon Canter recalls being in meetings about shows and people would literally say things like, what can we give the girl? 'It's astonishing to look back and think, what a boys' club it was and how strange that was. There were women in the revue but they didn't get a fair crack of the whip at all. I don't remember the women in our revues writing really. The men owned it.'[39]

Mary didn't get any sense that as a woman she wasn't welcome or shouldn't be there, 'none at all'.[40] And yet the committee remained exclusively male. 'To my mind that just shows women's good sense,' says Mary. 'I've sat on multitudinous committees through my life and they're incredibly boring. So, I'm extremely glad I didn't want to sit on any when I was at Cambridge.'[41] Mary became an arts administrator, Secretary General of the Arts Council and chief executive of the Royal Opera House in London.

To a degree, the Footlights reflected Cambridge itself. There were still very, very many more men than women at the university. Things were beginning to change, however. In October 1972, three previously male-only colleges, Churchill, Clare and King's, became co-educational. By the time Mary was to graduate things weren't noticeably any different, but over the next few years the number of women at the university grew rapidly.

At the time, Mary was dating a law student at Trinity by the name of John Lloyd. John had set his sights on going to Trinity for no other reason than he liked the name. 'It had a magic about it. And that magic has never lost me. Trinity changed my life. It changed the way I looked at the world. And it changed the possibilities of things.'[42] John arrived with the idea of being a crusading defence attorney, but his idealism fell flat within two weeks and he tried to change to English. 'The head of English said, "I know your type. You get in on an easy subject like law, which nobody wants to do, and then you try and change. I suppose you think we sit around on the banks of the Cam reading Keats all day!" I said, "No, no, sir, of course I don't." "Well, we don't." And of course they do, absolutely that's exactly what they do, or they did.'[43] John was stuck with law and managed to scrape through his exams.

The faculty quite liked the idea that their students pursued other interests and activities, and because John had enjoyed acting at school, he joined a few drama clubs. Unfortunately, he appeared in two notable disasters, quite accidentally. One was a production at Trinity of a short play called *The Death of Cuchulain* by W. B. Yeats. 'I was wearing a sort of leopard skin rug and a pair of my girlfriend's tights, and it was just hopeless, really. Apparently, the director cried every night; he's in the House of Lords now.'[44] An appearance in La Machine Infernale by Jean Cocteau fared even worse thanks to a hopeless papier-mâché rendering of the face of Anubis, the jackal-headed god, that sent audiences into hysterics whenever John came onto the stage wearing it. 'So, I thought, maybe comedy is for me.'[45]

Before his arrival at Cambridge, John had never heard of the Footlights but was asked to be in the Trinity revue, 'And I was completely hooked.'[46] By his second year, John was running it with Richard Burridge and writing sketches for their summer revue. For the big closing number John recruited Mary Allen, 'And I fell in love with her on the spot.'[47] It was Mary who suggested he and Burridge audition for the Footlights. They got in. According to Jon Canter, John Lloyd quickly endeared himself. 'I remember his opening monologue line in Footlights, which went, I was aborted at an early age in a sewer in Crewe. And we just loved that because he was this pretty boy, quite public school, saying this utter bizarre filth. He had a kind of confidence about him.'[48]

Roles in the panto followed, then John and Mary put on a smoker together. There were one or two auditionees that evening, one of whom John was to meet again several years later at a party given by Clive Anderson. 'Clive said to me, "Have you met Michael Portillo, John," and I said, "No, I don't think so, how do you do, minister." And he goes, "Oh yes, John, oh yes, we have met." He gave me a slightly sinister look. I said, "I'm sure we haven't." "Oh yes, you did a smoker at Cambridge and I auditioned and you turned me down, and you took Clive Anderson instead. And I've never forgotten it. And that's why I went into politics, John." And I went a bit cold all over.'[49]

John was happy to operate on the fringes of the Footlights. He had no ambition to be president or even to serve on the committee. 'I've always been somebody who likes pushing the boundaries. I like to be the person on the outside. I'm very uncomfortable being a brand leader, being the person who says no.'[50] He did get into the cast of *Every Packet*. 'It was very jolly and good hearted with lots of jokes, very *I'm Sorry, I'll Read That Again* kind of style.'[51] John did a punting skit. 'I came on in a boater and a blazer, miming that I was punting. "How well I remember the Girton May Ball in 1964 when Priscilla and I left the dance and punted off to Grantchester. The pole was heavy. I was tired from dancing and it was three miles down the A 11 to the river."'[52] That skit was always a banker for John, but he can't say whether it survived to Edinburgh because after the brief tour he was sacked. Stephen Wyatt took John to a pub to break the news that because of costs the cast had to be reduced by two and he had lost out. 'I started to get quite tearful,' John recalls, 'because having gone to Cambridge with no ambition at all, thinking I'm going to hate this place, this is not my style, and then in my last year I found something I could do and something I wanted to do and really enjoyed doing, and the rug had just been pulled. It was dreadful.'[53]

Stephen could see that John was devastated by the news, then a thought occurred to him. Ex-Footlight alumnus David Hatch had come to see the show, liked it, and wanted to put a version of it on the radio. Hatch had also offered Stephen a placement as a trainee producer in BBC Radio Light Entertainment. 'I turned it down,' he admits, 'which seems to this day a wise decision.'[54] It was Stephen's idea that John could do the radio version of *Every Packet* instead of going to Edinburgh. This met with very little enthusiasm on the part of John, who was fully aware that everyone from TV and radio saw the Footlights in Edinburgh and that his colleagues had a much better chance of being talent spotted. Then, the more John thought about it, the more the radio idea appealed. Growing up John went without a television set for many years and relied on the radio, listening especially to comedy shows. John agreed to Stephen's proposal and the radio version of *Every Packet* proved so popular that a series based on it was commissioned which also featured Jon Canter and Mary Allen. Thus began John's career in radio as a writer and then a producer.

John decided to travel to Edinburgh anyway where he caught the Oxford revue performing and came away impressed by Mel Smith and remembered him a few years later when he produced *Not the Nine O'Clock News*. Still pissed off not to be in the Footlight revue, John decided to gate crash a performance. The closing sketch was a Tarzan parody with Jon Canter as the ape man. John got six friends to dress up in silly loin cloths and walk on stage right at the end. 'It was awful because Jon went on and gave Tarzan's yell, then we all came on, aahuaaa uaaa uaaaaaaaa, and there was total silence. The audience were looking at their programme and thinking, I've really enjoyed this show but what is this! We stood there for about five seconds blushing hideously and left.'[55]

Despite this, John remained on friendly terms with the cast. He and Robert Benton playfully leaked to the local press that Benton was the nephew of Elizabeth Taylor and that the superstar was coming to see him in the revue and was arriving at this big fancy hotel on a certain day. Together with an actress called Kerry from Cambridge, who was a brilliant mimic, they hired an Austin Princess limo, and Kerry got a cheap black wig and a big pair of sunglasses. John assumed the role of Miss Taylor's press representative. 'We swept up in the limo and Kerry got out and there was a huge crowd of people, hundreds of people cheering Liz! Liz! Kerry didn't look anything like her, but because of the wig and dark glasses and people's expectations, and I literally had to fight our way through the crowd with a rolled-up newspaper, "Let Miss Taylor through, please. Miss Taylor is late for her appointment." And we got to the hotel room, and they called the police because of the crowd. Eventually they had to smuggle us out of the back, I think. That was good fun.'[56]

Disappointed not to be included in *Every Packet* in any capacity was Douglas Adams. Jon Canter was great friends with Adams and ended up sharing a flat with him. 'He was very ambitious. And that wasn't really the done thing in Footlights, to appear in any way aspirational in terms of career. It was not cool to say you wanted to go into showbiz. And we used to take the piss out of him mercilessly because Douglas was unashamedly ambitious and would go down to London to interview John Cleese for the college magazine and we'd all go, we'd never do that. Of course, we'd have loved to do that.'[57]

Mary Allen was another lifelong friend; she spoke the eulogy at Adams's funeral. 'Douglas was an absolutely delightful man, and a very funny comic, and like so many comics filled with anxieties about whether they were good enough.'[58] This trait was perhaps the reason why Adams tended to be late delivering his books, as Mary remembers. 'Once his publisher asked Douglas to meet them at this hotel. Douglas went up to his hotel room and the publisher nipped out of the door and locked it and said, "Right, I'm not letting you out until you've finished." And what he'd been trying to finish in two years he succeeded in finishing in eleven days.'[59]

As a performer, the consensus was that Adams wasn't good enough. 'We rather sort of edged him out,' admits Jon. 'We didn't want him in the shows. But he was a brilliant writer with his friends Martin and Will.'[60] Such was Adams's resentment that he hadn't been included in the revue yet again he, along with Will Adams and Martin Smith, organized their own alternative revue. It was performed over three nights at the School of Pythagoras in St John's College and proved a minor hit thanks to having more off-kilter humour than the Footlights revue. To publicize the show, the three of them wore fancy dress, Adams as a turkey, and strolled about the town centre getting their photographs taken. The show's success did not go unnoticed within the Footlights and all three were asked to be on the committee. As a writing team, their sketches became a regular feature in smokers. One sketch concerned a man who discovers that his idyllic cottage is to be demolished to make way for a motorway; an idea Adams would revisit for *Hitchhiker's Guide*.

While Douglas Adams did appear in that year's pantomime, *Cinderella*, playing Prince Charming's father, King Groovy, he did not feature in the 1974 revue, *Chox*. Again, he couldn't hide his bitter disappointment. The whole reason Adams went to Cambridge was to make his mark as a comedy writer-performer with the Footlights and his last chance of doing a revue had been denied him. He did, however, contribute some material. Later, Adams was to realize and appreciate the fact that perhaps he was never cut out to be a performer, anyway.

Chox ran for its customary two weeks at the Arts Theatre. Jon Canter was president that year and again featured in the cast and wrote material. In style and content, it very much followed on from previous revues. 'We were fitting into a great tradition. We weren't rocking any boats.'[61] After all, audiences came to see the Footlight revue with almost a preconceived notion of what to expect. 'You had the security of the audience,' says Jon, 'which is good and bad because you don't need to grab them in the same way, you don't need to prove yourself. You've already proved yourself just by appearing in the Cambridge Footlights. We didn't try to give them anything too radical.'[62]

Jon recalls one of the cast, Geoffrey McGivern, turning up fantastically drunk one night. 'We plied him with coffee before he went on stage and as a true professional he never missed a single word of the script, but he said it very s . . . l . . . o. . . w. . . l . . . y so you just had to stand there on stage and wait. Somebody from the audience told the theatre manager, Commander Blackwood, and there was a notice in the dressing room later: If anyone is drunk on stage again, I will cancel the show.'[63] Blackwood ran the Arts Theatre and was an old ex-naval commander, quite a tough character. Graeme Garden remembers him as, 'very naval.'[64]

Amongst the cast of *Chox* was Griff Rhys Jones, then more of a straight actor with the Marlowe Society before discovering his gift for comedy with the Footlights; he was also gaining a reputation as a director of some note. 'Everybody expected that Griff would become famous,' declares John Lloyd,[65] who helped that process by casting him in *Not the Nine O'Clock News*. And there was Clive Anderson, a law student at Selwyn College in his second year. Clive had been at Harrow County School for Boys where, along with his friend and classmate Geoffrey Perkins (later a comedy producer, writer and performer), he wrote a Christmas revue. While he harboured no real artistic ambitions, the Footlights did form part of his reasoning for going to Cambridge and he auditioned for a smoker in his first term. Taking along one of his old school sketches, on the panel was Jon Canter who dismissed it out of hand, something that Clive has fun occasionally reminding him of now that they are friends. Undeterred, Clive went back with the sketch to the next smoker, where a different person headed the auditioning panel, and he got through. Ironically, Clive was to perform that sketch, about a Soviet Union nuclear attack on the UK, not only in one of the revues but also on television years later. 'It's among the best things I've ever written, which admittedly is a low bar.'[66]

Clive admits that he was cast in *Chox* on the strength of a monologue he performed at a late-night revue, which was put on around Easter time to try out material that might make it into the May Week revue. 'It was based around a miners' strike that was going on at the time. I did it as a miner's leader, essentially Mick McGahey who was a Scottish equivalent of Arthur Scargill. It was topical and to an extent satirical.'[67] Unfortunately, by the time May Week came along the strike had been called off and so the monologue was no longer topical and was therefore cut. Clive was put into other sketches, and worse, into some of the songs and dance numbers. 'And I thought, this is ridiculous, I'm not doing what I can do, and I'll be doing things that I can only do vaguely well. So, I rewrote the thing, taking out all the topical references, and we called it the Scotsman monologue. I just did it in a kilt and strung together a load of jokes and it went down well. Douglas Adams liked it, he said it was a brilliant parody of the worst in Scottish comedy, only I didn't mean it as a parody.'[68]

Putting the revue together, Clive noticed a creative tension between those who were comedians or joke-smiths, or who just wanted to goof around, and those who were maybe better actors or better singers, or just technically superior. Of course, it's useful to have both. Clive didn't put himself in the top bracket as a performer. 'I'm a bit shambolic on stage, which I don't know if it's a cultivated style or just that I am shambolic.'[69] According to Jon Canter, though, Clive was the only member of the group capable of improvising on stage. 'And that gave him a relationship with the audience which none of the rest of us had. I was always impressed by that.'[70] Jon recalls during the run of *Chox* at the Arts Theatre there was a power cut one evening. 'And Clive was on the stage. The director came on and apologized and Clive just kind of wandered round being amusing.'[71]

Improvisation didn't feature in any of the revues. It wasn't really the done thing to ever deviate from the script. And in the Footlights, it hardly went on. In comedy generally, it wasn't something that caught the public's imagination until the 1980s and shows like *Whose Line Is It Anyway?*, hosted by Clive Anderson. 'I think I'm better at adlibbing than I am at learning lines,' Clive admits. 'It's what I like most and oddly enough in my career I've gone into things involved with improvisation, interviews where you're on the hoof, and I've done quite a lot of stand-up comedy as well where I like a bit of audience interaction. Some comedians do and some don't, but I've always liked a bit of reaction from an audience.'[72]

Thanks to the success of *Every Packet*, and the radio version, the BBC paid more attention to *Chox* than they had to any of the more recent revues, even sending their top comedy executive, Dennis Main Wilson, to see it. He liked it enough to commission a fifty-minute highlight show that was later broadcast on BBC 2. Producer Michael White also organized a four-week engagement at the Comedy Theatre in mid-July, the first time the club had been in the West End for a decade. 'I can't believe how we took it in our stride really,' recalls Jon.[73]

The opening night saw many former alumni in the audience. Graham Chapman came to see it and was so impressed by a sketch written by Douglas Adams, Martin Smith and Will Adams that he accosted them in the pub afterwards shouting: 'You bastards! I wish I'd written that.' Chapman soon struck up a writing partnership with Douglas Adams that lasted for a short while. The sketch in question centred on the Crawley and District Paranoid Society. 'It was a well worked through notion,' recalls Clive. 'We were all on stage and somebody was chairing and reading the minutes of this society, so it just worked round everybody obsessively being got at. It was well written and a great performance piece.'[74]

However, *Chox* did not go down well in the West End. 'It was pretty much a disaster in terms of critical reaction because it was just a student revue,' says Clive. 'We certainly got plenty of laughs and it was great fun to do, but it wasn't something that was breaking lots of solid new ground.'[75] Given the fact it was a limited run there was no time for previews to iron out any technical problems. 'And what looked like a jolly good revue in a Cambridge theatre or on tour,' claims Clive, 'probably looked a bit young and juvenile on the West End stage. And I think the reviewers pointed this out.'[76] None more so than Michael Billington in the *Guardian* who called it, 'dismal ... amateur vaudeville.'

When *Chox* moved to Edinburgh, cast member Crispin Thomas took over directorial duties. 'Crispin was very theatrical,' remembers Jon Canter. 'Very stylish. And just gifted as a theatrical force.'[77] Sadly, he was to die of Aids in the 1980s. Clive thinks the show worked better in Edinburgh because, as usual, it was cut from almost two hours to the best part of an hour. This process could be tricky, though, especially with bigger casts, what with sketches being cut and things recast people lost out and that sometimes led to a few feeling a bit bruised and wounded.

Something else, too. It had been the case that Cambridge presented a double-header at the Fringe, the Footlight revue and a heavyweight play from the ADC; most of the Footlight cast did both. This had always been something of a mixed bag, financially speaking, given that the revue was always more popular than, say, a Greek tragedy done in the original Greek. As Clive recalls, the year before *Chox*, a lot of money was lost and the idea of combining the two groups collapsed. 'So, we weren't expected to go to Edinburgh at all because the finances weren't there. And almost at the last minute somebody put together a deal that we went and sort of sub-let from wherever the Oxford revue were performing. That meant it was just the Footlights, so it meant that financially it was much better. We stayed in a big flat up near the castle. So, we had a good year. There was a little bit of Oxford and Cambridge rivalry, but my old school mate Geoffrey Perkins was in the Oxford revue.'[78] Jon Canter recalls meeting another up-and-coming comedy personality in the Oxford troupe – Mel Smith. 'It's interesting how some people are almost fully formed aged nineteen or twenty. I was only three months younger than Mel, but he seemed like a complete adult. He was this really worldly guy.'[79]

10

A Kick in the Stalls

Things had moved quite quickly for Clive Anderson after joining the Footlights, he managed to attend all the smokers and was put on the committee. 'The life of an undergraduate at Cambridge, as indeed most universities, is three years and so everything happens at a super-fast rate, whether its learning stuff, your love life, hobbies, your outside interests, studies, everything happens at this very fast rate. So, three years of three eight-week terms you go through about six lifetimes.'[1]

Hobbies and outside interests were quite important at the time. The faculty wanted people who had a hinterland, who had extracurricular ideas. In more modern times that same attitude is not so prevalent. 'When I was applying to go to university,' says Clive, 'you had to stress what you'd done, if you'd played rugby for your county, been in a play, or you'd chaired the stamp collecting club, or whatever, that was all seen as positives. When my children were applying the people said, to be honest, we're not interested in any of that. It was like, maybe you've climbed Kilimanjaro but only if you can say you were thinking about the sonnets of Shakespeare and you're applying to do English. But when I got there, I played football quite a bit, I edited a magazine and did a couple of plays.'[2]

Clive was also the designated driver for the cabaret team. A hire car was always used and on one occasion there was something wrong with the back light and returning from a gig Clive was stopped by the police. 'I was breathalysed. I knew I was in the clear and I knew why he was breathalysing me because of the light, but also because everybody else in the car had been drinking. I probably might have failed simply by breathing in the fumes of all the other passengers.'[3]

Now in his third year Clive wrote the 1974 panto, *Babes in the Wood*, along with Simon Levene, 'and we wrote huge parts for ourselves in it. And that was very enjoyable.'[4] Levene played the Dame and Clive played a kind of Buttons character. The previous year he had appeared in *Cinderella* as Baron Hardup. Griff Rhys Jones directed *Babes in the Wood*. 'He was a good director,' states Clive. 'Very forceful. But he got very cross with anybody who hadn't learnt their lines properly, which was me most of the time.'[5] Clive found that writing a panto one got the best of all worlds. 'You can put a corny old joke in it and half the people laugh because they haven't heard it before and the other half groan happily. And you can put topical references in that people go, oh, there's a topical reference even though it's set in oldie worldly times. Also, there is a structure to follow, a narrative, and lots of songs.'[6]

By his third year, it was generally accepted that Clive would make a good president. His main duties were making sure there were regular smokers producing plenty of material ready for the late-night revue and the main revue and, along with the committee, to find a director to direct the May Week revue. Clive recalled seeing John Lloyd doing some monologues and bits of performing in his first year. 'And he was the obvious person to ask to come and direct it.'[7]

In 1975 John Lloyd was working for BBC radio where David Hatch had made him a producer, a job at which he excelled. His later move into television produced hits like *The Hitchhiker's Guide to the Galaxy*, *Spitting Image*, *Blackadder* and he was the creator of *QI*. Being at the BBC gave John a bit of a profile to come back to Cambridge and direct the revue. 'But it was a terrifying experience. I'd never directed anything in my life.'[8] Still, he had no qualms about accepting the offer.

John Lloyd did not want a repeat of *Chox*, and so approached the task in a completely different manner. 'And in a much more assertive way,' testifies Clive. 'He said, well, it's comedy you should be doing, no more silly songs and pointless dance routines and things. And so, he had a structure to it, a story that linked everything together. From that point of view, I don't think it was that successful as a way of doing it, but it made it more interesting to do, and it enthused us.'[9]

Entitled, *Paradise Mislaid*, generally the theme was that it took place in hell. It was a structure that John thought, 'probably got in the way. On opening night, I couldn't bear to look because I thought it was going to be a disaster.'[10] It ran over, as revues tended to do, and needed polishing up but the result was an accomplished one; Griff Rhys Jones was to say that this was the most successful of the revues in which he featured.

Geoff McGivern played a sort of demonic quiz master running hell, and there were plenty of pyrotechnics, flashes and the like. At one point the horned wig McGivern was wearing caught fire and he was blasted by the wardrobe mistress because she had to make him another one. 'We had a lot of fun doing that show,' recalls Chris Keightley, making his revue debut. 'Audiences were remarkably forgiving, I thought. We did do some crap.'[11] There were several satirical targets, including the recent hit musical *Jesus Christ Superstar*, along with people like Ken Russell, Milton and Enoch Powell. The finale featured Clive Anderson as an American film director, complete with riding boots and megaphone, auditioning performers, which was a device for a series of short sketches, mostly the ones that didn't fit the revue's concept. One featured a ten-legged man, in fact Griff Rhys Jones, Geoff McGivern, Chris Keightley and two others inside a large suit shuffling onto the stage and performing a Greek dance, with all their legs crossing.

That always went down well with audiences. As did Chris, on his own on the stage, as a ventriloquist dummy operated by the invisible man.

Another skit, about giving out vouchers, almost cost Chris his life on tour. 'We had these different sized vouchers, and the punchline was that you get this bloody enormous voucher. And this ten foot by six foot blue voucher, which had a hole through it, would drop out of the flies and I was supposed to stick my head through it and say the final punchline. But when we set it up, and I think it was in Southampton, this thing was dropped in so fast, they just let it go, it came scything down and almost took my head off.'[12]

Chris went to Cambridge specifically because of the Footlights, being a huge fan of the *Beyond the Fringe* album, 'I practically knew it off by heart,'[13] and Monty Python. He'd been involved in school plays growing up and went into amateur dramatics in Middlesbrough where he lived. Chris was part of a new generation heavily influenced by Monty Python. One revue sketch he recalls went by the name of 'Luring the Poodle'. 'We all had Morris dancers' gear on and poodles on sticks. I think you would have to say that was Python inspired.'[14]

Chris also numbered amongst a wave of working-class northerners who came into the Footlights. Another notable example was the Liverpudlian Jimmy Mulville. 'Before that there had been quite a lot of luvviness going on in the Footlights,' states Chris. 'And there was a brief blossoming of northern comedy. But then the next lot came in and it went back to the luvvies again.'[15] Chris notes that while there was a fair sprinkling of state school kids around, it was still predominantly posh and privately-educated people at Cambridge. At one freshman party, Chris was asked by a fellow student what his father did. 'Oh, my dad's a docker,' said Chris. To which this kid replied, 'Oh, my dad's a doctor as well.'

Jimmy Mulville went to his local comprehensive, studied hard and got a place at Jesus studying French and Classics. Keen on acting, he looked to join one of the drama societies. What he thought might hold him back was his strong Scouse accent, along with a lack of confidence, especially compared to some of his contemporaries. 'I had a lot of front, but not real deep confidence. And so, I struggled in my first year trying to get my confidence up.'[16] He did, however, give the Footlights a try and auditioned in front of the president at the time, Clive Anderson. 'I still moan at him about this. He was doing a crossword with his girlfriend, and I did a monologue, which wasn't very funny, and he barely looked up from his crossword. And he said, "Have you got a sheet?" I said, "A sheet?" He said, "Yes, a bed sheet. Do you have a bed sheet?" I said, "Yeah, I've got a bed sheet. I've got a bed with sheets on it." And he said, "Well, turn up tonight at the Trinity theatre and you can be in the chorus." So, I turned up with the friggin' sheet, not knowing what the fuck it was, and Chris Keightley was doing a song about a guru and we were all his followers dressed in sheets. I had to strip off to my underpants, put a sheet on, and do these doo-wops in the background. That was my first taste of the Footlights.'[17]

As it turned out, Jimmy's Scouse accent was required for a play being put on at Christ's College. This led to him being asked in his second year to play Archie Rice in an ADC production of *The Entertainer*. In the audience one evening was Chris Keightley, who had taken over from Clive Anderson as president. He came backstage to compliment Jimmy on his performance and asked if he wanted to join the Footlights. And becoming a member gave Jimmy a little bit of status around the university. 'Along with a feeling that you'd found your tribe, that you'd found people who were like you.'[18] Status, too, amongst his tutors who afforded him some leeway as he usually gave in his essays late. 'I remember writing one essay for a Dr Peter Garnsey and he held it like it was toxic. And he handed it me back and said, "Did I see you in the Footlights pantomime? I took my family to see it. It was very funny, very good. We really enjoyed it. I've read your essay. I suggest you stay that side of the footlights." I took his advice.'[19]

Chris was also responsible for hooking Jimmy up with a modern languages student at Emmanuel called Rory McGrath. 'I was in my flat one afternoon,' recalls Jimmy, 'and this guy turns up with masses of hair, thin as a rake, and in his pocket, he had two cans of Tennent's lager. I thought, he's my kind of guy. And he came in and I said, "Why don't we get stuck into this Footlights thing?"'[20] Jimmy and Rory McGrath began writing and performing together. Within a year, Jimmy would be president and McGrath his vice president and pretty much running the club. Jon Canter was to describe them as, 'verbal hooligans'.[21] There was something quite rough and ready about the pair of them, along with the distinct aim to bring in what can only be described as a sort of laddish humour; certainly they wanted to get away from the image of Footlights as songs about punting. 'In *Varsity* there was an article saying the Footlights was once a very elegant and witty organization,' recalls Jimmy. 'It's now been taken over by two working class thugs.'[22]

Amongst the first things Jimmy did was perform in the panto, something he came to really appreciate and enjoy. 'I think the best thing the Footlights did in its year was the pantomime. The focus is on the revue, the summer revue is where you're judged. But the most fun you had was doing the pantomime. You could do cheesy jokes and songs. We did *Snow White and the Seven Dwarfs* one year. Most of the cast were on their knees; Robert Bathurst, who was six foot three, was one of the dwarfs. And he was called Shorty.'[23]

The panto earnt money for the club, too, selling out every night. Chris did just one panto, *Robinson Crusoe*, but still remembers this one choice slab of cheesy dialogue. Crusoe meets this native on an island inhabited by cannibals, who explains the edict, a girl on Monday, a little baby on Tuesday, and a man on Friday. Crusoe says, 'You were the man for man Friday.' The native says, 'Yes, I was the man Friday man.' Crusoe says, 'Well, that's what I'll call you.' He says, 'What?' Crusoe says, 'Man Friday.' He says, 'Oh, but my name's Benny.'

As president, Chris attended many college revues and shows looking for talent. In the Footlights there had always been hangers-on, those just there to have a good time, most of whom were not very good. Most of Chris's contemporaries had left, too, people like Clive Anderson, who had been quite dominant. 'I was a rather lonely figure. And I had to put a revue together. That's why I went out and sought other people.'[24] It was a lot of work and sometimes Chris found it difficult to keep the right balance between Footlights and the academic side. 'When I was an undergraduate I did far more work on the revues than I did on my studies. In fact, when I went in to do some revision, I did my first degree in psychology, I went in and said I'd like to borrow some books and the librarian asked, "Who are you?" I hadn't been in there all year.'[25]

Another of Chris's jobs was to work with the committee in choosing a director for that year's revue, entitled *A Kick in the Stalls*; quite an apt title for 1976, with the punk music explosion just starting. Their first choice was vice president Griff Rhys Jones but he had important exams looming. The next idea was to bring in someone like Graham Chapman, a big name from the past. They asked around with not much joy until it was decided to approach Douglas Adams, who had graduated in 1974. He said yes. 'It seemed a good idea to bring him in,' remarks Chris. 'He'd worked with Python, so it would be good publicity. Douglas was a hugely entertaining and witty man. I wouldn't say he was the world's best director. But he was very funny.'[26]

Returning after two years, Adams found the Footlights much changed. When he'd been there it had been tough getting into the club, and impossible to get into the revue, that had all changed and they were having difficulty drumming up business. 'I wound up knocking on people's doors saying, "Have you heard of the Footlights and would you like to be in the May Week revue?"'[27]

For Chris, the key thing was to collect enough material together for the revue. Normally, this was taking the best from the smokers. However, like *Paradise Mislaid*, *A Kick in the Stalls* had a loose theme, requiring additional writing, especially linking material. 'We'd be around at Harry Porter's house late at night sitting around with Douglas playing the guitar and coming up with ridiculous ideas.'[28]

Harry Porter lived in a large house in the city and was always accommodating if people needed a place to stay or hang out. He was entertaining and had a fund of amusing stories. 'Harry was lovely, a gentleman. And very funny,' recalls Jimmy Mulville. 'And usually quite drunk.'[29] He did perhaps take a little too much interest in some of the better-looking male students. They all played along and took the mickey out of him a bit. 'He loved kissing Griff,' reveals Jon Canter. 'It wasn't reciprocated. Harry was very fondly thought of, and it was fantastic to have him there.'[30]

The theme of *A Kick in the Stalls* was that of a Russian invasion of a fictional country called Bogoffia. 'I remember we had the muzzle of a tank gun coming on to the stage,' says Chris, 'which was the head of the Russian column coming up the road. They're stopped by some Bogoffian border guard saying, "We have to stop you in case you have concealed weapons. Igor, search the tanks for concealed weapons."'[31]

Without doubt, the hit of the show was Chris's Kamikaze sketch, which came about when he was on holiday in Malta and spotted a biography written by an ex-Kamikaze pilot in the airport book shop. 'It made me laugh because I thought they were all supposed to be dead.'[32] On stage there is a line-up of Kamikaze pilots, wearing their headbands, and they're being balled out by their commanding officer for not having sacrificed themselves. He wants to know why they haven't been successful locating aircraft carriers. 'And where exactly have you been looking for these aircraft carriers?' asks the officer. 'I can't but notice that you seem to more or less totally ignore the area of the sea. I would have thought the sea was quite a promising area.' The pilots come up with all manner of excuses as to why they haven't crashed into a ship, like their headband slipped over their eyes. Chris did the sketch first at a smoker and then he and Douglas Adams polished it up for the revue. 'And it went down a storm.'[33]

Not much of anything else did. '*Kick in the Stalls* got mullered in the press,' admits Jimmy Mulville.[34] The *Financial Times* pondered with this offering that the Footlights revue format, 'was past its heyday'. It certainly proved that Douglas Adams was not a born director. And according to Chris he did not enjoy the process. 'The whole thing just got so convoluted. Douglas overwrote everything and put so much into every sketch that they ended up twice as long as they needed to be.'[35] The result was that opening night ran something like four hours. 'Whole rows were getting up and leaving,' recalls Jimmy.[36] There was a running joke in the show where there would be a blast of martial music and these two border guards, one of whom was played by Jimmy, would goose step onto the stage. 'The third time the martial music comes on,' recalls Jimmy, 'we're in the wings and I hear this bloke in the third row say, "Oh fuck, not this again."'[37]

Backstage afterwards, Chris was confronted by the theatre manager, Commander Blackwood, demanding that if the show wasn't down to two-and-a-half hours by the following night – "You're out!" Drastic cuts were made and there was an improvement. Then Griff Rhys Jones was brought in to re-direct it for Edinburgh and it worked much better. 'Edinburgh was fun,' says Chris, 'but you were conscious of the huge pressure of competition and also the huge pressure on you as a Footlight because great things were expected from you.'[38] Chris went into the pharmaceutical industry but kept in touch with many of his former Footlights colleagues. 'We used to go to the Groucho Club and get as many of the old presidents together as we could and then have an appallingly drunken evening.'[39]

Succeeding Chris as president was Jimmy Mulville, who came in with ideas of his own, namely that the club needed to put on more regular smokers to get more people involved and to make them more of an event.

These smokers were held over at Trinity's theatre. Jimmy also felt that the revues of late had come over as a bit too derivative of Monty Python. 'So, there was a move away from that to go back to more proper revue.'[40] Sketches in the 1977 revue, entitled *Tag*, included *Dixon of Dock Green* (the BBC police drama series) in franglais and an ancient Roman bingo caller. Jimmy tried out *Tag* first in Uppingham, a market town in Rutland. The show included a monologue written and performed by Jimmy in the face of warnings that it wouldn't work because it didn't contain a single punchline. Jimmy was dressed as a northern working men's club comic, frilly shirt, bow tie, and proceeded to have a mental breakdown on stage. 'It did get funnier and funnier because you watched this comedian clinging onto joke formulations as he fell apart and told you how shit his life was.'[41] It went down well and stayed in. 'And when I now get frightened about doing something, about taking a risk, I always think, well, you did that, you were twenty years of age and you thought, fuck it, what's the worst that can happen.'[42]

For Jimmy, the coup of the show was getting Griff Rhys Jones to come back and direct. Griff Rhys Jones had left the year before and joined BBC Radio Light Entertainment. 'Griff's stage craft was extraordinary,' declares Jimmy. 'He was so good we all thought Griff would be the guy who'd end up running the National Theatre.'[43] Instead, that turned out to be Nicholas Hytner, Jimmy's fellow cast member in *Tag*.

Following its usual run at the Arts Theatre, *Tag* went on tour, including the Robin Hood Theatre in Newark. 'Very old people would come along,' recalls Jimmy. 'And they'd suffer whatever was on stage because it was a nice day out and they had a nice meal afterwards.'[44] It was while the show was at Newark that Griff Rhys Jones showed up to check everything was still ticking along nicely. One of the interesting features of the theatre was that it had an honesty bar. One evening after the show, the cast headed up there for a drink only to find it was closed. 'And I remember Griff jumping head first into the bar and smashing it open,' says Jimmy, 'and then us just drinking the place dry.'[45]

In Edinburgh, on the Sunday before the Festival kicks off, there is a procession of floats where people dress up in costumes and promote the various shows they are in. Martin Bergman was in the cast of *Tag* and informed everyone that he'd already decked out their lorry, and indeed he had, it was all silver and very impressive. After the procession was over it was back to St Mary's Hall, the venue the Footlights were sharing with the Oxford Theatre Group. As Jimmy got off the float, he was accosted by someone from the Oxford group, built like a rugby player, and accused of nicking his set. Jimmy didn't know what he was talking about, but then saw Martin Bergman skulking away in the corner. 'Martin had gone into the storeroom and taken this muslin-backed silver paper the Oxford lot were going to use to build the set for Richard Curtis' adaptation of Evelyn Waugh's *The Loved One*. And we'd just put it on our fucking lorry. And I thought this guy was going to hit me. I was so terrified. I'm a physical coward. And he came at me, and I held my fist out in front of me and he ran onto it and his lip just parted like the Red Sea and out came all the blood. I felt sick and the following day my wrist was swollen.'[46] The local paper was quick to accuse the pampered offspring of the upper classes of raging war on the streets, fostering the general misconception that if you were from Oxford or Cambridge, you were posh.

It was while sharing St Mary's Hall that some of the Footlights team caught a performance by the Oxford revue. 'And we saw Rowan Atkinson for the first time,' recalls Martin Bergman. 'At that point, I felt we might as well all give up! We had just witnessed the arrival of the premiere comedian of our generation.'[47]

Tag was a successful parting gift from Jimmy (a programme of highlights was broadcast on BBC 2), as he and Rory McGrath left to go and write comedy on BBC radio. It was a place where he had forged lifelong friendships, with Rory, Griff Rhys Jones and Clive Anderson, and learnt much about his chosen profession of comedy. 'Because you had deadlines to put shows on in front of paying customers, you weren't wanking around, you had to get it right. So, you'd play around with running orders. I produced the first two series of *Smith and Jones*, and I saw that what Griff and I were good at was coming up with running orders. It was just in our bones, of what works there, and what doesn't work there. And how to finish a show.'[48]

Jimmy's successor as president was Martin Bergman, whose comedy idols growing up were John Cleese and Peter Cook. 'I knew they had gone down the Footlights route, and following them was my teenage aim.'[49] His English teacher at his school, David Lund, had attended Selwyn College and was the musical director for the Footlights in the late 1960s. Martin appeared in numerous comedy revues at school with his writing/performing partner at the time, Owen Brenman. 'It was an all-boys school, so we imported a young friend of Owen's who made us laugh to do the female roles – Emma Thompson.'[50]

Martin auditioned for the Footlights, performing a sketch he'd written at school and was accepted. In the same college as Rory McGrath (Emmanuel), they began writing sketches together. Something did strike Martin about the club when he first arrived. 'I'd expected Footlights to be very sophisticated, and I was slightly surprised at how broad the humour was.'[51] Something else Martin was determined to do during his reign as president was to restore the club to former glories by having its own club room again.

Members knew that there had once been a club room, and several times attempts were made to recreate it. For others, they never missed what they had never had and so it didn't seem much of a hardship for committee meetings to take place in pubs or rented rooms, and for smokers to be held in Trinity's theatre; and there was always Harry Porter willing to open up his house for writing sessions and rehearsals. Martin came across one location that looked a possibility. It was the basement of the Cambridge Union Society in Round Church Street, not too far from the ADC Theatre. Chris Keightley recalls visiting the place along with Martin and not being terribly impressed. 'We all had a bit of a debate about whether it was suitable or not. It was rather dishevelled and had a very low ceiling. It was literally a cellar.'[52]

The space was rarely used by the Union and so Martin did a deal with them to pay an annual rent. 'I then contacted builders I knew through my parents and had them build a sort of rudimentary nightclub, with a stage at one end and a bar at the other. Then I raided Harry Porter's house for old Footlights photos, framed them and stuck them up on the walls. Voila! Club room!'[53]

The finished result, recalls Jan Ravens, resembled a sort of speakeasy. 'There were sofas along the walls and in front of them were these chrome framed tables with glass tops, flimsy as anything. Martin must have got them as a job lot. It was damp and always a bit yucky, and I think once it did actually flood.'[54] Paul Shearer was unimpressed. 'There was a brown carpet that sometimes squelched because it had beer spilt on it and it smelt of fags.'[55] Still, everyone made the best of it, and there was a rostrum stage at one end. 'That's all you needed,' admits Jimmy Mulville. 'You just needed a space that you could go, have a few drinks and just hang out and meet other people.'[56]

The grand opening took place in February 1978 and Martin wrote to invite all the ex-Footlight alumni he could think of. Most declined. 'I do remember one day getting a knock on my undergraduate door and finding Clive James on the other side. He was RSVP-ing in person! I think the evening was quite jolly. People got up and did sketches and monologues, and we all drank too much. We could only fit a hundred or so people in the place, so it was quite a hot ticket.'[57] Others in attendance included Pete Atkin, Jonathan Lynn, Robert Buckman, Rory McGrath and Griff Rhys Jones.

While the new club room didn't have many of the advantages of Falcon Yard, for starters it didn't have a late licence, Martin was keen to bring the place alive. 'Smokers only happened once or twice a term. To utilize the club room, I soon discovered that the bar alone was not a big enough draw. We needed to put something up on the stage.'[58] Martin brought in revue groups from other universities such as Durham, Bristol and Norwich. 'We tried a hypnotist we found in the back pages of *The Stage*. Anything to get the room full!'[59]

Martin had seen a new young comedienne on the ITV talent show *New Faces* called Victoria Wood. 'I thought she was wonderful. At that point, she was just doing songs. I contacted her agent and paid her fifty pounds to play the club room. I think it was the first solo gig she ever did. She stayed in a guest room at Emmanuel and the bed broke in the middle of the night! As I recall, about fifty people came to see her. A few years later, I produced her at the Edinburgh fringe when she was starting to get famous. Lovely woman, much missed.'[60]

11

The Cellar Tapes

It had become a recent tradition to invite ex-Footlight alumni to direct the revue, recent cases being Douglas Adams, John Lloyd and Griff Rhys Jones. Martin Bergman asked Clive Anderson if he was interested in directing the 1978 revue. Then practising as a barrister, so to an extent in charge of his own time, Clive agreed, even though he had never directed before. 'So, in that sense, I was totally unsuited to the role. But I thought I knew a bit about comedy, so if there was say six similar sketches, I think I was confident of being able to select the best three, or to say to somebody, that's quite good but it needs a better ending or let's rewrite that.'[1] Entitled *Stage Fright*, Clive wrote much of it, too, along with Martin and Rory McGrath, who had graduated but lived in Cambridge. 'I enjoyed the process,' says Clive. 'The main thing was selecting the right people but there were some talented people around. Martin Bergman was a sort of mover and shaker, and he was in it. I think Robert Bathurst was very much the centre of things.'[2]

While directing the revue, Clive stayed at Harry Porter's house and found him to be an interesting man. 'If you were writing a book about Oxbridge dons, he would certainly be a character you would want to have. He had been a don at my college, Selwyn, which he left, I don't know why, it was before my time. But he did visit me once in my room and it had been his room, for some reason it had been downgraded to be an undergraduate's room when I had it. He liked a drink. He was always very supportive of our efforts. He might offer the odd bit of advice. And he'd reminisce about people he thought were great performers. He liked Griff a lot.'[3]

Porter had taken on the role of club archivist, storing all manner of material, photographs, scripts, programmes etc, relating to the Footlights, past and present. It was all stored in his house. Clive spent hours going through it, finding himself particularly drawn to old reviews. Quite often when a new revue opened the cast was unfairly compared to greats from the past like Cook, Cleese or Jonathan Miller, or accusations that this year's crop were not as good as last year. 'I thought, I wonder if everybody got good or bad reviews when they were young. Obviously, I cherry picked a bit, but I found a bad review for Jonathan Miller, a bad review for John Cleese. I could have found a bad review for virtually everybody. Obviously in some cases it was a bit of a cheek because it might have been the only bad review.'[4]

One stinker from the mid-1960s came from the *Evening News* and read: 'This show can be recommended only to the parents and friends of those taking part. Very fond parents, very close friends only. This will probably be the only occasion the cast can be seen on the professional stage.' Clive presented these bad reviews for his cast to read, perhaps allaying any nervous thoughts they may have harboured about a critical onslaught.

Included in *Stage Fright*, and making her debut revue appearance, was Jan Ravens. 'We weren't really employing her as an impressionist, which became her great thing,' reveals Clive, 'but she was a great stage performer, she could sing, she could act, she was funny.'[5] Interested in drama at school, Jan also discovered a gift for mimicry and did spot on impersonations of the teachers that led to a certain celebrity status amongst her classmates. Determined to go to drama school, it was her art teacher, who directed all the school plays, who persuaded Jan to attend her old college at Cambridge, Homerton. Arriving on a drama teaching course, Jan first auditioned for the Marlowe Society and in her first year was in a production directed by Griff Rhys Jones, playing many of her scenes with Jimmy Mulville. 'And that's when I got into the whole Footlights crowd.'[6]

Coming from a grammar school, Jan had the presumptive notion of Cambridge being rather posh and privileged; instead, she found it to be a good mix of people, 'but everyone did seem to be very confident'.[7] It helped that when she started people like Jimmy Mulville were still around. 'We felt a bond with each other straight away,' states Jan, 'because he was from Liverpool and I was a plastic Scouser from Hoylake.'[8]

Something Jan couldn't help but notice was that the women in the Footlights were not really writing. *Stage Fright* featured no material written by a woman. 'It was just the way it was. It was the culture. It's like you need to see someone like you doing something in order for you to do it.'[9] Even so, it was exciting to be part of it and Jan's friend, Sarah Palmer, was also in the cast. 'It was quite old fashioned in a way. We had these terrible costumes, which were not very flattering to Sarah and me because they were white jeans, a white shirt and coloured tie, they were absolutely terrible.'[10] In one sketch Jan performed the Tammy Wynette song 'Stand by Your Man' in the persona of Margaret Thatcher singing to her husband Denis.

Jan was also involved in the final sketch; indeed, everyone was on stage for it and it lasted fifteen minutes. During the second week at the ADC Theatre, on the Saturday, Clive was there because some more senior barristers had come along to watch the show. Before curtain-up, Sarah Palmer reported ill and couldn't go on. Jan could cover Sarah's part in all the other sketches, save for this end sketch, which was a big chunk of the second half, so Clive stepped in. 'Which obviously got some extra laughs. The audience was told quite specifically that as an emergency measure I was playing in the end of the show, so they knew that I was therefore not word perfect, and I was a man in a dress. Which I have done over the years occasionally. I think I used to be a reasonably convincing, even good-looking woman.'[11]

The tour played the usual places. In Uppingham there wasn't an awful lot to do during the day except frequent the pub. One lunchtime Jan drank so much beer that by the time she was due on stage she felt dreadful. 'The stage manager said, "What you need is a port and brandy, that'll sort you out." So, inexplicably, I had this port and brandy, and I went on stage and I felt so drunk, and I never, ever wanted to feel like that again. It was such a good lesson. It was such a terrifying feeling.'[12]

That tour was Jan's first experience of the Edinburgh Fringe, where once again the Footlights shared a venue with the Oxford revue. And while Jan was thinking she'd much rather have been doing a Jean Genet play with the Marlowe Society, the Footlights was a lot of fun. 'It was your world, really. We did have a great laugh. But we were serious about doing a good show and the rehearsals were hard work.'[13] Jan involved herself in the pantos, too, which she enjoyed just as much as the revue. 'There wasn't as much pressure on it. I have fond memories of them. There was something very joyous about it. The pantomime was a real highlight. We all rallied round making props and costumes.'[14]

All this, of course, took up a lot of time, especially for anyone on the committee, or the secretary or president; Footlights was almost like a full-time job. There were smokers, trying out new material, there was the pantomime, the late-night revue, and the big May Week revue, which came at the same time as everyone was doing their exams. 'Footlights was the kind of backbone of my time at Cambridge,' declares Jan. 'I suppose, more than my course. In fact, it became more important than my studies.'[15] At one point, Jan was threatened with being kicked out of college because she was too busy with the Footlights. This is the reason, along with a heavy workload, why Jan didn't feature in 1979's revue, *Nightcap*, and she was gutted to miss out. Sarah Palmer was also too busy taking her final exams. Director Martin Bergman wanted at least two women in the cast, but ended up with just one, Emma Thompson. Studying English at Newnham, Emma made an instant impact when she arrived. 'I can remember her coming into the Footlights club room to do her first audition and just thinking – fucking hell!' recalls Jan. 'She's always had this amazing confidence and charisma.'[16] Martin very quickly labelled her a star and insisted she play the lead in the Christmas panto, *Aladdin*.

Another Footlight newcomer who featured in *Aladdin* was Hugh Laurie. 'The stage manager had found a man telling funny stories in her college bar and convinced him to come and audition for me,' recalls Martin. 'He was a rower, and I thought he was terrific. I put both Emma and Hugh in *Nightcap*.'[17] Laurie wasn't at all sure what the Footlights was all about before walking into the club room and seeing photographs of all his comedy heroes adorning the walls. 'I realized that I was in a hallowed space.'[18]

The cast of *Nightcap* also featured Robert Bathurst, then president, and Simon McBurney, an English literature student at Peterhouse. Sketches included a Stephen Sondheim parody sung by Emma Thompson, a Zulu monologue performed by Hugh Laurie and a Wild West sketch. '*Nightcap* was my favourite of the three revues I took part in,' says Martin. 'We later did a version of it on a BBC TV show called *Friday Night . . . Saturday Morning*.'[19]

Nightcap was halfway through its two-week run at the Arts Theatre when a familiar voice boomed into the dressing room where Martin was relaxing after the curtain call. 'I enjoyed that. That was really funny. Who's in charge? Is it you?' Peter Cook stumbled down the stairs, cigarette in hand, pointing at Martin. 'Peter Cook was my idol. I had grown up watching *Not Only . . . But Also* [the 1960s BBC sketch comedy show Cook did with his partner Dudley Moore] and had devoured the Derek and Clive recordings. I tried unsuccessfully to act cool when he asked if I'd like to have lunch with him the following day.'[20] A year later, when Martin was asked to guest host an edition of a BBC chat show, Cook agreed to appear. Martin and Rory McGrath also wrote some E. L. Wisty monologues for Cook that he performed on Radio One.

Martin graduated that year, going on to become a film and television producer and director. His final act was to make Footlights history by installing Jan Ravens as the first female president. 'Jan was an obvious choice because she was super-talented, but I did think a woman at the helm would be beneficial.'[21] Jan was delighted to accept. 'I was really pleased about it because Emma and another friend of mine, Sandi Toksvig, we were feminists obviously, and so it was, yes, about time. And we did try and get more female writers in, and I tried to be more open about auditions and more inclusive. I felt the responsibility of it because I felt if I screw this up, they won't ask another one.'[22]

As president, Jan oversaw 1980's revue, *Electric Voodoo*, which ended up a personal disappointment. Her choice of director was Crispin Thomas, ex-Footlights, then an assistant director at the Northcott Theatre in Exeter. His promise of colourful costumes and more singing and dancing had the effect of making the show come over as too camp and kitsch, which didn't suit a cast that had more of a strong sense of the ridiculous. Thomas introduced showbiz clichés like having his cast sweep the floor before going into a Broadway-type, 'waiting for the show to begin,' number. 'It was supposed to be ironic,' claims Jan, 'but it just came over as cheesy and terrible.'[23] One cast member, Simon McBurney, quickly realized where things were going and pulled out.

When *Electric Voodoo* went to Edinburgh Jan tried to fix the show but it remained unsatisfactory, which was especially disappointing as the revue the president helped organize in their final year acted very much as a calling card. 'That's one of the reasons I was so disappointed in mine because I thought, oh shit, this is really not what I wanted to be saying about myself.'[24] At least it broke a barrier of sorts, out of a cast of six, four were women, including Jan and Sandi Toksvig.

A much bigger success was that year's panto, *Cinderella*, which Jan co-wrote and directed. Most significantly of all there was *Woman's Hour*,

Cambridge's first all-female revue. *Woman's Hour* was prompted by the fact that it had always been predominantly men who did the writing in the Footlights, and people like Jan were beginning to question it. 'I remember the feeling that we weren't allowed or weren't good enough to write. Nobody was saying, you're not allowed to write, it was just the way things were.'[25]

Jan had always felt that the best way for a change to be made was to, 'dazzle them with excellence,'[26] and so together with her friends Emma Thompson and Sandi Toksvig, the idea for an all-woman revue was taken to the ADC Theatre, a nice 200-seat theatre, where it was enthusiastically welcomed. The show wasn't intended to be a feminist tract, although some of the sketches did veer in that direction, 'The main point was just to be women being funny,' says Jan, 'and for it to be our take on things.'[27] For example, there was a book programme parody, a sketch where Jan played a magician's assistant embarrassed about how awful her thighs look in leotards, and a quick skit about the perils of waxing.

With Hilary Duguid as the fourth member of the cast, *Woman's Hour* was performed 29 January to 2 February 1980. 'Sandi was quite annoyed with Emma,' claims Jan, 'because literally a few days before we were due to put the show on Emma shaved her head, so of course her look was quite extraordinary. I think Emma wore a baseball cap for most of it.'[28] Despite this minor handicap, the revue was a resounding success. 'It was exhilarating,' reveals Jan. 'And it did feel like something had happened. What was great about doing *Woman's Hour* was it was part of a wave of feminism that felt very exhilarating. It did feel like you were part of a bigger thing and that whole business, which we were only dimly aware of at the time, but nevertheless we were aware of it, about creating something that other people could then say, well they've done it, so we can.'[29]

Jan and Sandi did quite a lot of the writing together on *Woman's Hour*, and after leaving Cambridge that year formed an all-woman comedy sketch troupe called Flying Ducks. 'She's always been a one-off, Sandi,' says Jan. 'She had so much confidence as a writer.'[30]

Within a year, Jan was back in Cambridge. Hugh Laurie had been installed as Footlights president and wanted Jan to direct the 1981 revue. *The Cellar Tapes* proved to be the most successful Footlights show since *A Clump of Plinths* with a cast that included Stephen Fry, Hugh Laurie and Emma Thompson. And it was another barrier broken for Jan, as the first woman to direct a Footlights revue. 'I did feel a huge amount of pressure of being the first one and thinking, as I had done when I became president, I hope I don't fuck this up, because they'll never get another one.'[31] Even so, Jan arrived having directed several productions at Cambridge, 'and so they knew I wasn't a walkover. Although I felt very much that Hugh and Stephen were in charge of it because they were such a strong writing partnership. They did write separately but they did have this real rapport and a great affection and respect for each other.'[32]

It was Emma Thompson, a mutual friend, who had introduced Fry to Laurie, knowing that Laurie was looking for a writing partner. One evening she turned up at Fry's dorm room and together they walked over to Selwyn College and knocked on Hugh Laurie's door. Invited in, Fry's first glimpse of Laurie was of him sitting on his bed with a guitar playing a song he had written. Laurie's recollection of this first meeting is slightly different, that it was he who turned up at Fry's rooms. Whoever is right, the connection was immediate and one of the great comedy duos in British comedy was born.

With Emma already cast, Jan was keen to have two women in the show, 'not just the token bird, as it were'.[33] Penny Dwyer came through the auditions. A Footlights member, Penny spent more of her time with CULES, the club that went to schools and hospitals, 'Footlights with a social conscience,' observes Jan. 'And I thought she was quite gritty and earthy and she'll be a good foil to Emma, who was so sort of glossy. But actually, she got a bit lost in it.'[34] After leaving Cambridge, Penny decided against going into a career in entertainment and became an engineer.

As for the two remaining spots, one went to Tony Slattery, 'who was such a live wire on stage that he was already pretty much a given',[35] claims Paul Shearer, who auditioned for Jan and claimed the final place. Paul had never heard of the Footlights when he arrived at Cambridge. It was his friend, Richard Hytner, who introduced him to them and thought it might be fun to audition. They got a part in the panto. 'I was given the very glamorous role of the back legs of the dragon,' recalls Paul. 'So, it was a small start.'[36] The star of the panto was Emma Thompson. 'She was consummately professional,' remembers Paul. 'Her sheer discipline was incredible.'[37] Next, Paul and Richard Hytner wrote a sketch that they performed together at a smoker, playing two blokes chatting while stood at the urinals, backs to the audience. 'It was toilet humour, quite literally.'[38]

Paul was doing an engineering degree in his first year, then switched to computing science, 'because there were less lectures and it allowed me more time to fart about on stage, basically.'[39] Even so, Paul found it hard to juggle the two things, since by then he and Richard Hytner had set up their own revue company and were writing heavily together. 'I didn't pass my exams in the second year, and I was hauled in by the tutorial body and they did ask me one deadly question which was, "Do you feel your contribution to university life has been curricular or extracurricular." And I had to fess up, "Well, I have to say it's probably largely been extracurricular." So, then I had to stay for a few weeks in the summer and knuckle down to academics.'[40]

For Paul, the Footlights was an intense group. 'And you can get very upset if someone doesn't think that your idea is funny.'[41] And full of those peculiar obsessions that can creep into sketch comedy. 'I remember one group trying to work out what kind of biscuit is going to be the funniest line in a sketch, is it bourbon creams or is it fondant fancies.'[42] The membership was still by no means large, but there was a core element of people who were more serious about performing than the others, and involved themselves in the

FIGURE 11.1 *The cast of the 1981 revue,* The Cellar Tapes. *Actors (clockwise from back left): Stephen Fry, Tony Slattery, Paul Shearer, Hugh Laurie, Emma Thompson and Penny Dwyer in the BBC television show* The Cambridge Footlights Review, *6 February 1982. Photo by Don Smith/Radio Times via Getty Images.*

running of the club by being on the committee. And once you were on the committee you felt fairly secure in the knowledge that you would be involved in the May Week revue and the tour. Paul was on the committee and as such found himself organizing the odd smoker. He recalls one he put together with Emma Thompson in which Tilda Swinton performed. Tilda, a student at New Hall College, was on the fringes of the Footlights but in the end went down the drama route.

As *The Cellar Tapes* went into rehearsal, things were already starting to look promising. 'I was very aware that the calibre of the cast was really high,' confirms Jan Ravens. 'And the calibre of the writing was really high.'[43] Although Jan admits to sometimes losing her temper when some of the cast was late for rehearsals, for example. 'You had to be committed to it. And for most of us, as it turned out, that was a good thing because we were preparing for our careers.'[44]

Because the previous year had been a camp, singing/dancing kind of show, which Jan was not happy about, and would have been an absolute anathema to the likes of Stephen Fry and Hugh Laurie, the approach this time was very different. Jan brought in Kevin McCloud (later of Channel 4's *Grand Designs*) to be the designer and he gave the production a minimalist feel. 'It was sparse,' says Jan, 'and a bit grittier than the previous year, which the cast wanted.'[45]

This approach was reflected in the sketch material. 'I think Stephen and Hugh had a deliberate going away from Monty Python with its surrealistic overtones,' claims Paul. 'Stephen and Hugh were very much the creative engine of *The Cellar Tapes*.'[46] The pair had been particularly prolific in their writing that year and it was no real surprise that it was they who established the whole tone. 'They had a very strong idea of the kind of material they wanted,' confirms Jan. 'They were taking the piss out of quite a grown-up world. When I started in the Footlights it was more kind of like pure comedy, just for the fun of it kind of thing; doing things that made ourselves laugh and hoping that might translate to other people. By the time of *The Cellar Tapes*, it had got a bit more edgy, a bit darker and a bit more serious, in parts.'[47] There were sketches about suburban couples, spies, a song about the British Movement (a neo-Nazi organization) and Hugh Laurie performed a song about the IRA. At one point, Tony Slattery took on the persona of a loner contemplating killing someone in a song he performed entitled, 'I'm Going to Shoot Somebody Famous'.

In another way, *The Cellar Tapes* was also a throwback. After the, for want of a better word, laddish humour of the Mulville and McGrath years, here were sketches about chess and Shakespeare, very unashamedly going back to almost archetypal Oxbridge comedy. There was clever word play and lots of puns. In one sketch, Stephen Fry is sat down for dinner and his butler says, 'Cape on for dinner, sir.' Fry answers, 'Oh yummy, capon.' 'No, no, you will need to put a cape on for dinner, sir.' It's a joke that would have worked in the 1920s or 1930s. It reflected who they were, and comedy needs to reflect who you are as a person, to some extent, and Fry and Laurie were never going to be the next Alexei Sayle or Ben Elton, comedians who were at the forefront of the emerging alternative comedy. In a way, *The Cellar Tapes* was swimming against the tide of what was beginning to happen in British comedy. It was as though the cast thought they couldn't pretend they were part of alternative comedy scene. They were completely honest about who they were. Interestingly, these two worlds did meet in a 1984 episode of *The Young Ones* called 'Bambi', which parodied the BBC quiz show *University Challenge*. Fry, Laurie and Emma Thompson, along with Ben Elton, represented 'Footlights College', against the Young Ones' 'Scumbag College'.

Because Fry and Laurie had contributed so much of the writing it was difficult for anyone else to get much of a look in. 'Emma and I, we were fighting to get material on in *The Cellar Tapes*,' admits Jan. 'I wrote a sketch about a beauty salon.'[48] Paul contributed a sketch about a sad character sat in the corner at a disco trying to talk to girls, and performed a monologue based on a recent television series about the history of the British Navy that was presented by Lord Admiral Hill-Norton. 'And he had this ridiculously plummy voice.'[49] Later, when the group went off to do their own tour the following year, the Falklands War broke out. 'We tweaked the monologue,' reveals Paul, 'to include the line, "I'm standing here on the deck of this aircraft carrier and the engine under the bonnet of this beast means that we can steam anywhere in the world, within three weeks." And that was during the three weeks of the task force setting sail and heading towards the Falklands. And as they were getting closer and closer, the audiences were getting more and more uncomfortable with it, not surprisingly, and certainly when the *Sheffield* went down, we pulled it.'[50]

As a team everyone worked well together, between the bouts of mania and depression that can affect comedians. They bonded, too, in the adversity of performing as members of the Footlights cabaret group. Most memorably, when they were booked as the entertainment at the post-premiere party for *Chariots of Fire* at the Dorchester Hotel. For Paul, this was his first professional engagement. 'Although there were four palm trees that were dressing the corners of the ballroom that actually cost more to hire than we did.'[51] After dinner had been served, the team was asked to go on, but staff were still clearing away desert and serving coffee. 'So, the whole audience was a bit distracted,' Paul recalls. 'Just below us there was one table which had David Puttnam on it and Lindsay Anderson. And because they were round tables some people were facing away from the stage and I remember in the middle of one sketch Lindsay Anderson turned round and looked up with a face of utter disdain and turned back away. And we thought, oh dear, it's not going very well. Hugh was apoplectic. He thought it had gone terribly and was really moody afterwards.'[52]

The night before *The Cellar Tapes* opened, Jan was in a state of panic. She found a phone box and called her mother and cried down the line to her, 'Oh my God, I don't know if it's going to be OK. I don't want to let them down.' She needn't have worried; it was a huge success. 'And I remember getting a card from my mum the following day saying, you've done it.'[53] On the front was a cartoon of a little dachshund climbing a very tall staircase.

In Edinburgh, *The Cellar Tapes* stormed the Festival and won the inaugural Perrier Award, presented on stage by Rowan Atkinson. It came as a complete surprise to the cast who never thought they had any chance of winning. 'There was already a sort of anti-establishment backlash against the Footlights,' says Paul. 'We were seen as a kind of comedy establishment. But I think the quality of the show overcame any objection.'[54] In a way, by winning that first Perrier, the Footlights were legitimizing the award more than anything, and it became the most prestigious comedy prize in the UK.

Among the audience one evening was BBC producer Dennis Main Wilson, 'who was one of those guys who totally existed on Scotch and cigarettes and wore a huge sports jacket,' recalls Jan. 'But he was a proper comedy guy.'[55] In his day, Main Wilson produced *The Goon Show* and *Hancock's Half Hour* on radio, before moving to television and bringing us *Till Death Us Do Part*, *The Rag Trade* and discovering John Sullivan, who went on to write *Only Fools and Horses*. He liked *The Cellar Tapes* enough to put a pared down version of it on television.

There was also a tour of Australia, organized by Martin Bergman. The cast was minus Penny Dwyer and Tony Slattery, who had to go back to

Cambridge to continue their studies; their parts were taken by Bergman and Robert Bathurst. Paul Shearer was absent, too, sitting in his sister's flat in London having graduated and thinking, oh fuck, what do I do now? It was the agent Richard Armitage who came to the rescue. Armitage had signed up Emma Thompson while she was still at Cambridge, and also had Stephen Fry on his books. Along with Hugh Laurie, he wanted them to go on a revue tour of the UK, and Paul was brought back into the group. It was the start of his career as an actor and writer. He had never thought once about applying for a proper job. 'And I haven't, yet.'[56] That's what the Footlights gave him. Confidence; the mere fact that there was a path that had been trailblazed by others. 'Once you knew about the club and you were part of it, the fact that there were so many people who'd gone through and gone on to do stuff, and some of them hugely famous, it was just encouraging, you just sort of thought, oh, well, maybe I will give it a go.'[57]

12

Hawaiian Cheese Party

There was always an active idea within the Footlights that when the big guns left in their third year there should be someone ready to take over the reins sufficiently immersed in the lore and traditions of the club. It had already been decided that this was going to be Tony Slattery. He was duly made president and was the undisputed star of the 1982 revue, *Premises, Premises*. 'Tony was a giant figure at Cambridge,' states Peter Bradshaw, an English student at Pembroke. 'Maybe that's because all of us younger students were saucer-eyed at older students who had been there a long time and had huge reputations. He was the Olivier of comedy at Cambridge. He was a gigantic name.'[1]

Much of the show was written by Richard Turner and William Osborne, later a screenwriter in Hollywood; he co-wrote *Twins* (1988). Joining Slattery in the cast were Morwenna Banks, Kate Duchene, who did an amusing Joyce Grenfell-type monologue, Robert Harley, Neil Mullarkey and Will Osborne. Morwenna Banks and Neil Mullarkey were at the same college, Robinson. Morwenna had done some acting with the ADC and it was Neil who identified a talent for comedy and persuaded her to join the Footlights. Having two women in the cast was now the standard, though when told this the manager of the Arts Theatre enquired whether they were funny or whether they were attractive. 'It was a shocking thing to hear in 1982,' declares Neil. 'So, I told him the women were funny and the men were chosen for our beauty. I hoped we might have moved on from the old variety tropes of men are funny, and women are seen as either dolly birds or harridans.'[2]

Neil went to Cambridge, reading Economics, Social and Political Sciences, with the express intention of being in the Footlights and he joined in his first term. 'I'd heard of The Goodies and Monty Python so that was the place I wanted to be.'[3] Originally intending to be a doctor, Neil caught the comedy bug performing in school plays and enjoyed the sensation of getting laughs on stage. Having never written a comedy sketch before his audition ('I had to learn'), Neil performed a couple of monologues in front of a judging panel that included Stephen Fry and Hugh Laurie. 'One was a *Blue Peter* appeal, and the presenters were saying things like, send us the deeds to your house.'[4] It went down well enough for him to be asked to perform at the next smoker, then another. By the spring of his first year, Neil was invited to be on the committee, which tended to happen if a member did well at smokers.

As was tradition, *Premises, Premises* was put together from the best sketches of the year that had done well in the smokers or in the late-night spring revue. Then, usually around the Easter holidays, there was a week of intensive writing where some sketches would be developed further and new material added. Chris England, who was reading English at Pembroke, had failed to make the cast but managed to get some material in. Chris had always wanted to be involved in comedy. 'I was very much a Python baby. And all the people I most admired, like Peter Cook, seemed to have come out of Cambridge. And so, I set myself to get there.'[5]

Now in his second year, Chris found there were always more people than could ever hope to be included in any single revue; 'but that's part of the Footlights reputation as a proving school, the competition is part of it.'[6] Chris had found his first year especially competitive, partly because of the big guns of Fry, Laurie and Emma Thompson. 'It was kind of their territory, so there was a very definite sense that you bided your time. It was quite intimidating to begin with because Stephen and Hugh and Emma were so obviously accomplished at a level way beyond the school revue that I'd been doing.'[7]

Unusually, four of the sketches that featured in *Premises, Premises* were either written or co-written by a first year English student at St Catharine's by the name of Steve Punt. At his school's drama club, Steve had persuaded his teacher to allow him and a friend to write and perform their own sketch show. 'It went down so well that it gave me just enough confidence to think when I got to Cambridge, on the basis that I know I can make some school parents laugh, well at least let's try it.'[8] Keen to join the Footlights as soon as possible, Steve attended the Societies' Fair, now held at a sports hall. Next, he caught a smoker at the club room. 'I stood at the back and watched. It was a very crowded, hot cellar. People packed in. The stage was tiny and there was a very low ceiling.'[9] Taking the plunge, at the next smoker Steve performed a sketch about government cuts in education, quite topical at the time, the joke being that all university courses had been cut back so much that English was now a course on one single book and that the history degree was just about Henry VII.

Another smoker Steve attended turned out to be a revelation. Tony Slattery performed a sketch called 'Economy *Star Trek*', which ended up in *Premises, Premises*. 'It was a one-man *Star Trek*,' Steve recalls, 'where Tony played all the characters. And he hurled himself from side to side on the stage, like they used to do on the show when the ship was under attack. It was full of silly jokes ("Chekov, stop writing plays!" was one of the lines), but it was so confidently done, and so visual.'[10] It was the visual nature of the piece that made the biggest impact. 'A typical Footlights monologue was someone standing stock still talking clever funny words,' says Steve. 'That was the classic Footlight style, Peter Cook's style, really. No visual content at all. That's why Tony's sketch really stood out. And it was quite influential because I think those of us who were the newer members saw that and thought, oh, you don't have to just stand stock still.'[11]

Together with David Dickinson and James Bourne, Steve developed a sketch that was highly visual in nature, a parody of the photo love stories in girls' magazines that were very popular at the time. They performed it at a smoker and it featured in a revue show that Steve participated in at Edinburgh, which made up for missing out on the cast of *Premises, Premises*. It played in a small venue with barely eighty seats. 'We literally had to build our own stage out of beer crates. I've always regarded that as my proper Edinburgh because when you go to Edinburgh with Footlights, that's not the real Edinburgh, and you feel like saying, I did do this for real before pitching up with Footlights and doing a 350-seat theatre. It's weird doing it with Footlights because you know it's nothing to do with you. You're just there as part of a tradition.'[12]

One evening a BBC producer called Paul Mayhew-Archer saw the show and asked the cast to perform a sketch on Radio 4. After the broadcast, Mayhew-Archer suggested that Steve send some of his scripts to *Week Ending*, a satirical sketch radio show devised by Footlights alumnus David Hatch, that Mayhew-Archer was currently producing. Now in his second year at Cambridge, Steve sent off a succession of scripts only for nothing to be used. 'Then one week I was listening to the show thinking, oh, I didn't get anything on again, when right at the end there was a joke and I went, hang on, I recognize this, and it was my joke.'[13] Steve began to write regularly for *Week Ending*, and then in his third year wrote material for TV's *Spitting Image*, becoming, along with Peter Cook, one of the few Footlight members to write professionally while still at Cambridge.

Neil Mullarkey also experienced the Fringe before going there with *Premises, Premises*, as part of a team from CULES. 'That was fourteen people, one flat, one toilet, one bathroom. But in hindsight, of course, that was my favourite year because I'd never been to Edinburgh, and it was so exciting.'[14] And just like Steve, he noticed a big change when he returned there twelve months later with the Footlights. 'It was much easier because you don't have to do any flyering, you just sell out, you get reviews, you're in decent accommodation, and a good theatre. Edinburgh was a very different experience if you were in the Footlights in that era.'[15]

In his final year, Neil was made president and didn't waste any time going to see his director of studies, knowing how busy he was going to be, to explain that he was not going to do very well in his degree. Oh well, fair enough, was the reply. It turned out the teacher had been a Footlight contemporary of Germaine Greer. As it was, Neil ended up with a respectable 2:2.

As president, Neil oversaw the revue and also directed the panto. 'That was probably my favourite endeavour of the Footlights because we were all in it together.'[16] With its much larger cast, Neil was working with people who weren't particularly looking to make showbiz their career; they were in the Footlights just to have fun and so weren't natural performers. 'I loved helping those people to feel empowered, to not be scared and to bring out the best of them.'[17]

For the 1983 revue, entitled *Hawaiian Cheese Party* for no obvious reason, Neil brought in ex-Footlight Nick Symons to direct, who later produced *A Bit of Fry & Laurie* for the BBC. The cast featured the returning Morwenna Banks and Robert Harley, along with Chris England, making his revue debut.

One of Chris's contributions was a spoof England World Cup song (music by Mark Warman) which had the cast in matching pullovers doing some dopey Kevin-Keegan-style dancing and mugging. Chris co-wrote the song with Nick Hancock, a second-year student from Homerton, formerly a woman-only college that had recently begun to accept men. Performing in many plays in his first year, Nick met Chris and Robert Harley and was

FIGURE 12.1 *The cast of the 1983 revue,* Hawaiian Cheese Party, *perform a spoof World Cup song.* © Chris England.

encouraged to audition for the Footlights. Naturally, there was more at stake when Nick decided to try to get into the revue. 'Although auditions are a really good life lesson,' he says, 'because you're going to do a lot of them and you get told no a lot of times, and that's not the worst thing in the world when you're a cocky nineteen-year-old.'[18] Usually, it was the director and president who had the final casting vote, although by this stage it was generally known who were the favourites to get in, and there was always one or two very strong candidates who missed out. 'And there was always a feeling of regret for them and of imposter syndrome for you,' admits Nick, who made the cast.[19]

Nick recalls performing a monologue as a David Coleman-type broadcaster commentating on the Olympics opening ceremony; in another sketch he was one of two Shakespearean actors who can't remember their lines and start making them up as they go along. Other sketches included a writer creating the opening of a book, with it being acted out behind him, and so every time he crossed things out the actors left the stage, and Neil Mullarkey as a Hollywood silent movie star who literally can't talk and can only express himself with exaggerated movements.

At the time *Hawaiian Cheese Party* was being put on, the landscape of British comedy was changing, as alternative comedy began to take root. 'That's what really characterized the era I was there,' argues Steve Punt. 'We all knew alternative comedy was happening. Nick Hancock and I used to sit and listen to the Comic Strip album. And we thought, we don't want to look completely out of touch Oxbridge wankers, but at the same time you're aware of what the Footlights brand is. And the one thing I don't think audiences will ever forgive in comedy is falsity. We wanted to at least acknowledge that we knew alternative comedy was going on, but without it looking fake or obvious.'[20]

As it was, *Hawaiian Cheese Party* was not so different from the revues of previous years, a sketch, a quickie, a song, a character monologue, finish the first half with a song, finish the second half with a song. Still, Neil attempted to do something edgier, the result of a dinner he attended at his college where one of the guests hailed from the Cambridge Conservative Association. The conversation turned to the troubles in Northern Ireland and the guest asked, quite innocently, which side the IRA were on. Neil wrote a sketch where a P. G. Woodhouse-type character featured as a British government minister who doesn't really understand the political complexities of what's going on – 'I'm so glad we got together. I know you're a Catholic and I know you're a Protestant, but let's have a nice chat shall we. And which one are you?' 'I thought it was brilliant biting satire because that was an important issue at the time,' says Neil. 'But the audience found it too uncomfortable.'[21] Despite this setback, Neil continued to try to push these types of sketches. 'Because I thought they had something to say and the riposte was, quite rightly, well, they're not laughing that much. They're not laughing as much as the silly one where you fall over.'[22]

To be fair, doing an edgy student-type show would never have worked. Audiences at the Arts Theatre tended to be a mixture of students and members of the public, while on tour, playing provincial theatres, it was predominantly middle class. 'We had to think about the mainstream audience,' admits Neil.[23] As president, Neil didn't feel the club required too much running, but he did identify the tour as something that could be improved. For years the tour had been playing the same old venues, usually with a gap between each gig. Why not, he thought, extend the tour by playing more engagements. 'I had this book of agents and theatres, and I would just ring them up and say, would you like to have us and would you pay us a guarantee. Yeah, alright.'[24] In this way, places like Norwich and Newcastle were added to the itinerary. Nick Hancock has a memory of playing Bury St Edmunds and on an afternoon off pottered round the market where he found and bought an album of old TV themes. Back home he put the record on and started acting out the titles. This became the basis of a very popular sketch he did with Neil over several years. 'Just buying that record and pissing about, that served Neil and me really well. We ended up on *Saturday Live* doing that.'[25]

More gigs inevitably lead to more money in the coffers of the Footlights, which as an organization already had more money than other university societies. 'That was one of the nice things about it,' claims Nick, 'that the Footlights was a going concern. You actually got money out of it. We were paid when we were on tour and if we did cabaret shows that money would be split between us, and when you're a student that's a real bonus.'[26]

Steve Punt enjoyed being part of the cabaret team, whether it was playing charity fundraisers or a private party at the Inner Temple for a room full of lawyers. 'It was quite a stern test of material. It wasn't your comfortable audience of students. But it was good experience. One of the things about Footlights, and one of the reasons I think why Footlights has consistently produced, is that you do in the end, end up performing to real audiences, on the tour, for example, as opposed to just doing everything to students.'[27]

With money coming in from the tour and cabaret, the club decided to buy its own car. Previously it always hired a car to ferry everyone around on tour and for cabaret dates. This was now deemed to be a waste of money and that it made more financial sense to invest in their own transport. Another change, instigated by Neil, was to no longer continue the practice of sharing a venue at Edinburgh with the Oxford revue group, and plans were made for the Footlights to have their own venue.

Following its run at Edinburgh, Martin Bergman, who by then was producing live arena productions, along with comedy shows, organized a scaled down version of *Hawaiian Cheese Party* that had toured the UK, playing theatres and student unions. A version was recorded at Liverpool University and broadcast on BBC Radio 4. The cast was the same, all except Nick Hancock who had to return to Cambridge to continue his studies, everyone else having graduated. 'This is why people at the time were envious of the Footlights,' says Neil. 'Just because of John Cleese, Monty Python and Peter Cook we could sell out Edinburgh and go on tours.'[28]

West End transfers, however, had become something of a rarity. The cast became aware that Martin Bergman had organized the cast of *The Cellar Tapes* to go on tour to Australia and kept badgering him about doing the same for them, only for their enquiries to be deftly batted away. In the end, Chris England took it upon himself to ask Bergman how he'd gone about arranging that Australian tour. The answer was simple enough, he'd written letters to theatres and student unions, and offers came back. 'So, that's what I did,' reveals Chris. 'I wrote to all the student unions in Australia and all the theatres I could find. I said, we're the Cambridge Footlights and we're going to come to Australia. Can we do a gig at your place? Get in touch. And letters and offers started coming in. I said to Martin, with a fistful of these letters, "Heh, Martin, we're going to Australia, look at this." And he said, "Oh come on, give them to me." And he took the whole thing over and around the ones that I'd set up he set up some better ones.'[29] The group stayed in Australia for two months playing places like Brisbane, Sydney, Wollongong, Canberra, Tasmania and Hobart. 'It was a fantastic experience,' says Chris.[30]

The year of *Hawaiian Cheese Party*, 1983, also marked the centenary of the birth of the Footlights. 'There was a lot of fuss about Footlights that year,' recalls Chris, 'about the history of the club.'[31] Cultural historian and writer Robert Hewison was writing a book about the Footlights and was much in evidence around the university. For years afterwards, Harry Porter kept a stack of them and when people came on to the committee he would say, 'Have you got the Robert Hewison book?' and give them a copy. Television producer Tom Gutteridge was also making a BBC documentary on the Footlights and his cameras filmed auditions for that year's panto and a couple of smokers. On one occasion Gutteridge brought Peter Cook along with him to shoot a few inserts and to watch a smoker. 'It was a huge thing and he was tremendously aloof,' recalls Chris. 'It felt like a giant had arrived; an aura had arrived.'[32] Afterwards, Cook came to the club room where everyone nervously huddled round the bar. 'We were all trying to think, what are we going to say to him, what are we going to ask,' recalls Steve Punt.[33] Then someone piped up, 'What do you say to the man who invented satire?'

The centenary was a big deal, and the fact was prominently displayed on the poster for that year's revue. Only when it came back from the printers, and the director was showing it off to the cast in the club room, that Chris spotted a glaring error, 'Well, that's not how you spell centenary.' It sported an extra R. The poster had to be hurriedly fixed.

For some, the buzz surrounding the Footlights centenary celebrations only served to highlight its privileged reputation. Especially in the world of alternative comedy, the club was viewed as an anachronism. 'There was quite a lot of looking down the noses at a lot of my contemporaries on the comedy circuit at the very beginning,' says Nick Hancock. 'And when I started doing the Comedy Store and things like that, it was very unfashionable to have been at Cambridge and in the Footlights. I was lucky because I was quite stupid and had a vague Northern accent so everybody presumed I hadn't been to Cambridge, so that was alright. I got away with it.'[34] Ironically, sometime in the late 1980s Nick got a call for a gig at a May Ball at somewhere like St John's and the guy who booked it told him, 'Yeah, you go and give 'em what for with your Northern working-class sense of humour,' utterly ignorant to the fact that Nick had been president of Footlights. Steve Punt noticed something very similar when he began on the circuit. 'It was not a thing to boast about if you were on at the Comedy Store because London was very much in the grip of the backwash of alternative comedy, and that was the big thing.'[35]

In this atmosphere, Nick took over as president, with Steve Punt as his vice president. 'And I think that we both had a feeling that we wanted to do things differently,' asserts Nick. 'We did try quite hard to, at the very least, frame things differently.'[36] For example, both oversaw the revue, determined not to follow convention. '*The Young Ones* was on TV, and *The Comic Strip*, so we were trying to look as if we were if not moving with the times, moving towards the times,' asserts Nick.[37] There was also a partial reaction against *Hawaiian Cheese Party*. 'We wanted to be different,' admits Steve. 'And also, *Cheese Party*, like *Premises, Premises*, was very much modelled on *The Cellar Tapes*. They were so marked by *Cellar Tapes* in terms of thinking, this is what a Footlights revue must have.'[38] Even new members, such as Christopher Luscombe, felt the impact of *The Cellar Tapes*. 'I think I always felt under the shadow of those people.'[39] Fourteen years later, when Lucy Montgomery arrived, not much had changed. '*The Cellar Tapes* was still the gold standard. Their poster was up in the club room, so you always saw it.'[40]

The decision was made to ditch the idea of just presenting the best sketches of the year and instead conceive and write a new production almost from scratch. The fact the year was 1984 inevitably led to having a strong Orwellian political theme running through the piece. *The Story So Far* was about a man who becomes prime minister and was set slightly in the future, which opened a lot of comic potential according to Nick. 'It was a way of taking things that were developing at the time in politics and moving them into the future and saying, if it carries on like this, this is where it could end up.'[41] For example, the general election was carried out entirely on television and conducted rather like the reality television shows of today, with audiences voting at home through their phones, and campaigning done almost like a talent show. One joke had the compere saying, 'Each candidate tonight you'll see once in a swimsuit and once in evening wear.' And there was a family, sat at the corner of the stage, which watched television throughout. 'In fact, all those four characters,' says Nick, 'the dad and mum, and the two kids, the two kids were me and

Steve, all we did was talk about television, so it was kind of like Gogglebox in a way.'[42]

Once in power, the new prime minister conducts a slightly sinister overview or survey of the country, of everybody and everything, a sort of new Doomsday Book, but this time by computer. Having this framework, the fact that it could be any aspect of British life, allowed the writers to use some of their favourite sketches. The show ends with the prospect of an imminent nuclear attack. This was a mild political comment, given the fact that cruise missiles were kept at a US military air base at Molesworth, just thirty miles from Cambridge.

The cast was bigger than usual, and Nick brought in Christopher Luscombe, who was seen as more of a straight actor, to play the PM. Christopher had come to Cambridge precisely for the purpose of joining the Footlights. 'I heard about the Footlights when I was very young and the tradition of people like Peter Cook and Graeme Garden. I was absolutely determined to perform and very stage struck. And I realized that if I worked hard enough, English was my subject, I could get to Cambridge and be in the Footlights and that would be my way into the business.'[43]

On his first day at Cambridge, Christopher attended the Societies' Fair and was wandering around all the different stalls when he came across the desk for CULES. He got talking to them and they seemed very keen for him to join. 'It doesn't matter if you're not very good you can still be in it,' they stressed. 'And I thought, well I don't want to be in your group. I'm sure they were very good and delightful, but I wanted to be in the professional outfit.'[44] And that meant the Footlights. However, having worked so hard getting there and been so determined to join, it was a case of how the hell to get it. The confidence was just lacking to dare to even try and audition, and so in his first year Christopher appeared in plays.

When he finally got in, his first impression of the club was that it was, 'a little bit cliquey. Inevitably, the people in the third year felt very grown up, and you felt like you couldn't even talk to them. In a way, I always thought the Footlights was a microcosm of the business. In the first year you felt like you were just starting out, but by the third year you felt like you ran the place. If you were in the Footlights in your third year you were a bit of a star. People recognized you in the street. It was a very heady experience.'[45]

In a very real sense, the Footlights helped Christopher to find his voice, not least the fact that to be a member one was obliged to be a writer and not just a performer. 'And that flummoxed me a bit because I was happier if you gave me a script.'[46] Writing was a whole other skill, one Christopher wasn't used to at all. Looking around for inspiration he came up with the idea of writing a sketch about a 'bedder', a term used for a housekeeper at the university. The idea was very traditional, almost archaic. 'But I happened to have a bedder who was a great character, and I talked to her a lot and in a way found that I got rather into her head and could talk like her. It just came out of me. So, I wrote a sketch about her.'[47]

At the time, Prince Edward was a student at Jesus College and so the sketch was made about a bedder cleaning the rooms of this member of the royal family and this clash of cultures. Christopher wrote it as a monologue, performed it and was invited to appear at the next smoker. 'And that inspired me then to write other Cambridge monologues. I did one about a don, a porter, a student, the master and his wife, all these characters. I usually did one a term.'[48]

Hardly anyone was doing this kind of material at the time, which harked back to the Footlights past, and it was no surprise that Harry Porter turned out to be a fan. Ever since joining the Footlights, Christopher had heard stories about Harry Porter, about his knowledge and importance to the club's history, and had wanted to get to know him. 'When I was at school, I had a teacher who was very important and took me under his wing. And at Cambridge I never felt that I had anyone like that. The dons aren't really that interested. But Harry became that person. He did love my material because it was so traditional and he took me under his wing a bit. We used to go out to dinner, and we used to go to London to see shows. And he introduced me to other old Footlights people. Harry was very self-effacing. Very shy. I was very fond of him.'[49]

When Christopher left Cambridge and became an actor, sometimes Harry Porter travelled to London to see him perform. 'I remember him maybe being a little bit of a fish out of water coming to the stage door at places like the Barbican. He felt like he didn't really belong there. He belonged in Cambridge.'[50] Eventually, they lost touch, and Christopher never saw him again. 'There was something very vulnerable about Harry. I think we all felt slightly sorry for him. I think he'd had a slightly chequered history. And maybe his academic career hadn't been quite what it should have been.'[51] It did seem that he lived vicariously through the Footlights and the young people involved in it. 'I think he rather worshipped us all really.'[52]

Left entirely to his own devices to create the character of the prime minister in *The Story So Far*, Christopher doesn't believe that the production was altogether a great success. 'It was a bit of a curate's egg as a show. And I think in a way maybe the audience didn't really come for that; they wanted an old fashioned revue. But it was ambitious. And I loved doing it.'[53]

For Nick Hancock it was his last appearance for the Footlights. By this stage, Nick had grown tired of the club and made it known that in his final year he no longer wanted to be involved. Most of his spare time away from his studies was now largely spent playing football; a career in comedy was the furthest thing from his mind. He did meet up again with Neil Mullarkey, 'who was a great champion of mine'.[54] Neil often popped back to Cambridge and suggested to Nick they write a show together. The result became the basis for a short-lived double act. Short-lived because Neil was to team up with a young Canadian comedian just arrived in London called Mike Myers. By chance, one evening Myers saw a poster for a comedy revue Neil was in that had the wording, 'Ex-Footlights' on the poster. The name had a certain resonance for Myers, 'I knew they were the top outfit,' he said, 'so I went along and introduced myself.'[55] Myers was put to work in the box office selling tickets and helping paint the sets. He got friendly with Neil and together they started a double act, along with helping to form the Comedy Store Players in late 1985. When Myers went back to Canada there were some gigs to fill so Neil went back to Nick, who wasn't doing comedy then, and the partnership was resurrected with great success.

Another comedy partnership sprang out of *The Story So Far*. Halfway through his second year, Steve Punt caught a late-night college revue and was left particularly impressed by one of the cast members who excelled at accents and comedy voices, a skill not usually associated with the Footlights. His name was Hugh Dennis. Steve encouraged him to perform at a few smokers, and Hugh was in the cast of *The Story So Far*, but as a partnership they rarely performed together on stage. That was soon to change. Quite often a Footlights revue team would leave at the same time but stay together to carry on touring, like the cast of *The Cellar Tapes* who, minus Tony Slattery, did a UK tour. The same thing happened with *Hawaiian Cheese Party*. Steve's year was a bit fractured, literally it was just him and Hugh. Obviously, nothing from *The Story So Far* was really suitable, so the two of them went away and spent several months trying to come up with some material they could do as a pair. Finally, they booked a week at the ADC Theatre and put on a late-night show. 'And we found that most of it worked,' says Steve. 'And that gave us the confidence to go and start doing open spots at clubs.'[56] It was the beginning of a comedy partnership that still endures today.

With most of the cast of *The Story So Far* having graduated and Nick Hancock no longer associated with the Footlights, the club was left in the capable hands of Kathryn Crew, who had appeared in the revue and been installed as the new president, and Christopher Luscombe, who was her vice president. Kathryn became only the second female president of the Footlights and the first since Jan Ravens. The general feeling had been that it was time for another woman to take up the position, that politically it was a good move. 'And she was very funny,' confirms Christopher.[57]

Christopher hadn't felt entirely comfortable in *A Story So Far*. Being something of a traditionalist he was happier in the more old-fashioned type of revue. His dream, and he pushed Kathryn in this direction, was to do a revue more along the lines of the great Footlight revues of the past like *Cambridge Circus*. 'That was the template.'[58] To helm the revue, Christopher remembered being directed in a play in his first year by Charlie Pattinson, who had since graduated. 'He had a real charisma, and I begged him to do the show; he was really professional.'[59] Going on to become a television producer, Pattinson made the cast return to Cambridge in the holidays where they spent almost two weeks writing sketches, on their own, in pairs or in larger groups. 'And he was really tough on us. You'd work all day on a sketch, bring it in and read it out and he'd go, No. It's crap. Try again.'[60]

As a way into writing sketches, it was often a case of just looking at what was in the news that day and writing something topical, in this way it became almost by accident a topical revue, thus the title *Topical Heatwave*. 'Which, of course, is a difficult thing,' stresses Christopher, 'because by the time you've been on tour for a while it's not topical anymore. We had to keep writing new stuff.'[61] Along with the usual pastiches, such as a gentle ribbing of Andrew Lloyd Webber musicals, Christopher developed one of his Cambridge monologues for the show. There was also some more consequential material. 'We dared to be a bit serious and political,' claims Christopher.[62] For example, reference was made to the recent Bhopal disaster, a huge toxic chemical accident in India that claimed many lives. 'We did a serious song about that which used to finish the first act,' Christopher confirms. 'And we did a sketch about the exploitation of India in movies like *Gandhi* and *A Passage to India* which led into this thing about the Bhopal disaster and it was very moving. It was probably a bit naïve, but it was very effective.'[63]

Christopher remembers playing to good houses during the tour and enjoying appearing in some wonderful old theatres and feeling like a professional actor. He was less enamoured of the Edinburgh Fringe. 'I felt Edinburgh was a bit more competitive. And I was a little bit aware that we were regarded by other groups as being a bit privileged and elitist. I never felt that we were better than them at all, quite the reverse. I suppose there was an element of jealousy because we had guaranteed houses and didn't have to do any leafletting. As a result, I didn't really enjoy that experience as much because I felt a bit embarrassed and a bit pampered in a way.'[64]

For a while there was the tantalizing prospect of a West End transfer. The owner of the Fortune Theatre, the original venue for *Beyond the Fringe*, liked the show and for a while considered taking it on. In the end, it never transpired but the show did go into the Bloomsbury Theatre for a short run. By then Christopher had already made his TV debut. BBC presenter Russell Harty hosted a programme from the Edinburgh Festival and invited him to be on the show, where he performed his Cambridge monologue. The other guests were the actor Ian Charleson and a young Hugh Grant, who was in a sketch comedy group called The Jockeys of Norfolk, made up of Oxford graduates. 'That was a brilliant revue, and Hugh Grant was wonderful in it. And I remember thinking, he's going to be a big star.'[65] As it happened, watching that evening was the comedy actor Terry Scott who got in touch with Christopher and asked him to be in pantomime. 'And it was amazing because my first experience of the theatre was seeing Terry Scott in pantomime at the Palladium. So, I just couldn't believe it. And I did pantomime with him that Christmas in Bath and the following Christmas in Guildford, and that was really my way into the business.'[66] Christopher went on to an acting career, then switched to becoming today a theatre and opera director.

As usual, the Footlights revue had debuted at the Arts Theatre very close to most people's finals. Indeed, one of the cast members had an exam on the day it opened. Christoper was at Pembroke and had a particularly strict English tutor who was not at all impressed by all the theatre he was doing. 'Then, when I did the finals and the May Week revue, I found out that I'd got my degree when he put a note in my pigeonhole and it said: "I saw the Footlights last night, you were fantastic, it was a wonderful evening." Which was all unbelievable because he wasn't a theatrical man at all. "And by the way you've got a 2:1." It was a special moment. And very generous because in a way by doing that he was saying, what matters is the Footlights. That's all you really care about. I know that. I accept that. You're going into the theatre. Good luck. But you did get your degree.'[67]

13

Another Fine Mess

Outside of the Footlights there had been a gradual transition away from character/sketch comedy to more personality-based comedy or stand-up. Monologues had always been a popular form of entertainment within the Footlights, going all the way back to Peter Cook and his characters like E. L Wisty. Monologues were always done in character; the performer was never themselves. This is perhaps the reason why stand-up was never a feature of smokers or the revue. There was no tradition of it whatsoever. Maybe stand-up in its earliest form was seen as the province of the variety and music halls, then in the 1960s and 1970s as being performed either by middle-aged comedians in dinner suits or broad working-class comics in northern clubs. Stand-up before 1980 didn't exist as we know it today. And while alternative comedy did marginally infiltrate the Footlights, the kind of stand-up as presented by new comedians such as Alexei Sayle and Ben Elton singularly failed to do so. That was until the arrival of David Baddiel, who was determined to bring the art of stand-up to the Footlights.

Before arriving at Cambridge, David was already obsessed with stand-up, having gone to the Comedy Store in London as a punter in 1982. It was David's older brother who first got him into comedy, playing him the Derek and Clive albums. 'So, I already had a kind of punk, as it were, aesthetic as regards comedy rather than a character and songs idea of what it was.'[1] At Haberdashers' Aske's, a very middle-class boys' school in Hertfordshire he attended thanks to a grant, David and a friend, Nick Golson, along with a couple of others, wrote the school revue one year. It was the usual practice that the revue was written by older boys on their way to Oxbridge and would be full of gentle songs and sketches about school life. 'Me and Nick made it a very, very vicious series of sketches about teachers who everyone hated,' says David. 'And it stormed it. And I so loved doing it, I thought, oh I would love to be a comedian.'[2] David had a sense that places like the Comedy Store were a possible route into the business, 'but I also came from too much of a Jewish, lower middle class immigrant background not to go to university. So, I thought, I'm definitely going to university, and so how can I marry those two things, and going to Cambridge and being in the Footlights felt like the thing to do.'[3]

Nick Golson was also at Cambridge and he and David auditioned three times to get into a smoker. Finally, it was Nick Hancock who put them through. It was the beginning of a lifelong friendship between David and Nick, a friendship tinged by their Footlights experience. There's a strange thing that happens in the Footlights, a sense of seniority that some members claim over others. Obviously, somebody who has been a club member for two or three years is going to be more senior than a person in their first year. 'But as with all things, the longer you've been there the more the lines blur, and you don't need to impress people so much,' declares Nick. 'Although David Baddiel, who came into it in my last year, I always say to him, "You still kind of treat me like I'm more grown up than you and it's just ridiculous, you are a major author and public figure." Something remains somehow.'[4]

Together, Nick Golson and David started writing sketches and formed a comedy double act. One of these sketches even ended up on a television show, it was about two people trying to do what appears to be a cryptic crossword, but every answer is the same word: fart. They also did a lot of what were called 'quickies'. These were, unsurprisingly, 'quick' sketches, sometimes no more than a single line gag: the house lights would be brought up, the performer would go on, do their bit and then – cut to black. 'And if you had a funny one, they would go like gangbusters,' recalls Peter Bradshaw. 'I remember this one guy came on and went, "Ladies and gentlemen, I want to do an impression. Here we go." And in total silence he moved about the stage doing weird movements, like a sort of experimental jazz mime. And after ten seconds or so of doing this, he stopped and said, "There it is, I was God, I was moving in a mysterious way." And then black out. Huge laugh.'[5] The only 'quickie' that David can recall writing and performing with Nick had them both talking to each other as if looking out over the horizon. One remarks, 'Red sky at night, shepherd's delight, red sky in the morning, shepherd's warning.' And then the other says, 'Mince beef and mashed potato, shepherd's pie.' That always got a big laugh.

David and Nick tried and failed to get into the summer revue but were compensated by being cast as comedy policemen in the panto, *Aladdin*. The following year they were given the task of writing the panto, *Robin Hood*, and David played the lead. At one point, he performed a semi-serious protest song, something that causes him a modicum of embarrassment today. It was partly about RAF Molesworth, which was the local CND site of activism, one of two British bases to house American cruise missiles; it was very much Cambridge's Greenham Common. 'I'm not embarrassed about the sentiment of the song,' admits David, 'but I'm quite embarrassed – (A), about doing something as pompous as a serious song in a panto, and (B), me singing. But the panto was really funny.'[6]

Featured in the cast was a philosophy student at King's, Michael Marshall Smith. 'I played Friar Tuck. The idea, very un-pc now, was that Friar Tuck became anorexic over the course of the production. So, I started out pretty bulky with this very uncomfortable Styrofoam and then in each scene we would remove a layer to the point where I was actually slim at the end.'[7]

David and Nick brought in quite an eminent Cambridge drama director to oversee matters. 'And that was my first experience of something that has plagued my career ever since,' claims David, 'which is employing a director and then thinking, they don't know what's funny. They may be able to direct a play. They may be able to direct Shakespeare. But they are ruining this joke.'[8] In the end, both took the decision to sack him, despite his reputation. And he was not at all happy about the situation. 'I remember Nick saying to me, "Can we sack this guy. He's not funny and he's ruining the panto, but if we sack him, we will be known as Mr Cunt and Mr Cunt. But we took that risk, and we did sack him and I directed the panto.'[9]

One of the first smokers David attended was hosted by Nick Hancock. 'And his attitude was just unbelievably modern funny, not at all like straw boaters, or songs about punting, not at all like that, but an aggressive, funny, muscular form of comedy. And I remember feeling when I saw it that Footlights had clearly imbibed some of Alexei Sayle's attitude.'[10] The revue of 1985, *Topical Heatwave*, however, was a return to something trad after the modernity from the likes of Hancock, Steve Punt and Hugh Dennis with *The Story So Far* revue. 'And one of the things about Footlights,' says David, 'is that quite a lot of what happens is either continuation or reaction to what's gone before.'[11] David would soon be in position to affect change.

At the end of 1985, the Footlights committee faced something of a dilemma, with members split between looking for leadership from a candidate very much in the old school mould, or someone a bit more progressive. In the end, they chose Nick Golson as the new president, with David Baddiel as his vice president. It was a realization that the club needed a change of direction and wanted to see the kind of alternative comedy that someone like Baddiel represented being something that the Footlights did. One of the first things David did as vice president was to organize many outside comedians to come and play the club room, people like Jeremy Hardy, Roy Hutchins and John Sparkes. These were proper stand-up cabaret nights. David compered the evenings and they were always a sell-out.

Exerting control over the summer revue, David and Nick brought in Chris England as director. Since leaving Cambridge, Chris had directed a few Edinburgh Fringe shows and was happy to take the job, coming down early to help with the writing. And while he was only three years older than the cast, 'I felt it. I felt like the grandfather of the troupe.'[12]

During his stay in Cambridge, Chris lodged at the home of Harry Porter, who always obligingly put people up in his large home. 'He was the most tremendously positive and supportive influence,' says Chris. 'He always made sure never to miss any opening night. Everyone was tremendously fond of him.'[13] Porter was still very much the club archivist, the source of all knowledge about its past. In truth, Porter only really liked pre-war Footlights and was much more likely to sing the praises of Jack Hulbert than Cook or

Cleese. 'Still, having an archivist for a comedy club just made it feel like a different thing to anything else,' states Chris. 'You felt like there was a history that you were part of.'[14] At that time, the archive was stored in a cupboard in the basement under the stairs of Porter's home. 'It wasn't like a museum,' recalls Chris. 'It was piles of stuff, but there was a certain order to it. He could find things in it.'[15]

Steve Punt recalls rummaging through it often. In 1983 he was the junior archivist, a newly created role. It sounded much grander than it was, in fact all Steve had to do was to make sure that a copy of each programme got delivered to Harry Porter. One day while looking inside he came across a box of tapes. One of them especially caught his eye, a recording of the 1959 revue *The Last Laugh*, which he found, 'Very political, and a fascinating listen.'[16] Peter Bradshaw once came across a box of fascinating photographs. 'When he was a younger man Harry Porter invited Alfred Hitchcock to speak at Cambridge, and there were some very funny photographs of him with Hitchcock, I think in the cloisters of Queens'. Hitchcock was clowning around and going into his weird, creepy persona in these photographs.'[17]

Chris assembled his cast for *Another Fine Mess*. It included Russell Churney, later one of the most admired musicians on the London theatre and cabaret circuit. Tragically, he died in 2007 of pancreatic cancer aged only forty-two. Unusually, this revue featured two Americans: Ben Liston, who performed very surreal sketches, and lots of monologues, and Katy Furshpan, who at one point during her time at Cambridge was in a relationship with Prince Edward. Like Charles before him, Prince Edward did not attempt to get into the Footlights. 'I think probably Edward would have liked to have been in Footlights,' says David Baddiel. 'But like many members of the royal family he had no actual talent.'[18]

Christopher Luscombe thinks this is a tad unfair. His memory was that most people liked Edward. 'He was very nice. And I became quite good friends with him and went to his twenty-first birthday party. He clearly had a leaning towards the arts. He clearly loved it.'[19] Christopher had a little slot on local radio each week that he called 'University Notebook'. When he played Widow Twankey in the panto he took it upon himself to interview past Footlights dames such as Richard Murdoch and Griff Rhys Jones. Because Christopher had got quite close to Edward he asked if he could interview him for his radio show and the prince agreed. 'I don't think he did any other interviews in the whole time he was at Cambridge. I remember the journalists at BBC radio were so jealous of the fact that I'd got him that they tried to prime me with questions to ask him. I didn't want to put him in an awkward position, so I was very clear what the questions were going to be.'[20] Most questions revolved around his interests in theatrics and what he hoped to achieve and what he enjoyed about Cambridge. 'It was probably very anodyne, but nonetheless we got to hear him speak. And we had a laugh together. He was quite light-hearted.'[21] Christopher doesn't know if Edward would have liked to have been in the Footlights. 'I wonder if in a way Footlights did seem a bit too professional. I think maybe Footlights had a bit more edge. Maybe in his position he couldn't really have been satirical in the way that we could be. Iconoclastic. Subversive.'[22] Edward did attend some smokers though.

However, as royalty, Edward was afforded some entrance into that world via membership to CULES, which had a much lower profile. 'And was more a bit fun,' claims Peter Bradshaw. 'Whereas Footlights was a bit too obviously for careerist people who in all deadly seriousness wanted to be famous comedians.'[23] David recalls seeing Prince Edward compere a CULES show at a May Ball. 'He was utterly terrible. And not only was he utterly terrible, as it was going badly, he became very tetchy and royal, saying things like, "You could bloody laugh. Bloody hell." Things like that, and "Come on." And that was funny.'[24]

Despite CULES being very much in the Footlights shadow, a night was organized at the ADC Theatre for CULES to put on a performance in aid of charity and the Footlights were relegated to a support act. 'And the reason for that,' according to David, 'was the Queen and 'Princess Margaret' were coming up to see Edward perform, so obviously he had to be the headline act. So, it was a bit of a humiliation for the Footlights.'[25] Before the curtain went up Prince Edward visited the dressing room to give everyone a lecture about protocol. If, he explained, the Queen approached you and spoke to you, the correct way to reply was to say, Your Majesty and after that Ma'am. And if Princess Margaret spoke to you, it was Your Highness and after that Ma'am. 'And I thought, this is fucking ridiculous but whatever,' says David. 'I did a routine about my hair. I had this massive hair at the time, sort of 1980s hair. After the show, we're standing on the ADC stage and the Queen wafts past me, doesn't say anything, and then Princess Margaret stops and says to me, "I recognize you, from your hairdo." And I was so surprised that she had spoken to me at all I forgot what to call her. And I said, "Do you, Princess Margaret." And she looked at me like, who is that. No one had ever addressed her by her own name – ever. It was a very peculiar event.'[26]

For Christopher Luscombe the event was notable for the fact that a friend of his, who played the piano for the Footlights, approached the Queen with what turned out to be a very awkward question. 'We all mingled after the performance over drinks, and he said to the Queen, "Your Majesty, which act did you prefer, Footlights or CULES." And she didn't say anything, she just turned to him and she got her programme and just bopped him on the head with it. It was a brilliant moment and showed that she was very witty.'[27]

Along with Nick Golson, David also featured in the cast of *Another Fine Mess*, and having performed stand-up in some smokers was determined to do the same in the revue. 'David was very keen then to be a solo comedian,' points out Chris England. 'He wasn't really someone that you put in a big sketch. So, what I did with him was I arranged two stand-up spots. One in the middle of the first half and one in the middle of the second half where he could come out and be himself and do a few minutes.'[28]

It was a significant moment; the first time a Footlights revue had ever accommodated stand-up. 'I literally would come on just with a microphone,' reveals David, 'quite importantly with a microphone because most Footlights sketches were either just projected or with hidden mics. Either way, the symbol of the microphone meant that I was going to be talking just like a stand-up. And I talked about being Jewish and masturbating.'[29] Neil Mullarkey saw one performance and was struck by David's performance, especially the subjects he chose to talk about. 'I remember thinking, this is out there. Going into that territory felt very unusual for the Footlights.'[30]

Even though David was still learning his trade, he had a natural knack for it. 'I would land the jokes in a very emphatic way that I picked up from say Alexei Sayle. It was a much more aggressive, out-front form of comedy.'[31] As a result, both sets went down well. There was no push back at all from audiences, much more used to monologues done in character. Here was somebody quite blatantly not in character, but as themselves. 'I am interested, in general, in authenticity and talking directly about your life and trying to make that funny,' affirms David.[32] The idea that Footlights had to be mainly performing as a character because what these people were who came out of Footlights were basically comedy actors, David always thought to be a grey area. Take someone like John Cleese, a great comedian, who happens to perform in a particular character, but the character is very close to who they are anyway. The same can be said of Stephen Fry. 'They find a voice that's within them and sometimes it is a character, but it feels close to who they are. I just happened to be the first person in the Footlights to say, hi I'm David Baddiel, I want to talk about something from my actual life and there's no artifice at all.'[33]

David did feature in a few sketches; he wasn't averse to sketch comedy. He and Nick Golson played two stupid characters talking to each other, a bit Smith and Jones-like. 'At one point we're discussing the new toilet at the library, and how it was a fantastic new toilet, very flashy, you lift up the lid, there's a kind of light on it, it's amazing. And then he says, "I tell you what's really lovely, which is after I'd finished, I pressed the electric flush button and outside comes a lovely little picture of my turd." And I said, "No, what you've done is you've shat on a photocopier." It got a massive laugh. But it was also very much not in a Footlights tradition of genteel comedy.'[34] That, along with David's stand- up about masturbation, led to Owen Dudley Edwards in the *Scotsman* saying of the revue, upon its arrival at the Edinburgh Fringe, that on this evidence the Cam was an open sewer. 'I think I was upset at the time,' reveals David. 'Now I think it's totally brilliant. *Another Fine Mess* was probably by the standards of Footlight shows a fairly punky, sweary show, but nothing compared to what you could have gone out and seen at the same time, like Jerry Sadowitz. Nevertheless, Owen Dudley Edwards felt it was awful.'[35]

Before its run at Edinburgh, the tour had been going well when halfway through Ben Liston had to go back to America and was replaced by Peter

Bradshaw. This was Peter's first taste of appearing in the revue and he enjoyed it immensely; 'It was an amazing experience.'[36] Peter was first at Cambridge between 1981 and 1984, reading English at Pembroke. Back then he saw himself much more as a straight actor, doing Shakespeare and putting on a production of a Kafka play. Taking a year's break, he returned to do a PhD, 'I was a real lifer,'[37] and was encouraged to become more involved in the Footlights, 'which you could do in those days because they had a much more gentlemanly, laid-back approach to people doing PhDs; they just let you get on with it. And it was different from being an undergraduate where you had lots of things to do in every term.'[38]

Peter was glad to be back, especially the thrill of going to smokers. 'They were terrifically exciting and incredibly atmospheric. However, the process of auditioning for smokers was sort of terrifying, but also rather brilliant and rather creative in that we would announce a smoker on, let's say, a Thursday night in the club room, and in what must have been a pretty lax relationship with the fire regulations people would cram in down there. And you would audition the day before the smoker. You would turn up and, absolutely quaking with fear, you would perform your funny sketch or song or monologue in front of a pretty hatchet-faced panel.'[39] Peter clearly remembers his own audition, in front of a panel that looked as if they would rather be at a funeral. 'It was terrifying.'[40]

If the panel thought the auditionee was funny or had enough merit, they were literally put on the next day. 'And the whole of the next day was utterly obliterated by your nerves and your jittery excitement,' recalls Peter. 'All the lectures and the work you had utterly obliterated, because at six o'clock you had to turn up, and this running order would be thrust into your hand, and you were sixth on, before the break, because there would be about fifteen or sixteen turns altogether, and you would be terrified. But, of course, if it went well, you would be utterly euphoric in a way that performing in plays never made you feel. It was total cocaine.'[41]

In that year between doing his first degree and his PhD, Peter worked for a US publishing company as the London editor of a financial newsletter. It was that experience that made David Baddiel ask Peter to be editor of the recently founded Footlights newsletter. 'Every couple of weeks I would host newsletter night at my house, and it was amazing fun, everybody came to it.'[42] The aim of the newsletter was to alert members about such things as upcoming smokers. 'It was a single sheet of paper which I remember I typed on my housemates' electric typewriter. We put the Footlights crest at the top and wrote a lot of facetious nonsense and literally photocopied it and then sent it out using the UMS, the university mailing system, to everybody at their college addresses.'[43] It would land in their pigeonholes in the porter's lodge in each college. Peter is unclear if anyone carried on with the newsletter after he left. 'We invented it and I think it might have died with us.'[44]

Peter's work on the newsletter tapped into his love for writing, since 1999 he has been the chief film critic at the *Guardian*. He wrote material, too, for

Another Fine Mess. 'Everything about comedy writing in Cambridge in those days, there was a kind of amateur aspect to it, which is that you just watched other people doing it and you imitated them and hopefully whatever innate little talent you had would modify that template.'[45] In a few years' time, the Footlights would bring in writers' workshops, back then there was no such thing according to Peter. 'In those days, rightly or wrongly, it was purely, either you can do it or you can't. You don't need a workshop, just watch other people. You know what to do, now do it. It was trial and error. Nobody knows, and this is still true, nobody knows what's funny until you do it. And then some lines get a laugh and you realize, that's funny, and some things don't.'[46]

One sketch Peter especially recalls writing and performing was a monologue. 'I come on stage as this weird, nerdy bloke, in a pretty familiar Peter Cook style, if I'm honest. And the idea is this guy who I'm playing is a poet and he's invented a new form, which is the serious limerick. And with a stricken dead-pan expression I would then recite these grotesquely inappropriate limericks on terribly offensive subjects. And it absolutely stormed it every time I did it.'[47]

One of the joys of going on tour was always the chance it afforded to play some of the country's grandest theatres, such as the Theatre Royal Bury St Edmonds, 'a lovely little theatre,' says Peter, 'which Footlights played every year and always did well at.'[48] The audiences they played to were still largely middle class. 'And they would get upset at chancy material in a way that surprised us and sort of disconcerted us,' Peter reveals, 'because we were playing some quite chancy material which of course had gone over very well with students.'[49] Sometimes the cast would think they had done a great show, with loads of laughs, and then buy the local paper the next day to find that the theatre reviewer was furious about it, 'saying absolutely disgusting toilet humour,' recalls Peter. 'I should think if somebody watched it now, they would think it's about as edgy as a nursery school show. But in those days, they thought it was pretty edgy.'[50]

Before Edinburgh, *Another Fine Mess* had a week's run at the Bloomsbury Theatre in London. It just so happened that at the same time David Baddiel landed a small part in an episode of *Filthy Rich & Catflap*, the follow up to *The Young Ones*. 'I basically had to get up to Manchester where they were filming, which was a nightmare, to be with Ben Elton and Rik Mayall and all the others, and then come back and just make it in time. In fact, I missed one of the shows.'[51]

David had already experienced the Edinburgh Fringe, having earlier done some street theatre, and while there with the Footlights he and Nick Golson put on their own lunchtime show entitled 'Super Lads', which presaged the whole lad culture of the early 1990s. As David remembers it, *Another Fine Mess* went down well with the Edinburgh crowd. 'Although it was very depressing that we got that review in the *Scotsman*, people were very upset.'[52]

FIGURE 13.1 *Poster for the 1986 revue,* Another Fine Mess. *Reproduced with the permission of Chris England.*

Given the edgier material in *Another Fine Mess*, the cast was anxious to mix with the alternative comedy vibe of the festival; that's where they wanted to be rather than part of the mainstream. For Chris England, this was in direct contrast to when he was in Edinburgh back in 1983 with *Hawaiian Cheese Party*, when the Footlights felt to him almost separate from the rest of the Fringe. 'We were in the George Square Theatre, which was a big venue for Edinburgh, and it was almost like the festival was happening and the Fringe was happening and we were pulling an audience from the city and not really part of the flow of the alternative comedy.'[53] A new venue was found at the Assembly Rooms, a premier location. 'And we kind of exposed ourselves to a lot more scrutiny than we previously had,' reveals Chris, 'and were measured up against different things as a result of that.'[54]

Something else had changed for Chris since 1983, when the Footlights, 'was a mainstream banker.'[55] As alternative comedy grew more popular, the Footlights acquired a lot of baggage, a dark stigma of privilege and entitlement. 'I think we all felt at that time that obviously it was a privileged way to break into the business because you were standing on the shoulders of giants,' suggests Chris. 'You were able to put in your publicity material, from the company that brought you Peter Cook, John Cleese etc.'[56] This fostered resentment from other comedians. And it wasn't just aimed at the Footlights, either, claims Chris, but any form of Oxbridge humour. 'I remember very clearly at Edinburgh, late nights at the Gilded Balloon, where the Oxford revue had ventured on stage and were absolutely persecuted.'[57]

This view of the Footlights meant that by the mid-1980s the club was very much on the back foot and no longer thought of as helping to lead comedy in the way that it had done for twenty years up to and including *The Cellar Tapes*. 'Suddenly, Footlights was the pariah,' argues David Baddiel. 'As could be seen in the 1984 episode of *The Young Ones* where Stephen and Hugh and Emma are all being posh twats being utterly humiliated. And that was sort of what things were like.'[58] When David left Cambridge that year to begin his career there was now a very clear divide between alternative comedy and stand-up as happened at places like the Comedy Store and the Footlights, this posh sketch Oxbridge tradition which was now incredibly unfashionable. It hit home for David when he called up the Comedy Store to ask for an open spot. 'And they said, "Have you got any experience in comedy." And I very proudly said, "I was vice president of the Cambridge Footlights," and they put the phone down. So, I just never mentioned it again.'[59]

Whatever the difficulty of coming from the Footlights in the mid-1980s as a performer and a comedy writer, the advantages were self-evident. 'It was the first time that I had the regular chance to perform comedy in front of people on stage,' says David. 'Which to be honest was more about the club room, it being really like a comedy club because it was downstairs, it was packed, it felt totally like a comedy club and that gave me lots and lots of experience, and yes some confidence I guess.'[60]

After appearing in the David Baddiel directed *Robin Hood* panto, Michael Marshall Smith was one of the main writers on the next one, *The Three Musketeers*, as well as playing one of the leads. 'It was such a learning experience. I learnt a lot about timing, and how on a good night you can stretch out the pause before a line and it just gets funnier.'[61]

As a teenager, Michael was greatly influenced by radio comedy, stuff like The *Hitchhiker's Guide to the Galaxy*, *The Burkiss Way*, old *Goon Show* episodes, and things like Bob Newhart and Woody Allen tapes that he'd listen to over and over again. When the possibility arose that this might be something he wanted to do as a career, it played a factor in his choosing to go to Cambridge. 'I had become aware that there was this rich tradition of the Footlights. It was a kind of, oh cool, this is where the heart of a certain type of comedy is, so I want to get involved in that.'[62]

He arrived at King's to study Philosophy, Social and Political Science, but more importantly with half a dozen comedy sketches that he'd written. 'I was somewhat laser-focused on joining the Footlights, so I found out when the audition for the first smoker was and turned up with my sketches written out only to be told, oh no, you can't just be a writer, you've got to perform it as well.'[63] It just so happened that Michael had befriended fellow King's student Tim Firth, later a dramatist and screenwriter; he co-wrote the film, *Calendar Girls*. 'Tim was a brilliant musician and songwriter,' states Peter Bradshaw. 'You could put him down at the piano, and this is an amazing skill which Footlights did seem to attract the people that could do this, and he could compose a hilarious song for you.'[64] Michael asked Firth to appear with him in a sketch that was called 'Olympic Bathing'. It was a take on the idea that having a bath had become an Olympic sport, so it was all to do with whether people were towelling effectively, their use of bubble bath etc.

Michael was never an acting kid at school. It was always writing rather than performing that was his focus, and he subsequently became a novelist and screenwriter. But he did enjoy performing with the Footlights, for him that was an essential part of it. 'Because there is no better way of finding out what's funny than being the person who has to stand up in front of a hundred drunk people and make them laugh. It's all very well just typing stuff out, but learning the way in which you deliver things, and even simple things like putting the funny word at the end of the sentence, that's a craft that is best honed through having to make people laugh and dealing with it when they don't.'[65]

The overall comedy vibe at that time, according to Michael, was fairly traditional, which, as it happened, was what most of the new intake of members leaned towards. 'There were a few who were trying to push it a tiny bit more alternative, and a little bit more drama, but overall it was still very much old school, carefully worded sketch comedy.'[66] This certainly suited Michael and Tim Firth, who along with William Vandyck, a law student, and Mike Smith, had formed their own comedy troupe called The Throbbs, putting on shows and late-night revues. Later, they even started to get paid gigs, with varying levels of success. 'You do a wedding,' says Michael, 'and everybody's already hammered and you stop the disco and go, OK, here are three amusing young gentlemen from Cambridge to entertain you, and people just start chucking stuff at you. We had some of those nights. But that's how you build up resilience.'[67]

The team of Michael, Firth, Vandyck and Smith, along with Tim Scott, who was president in 1987, were very much the dominant force inside the Footlights at that time, performing a lot together and fully expected to make the revue. Indeed Firth, Scott and Vandyck did, along with Richard Thomas, while Smith and Michael did not. It was an unusually small cast this time and included not one woman.

The Footlights continued to be a resolutely male domain. 'There were women involved but the centre of gravity was still pretty male,' admits Peter

Bradshaw. 'And of course we were excruciatingly aware of that.'[68] Peter is of the opinion that many women in the Footlights were reluctant to put themselves forward in case they failed. 'And for reasons I understand entirely. If a man failed, they had the male super structure of support to help them through it, whereas a woman failing didn't have that. It wasn't a protective or supportive environment for women. Although there were some brilliant women who came through it. But I think a lot of the women that I knew, creative, performing women, would rather do straight drama and control the narrative in a way.'[69]

One such woman was Tanya Seghatchian, who was on the Footlights committee but never in any of the revues. She went on to be a film producer. 'She was an amazing force of nature even in those days,' says Peter.[70] In the 1990s, Tanya went to work for producer David Heyman whose production company had a deal with Warner Brothers. It was Tanya who read an article on a book that was due to be published, about a boy who discovers he's a wizard. She rang the author's agent and asked for a proof copy to be sent to the office. The author was J. K. Rowling and the book was Harry Potter. Heyman and the rest of his staff loved the book – and the rest is history. Tanya became a co-producer and then executive producer for the first four Harry Potter films.

Michael may have failed his audition to get into the cast of the revue, entitled *Backwards into the Limelight*, but at least some of the material he had written or co-written was going to be used. Even so, it was tough to take. 'I thought, I've been working so hard with these guys and this is what I probably want to do at this stage. It was one of those things where you say, OK, if you want to keep doing this, you're going to have to take the ego hit of having been rejected by the director and get yourself on the tour somehow.'[71] That's exactly what he did and he landed a place in the band as a guitarist and pianist and went on tour. 'And I'm really glad I did because it was a fun thing to do.'[72] Staying at one lodging house, William Vandyck decided to check out the local courthouse to watch proceedings. To his astonishment he saw his landlady sat in the dock on some charge. Then, the woman's husband came to sit next to him and said, 'It's funny because it's normally me that's up there and not her.'

Hitting Edinburgh, *Backwards into the Limelight* did well enough. 'But we felt we were being positioned as overly privileged toffs doing this rather old-fashioned comedy,' admits Michael.[73] This contrast was made even more apparent when, following Edinburgh, Michael and a few others went to the US on a short tour of colleges. 'And that was an interesting contrast as well because again we would stand up and do our immaculately worded skits, or so we thought, and then some of the American guys of our age would just come crashing on and do improv and all the rest of it. It was a transitional time in comedy, and I don't think we were ever going to join the new wave, really. We liked writing sketch comedy.'[74] That led to Michael's involvement with Tim Firth and Vandyck in the BBC Radio 4 comedy series *And Now in*

Colour. 'And that was a continuation of what we'd done at college.'[75] In any case, by that stage Michael was positioning himself as more of an author than working in comedy. On the Footlights tour, at the suggestion of a mate, he'd taken a Stephen King novel along with him to read. 'I then looked down a bit on Stephen King, but that flicked a switch and I spent the whole tour, because you know what tours are like, there is a lot of dead time, I just got a ton of reading done. And then while we were in Edinburgh, I wrote my first short story. And from that moment on I realized this is what I really want to do.'[76]

In his final year at Cambridge, Peter Bradshaw was made Footlight president, a decision that he couldn't help but feel slightly self-conscious about, 'because I thought, well this looks like kind of Buggins' turn, and I think it was a bit like that if I'm honest.'[77] In his mid-twenties by this stage, 'which for a student is absolutely Methuselah,'[78] Peter was conscious of the fact that he ought really to move on and let somebody else have a go. In the end he did accept the position but decided against trying out for any of the shows, preferring to give those with much less experience a chance. 'My position by that stage when I was president was more directing and administrating and bringing everything together rather than performing.'[79]

From the beginning of Peter's presidency, 'really from the first day of the first term,'[80] the search was on for material for the summer revue. 'You think, by the end of the year we have got to find enough material to fill a two-hour show. So, you're desperate for material, that's what it's all about.'[81] That material could only really be sourced from the two smokers held every term, and then in the Lent term there was a late-night revue at the ADC Theatre, which usually went on at 11 o'clock and lasted for an hour. 'That was the main precursor of the May Week show,' says Peter. 'That's when you tried out a lot of material.'[82]

Such a deadline usually put a dampener on any temptation to try to experiment with the revue format. It was often a case of, let's not re-invent the wheel here. All things considered the revue, for all its faults, was an efficient form of delivering a lot of comedy very effectively to lots of different audiences, captive audiences in the case of the Footlights. However, revue as a format had virtually died out. Just a few decades before it wasn't unusual to see revues performed by professional actors on the West End stage. Now it only really existed in the Footlights and in other university troupes.

As for talent, Peter was always on the lookout for new people and it was obvious from the word go who could do it and who couldn't. Of course, talented people can have off days, or they can have off moments, but generally the people who could do it were the people who wanted to do it. 'And they generally tended to be the people who had been fascinated with comedy and Footlights forever before they turned up. And usually, the people who turned up and kept on doing smokers were the people who would be invited to join the committee and they would get into the revue.'[83]

Someone who especially stood out for Peter was Simon Munnery. Like David Baddiel before him, Simon's preference was for stand-up over sketch comedy, which he disliked intensely. His material was dark and edgy. 'And sometimes he gave incredible offence, but he completely didn't care,' says Peter. 'The rest of us were much more nervously concerned with what the audience thought, what was getting a laugh and what wasn't, but Simon absolutely did not give a shit, he just did his own thing.'[84] As Simon explains, 'I like to skirt the borders of outrage.'[85]

Simon was asked to go on the committee, much to his surprise and consternation, and was made Peter's vice president. 'I came back that autumn and there was a note in my pigeonhole saying you're Footlights vice president. I didn't know anyone on the committee. I didn't like them. My first suggestion on the committee was that we change the name of the Footlights.'[86] That was never going to fly. Something that went down much better was a week of stand-up that Simon organized at the ADC Theatre. He invited acts from London and got local acts to support them, the likes of Ian MacPherson, Malcom Hardee, Andrew Bailey and Jeremy Hardy.

At school, Simon had no sense of doing comedy as a career, he was much more into science and maths and did Natural Sciences at Trinity, which he ultimately found to be unfulfilling. A member of his debating society at school, Simon went along to the debating club at Trinity where he befriended Stephen Cheeke. They shared a very similar sense of humour and were to form a comedy double act that went by the name of God and Jesus. 'We used to sit around the pub with three others trying to think of the most offensive jokes we could,' recalls Simon. 'And then we'd do them. There was a joke we used to do, it's awful, and it used to get a massive laugh or a massive urgh. The joke is – What do you get if you put a baby in a liquidizer. An erection.'[87] Comedy was starting to get dark and more dangerous. For one gig at the ADC Theatre, Simon hired a moped and brought it along. 'For our entrance we had 'Born to be Wild' playing and the two of us just going round and round the stage on this moped. It's utterly illegal, you're not allowed to have petrol on a stage, obviously, let alone a moped which you could just slide off and kill people.'[88]

It was Cheeke who mentioned the Footlights to Simon, who was not altogether familiar with them. After being accepted, more than anything else Simon loved was the buzz of doing smokers because there were no rules or conditions. 'You could say anything you liked.'[89] The smokers had always been the environment for experimental material, and in more recent years for hard edged humour. Chris England recalls in his third year, when he was part of the group that oversaw things, there was a feeling that there was more fun in undermining it, in pushing the boundaries. 'I remember doing a sketch about Christopher Columbus explaining to the king of Portugal that he'd discovered America which was all swearing. You couldn't ever have done it at any of the other places that we went, but part of the purpose of it was to undermine the evening. And so, the smokers were a little rougher.'[90]

Curiously, back in 1965, shortly after Richard Crane was elected to the Footlights, he saw a fellow applicant stand up at a smoker and perform a sketch that was basically all fuck and shit. 'And he got laughs for his daring. I and others thought this was definitely a downward slide, but he was elected anyway.'[91]

As subversive as smokers may have been sometimes, tradition always held sway and attendees were required to wear a dinner jacket and bow tie. Although by the time Simon Munnery arrived that had long gone.

Simon was hooked after his first smoker appearance. 'I liken it to, if you walk into a casino and you are unlucky enough to win, then it's too late, you're a gambler. And my first gig went very well. I remember how it began, very dead pan, with a kind of aggression. I had a lot of pent-up anger. "Hello. My name's Matthew . . . No, it isn't. That's a joke for you there." And the last joke I remember, I said, "I'd like to do a different sort of joke for you now." And all the way through I had in my hand a cooked tomato. And I just mashed it on my forehead, and covered the front row in tomato, and I said – "Slapstick lives." And walked off. And it stormed it.'[92]

Unlike David Baddiel, who was into total authenticity when it came to his stand-up, Simon was in essence playing a character. 'I wasn't being me. I was being a version of me.'[93] It wasn't long before he introduced a complete character into his stand-up, a character he called the security guard. One summer while at Cambridge, Simon got a job as a security guard in a factory. 'One morning the big chief came in and I had my tie loose, I'd been up all night, and he takes me into a little room and criticizes how I appeared, and I said, "The only person who's going to see me is a burglar. It doesn't matter that during the night I've got my tie loose." Sacked. But they never asked for the uniform back, and I thought, that could be an act.'[94] Simon wrote a whole bunch of jokes: 'Good evening. I am a security guard. I've got lots of security guard jokes for you. How many security guards does it take to change a light bulb? One. We're not stupid. Three security guards go into a pub. Nothing happens. That's what we get paid for. What do you get if you cross a security guard? Trouble.'

Being vice president almost guaranteed Simon being in the 1988 revue, *Sheep Go Bare*, in a cast that also included Tom Hollander and Mel Giedroyc. Simon performed two stand-up spots, and against his will appeared in a sketch. 'I was against sketches. I didn't like them. I liked doing stand-up. I was prejudiced against sketches.'[95] He did enjoy the tour. At times, the edgier humour did not go down well with a provincial audience. At a matinee in Ilfracombe there was a set of twin doors at the back of the theatre and during the show elderly members of the audience with Zimmer frames were seen to leave and the doors would swing open and closed like a saloon bar. 'The trouble with the Footlights revue is that audiences come to see it because it's the Footlights revue. They don't come and see it because of what it is. That's why I said change the name. Let the show live on its own merits, otherwise you're going to disappoint people because they want songs with people wearing boaters, singing about punting down the river. There were lots of sketches, but then there were things like me doing vicious dead pan stand-up and hardly any mentions of tutors.'[96]

When the tour arrived in Edinburgh, Simon was already no stranger to the Festival, having appeared there with Stephen Cheeke as God and Jesus, in front of a confrontational crowd. 'The last thing Stephen said on stage was, "We'll only go when you throw glass." And they did.'[97] Simon went on to become something of a veteran at Edinburgh, a 'Perennial fringe maverick' in the words of the *Guardian*. Performing with the Footlights was different, of course, with the added sport of members of the audience going there to star spot. 'People like to see, I think, someone who will be a star in the future.'[98] This happened within the Footlights itself, too, according to Jon Canter. 'It always came down to the same thing, you wanted to see somebody before anybody else, and you wanted to see their talent and kind of revel in it.'[99]

A scratched together team of committee members, including Simon, also undertook a short US tour, playing Princeton and a club in Boston, before ending up at a club called Catch a Rising Star in New York, where they were picked up from the airport in a stretch limo. *Sheep Go Bare* also enjoyed a short run at the Richmond Theatre. Halfway through a performance, Tom Hollander was handed a note scrawled in red ink that said: You're great. Call me. It was from Michael Foster, one of London's most powerful agents. A man whose legendary temper had caused him, telephone in hand, to break his own finger while dialling. Foster had seen the show and although he had to leave in the interval wanted to represent Hollander, promising great things. It didn't quite work out that way. What actually followed for Hollander was a year-and-a-half working in Hamleys as a toy demonstrator and whenever he called Foster in his lunch break to see if there were any jobs or auditions lined up was told to, get off the phone. Foster eventually sacked him.

14

Back and Beyond

The American university of Valparaiso, Indiana, ran an exchange programme where a collection of students would be sent over to Cambridge University to study for a semester. Joel Jeske arrived in January 1989. 'I specifically went on the Cambridge programme because I knew about the Footlights. That was very much my whole intention when I went to England, I want to get involved with this group, I want to see how they cultivate their talent, I want to be cultivated by them, and learn from that.'[1]

Joel was a big fan of British comedy. Growing up outside of Chicago, the local public broadcasting station showed many UK programmes, things like *The Two Ronnies*, Dave Allen, sit coms, and, of course, Monty Python. 'At an early age I was a tremendous fan of Monty Python. And we also had *The Goodies*. Then as I got into high school, I discovered people like Peter Cook and *Beyond the Fringe* and being the comedy nerd that I am started researching all this. I got to know about the *Cambridge Circus* show that came to Broadway. And then we had *The Young Ones* and I started to get into the alternative scene and watching things like *Blackadder* and *The Comic Strip*.'[2]

Hoping to soak up everything there was to know about British comedy, Joel had only been in Cambridge a few days when he found an audition notice from the Footlights hanging up at the Student Union. He went along to the club room and auditioned. His acceptance came at an interesting time when discussions were taking place within the club as to where to pivot itself as regards its approach to comedy. 'They were trying to break out of the two people sitting in chairs and talking their way through a sketch,' says Joel. 'They were looking to embrace more of the alternative cabaret movement. There were all these splinter groups trying to do all this off the wall extreme alternative comedy. And so, Footlights was trying to do that.'[3]

One of those operating beyond the Footlights sphere was a comedy double act comprising Henry Naylor and Andy Parsons. In their first year both had tried to make an impact in the Footlights by doing a few smokers in the club room, 'which was dank and gloomy and smelt of cabbage,' recalls Henry, 'but it was a great place to do comedy. Anywhere with a low ceiling and a bit grimy, it had a London club vibe.'[4] And there were all those posters and photographs on the wall that gave the place a sense of history, which

Henry quite liked. But to him it felt too much like a closed shop. 'It was extremely cliquey. And there was very much still a public school bias and I don't think Andy and I fitted the typical mould.'⁵ Sharing a very similar sense of humour, and political outlook, Henry and Andy joined forces and started doing gigs around the university, taking advantage of the something like thirty theatres housed in the various colleges. It was almost like a mini-circuit, and this is one of the reasons why Cambridge produces so many comedians. 'I'm sure Andy and myself had done over a hundred gigs before we'd left university. And then you come out on to the London circuit and they'll be people who've been trying to get open spots and they've probably done ten or twenty gigs. You would have an enormous advantage already because of that.'⁶ Henry, though, was always careful never to admit he came from Footlights. Even today he leaves it off his CV.

Their material was quite surreal and left field. One routine had Henry pushing Andy around on an office chair as they parodied a Torvill and Dean ice dance. Along with the silly stuff was more edgy material and even a bit of social politics. 'We did a routine called first and second-class comedy,' Henry recalls. 'We'd have a curtain and we'd pull it across the front row of the audience, separating them from the rest of the audience, and one of us would be stood behind saying, "I'm doing the first-class comedy and tell a really good joke," And the other, "I'll be doing the second class and I'll be telling something a little bit more shit." '⁷

Like Joel, Henry grew up a fan of Python and The Goodies and remembers watching the Footlights 100-year anniversary documentary on the television and thinking that that was what he wanted to do. At school growing up in Barnsley he had written comedy and performed sketches in his final school revue. Arriving at Downing College to read history of art, Henry made a breakthrough in his second year when both he and Joel made the cast of the Footlights late-night revue, which went by the title of 'The Unwatchables.' Put on at the ADC Theatre, they were joined by Roland Kenyon (the current president), Chris Wickham, Nick Wood, who was a drool stand-up and impressionist, and a pianist and songwriter called Dai Jenkins. All six of them would later make up the cast of that summer's revue *Back and Beyond*.

For once, the title of the summer revue contained some meaning. President Roland Kenyon wanted the show to feel like they were dealing with the traditions of Footlights but at the same time moving forward, hence *Back and Beyond*. As a result, Kenyon brought in a Commedia dell'arte actor and professional mime named Geoffrey Buckley to direct. 'Geoff very much got us into our bodies,' says Joel. 'And so, if we had a more intellectual idea, like there was one sketch Roland and Nick did where they were executives trying to sell water and they were acquainting it with beer. The joke was, it's a fizz free, alcohol free, taste free lager, and they kept on getting more and more ridiculous with everything that beer isn't and water is. And so, Geoff was like, that's great, now how can you physicalize that. How can you not just sit in two chairs and talk to each other.'⁸

At times the humour became almost pantomimic. In one sketch, Joel and Chris Wickham played feuding street mime artists and mimed increasingly more elaborate weapons to take the other one out. Another sketch had Chris sitting on a chair peeling and juicing an orange, with Joel off stage on a microphone screaming in agony. 'It was basically the slow and desperate torture and death of an orange.'[9] This push towards much more physical comedy and clowning wasn't mere slapstick, like custard pies in the face, it was character based, it was situational, and not necessarily dependent on a verbal joke. 'And in a slight reference to the alternative cabaret movement we were all dressed in electric blue, Lenny Henry-type suits,' recalls Joel. 'That was our basic costume. I understood it. It was very much that kind of Second City tradition, or even *Beyond the Fringe*, of just the generic suit.'[10]

The one and only female in the late-night revue cast was Anna Cottis with whom Joel struck up a writing partnership. 'In terms of writing, once you attached yourself with somebody that you realized you shared a wavelength, you kind of hung out with them all the time.'[11] Both Anna and Joel were naturally inclined towards a more physical approach to comedy. 'The one sketch that we did and that we were both fearfully proud of was the idea of the ancient Greek poet Homer as a beat poet in a New York coffee shop. So, we'd do the Odyssey like beat poetry. Anna was doing interpretive dance and there was a guy on bongos.'[12] One of the lines in the sketch went: I wonder how deep the oceans would be if you took all the sponges out.

However, as the writing process continued Anna began to feel uncomfortable. As the only woman amongst six blokes, when it came time to cast the various parts in a sketch invariably Anna had to play the 'female' role, no matter whether she would have been better or funnier in another part, 'And they weren't really writing funny lines for those female roles.'[13] What she did enjoy was working with Geoffrey Buckley. Anna had previously done a clown and movement workshop, which gave her some experience coming into this revue. Working with Buckley encouraged Anna to persevere, 'because I was good at it. I understood physical comedy and I understand physical timing. But we didn't move into doing a physical comedy thing particularly. That revue was still very wordy.'[14] Doubts remained, still, and Anna confided in Henry Naylor. Henry's advice was for her to do the late night try out at Easter and see what happens. Anna was of a mind to do that anyway, not wanting to leave without doing something, to see if she got a laugh, to see if she had a good rapport with the audience.

Anna had been to a Froebel school, where children are free to explore, play, create, participate and learn at their own pace. There were other artistic children there and Anna developed an interest in performing. Leaning towards going to drama school it was her mother who insisted she go to Cambridge when she won a place there. Cambridge interested Anna because of the Footlights and the presence of other drama clubs. She had a grant and did engineering and philosophy, choosing King's because it was one of the first all-male colleges to admit women. Encountering her first smoker, Anna's initial reaction was, 'What the fuck is this?' The room was largely full of men, and the air was thick with smoke, some of the sketches she found funny, some less so. 'But I thought, these are just not my people. I'd never met so many posh people. And I'd never really met public school people. There were some people there who were from comprehensives or up north, like Henry, who I could connect more with, and others like Maeve Murphy.'[15] Maeve came from Ireland and was quite involved in the Footlights, with a place on the committee. They met when both appeared together in an all-woman feminist cabaret put on by a left-wing group; Anna performed a song in it and did stand-up. Maeve encouraged Anna to continue to hang around the Footlights, 'Don't leave me alone with these,' Maeve would plea. 'You've got to stay. They need women!' Anna successfully auditioned for the panto and was encouraged to audition for the summer revue and got in. 'And I was like, great. And then I was the only woman. Oh, that's going to be weird.'[16]

Anna did the Easter try out and enjoyed it. But if anything, it crystalized her intention not to do the revue tour, that it was simply going to be the same show with only a couple of extra sketches. 'We were not going to develop the work any better than that.'[17] There had been some discussion about Anna writing sketches herself. 'I thought OK, and I wrote a sketch about a woman who went to a party in a white skirt and sat on a white sofa and got her period and stood up and had red on the back of her skirt and gets all these different reactions. I said, let's work on it, it'll be really funny. I was told our audiences came mostly from small towns, and that something like this was not going to work in, say, Bury St Edmonds; it was too radical. I think I knew when I submitted it that they were going to say no, I just wanted to poke them a bit.'[18]

When Anna articulated to the rest of the cast her issue with having to play all the female roles, because she was the only woman, there was sympathy and there was understanding, but not much else. 'So, what are you going to do?' she asked. The answer was there simply wasn't the budget to put in another female cast member. 'Well, somebody could leave,' Anna suggested. 'And they were all really nice, but they were all uncomfortable and shifting in their seats. And nobody was going to be the one to sacrifice themselves and put another woman in.'[19]

Anna now had a decision to make for herself. Could she justify to herself being in the show as the 'token' woman. Was she going to be OK with it? In the end the answer was no. 'I would just feel awful the whole time. So, I decided to leave. It was a gut decision. And thinking rationally, I just felt like I would be dead, and I thought, it's not worth it, life's more than that.'[20] In her room, she wrote a letter, photocopied it and handed them out to the cast. 'I did like them, and I thought, if I'm going to go, I could just go and slam the door. But I wanted to give them the information, maybe it won't be any use now but just so they get it, that it's not a personal thing, you just want to get your position straight. And when I wrote it, I thought, maybe I won't send it, but looking at it, I said, well, that's the truth. And I've got to stick with the truth.'[21] She never regretted the decision.

Years later, Anna was in Spain for an arts festival with her theatre group performing Kafka's *The Trial* as Commedia dell'arte. This was just before the Covid pandemic struck. She was sitting in the festival canteen when she heard an American voice saying loudly, 'Anna? Anna Cottis?' She turned round and it was Joel Jeske, although she couldn't place him at first. 'You weren't in the Cambridge Footlights in 1989?' asked Joel. Anna said she was. 'And you did a sketch where you were a beat interpretative dancer,' Joel carried on. Then it all came back. 'And so literally thirty years later we ran into each other in Spain,' recalls Joel.[22] And it was a joy to discover that like himself, Anna had continued a career in clowning and physical comedy. Straight after Cambridge she had gone to France to study physical theatre and now runs her own theatre company.

As the revue prepared to go on tour, the club's finances received a shot in the arm thanks to a sponsorship deal with Holsten Pils lager. At the time the company was very much of the mind that comedy was the new rock 'n' roll; Griff Rhys Jones was starring in a series of Holsten adverts on television. 'There was a lot of product that rolled with us on tour,' reveals Joel. 'There was a lot of pilsner consumption.'[23] The cast was all required to sport T-shirts advertising the brand, banners were put up in venues, the logo appeared on posters and the company also printed the programme. 'The amount of material and the amount of creativity and comedy generation that happened while slinging back round after round after round of pilsner,' says Joel. 'You wouldn't even remember it the following day, you'd have like napkins with scrawled handwriting on them. It was fascinating how prolific we all were.'[24]

On tour, Joel had a monologue that he wrote about a restaurant critic going to a literary themed restaurant. It was all literature references and puns relating to food, and he played various characters. 'Audiences loved it up until the middle of July and then it just bombed. It played to silence for five shows in a row.'[25] What was happening was the show was travelling further north. Joel cut the sketch and ended up doing a kind of ugly American monologue of a middle-aged mid-western couple seeing England for the first time. 'That seemed to register more than a lot of literary puns.'[26]

As the show made its way up to Edinburgh, Joel noticed that whenever they arrived at their hotel or B&B, or showed up at the theatre, 'we would be greeted by just this natural joy'.[27] Much of it, he figured, was people speculating who might be a star of the future. 'So, there was a little bit of celebrity there, and being heralded through association, as it were.'[28] This feeling was much the same when they arrived at the Festival. 'People looked forward to the Footlights revue at Edinburgh every year,' affirms Joel. 'When we walked in the door and we were setting it up, we were at the Pleasance Theatre, the upstairs room, the manager came in and said, "Well, you guys are sold out for the week, so have fun."'[29] And hanging out with all those comedians and professional artists, the mere fact that Joel was a Footlight opened those kinds of people up to him a lot more, as opposed to just being a token American who had a show playing Edinburgh. 'It got me insight and it got me inside to a lot of their conversations, and that made it really special.'[30]

The revue tour and his stay at Edinburgh meant that Joel's visa had expired. 'Flying back to the states, at Heathrow airport they looked at my passport, it was, "So what have you been doing for the past three and a half months?" And I said, "What do you mean?" "You've overstayed your visa. Could you come over into this room we have some questions to ask you." Thankfully I had all the materials from the tour that I could show them.'[31]

Back and Beyond was modestly received. A thirty-minute version was aired on BBC 2. Henry Naylor remembers it less fondly. For all the talk of moving the club forwards, he found it something of a throwback and that the club still hadn't embraced what was happening in comedy. For example, there was a sketch about Plato in the revue. 'There's something about that which just shows how cosseted and remote and intellectual and out of date some of the comedy could be. If you look at what was coming on in the London circuit at the time, it was for real people in a pub setting rather than just intellectuals being incredibly witty.'[32]

And following the departure of Anna Cottis, the cast was all men; another backwards step. 'I didn't like it from a personal standpoint,' declares Henry. 'And it was an issue in comedy generally. At the time most comics on the London circuit were men. But I also thought it wasn't good for the club. It was confirming what people thought not just about Footlights but about Cambridge.'[33]

Taking over from Roland Kenyon as president, Henry's belief was that this attitude could no longer continue. What was required was a radical rethink, an almost systemic change. When Anna Cottis was in the Footlights she had come up against tradition. This is how we do it here. 'Which is another way of saying, fuck off, isn't it.'[34] It wasn't deliberate in any way or malicious. 'In general, when you have all-male environments,' she explains, 'some blokes are aware that somebody's not there, and some blokes just aren't. They're just fine. And if you tell them, look, there's no women here, they'll go, oh yeah, but they don't think about it. They're really comfortable. And they don't know what to do about it. And some of them go, oh that's important, like Henry. Henry wanted to make a difference. And that was partly because he was already a step out because he had an accent. So, if you're already partly out you can see why it matters.'[35]

Even in the late 1980s there was still an enormous sexual imbalance in terms of there being something like three men to every female student at Cambridge. Both Henry and Andy Parsons shared very similar thoughts politically in terms of how things needed to change and approached the matter in the same way. 'Because Footlights had a problem in attracting female performers,' states Henry, 'because it did just feel like a boys' club, as did the whole university at that time, I think it was important to develop female comedy and bring more female performers on board.'[36] One of the first things Henry did as president was to appoint a women's representative on the committee, declaring, 'Until the number of women in Footlights reflects the number of women in society the role of women's representative will remain on the committee.' Another thing he did early on was to name Tanya Seghatchian as vice president, the first woman to fill that role since Emma Thompson almost a decade earlier. Henry wanted to get as many women on the male dominated committee as possible; the hope, which went unrealized, was to make it at least fifty/fifty. Someone not entirely won over by these plans was Harry Porter. 'Harry was very much a traditionalist,' says Henry. 'I don't think he was wild about us finding loads of women for the club.'[37]

Next, the plan was to seek out and encourage talented women at auditions and other college productions. 'And we found Sue Perkins,' says Henry, 'who from the get go was excellent.'[38] Sue was studying English at New Hall College and Henry put her on the committee. Other finds included Kirsty Peart and Sarah Gold, who ended up being a leading figure in British advertising.

There was also a first-year student, an aspiring actress, called Nicola Walker, who impressed Henry. 'You see somebody of that quality turn up in an audition, you think, we've got to find a role for her.'[39] Nicola arrived at Cambridge with her father, both lugging around a ridiculously old-fashioned trunk, 'because we thought, maybe that's what you're meant to take,'[40] as if Cambridge were some kind of embryonic Hogwarts. Nicola had other preconceived notions about the place, that it was totally elitist and full of posh people. 'But I arrived at this brilliant, brutalist architecture that is New Hall, this amazing building up on the hill. It wasn't the lofty towers and cloisters of places like King's, but it was the right place for me.'[41]

Lugging this trunk into her room, one of the first people she met that day was Sue Perkins. In her second year, Sue had been prescribed a first year to look after; her job description was quaintly referred to as – college mother. 'It was her job to make me feel welcome,' says Nicola.[42] This terminology harked back to the past, encompassing things like bedders and was slightly at odds with New Hall being this extremely progressive college. Slightly in awe of her surroundings, it was Nicola's father who got chatting to Sue, telling her how interested his daughter was in acting. It was Sue who suggested Nicola come along to a Footlights smoker. 'And that changed everything for me. Susan was the one that absolutely opened the door.'[43]

Nicola was the first in her family to go to university or even have any allusions about going. 'I come from a background where it just wasn't offered as an option for them. It should have been. But it wasn't.'[44] She was born in Stepney, in the East End of London, her father was a scrap metal dealer, her mother an interior designer. When Nicola's A levels came up and people began to raise the possibility of her going to university, the family went through the process with a sense of complete confusion and real excitement. Nicola's preferred choice was the University of East Anglia, but when her results came through it was one of her English teachers who suggested Cambridge and got her an interview at New Hall.

While the primary drive of going to university was to study English, the hope was to join drama clubs and do as much acting as possible. Nicola knew nothing of say the Marlow Society, but had heard of the Footlights. 'And that's interesting. Even though I didn't understand the collegiate system of Cambridge, or the ins and outs of it at all, I knew about the Footlights. And I think that's what's incredible about Footlights, my mum and dad knew about it. We all knew about Footlights.'[45]

It was Sue who took Nicola to her first smoker. 'I thought, this is an amazing room. And not what I expected. It was intoxicating. I hadn't ever seen anything like it.'[46] The first surprise was the less than grand surroundings of the club room, which had just a small sign on the door outside with the name Footlights on it, 'An insignificant sign.'[47] The sheer ordinariness of it all made the place seem totally accessible right away. In Nicola's head she had presumed the Footlights was filled with a certain type of person. 'Of course, it's only a reflection of its intake at the time, it fluctuates, it is just a mirror of a wider world, but in 1989 it felt to me to be very inclusive and diverse and welcoming. And I was immediately offered, what do you want to do, do you want to write, do you want to perform, do you want to be on the technical side.'[48]

At that very first smoker, one act stood out from all the others, Saurabh Kakkar, who went on to become a television executive. Kakkar came on stage holding a baseball bat and went into a stand-up routine that was funny and at the same time shocking and biting about racism. Right away Nicola knew she wanted to do every smoker, she wanted to be around these incredibly talented people. At the same time, she was fully aware that she wasn't a writer. She could perform sketches well, she just couldn't write them, that wasn't her skill set. Despite that, Nicola was encouraged to get involved, especially by Sue and Henry, who realized the club required performers as much as they did writers; people who writers could write for. It was a smart move and showed an understanding of how the industry worked. Even so, Nicola was encouraged to try to write. 'The constant refrain was, you should write because most everybody else wrote. But I don't ever remember being made to feel as though I weren't absolutely part of the group.'[49]

It was Henry who encouraged Nicola in her first year to audition for shows. The first of these was called *Daughters of England*, which was an all-female revue, the first the Footlights club had ever put on. To bring forward female writers and performers, and to help develop a female voice, Henry had brought in Lizbeth Goodman to develop the show. 'Partly to try and get more women into the main shows but also to create a space which wasn't just a boy's club. We gave Lizbeth some of the club's budget and said, do what you want, and didn't interfere in any way.'[50]

Lizbeth knew a budding writer called Ali Smith who was studying for a PhD in American and Irish modernism at Newnham College. Raised in a council house in Inverness, Ali had begun writing plays while at Cambridge and Lizbeth brought her in to co-direct the show with Sarah Wood, and to write a lot of the material. Put on at the ADC Theatre, the cast featured Gina Clarke, Emily Gray, Sarah Grigor, Jane Tonge and Nicola, who thoroughly enjoyed the experience and remembers it going down very well with audiences. 'The intention of the show was very clear. It was that Footlights had been a totally male dominated environment, that women hadn't been involved enough in the group, or the university often. It was a very forward-thinking moment.'[51] The following year Lizbeth put on another all-female revue, *Amazons!* again co-directed by Ali Smith and Sarah Wood. The hope had been that these would become a regular occurrence, but this proved to be the last.

Women were also well represented in the revue that summer, *Absurd Persons Plural*, with Nicola, Sue Perkins and Sarah Gold amongst the cast. For the cast there was no sense, certainly for Nicola, that they were being crusaders, it was just obvious there should be more women in the show. 'I think youthful ignorance and idealism meant that we thought this was obvious. Certainly, I came into an atmosphere at Footlights that felt we were moving forward, we're going to have more women. They had to be proactive about it because of Footlights history, but it felt very natural.'[52]

Looking for the best material, Henry put out an open invitation for as many writers as possible to come in and submit sketches. Ultimately, though, it was the cast who ended up writing most of the show. One writer who turned up was Ben Miller, a Natural Science student at St Catharine's College. 'I found him very funny,' recalls Henry, 'and I said to him, look, you shouldn't just be writing, you should be performing comedy. And we got him to do some stuff at a smoker and he was excellent. And he went on to become one of the stand out performers of that show.'[53] At the time, Miller was participating in straight theatre. 'He came to the writer's thing just to have a crack at comedy,' recalls Henry.[54] Others featured in the cast were Nick Ball and James Hickish. And with Henry and Andy Parsons by now well established as a comedy team it made sense for them both to appear, too.

Nicola enjoyed rehearsals and being part of the company. 'I loved it. It was a fabulous combination of real commitment and complete laziness. One of the writers would come in with a piece of grubby paper, and say, I wrote this last night, and you'd get to give it a go. And I do thank the Footlights for this, it's still the most thrilling thing for me when you get a new piece of writing.'[55] At rehearsals, the feeling in the room was, let's just be funny, nobody was really interested in doing edgy stuff, or politics. 'No regional theatres want a bunch of youngsters from Cambridge to turn up and fire political jokes at them,' argues Nicola. 'We were young, and we were all quite politically motivated, but to say it within the framework of a Footlight comedy show would to me have felt ridiculous. I just felt proud and pleased that I found myself stood on a stage with the Footlights name attached to it, that to me felt like a political statement. It was just a personal one.'[56]

People like Andy Parsons have gone on to have a lot of political content in his stand-up shows, and Henry, too, is comfortable writing political stuff today in his plays, but back when he was eighteen and nineteen, and this maybe is the reason why the Footlights generally shied away from doing political material, he didn't really know enough about the world. 'I think you need to see a few governments come in and fail to properly understand it and have a perspective that's worth listening to. I think at that age I would have been in danger of just writing cliches.'[57]

Absurd Persons Plural was the usual combination of good, some great and some poor sketches that were quite hard work every night to get right. Sketch shows by their very nature are inconsistent, and that is certainly true of Footlight revues. The problem being that there is so much material that needs to be collated for what are two-hour shows that inevitably a lot of stuff gets in that isn't quite up to par. Still, Henry recalls many positive reviews and good audience reaction. 'I think there was a feeling that people noticed we were trying to change things and shake things up a bit.'[58] Andy Parsons wrote Nicola's main sketch, a pastiche of a jazzy late-night singer who introduces a song by just droning on and on about their own miserable life. Sue Perkins had written a rap based on Vivaldi's 'Four Seasons' that she and Nicola performed. Henry did an impersonation of the Queen talking about a visit to a South Yorkshire colliery, and with Andy performed a skit on hard Northen comedians.

The tour began at the Arts Theatre; Stephen Hawking was spotted in the audience one night. Then everyone loaded their goods into the boot of a van, and like a rock band gigging round the country, off they went. 'It was utterly joyful and innocent and full of hope,' says Nicola. 'But with this real desire to actually give a good show.'[59] They even had a truck following them everywhere loaded with Holsten Pils. 'It was rather crazy,' Nicola admits. 'And there were many funny, drunken, joyful stories, but also what was running alongside that was that it was a job and it taught me to be respectful of the writing, the audience, the other actors on stage. It was a heady combination of feeling completely free and there being nothing at stake, which you don't ever get again. You had a safety net, because you were Footlights, and it meant something to people when you arrived at the theatre.'[60]

Some of the writers on that show were keen to play around with the idea of what Footlights is, and what an audience member imagines a Footlights person to be. Ben Miller wrote a song, 'We've Written All Our Essays, Now We're Punting on the Thames', that totally subverted the idea that what the audience was going to get was a cast dripping with privilege. 'We were from very ordinary and varied backgrounds that cast,' affirms Nicola.[61] They fought against that perception at Edinburgh, too, where the antagonism towards them had mostly gone, replaced by a sense that a lot of pro comics were pissed that the Footlights got the best venue and time slot, just because of its heritage. 'Because of the type of people we all were,' stresses Nicola, 'we were *so* not that and it made all of us stand shoulders back, feet squared; we're not that, we're going to show you what we are. That was our feeling in the group. You think you know what Footlights is, but we're here now.'[62]

Absurd Persons Plural turned out to be the only revue in which Nicola appeared. In her second and third years she gravitated towards drama and new writers, especially Sarah Phelps, an English student at New Hall with whom she and Sue Perkins shared a flat. Nicola didn't fully turn her back on the Footlights, as she helped out with auditions and took over Sue's position on the committee as falconer. Sadly, this did not mean looking after a bird of prey; the name derived from the old club room, Falcon Yard. 'You basically go around with a bin bag at the end of the smokers and pick up all the fag butts and empty beer bottles.'[63] The reason why Nicola did not perform with the club again, despite the gratitude she felt being allowed to join, was that there was only so much she could do within Footlights if she didn't write. It was very writer-centric, and had been for many years. Indeed, you would never become president or go far in the committee if you weren't a writer. Nicola observed the new intake of writer/performers coming through and the current writers in the club encouraging them. It was a system that worked. 'It felt very natural, it was organic and moving, and it had to be to stay alive. It was very aware of wanting to be relevant, wanting to move forward, wanting to not be perceived as being preserved in time.'[64]

Sue Perkins was to succeed Henry Naylor as president and brought in Ben Miller to direct the 1991 revue, entitled *Cambridge Underground*. Miller only wanted a cast of four, a reaction perhaps against *Absurd Persons Plural* whose cast of eight was perhaps too large and unwieldy. Three of that cast, Nick Ball, James Hickish and Sue Perkins returned, which left just one place left. Mark Evans didn't fancy his chances much. In fact, he was already planning to go to Edinburgh with a sketch group he had set up with a couple of friends. 'And when I got in, it was a genuine shock.'[65]

Mark grew up a fan of Python and The Goodies and reading about those shows introduced him to the Footlights and that played some part in him choosing Cambridge. 'I remember thinking, I'd like to try for that. But I don't think I ever thought I'd get in and do well, probably because you only ever hear of the famous people who came out of it, it becomes almost this mythical thing.'[66] There was, however, something called 'the virgin smoker' that was held very early on in the first term. It was sort of an 'open mic' night for those who had never taken part in a smoker before. You came along and got five minutes to show what you could do. Convinced the event would be packed out, Mark was surprised to find it sparsely attended and he performed several of his sketches. He continued to write that year and was invited to be part of the writing team on *Absurd Persons Plural*.

It was only when Mark got cast in the tour show, and returned to his room, sitting there for quite a while, that he realized, this is a possibility, isn't it, because others have done the revue and gone on to have careers. 'I remember feeling a mix of exhilaration and fear, a whole new world had opened up in a way I didn't quite realize until it crystallised in that moment.'[67] Mark hadn't worked with any of the cast before but knew them and already had an association with Ben Miller. 'Ben was quite good at bringing on the next generation. He offered me a sketch to do in a smoker, and I always felt like he kept an eye on me.'[68] Becoming president, Mark did that too, knocking on people's doors, telling them they'd done well in a smoker or an audition, and to keep going, bringing new funny people through and helping them because as Footlights they were something of a target around Cambridge. 'Everyone is very keen to stop you in the street and say, I saw you in that show, you were terrible. I do remember that happening quite a bit.'[69]

Mark contributed a lot of material to *Cambridge Underground*, including a skit on Ray Cooney's *Run for Your Wife* as directed by Ingmar Bergman, 'even though I'd never seen an Ingmar Bergman film, or a Ray Cooney farce.'[70] It was done in a very po-faced way and Death arrives for dinner at a typical suburban couple's house. The tour played Manchester at a small venue just round the corner from the Hacienda. 'We'd be going home,' says Mark, 'and these long queues would be going into the club, and I do remember thinking, we're doing nerdy middle class sketch comedy, and this is the 1990s happening right in front of us.'[71] And they played Buxton, in a basement space after a very long opera. 'And we'd been sitting in a dressing room that stank of effluent because of a cracked pipe somewhere that no one had been able to locate, and we went on to a bunch of very tired posh people who'd just come from the opera in evening gowns and black tie, and we died on our arses. At some point, I thought, this will be a funny story one day.'[72]

Edinburgh was a real eye-opener for Mark, a brilliant adventure, and the team stayed in a nice flat in Morningside. 'This was just before the time that the fringe became this insanely overinflated, massively expensive thing.'[73] They played the Gilded Balloon, a top venue, and with pithy irony wrote in the official fringe programme: 'No one performs revue like the Footlights, because anyone with any sense stopped performing revue in 1967. The songs, the sketches and the monologues are still there in the show, only for once with the sneaking feeling that it's all been done before. Much better. Somewhere else.'[74]

When Mark returned to Cambridge and hosted the first smoker of the new term, he noticed something very interesting. He felt bulletproof. 'Because I'd done seventy-odd nights of the tour show, it took my nerves away. By the end of that summer, without realizing, it's that subliminal learning, I just went, oh, that's taught me a lot, things have changed. There was a lot of confidence you got as a performer doing the tour.'[75]

Mark appeared in the 1992 revue, *And Don't Come Back*. As usual, members were obliged to audition in front of a judging panel, which included the director. William Sutcliffe was in his second year reading English at Emmanuel when he bumped into Sacha Baron Cohen. Both had attended Haberdashers' Aske's Boys' School. Matt Lucas was also a pupil there, as David Baddiel had been, all Jewish. 'Haberdashers' was to Jewish comedy in the UK what Eton is to the Tory cabinet,' declares William.[76] Cohen was reading history at Christ's and had lodgings close to his old school friend. He was on his way to audition for the revue and asked if William fancied coming along to lend a bit of support. William, who had no aspirations to be a performer, but a writer, replied along the lines of, 'Footlights, are you serious, isn't that a bunch of public-school tossers who think they're funny.' 'No, no,' insisted Cohen, who by then knew he wanted to be a comedian. 'You've got to come.' William ended up going to the audition with Cohen. 'And amazingly enough, and this doesn't reflect well on the talent spotting skills of the Footlights panel, Sacha didn't get in, and I did.'[77] Cohen was to audition for other Footlight shows during his time at Cambridge and was never chosen, something that left a modicum of resentment for years. And there was a reason for that. No one denied his obvious talent, the thought was perhaps he was too much of a maverick, that he might not be able to operate within a team. There had been stories of people falling out or getting a bit too big for their boots on previous tours. 'In almost all institutions,' says William, 'and Footlights was that kind of institution, you start at the bottom, you toe the line a bit, you do it other people's way and eventually you get to do it your way. Sasha's not made that way.'[78]

It was a matter of tone, too. Cohen's humour was perhaps too crude and smutty. He and William did a couple of smokers together as a double act. One sketch was going great guns, getting lots of laughs, until the punchline repulsed almost the entire audience. 'That wasn't accidental,' states William. 'That was the reaction we wanted.'[79] The issue, then, or perhaps the fear, was that someone as powerful as Cohen might have taken over, and not just taken over as an individual but would have taken the revue into territory that the people who ran it didn't want to take it into. 'If you look at what he ended up doing it's very distinct and it's very different from the history of Footlights,' says William. 'Even so, he would have been brilliant and he should have got in.'[80]

And so, the Sacha Baron Cohen-less *And Don't Come Back* went ahead. There had been a bit of a backlash about the show's director David Wolstencroft insisting on casting William. 'I think the committee people were a bit annoyed that I got picked. It was, who is this guy, he hasn't even done a smoker.'[81] William soon pulled his weight, writing a chunk of the material. One monologue he wrote and performed had Shakespeare as a northern working men's club comedian. 'It was very Footlights, and it slightly makes me cringe now. He's telling "my wife, my wife" jokes but every punchline is the title of a Shakespeare play.'[82]

Wolstencroft was then a history student at Emmanuel but had done several smokers. 'He was very serious and professional about it,' recalls William.[83] Likewise, Mark thinks Wolstencroft made a good job at making it slightly thematic and tying things together with call backs. 'We did a neat routine at the beginning and the end of the show with briefcase swapping like we were spies, and oddly he went on to create and write the BBC series *Spooks*. He had some really good ideas that just lifted it from just being lights up, sketch, lights down.'[84]

At the time Mark was in a double act with fellow cast member Dan Gaster. In one sketch they wrote together, Mark played a journalist who went by the name of Front Page Willis, the lead guy on his local newspaper. Along with lots of silly jokes, the idea was that in each location they played they would try and put in an amusing local reference. 'In one place we had the mayor of the town in,' Mark recalls. 'He'd come in his full regalia and was sitting in the front row laughing away very happily. And we made a joke about him, a very nice joke, not offensive, and he went stony-faced and then sat there grumpy and in silence for the rest of the show, which just made us laugh more and more backstage.'[85]

In Edinburgh, they played Southside, a larger venue than the Pleasance, but it somewhat lacked the kudos, which resulted in them grabbing a bigger audience but not necessarily a comedy audience. 'There would be a lot of tourists, who think, oh Footlights, John Cleese,' observes William. 'And so, Footlights would tend to get quite snotty reviews. By that point we very much were not the "in" crowd at all. And quite rightly so really because we were just a bunch of students. But it had the kudos of something else which was possibly not earnt, or just earned by the history of it.'[86]

15

Barracuda Jazz Option

The first time Katie Breathwick heard the word Cambridge mentioned was when she was eleven and her parents took her to a West End try out of *Me and My Girl* starring Emma Thompson and Robert Lindsay at the Leicester Haymarket Theatre. She was allowed backstage to meet the stars, 'and two days later I remember saying to my mum, I want to be an actress. And my mother, who was a teacher and knew the power of these things, said, well Emma Thompson did this thing called Footlights so maybe that's what you should do.'[1] In sixth form, Katie was to meet her future husband, Robert Thorogood, both revealing to each other their determination to go to Cambridge to be in the Footlights. 'By the time I was involved in Footlights,' says Katie, 'everybody I spoke to quietly admitted that's why they wanted to be at Cambridge.'[2] Not everyone was to make a career from it. Katie had a good friend, Michael Brierley. 'He was a very funny guy. A Christian. He auditioned for the revue, did not get cast, took this as a sign from God that he should not be doing Footlights and ended up the Reverend Canon at Ripon College.'[3]

Katie took inspiration from past Footlights women like Jan Ravens and Sue Perkins. Going to see *Cambridge Underground* gave her the confidence to turn up for that first audition. 'Because I knew that there were women involved because I'd seen that show. It made me think, I know I can do this. There is no barrier. I've just got to get on with it.'[4] Unfortunately, it was a no from the two guys on the panel. Next, Katie auditioned for the panto, and again failed, while Robert Thorogood got in. Learning there were no jobs backstage either, she and her friend, Tamsin Stanley, painted the rolled-out backdrop late at night on the top floor of a multi-storey car park next door to the ADC Theatre. These efforts got them invited to the after-show party where they got chatting to the president, Dan Gaster. Katie was reading social and political sciences at Newnham but wanted to live out of college in her second year and be closer to the ADC. Gaster said that he lived in a three-storey house nearby. 'If you can find enough people to take it on next year maybe you should talk to the landlord.' There was one proviso, the president always lived in that house, because there was a phone line in one of the downstairs rooms. 'And I remember thinking,' says Katie, 'my God, whoever the president is, imagine if I happen to be living in one of those bedrooms, feeling ambitious, having only just picked up a paintbrush and painted the set.'[5]

Robert Thorogood did indeed manage to get two rooms on the top floor for himself and Katie and filled out the rest of the house with Footlights Dan Mazer, Tamsin Stanley and Georgie Bevan, while the new president, Mark Evans, inherited the downstairs room with the phone. 'It became a bit of a Footlights village,' says Katie.[6] And a social hub thanks to regular deliveries of Holsten Pils. 'Twelve crates got delivered to that house every month,' Katie reveals. 'It was like a pub.'[7] The beer would arrive and be immediately taken up to the top floor kitchen. And thanks to an open-door policy there would be somebody there drinking until four or five in the morning every night. Not a lot of actual comedy writing went on. 'But what we were doing was sitting round that kitchen table making each other laugh,' recalls Katie. 'And we laughed like bloody drains around that kitchen table, absolutely knackered and pissed. None of us were handing in essays, we were all missing our lectures. But we were getting to know each other extremely well, and it meant that by the time you got into that rehearsal room or that writing room you already had a shorthand, and you already knew the other person's sense of humour and you already could leap ahead to what you knew they found funny.'[8] It's no surprise that everyone living in that house formed the cast of that summer's revue, entitled *Some Wood and A Pie*, including Katie. It had taken her five terms to get into a show, all the while doing smokers and working backstage. 'You had to hustle. I think it did require a hell of a lot of delusional self-belief. You just believed that you deserved to be there.'[9]

Of course, it was quite advantageous to be in that house, and probably from the outside it all looked a bit cliquey. James Bachman tried to get rooms there but there was no space. 'There were certainly people who could have been welcomed in more to the whole thing but weren't part of the gang,' he argues, 'or who maybe felt that.'[10] James was studying natural sciences at Emmanuel, focusing on physics and mathematics. A huge comedy fan, especially things like Python and The Goodies, he'd done a few revues at school but hadn't really given a career in the business much thought. Nor did he know a great deal about the Footlights. 'In my first year I didn't audition for the panto or any smokers, I had no idea that any of that was happening. But as I became more involved with it, I would see people who clearly had done all of the research about how Footlights worked before they arrived there, just freshers who would turn up to everything. And I'd think, OK, you really want this, rather than stumbling into it a bit.'[11]

James decided to go to a Footlights writers' workshop where he met Rory Ewins, an Australian studying at Cambridge just for a year. They clicked and started writing together, deciding to audition for a smoker. 'It went well, but I still didn't think, oh this is what I want to do. But it was fun.'[12] Along with two other writers, James and Ewins put on their own revue which went down well. 'And I remember coming off after the first night thinking, OK, that's really good. I feel amazing,' says James. 'And I was very aware that every performance I ever did after that was an attempt to recreate that feeling.'[13]

James did more smokers and was asked on the committee, 'where you had a feeling that you were nearer the front of the queue whenever anything was happening; who might write the panto or be in the revue.'[14] He was also asked, along with Dan Mazer, to run the writers' workshops, just six months after first doing one. This led to James becoming involved in the writing process for *Some Wood and A Pie*.

As we've seen, in the past, revues had largely been made up from the best sketches from that year's smokers, with a bit of new writing thrown in. Now it was very different. 'Smokers were places to find good writers or performers, but not necessarily material,' states James.[15] Instead, the cast, along with a few invited writers, would usually meet up in the club room, the director would chat through some thoughts and then everyone would be split into pairs and go off somewhere to write. After something like an hour-and-a-half everyone came back and read out what they'd written to see how it went down. There would be one session in the morning and another in the afternoon so everybody would get a go with everybody else. This way people got to slowly know who they wrote well with and which people shared that same sense of humour. It was also a great way of generating material and meant you had the beginnings of a show and a lot of sketches quite quickly that the director could then try and work out what went well together and what was good and what was bad. This process was the same for the spring revue as well as the tour and many people found it both incredibly useful and exhilarating. Having to make something out of nothing and then immediately put it up to scrutiny.

Except for William Sutcliffe, the cast of *Some Wood and A Pie*, as already mentioned, were all housemates, which according to Katie led to a great atmosphere on tour. 'It was a laugh. Obviously, there were flashpoints, there are in any group of people.'[16] The show met with a mixed response. 'In some theatres we went down like a lead balloon,' recalls Katie, 'and then others where they loved us.'[17] It was quite traditional in nature. William and Dan Mazer wrote a sketch performed by Mazer and Georgie Bevan about a mum coming into the bedroom of her teenage son trying to get him up for school, but he can't get up because he's got an all too obvious morning glory. There was a silly song to open and close the show, which the cast sang backwards at the finale. 'We had to dance backwards and sing it backwards,' says William, 'which was one of those things that seemed funny but was not necessarily that funny and was incredibly difficult to do and slightly pointless.'[18] In another sketch, Katie and Georgie played two women with shopping trolleys where it transpires that they are murdering people and putting their dismembered body parts in their trolleys.

Katie and Georgie were good friends. Georgie hankered for a career in radio journalism and during one term landed a gig on the student radio station, based at Churchill College. It was only an hour on a Wednesday afternoon but Georgie, along with Katie, turned it into a comedy show by inviting their Footlights friends to appear as fictional guests. It was during that term Katie fell in love with radio broadcasting, a job she still does to this day.

In another sketch, Katie played a girl being emotionally abused by her partner. It was co-written with William Sutcliffe, but overall, Katie didn't enjoy the writing process. The first person who wrote a sketch for Katie to perform at a smoker was Charlie Hartill. A future Footlights president, Hartill was to most people's minds, an eccentric. 'But his comedy was extraordinary,' recalls Katie. 'He wrote unbelievable sketches.'[19] Despite an obvious talent, like so many others, Hartill never made a revue cast. In his case, it may have been the fact he was already an alcoholic. 'You'd turn up in his room,' says Katie, 'and his curtains were closed and there'd be twenty-five red wine bottles scattered all over the floor. He was fucked, really. And we kind of knew that, even then, but he was an extraordinary person and extraordinarily creative.'[20] Also very tech-minded. He was one of the first people Katie knew who had an Apple computer, so all the revue posters and programmes were designed on that. Hartill went on to serve for many years on the board of directors at the Edinburgh Fringe but tragically died in 2004 aged just thirty-two.

Katie didn't possess enough confidence to write as much as she should have, in large part because of her experiences as a woman in the Footlights. 'There was definitely a difficulty with numbers, in auditioning, at the very gateway level, but also then being cast in shows, women were always in the minority.'[21] It didn't help that this was the era of the lads' mags and lad culture. 'So, some of the humour was downright offensive.'[22] In *Some Wood and A Pie* Katie recalls a sketch where Georgie Bevan's character was hit whenever she got something wrong. 'You couldn't do that now, could you, and we didn't have a similar sketch where a bloke got hit. And what is shocking to me now, is the memory that in certain locations that sketch got the biggest laugh.'[23]

When it came to auditions, Katie identified almost a fear factor, of entering a space where men were on the committee and largely men waiting to audition, there were not many women doing what Katie was trying to do. 'I'm sure there would have been people, sort of non-white males, who all felt that if you walked into a room who is going to laugh at your humour if there's not somebody who looks like you represented behind the desk that is judging you. And so often it was two boys. And they were all lovely. All these people went on to become my friends, but they can't help not necessarily finding female humour funny.'[24] This is why, in her final year, when Katie was on the committee, she tried her damnedest to be in every single audition room. 'So that if a female student walked in, she saw another woman on that audition committee and felt supported and represented because I never wanted a woman to walk in to feel that wall of maleness that I had felt at my first audition.'[25] Katie also organized an all-woman smoker in her third year. 'And out from the shadows came all of these wonderful women, youngsters who hadn't had the courage to turn up to audition, or maybe weren't performers but were writers, and we packed out the club room.'[26]

Since Henry Naylor appointed a women's representative to the committee back in 1990, things had regressed somewhat. Not least the fact that by the time Katie arrived that role no longer existed. This led to her writing a dissertation for her social and political sciences course, the subject: The Participation of Women in Footlights. She asked Harry Porter for access to the archives as part of her research. 'And bless him he gave me a key to his front door and said, come and go as you please.'[27] The archive was still located in a basement cupboard. 'I thought, this will take a couple of days, but the moment I went down there I realized what a juicy resource this was, and I spent most of a term there, elbow deep in all that information. Just because it was so interesting, and it was so fascinating.'[28]

It was this experience that led Katie to become junior archivist in her third term where she got to know Harry Porter much better. 'You had to break down Harry's barriers if you dared to be a woman.'[29] As for Lucy Montgomery, when she was in Footlights, Porter would not even talk to women. 'It was like you were invisible. They didn't exist.'[30] Porter knew that he had a reputation for, shall we say, an indifference to the opposite sex. He confessed to Mark Evans that he found Germaine Greer especially frightening and told an amusing story of when she was sat on a radiator in Falcon Yard one wintry morning. Commenting on how chilly it was, Germaine replied, 'Not for me and my clitty, Harry.' Porter told Mark, 'And do you know what, I didn't have a clue what she was on about. And to be honest, I still don't.' This was said with a twinkle in his eye. Porter was very good at playing the doddery old don. 'I was very fond of him,' says Mark. 'There were periods when he wasn't involved in Footlights. He told me, "They just didn't want me to be involved, so I wasn't."'[31] Mark brought him back into the fold. 'He was the institutional memory.'[32] A self-confessed Footlights nerd, Mark spent hours with Porter and in the archive, looking at old scripts and old minutes of meetings. And whenever he visited Cambridge would always pop in for a cup of tea or a glass of wine. At Porter's funeral, Mark shared the eulogy with Neil Mullarkey.

Being a traditionalist, Mark was responsible for reintroducing the club tie during his term as president, alas the president's jacket was no more. He'd also been in charge of performers' workshops, these included things like a circus skills' workshop and lectures given by industry professionals. Mark remembers bringing in Huw Thomas, a teacher at Middlesex Poly, but also compere of the King's Head comedy club in Crouch End. His advice was invaluable. To one student, who everyone thought was funny but lacked stage presence, Huw told him, 'The thing is, what you're doing is your shuffling on stage nervously. You either stand still or you pace like you own the space. And you're doing in-between.' This student started pacing, and it worked and he went on to have a decent career on the circuit. 'If Huw thought you were any good,' claims Mark, 'he'd invite you to do five minutes at the King's Head, to which most people replied, where's Crouch End?'[33]

Mark returned the year after graduation to direct the 1994 revue, *The Barracuda Jazz Option*. Katie was in the cast, so too was James Bachman. James had been very active in Footlights, writing the panto, *Cinderella*, with Dan Mazer. 'The panto was much more open to the general theatre community in Cambridge than the revue, so you ended up with many fun people in there who you got to know, but who weren't really Footlights people who could enjoy letting loose being in a ridiculous show.'[34]

Olivia Colman, then training to be a teacher at Homerton, played the Queen. In the cast was first year student Lucy Montgomery. 'I remember watching her and thinking, she was already fully formed brilliant. Everybody else was obviously a little bit crap, or at a certain level, but she was head and shoulders above everybody else already and stole the show.'[35] Katie was in that panto, too, and remembers at one rehearsal a huge buzz backstage when news broke that Emma Thompson was in the auditorium. She only stayed an hour but left a note in the clubroom: 'Darlings, it's been a bloody pleasure. I've left two crates of beer for you in the local Oddbins.'

A lot of money went into the panto, with big sets and costumes. The year before writing *Cinderella*, James was in *Peter Pan* and recalls there was a set of half a ship. 'It was far too big and took up too much space backstage for anything else, just blocked everybody constantly. And it didn't look that great on stage. But the panto was a real opportunity for anybody involved to try out every bit of doing a production in a way that footlight people didn't really get to do that much. I remember staying up late the night before the dress rehearsal of *Cinderella* helping build the sets.'[36]

All this work in Footlights almost resulted in James being thrown out of university when he failed his second year. Called back in the summer, he was presented in front of a panel of lecturers to put his case as to why he should stay. 'And I do remember a moment in that meeting where they asked me what else I was doing, and I said I'd been doing a lot of stuff with the Footlights, which I guess had replaced a lot of my academic work. There was a pause, and the head of studies said to me, "Do you think you might be president next year." I said, "Yes, I might be." And they were like, umm, OK. And I suddenly thought, I wonder if you think if I might become famous then you won't want to have thrown me out of this college, and also if I get rich you don't want to be unable to ask me for money. I remember that feeling of, oh, this matters to you. So, in the end they let me stick around.'[37]

Other cast members included Liz Hurran and Dan Mazer, and there was a second-year English student at Robinson College called Robert Webb. 'The very first time I ever met Rob,' recalls Katie, 'we were on the auditioning panel together, sat in the club room waiting for people to turn up, and I have to say I think that morning nobody did. In the end I went round the corner and bought some cans of beer and some crisps so the two of us could chat.

FIGURE 15.1 *Poster for the 1992 Footlights panto*, Peter Pan. *Reproduced with the permission of James Bachman.*

And he and I hit it off immediately. But fuck me, the moment he walked on stage he was extraordinary. You just kind of took a step back going, oh, OK, I'm never going to be as good as that.'[38] In *Barracuda Jazz Option*, Webb performed a couple of monologues playing different characters. 'And they brought the house down every single night,' Katie recalls.[39]

Comedy wise, James thinks the taste at the time was, 'silly and surreal'.[40] In one sketch, he played a policeman pulling someone over for speeding. Buying a police helmet he taped a blue and red light to it so he was the policeman and the police car rolled into one. He'd also carved out a reputation for comedy songs. In the revue he performed a protest song that whales should live in Wales ('There's no whaling ships in Aberystwyth') which became something of a signature item; he was to perform it at Harry Porter's memorial service. 'There was a gleeful stupidity, we just really liked jokes more than anti-humour or messages or shocking people.'⁴¹ A few bucked that trend. Dan Mazer, one of the few doing stand-up at the time, did try and push things to the edge, with an almost joyful exuberance. 'There certainly was stuff that Dan did that was deliberately done to annoy the audience,' says James.⁴² Mazer went on to become best known for helping co-create, with Sacha Baron Cohen, Ali G, Borat and Bruno.

However, if Mark Evans had his way things were going to be much darker. One afternoon he took the cast out for afternoon tea to explain his idea to do a themed show called, *A Taste of Armageddon*. 'And his opening idea,' recalls James, 'was to have a clown come on and then me come on with a baseball bat and beat the clown to death. And he got weird looks from everybody.'⁴³ Sensing disapproval in the room, Mark said, 'OK, well, there's that option, or what I call the *Barracuda Jazz Option*, which is just to do the best group of fun sketches that you can do.' This idea went down much better.

Again, the show was created in writing workshops, with other writers not in the cast, invited to collaborate. One of these writers was a first-year student called David Mitchell. David knew all about the Footlights but followed many of his school friends by applying to Oxford, figuring there must be the equivalent comedy and drama happening, given how fundamentally similar both universities were. After being rejected by Merton College, David took a year off and then applied to study history at Cambridge, having thought even more about becoming a comedian or an actor. Growing up he'd enjoyed the likes of *The Two Ronnies*, before gradually getting into things like Monty Python and *Blackadder*, identifying how many of these shows contained Footlight people. 'When I was a teenager, I thought of myself as a comedy nerd.'⁴⁴

David auditioned for pretty much everything in his first term. And it was at a recall audition for the pantomime that he first met Robert Webb. 'He was a year ahead of me and on the committee. I remember thinking he was very funny.'⁴⁵ They ended up writing some stuff together for the summer show. 'We wrote a dreadful sketch. Our idea was that it would be like a Ray Cooney farce but set in the trenches during the First World War. We also tried to put a song in it. We were a bit confused because I don't think we'd quite twigged that Ray Cooney farces, of which we had seen precisely none, didn't have songs. This sketch was awful, but we enjoyed writing it and then we hung out a bit in Edinburgh and decided to do our own show the following year.'⁴⁶

David found the workshops for *Barracuda Jazz Option* a relatively trusting environment. 'Nobody was going to take the piss out of you for writing something shit. The only thing that would go down badly was if you came back and you hadn't written anything. And so, you didn't, you wrote something. And the thing about comedy is you've just got to start bashing something down and something usually comes of that. So, there were a lot of unusable sketches. And a lot of sketches that were largely unusable with the odd bit that could be salvaged. And quite a few sketches that were pretty good and just needed a bit of a trim.'[47]

Somebody expected to have been in the cast was current president Robert Thorogood; his vice president was James. Thorogood chose not to appear and instead co-ordinated the tour. He would go on to become a successful television writer. One of the biggest headaches facing him was that Holsten Pils had ended their sponsorship deal. The beer company had tried to pull out the previous year, during Mark's presidency. 'I got a call from them one morning, "Just to let you know we're not going to sponsor you this year." And I went, "But we've booked a whole tour on the premise that we're getting the money." I had to talk them into it – can you keep it going please because otherwise our tour collapses. I averted that from happening.'[48] This time they meant it and the club went from being well off to not having very much at all. Stories of misuse of their product had perhaps filtered back to the company. 'I remember one time,' says James, 'hearing that a bunch of people went on top of the multi-storey car park next to the Maypole pub in Cambridge very late at night and just spent a couple of hours dropping beers off the top. We had too many we didn't know what to do with them.'[49]

Minus Holsten, *Barracuda Jazz Option* toured the country as normal. Of course, the days of producers turning up and saying, let's transfer this to the West End were long gone. 'We all hoped that it would happen,' laments James. 'The mythology of the ones who had come from where it had happened still hung around.'[50] As can sometimes be the case performing the same show night after night, the cast got bored and started messing around. James remembers Mark turning up at Bury St Edmonds for a performance, with Griff Rhys Jones. 'And he came round to see us in the interval and went, "Griff Rhys Jones is fucking here and you guys are not doing a good show." We were just dicking around, so we said sorry and did a much better second half.'[51] Ironically, when James was invited back the following year to direct the revue, *Fall from Grace*, he caught a performance at the same theatre and going backstage at the interval admonished his cast. 'This is really boring, can you dick around a bit and entertain me please.' Years afterwards David Mitchell admitted to him, 'We didn't know what to do when you came back and said that because some of us thought we shouldn't do that, and some of us thought that we really wanted to.'

Cast in his first revue, David Mitchell recalls that the original idea for *Fall from Grace* was to do a Christmas show and call it, *Deep and Crisp and Even*, and have a big picture of a snow-topped pizza on the poster. 'And I thought that was a good idea because it's not what you're expecting, and that's a good start for comedy, something that's not what people are expecting.'[52] It turned out not to be something tour venues were expecting either and they informed the Footlights that audiences would be puzzled by a Christmas show playing over the summer. The idea was abandoned.

Someone else making their revue debut was Matthew Holness, who had spent the whole of his first year vainly trying to get into Footlights. It was the reason he went to Cambridge in the first place. 'I'd grown up absolutely obsessed with Python, Peter Cook and all those Footlights, so I had this awful year of total anxiety when I first got there of not being in Footlights, and worried if I'd get in or not, and didn't really think I would. I was obsessed with it.'[53]

Matthew had always wanted to perform, having done plays at school and in local theatre where he grew up in Whitstable. During sixth form, shows like *The Mary Whitehouse Experience* and *A Bit of Fry & Laurie* were popular, 'and it felt like, if you wanted to get on in TV comedy a great way to do it would be to get into Footlights.'[54] Matthew first auditioned for the panto, unsuccessfully, and was heartbroken, 'because my understanding was that was the way you started to get into Footlights.'[55] Desperate to be involved somehow, he played guitar in the band. 'And I remember sitting in the band and hearing David Mitchell absolutely going great guns out on stage, he was always a star from the word go, and feeling sort of quietly panicked and slightly jealous that there was someone else who had come up and was clearly going to get into Footlights and I wasn't.'[56] Matthew went so far as to walk over to David's college, Peterhouse, and finding out which were his rooms, knocked on the door and introduced himself. Trying to sound confident, Matthew suggested since both were in line possibly for getting into Footlights, they should do a show together. 'Basically saying, please, please can I hang around with you so that I can get in as well. I remember being heartbroken again when he said, "That's absolutely wonderful, Matt, but I have just agreed to do a show with Rob Webb." I thought, oh Christ.'[57]

Would Matthew ever get in? Would he ever get to know the people that he'd been slightly obsessing over for the whole year. 'I can remember being in a phone box and seeing the Footlights committee walk past, a bit like that shot from *Reservoir Dogs*, it was like slow motion in my head. And I sort of hesitatingly put my hand up and they waved back.'[58]

Matthew knew a lot about Footlights history, that what he had to do was, yes go to smokers, but also to be proactive and put on his own show to get spotted or foster interest. With a couple of guys from his college, Matthew put together a revue that went to Edinburgh, where it won a few good reviews and came to the attention of the Footlights committee who came to see it. 'It was a bit like being summoned by the Secret Service, it was, would you go over to the other side of the Pleasance Courtyard, Footlights would like to speak to you. And they were lovely, and they invited me on to the committee for the following year and I remember just feeling absolutely overjoyed and elated because that was everything I'd always wanted.'[59]

This time the writers' workshop also involved a week away at a cottage on the Norfolk coast. There were big dinners and walks along the beach. 'It was lovely,' recalls David. 'You filled the house with microwavable food and booze, and we'd do three writing sessions there, so we increased the output a bit, but basically, we were just on a bit of a jolly. We behaved like basically overgrown children and the house was an absolute tip that we'd desperately try and clean in the remaining hours before leaving.'[60]

James enjoyed the challenge of coming back to direct, although he had hung around the university and Cambridge since graduation. 'There was a feeling that Footlights can give you of being a big fish in a small pond and it's quite tempting to not leave, in a way. There certainly were people who graduated who were still about for a while.'[61] He had decided on a theme for *Fall from Grace*, the seven deadly sins. And since comedy at the time was very personality led, with people like Newman and Baddiel, and Lee and Herring, the idea was for a Footlights tour that was presented by its cast as much as performed. 'So, we did have little bits of pseudo stand-up.'[62] The show was split into seven sections with an introductory short film for each sin, and had dark overtones, despite an underlying silliness to the whole thing, such as a send up of Take That. In the wrath section, David Mitchell played a surgeon getting angry in the middle of surgery, with lots of fake blood spraying everywhere. On tour this sketch wasn't nearly as effective, as they lacked the facilities to use fake blood and had to mime it instead. James had also brought back several replica guns from a trip to the US for the cast to use on the tour, 'because it all ended with us doing a *Reservoir Dogs* stand-off,' recalls Matthew.[63]

FIGURE 15.2 *The Footlights writing cottage in Bacton, Norfolk. Left to right: Leila Hackett, Robert Webb, Beth Chalmers, Matthew Holness, Jonathan Dryden Taylor, Barunka O'Shaughnessy, James Bachman and David Mitchell.* © *Lucy Montgomery.*

Matthew had always found sketch writing difficult. What he could do very well was character material and in smokers he mainly performed character monologues that were a bit hit and miss, like one character who was a bomb disposal expert. 'I was desperately trying to find something that would work.'[64] In his dressing room during the panto in his second year there were some props lying around and he popped on a pair of brown tinted shades. 'I looked in the mirror and thought, oh, that looks quite interesting for a character, and I just thought, that's like a sleazy horror fiction writer. OK, I'll do that for the next smoker.'[65] Garth Marenghi was born. Matthew wrote it first as a monologue and it was very different from how Garth ended up, and even when Matthew performed it in *Fall from Grace* it was more about the character being this sleazebag writer than the world that he inhabited later in the Channel 4 TV series.

Instead of the Arts Theatre, the tour show kicked off at its new home, the ADC Theatre. Matthew found the tour a slog at times. 'It's the end of the academic year. You have to hang around. You're already rehearsing for the show so you're not really having a big release at the end of your exam year. It's exciting, but then once you're out of Cambridge and you're touring theatres and you're all in the back of a bus and everyone's squabbling, it's like, oh Christ.'[66]

The cast still stayed in hotels or private houses and encountered the bizarre and the strange. In Plymouth, they stayed at one hotel and were warned about the landlord from his wife. 'Don't upset Roy,' she said. 'Why! What have we done?' She said, 'Just don't upset him. He gets violent. That's Roy's way. He's violent.' Roy ended up as a character in the following year's panto. 'It was like Basil Fawlty territory,' recalls Matthew.[67]

Another tradition was scouring the local papers to see if the critics had picked anyone out for individual praise, and then everyone feeling a bit down when reviews were lacklustre or thin on the ground. More depressing was the fact that in the regions, while people still turned out, it wasn't in huge numbers. Back in the glory days of the 1960s, 1970s and 1980s it was relatively easy for the tour show to pack theatres out. 'By the time we were doing it,' says David Mitchell, 'the whole world we know now of touring stand-up comedy, while it might not be quite as big as it is now, was very much up and running and we student amateurs were trying to compete with that. I remember Eddie Izzard coming on tour to the Corn Exchange while I was at Cambridge and what Footlights had to offer was comparatively amateurish.'[68]

There was another problem, too, provincial audiences still expected a traditional revue. 'What they basically wanted was Gilbert and Sullivan with a few more jokes,' offers David. 'And what Footlights was producing wasn't that. We were all nineteen-, twenty-, twenty-one-year-olds who were obsessed with comedy, and obsessed with recent comedy.'[69] The dilemma, as it had been for many years, was being hamstrung by tradition, while at the same time not being as good at the edgy comedy they wanted to do and what the professional comedians were doing. 'What we were doing,' says David, 'was a show with some edgy material and swearing, and not many comic songs, to an audience that wanted to watch *Salad Days*. So, we would do the show in Cambridge, and it would go down very well, and then we would go to the provinces, and they would disapprove and clap politely at the end. Then we would end up in Edinburgh and certainly the reviewers had their knives sharpened, because we were horrendous, privileged twats in their view, but we would get an audience that was a bit more in tune to what we were putting on stage.'[70]

Matthew and David were very much the force behind next year's revue, *Rainbow Stranglers*. Since arriving at Cambridge, David's desire to go into the comedy business didn't appear too unreachable since it seemed to be the aspiration of pretty much everybody else. 'And part of believing that that might come off was, if I become president of Footlights, that's a really good sign. That means I might make it in this career. So, that came to massively matter to me.'[71]

David was very much the heir apparent anyway, having joined earlier than anyone else. His only real challenger was Matthew who didn't fancy his chances. 'I knew I wasn't going to get it, but I thought, if I don't go for it, I'll never know.'[72] David was indeed elected, and Matthew became vice president. 'I really enjoyed running the club with David. We kind of had very good personalities together, but at the same time quite bad personalities. I remember us bickering a lot, but in a nice way.'[73] Indeed, their bickering was a feature of the spring revue's programme. 'We decided,' recalls Matthew, 'because we were bickering so much, to write a little sketch. We literally wrote it one line at a time. He would write something then I would write my response and pass it over, and it was basically just a very nice little version of our arguing.'[74] They also wrote the panto together, *Snow White*, which included the gratuitous death within the first ten pages of a dwarf named Pervy. Act Two opens with a song by fifteen dwarves who all die before the last verse.

For David, the biggest challenge facing his presidency was the club's finances. Having come out of a long period of receiving sponsorship money from Holsten, the club had to some extent restructure itself. Since Holsten's departure, the tour had lost money, and nothing had been saved during those sponsored years. David was determined this would not happen this time. That meant cutting overheads and working on a strict budget. One of the things he did was install a local coordinator at each venue and town whose job it was to find local sponsorship to advertise in the programme and to get free accommodation. Thanks to this astute management the tour that year did indeed turn a profit.

Matthew did his bit, too, as junior treasurer, although David was to enjoy telling the story of when Matthew kept the takings for a smoker in his room under the sink. 'I shouldn't have been junior treasurer,' Matthew confesses. 'I was planning to bank it, don't get me wrong. I just thought, it's fine under there for a bit, I'll go and bank it when I'm in town next.'[75]

Organizing the revue and taking on the presidency, David didn't have a lot of time for work in his final year. 'I became a past master at apologizing and wriggling out of doing essays and then would desperately cram in the three weeks before the exam and scrapped through with a 2:2.'[76] As much as he loves history today, at the time all he wanted to do was concentrate on comedy. 'And that turned out to be the most important for my life.'[77] As luck would have it, Harry Porter was a good friend of David's director of studies and took him to see a production of *Jeffrey Bernard is Unwell* with David in the lead role, basically to curry favour with him on David's behalf, 'and it totally worked. And that got me out of trouble for my last term and I was always very grateful to Harry for that. Harry was a sort of magical figure, really. And a link to the past. He had this large house in central Cambridge and basically every room was full of his books and things he was typing. And it had all the mod cons of when he bought it in the 1960s. It really was like a time capsule.'[78]

There wasn't very much David could do with the club room as president, which in the view of most members was never really a successful recreation of what it had been in Falcon Yard. 'It was just a rehearsal room that was always in desperate need of clearing of spiders' webs and general filth. And it cost quite a lot of money to rent for the godforsaken place it was. Occasionally we put on a low-key smoker or cabaret night in there in violation of God knows how many fire regulations.'[79]

Now very much a comedy team, it made perfect sense for David to install Robert Webb as director of the revue. 'Because both David and I really respected Rob's talents,' says Matthew, 'we knew he was very good, was a very good writer, we just said to him, go ahead and do what you want with it. It was a good fun show.'[80]

Along with David and Matthew, Webb cast three women in the show, Ali Chalmers, Leila Hackett and Lucy Montgomery. For Lucy, this was her final year and last revue opportunity. Like David, Lucy had first applied to Oxford. 'And then I was so shy at the interview I couldn't even really speak, so I didn't get in there. And when I got my A level results I then applied for Cambridge and that was much better, it felt like the right fit because I love doing comedy and acting.'[81]

When Lucy arrived, she was slightly taken aback by how everyone around the university took things seriously. 'If you joined the Union you wanted to be a politician. Everybody doing Shakespeare wanted to be at the National Theatre. And everybody in Footlights wanted to be a top comedian. You felt that this was them trying out their jobs before they went out into the big wide world.'[82]

It was made obvious to Lucy that you never got into the main revue in your first year, so the panto was the best way in. Lucy got a small part in *Cinderella*, and the following year was Prince Charming in *Snow White*. 'One of the cast playing a dwarf permanently fucked up his knees,' she recalls. 'They didn't give him proper knee pads and he's actually had to have knee surgery as a result.'[83]

In her second year, Lucy was asked to be on the committee. 'I really did not want to be on the committee because I had no interest in any of that, but you felt like a proper member if you were on the committee.'[84] She took on the position of social secretary, which really only meant that she oversaw the organization of black-tie dinners. These dinners were a nod to Footlights traditions of old, although in her time there Lucy found her fellow members not at all 'posh', certainly compared to many other Cambridge students. 'For example, the rowers were like another breed. You didn't get the old Etonian crowd when I was in the Footlights, those type of people were not moving towards comedy. The posh contingent wasn't there. That's why it felt like normal people trying to make each other laugh. It didn't feel like, oh let's put on a funny song, and all of that. It felt more egalitarian.'[85] Lucy went to a comprehensive and then a private school, but Cambridge was another level of privilege. 'Someone I went on a bad date with asked me if I had an inheritance. I went, sorry, what! Footlights was not of that world.'[86]

Reading English literature, Lucy was conscious of the fact that there was a balance to be struck between studies and Footlights, but by the end didn't give much thought to what she got for her degree. 'By then it's what you do with these other things that will get you your career rather than the actual degree itself.'[87] Also reading English, Matthew Holness felt the same. 'I think we all prioritized Footlights over our academic careers.'[88] Matthew recalls one encounter with his tutor, Peter Holland, about an essay he'd done. 'Because I was doing so much for Footlights that week, I had just tossed off a rewrite of one of my sixth form essays. So, a plan destined for complete disaster. And he just picked up the essay and said, "Well, I read a page of this and I'm not going to bother to read anymore."'[89] Holland asked what the problem was. 'Is it Footlights?' Obviously, yes. Holland had some sympathy, having in years past been senior treasurer. 'And he did say to me, bottom line is, your career is going to be in Footlights, make an effort but if you want to prioritize Footlights, I'll totally understand. So, he was very good about that. But he did sort of say, "But this is a shit essay."'[90] After that meeting, Matthew did buck his ideas up a bit, but had the feeling he was going to totally mess up his exams, having just not done the work. 'The irony being that I've never used my degree once since leaving, but all the experience that I'd gained from Footlights has been invaluable.'[91]

Like *Fall from Grace*, *Rainbow Stranglers* had a theme, vaguer though. 'It was something about totalitarianism,' offers David, not quite sure if it made any sense.[92] The problem with themes was it presented writers with something of a dilemma, how much material should adhere to the concept and how much was just a matter of picking the funniest sketches, and how much do you compromise between the two things? David remembers one sketch he wrote with Robert Webb, about a man going into a shop where he's clearly trying to buy the means to murder his wife, that was later adapted for their 2000 BBC TV comedy sketch show *Bruiser*. In another sketch, David played a librarian who goes mad with a gun. 'He's sitting there quietly, saying how restful he finds the library, and slowly it transpires that he's gone on a shooting spree. I did that sketch a lot in smokers. It was the sketch I performed most at Cambridge.'[93]

For Lucy, touring the revue was exciting and a great new experience. 'It was amazing training. You learn about the slog of putting a show on as well as the fun of having an audience.'[94] They did play some odd places, though, such as the Royal Naval College in Portsmouth in front of trainee cadets, who were a bit baffled by the material, and, not for the first time, Uppingham School, 'where the students clearly didn't want to watch it, and had been forced to by their teachers.'[95] In the show, Lucy performed the song 'As Long as He Needs Me' from the musical *Oliver!* as Eva Braun to someone dressed up as Hitler.

Edinburgh wasn't that new an experience, the previous year Lucy had written and performed in a sketch show with her friend Anna Bengo, something she found more personally rewarding than turning up with the Footlights. 'Because there was that thing of, you hadn't earnt the audience yourself. You do feel like they've only come because of the heritage thing. If you do your own show, you've earnt it.'[96] One can argue that the automatic interest from audiences justifies Footlights being in a top venue like the Pleasance at Edinburgh, but some, like Lucy, felt slightly unworthy of it. 'You're just basically slightly nerdy inexperienced teenagers with this unbelievable slot.'[97] It bred animosity and jealousy from some professional comedians who had slogged their guts out on the circuit for years to earn something like that. 'It's crazy that a student company ever got to play that room,' states Matt Green.[98]

And there was still a feeling that the Footlights simply weren't cool, especially around the edges of the fringe. 'We'd all be desperate trying to get into a conversation with all the people who you're idolizing doing their shows,' says Matthew, 'and we would just meet instant kind of, rush away little Footlighter. Go away. So, it was very much knowing your place when you got to Edinburgh.'[99]

16

Emotional Baggage

Matthew, David and Lucy all left Cambridge in 1996, leaving a massive talent vacuum at the centre of the club. But there had always been a sense of care within Footlights for the people coming up. 'There is this sense about; yes, the club will go on and it needs good people to keep it going,' argues Matthew. 'I suppose now, looking back, that's quite sweet isn't it us all thinking that Footlights is this grand institution, when it's just a comedy club. But at the time you're very invested in that, because that was your whole world.'[1]

The new intake was to bring a very different kind of comedy vibe, heavily influenced by what they were all watching on television. 'There was a big sea change,' claims Matthew, 'between the Smashie and Nicey era of slightly large character sketchy comedy and then *The Day Today* and Alan Partridge

FIGURE 16.1 *Jesus College May Ball, 1996. Left to right: Richard Ayoade, John Oliver, Lucy Montgomery and Neda Daneshzadeh. © Lucy Montgomery.*

came in and completely changed how everything was done. I noticed that far more with the generation coming up under me, they were huge Chris Morris obsessives.'[2] Suddenly, there was a move towards making a show that was more connected, more authored, where you felt there was a particular voice behind it all rather than just parachuting into someone's funny monologue or sketch that had done well at smokers. That now seemed less satisfying than making something that meshed more together. Matthew's contemporaries had leant towards traditional sketch comedy, enamoured of things like Python. 'I think the generation that came up after us hated that. Their material was very different. There was a real reaction against sketch comedy.'[3]

Amongst that new intake was John Oliver, an English student at Christ's College, and Richard Ayoade, who studied law at St Catharine's. Matthew first met Richard Ayoade when he auditioned him for a smoker and put him through. 'I found him very funny and that he wrote very similar stuff to me. He felt much more my comic sensibility than the people who I was doing the Footlights show with. The jolly sketch comedy that I was part of I didn't really feel was my thing. That's why I was drawn to Richard and John.'[4]

It was no surprise then that it was Matthew who was asked back to direct the 1997 revue, *Emotional Baggage*. It turned out to be a bad experience. The problem Matthew faced as a director coming in was a lack of autonomy. 'You have to slightly do that job in conjunction with keeping the current committee happy, so you weren't exactly in charge, even though actually you needed to be in charge.'[5] This became a huge issue when it emerged that certain cast members didn't want to tour with some of the others. Matthew found he was in no real position to be able to say, this is the cast, and if you don't like it, you're not touring. 'And that's what I should have done. But what I did was go to the various parties and say, well, he doesn't want to tour with you, blah blah, which made it an absolute nightmare.'[6] In the end, he resigned and the committee took over, then urged Matthew to return where he found himself directing a cast he hadn't really put together. The final cast were Richard Ayoade, Rebecca Morahan, John Oliver, Vicky Shepherd, Jerome Smith and Spencer Brown.

For the duration of rehearsals Matthew stayed, as was tradition, at Harry Porter's house. He'd heard about the archive and spent enjoyable hours looking through it, especially at old reviews. 'The Footlights have always had an absolute slamming in certain papers, and I remember sitting there with Richard Ayoade and rolling around on the floor with laughter just reading out these terrible reviews. I always find bad reviews very funny because it's amusing just how many people get so angry about what essentially is an attempt to make you laugh.'[7] Matthew got to know and like Porter, and that he was always happy to talk about the history. 'We must have seemed almost like kids just going, and you knew Eric Idle did you? But for our generation he was a link to that past.'[8] At this time, Porter was showing the ravages of a recent stroke. 'I think he was a shadow of his exuberant former self,' recalls Spencer Brown. 'But I always found him very nice.'[9]

Emotional Baggage ended up very much influenced not only by the likes of Chris Morris, but also American TV comedy shows, especially *Seinfeld*. 'There was a seriousness to it, in a way,' says Spencer. 'It was like serious comedy, whereas I wanted to be sillier. I liked Python. I liked Spike Milligan. Silly comedians. I wanted to do stuff like that, but it wasn't quite the right vibe at the time.'[10] Very much the focal point of the show was Richard Ayoade and John Oliver, who were in a double act at the time. 'They were the cool kids,' declares Spencer, 'and I think they did feel quite dominant in terms of our year.'[11] Spencer gravitated towards Jerome Smith, who shared a similar sense of humour, and together they wrote a sketch for the revue about someone with a catching disorder where the stakes are raised to teach him to catch. 'And we just ended up throwing bricks at each other.'[12]

As director, Matthew balanced some of the serious material with the sillier stuff, although a line was drawn regarding a song Spencer wrote and performed on his guitar. It was about sitting on an island and being in love with a girl who was on another island, both could see each other but neither could swim. 'The idea was the fish in-between us, I wanted them to come and do a dance routine and then carry me across. Richard and John were like, "We're not doing that!" And I remember a few years later Rich saying, "Do you know, we should have done that, I'm really sorry."'[13] Minus the fish dance, Spencer's song was the only song in the show.

It was a chance encounter with Robert Hewison's book about the Footlights, in Kidderminster Library, that decided Spencer that he wanted to go to Cambridge. 'I read it and went, oh, that's cool. There's a place where all these amazing comedians who I'd admired had gone.'[14] Spencer didn't have it in his head to be a comedian then, as a teenager he did magic shows at school. Even so, when he attended the Societies' Fair he sought out the Footlights stall, manned by David Mitchell. It took a while for him to start applying and attending smokers, suffering as he did, early on, by a lack of confidence. There remained a reassuring and encouraging atmosphere at smokers. For many it was seen as a safe space to experiment and fail in. 'But you felt like you didn't want to fail,' stresses Spencer. 'It's always excruciating if you're telling jokes and it's not working on stage, less so with sketches than stand-up because you've got somebody else there, but you were always trying not to fail.'[15]

Spencer recalls the club room as especially grim and damp, but with a strange sort of charm to it. 'When you had writing sessions, you'd all go down there, and you'd sit in a circle and it felt like your place. Even though it was probably objectively quite grubby, and it was the kind of place where in my first few years of doing stand-up, if I'd turned up I would have gone, urghh, this venue!'[16]

Another reason for feeling low on confidence at the beginning was that Spencer had never performed in a sketch before Footlights, and only written the patter for his magic act. 'That was one of the things that scared me really about joining, sitting down and writing a sketch for the first time.'[17] Although

Spencer got some material into *Rainbow Stranglers,* he missed out on tour shows before being cast in *Emotional Baggage.* 'It did feel like you had to be in with the Footlights people.'[18]

As usual, the revue opened first at the Arts Theatre, which had just undergone a major renovation, thanks to a Lottery grant. Barry Brown, a former Footlights president, was appointed architect of the refurbishment by the trust. It was a wise move. Andrew Blackwood, manager of the Arts Theatre, knew Barry was an architect and that he was the natural person to turn to. It was a huge undertaking, and Barry's connection and emotional ties to the building served as a huge positive. 'It goes back to that first revue night. It was so exciting and such a wonderful time that you really understood what theatre was about.'[19]

As the show made its way to Edinburgh, the message for audiences was not to come expecting to see John Cleese and Fry and Laurie. In a way this played into a prevailing attitude amongst some of the cast to distance themselves from past revues, and even Footlights itself, as if they weren't really part of it. 'At Edinburgh, there was a big attempt to integrate with the wider comedy scene rather than be viewed as a comedy team from Cambridge,' states Spencer.[20]

The big set piece of the show was a physical mime performed by Ayoade and Oliver, of two people being chased, on foot, on skis, in a car, and the music cutting from one crime funk track to another. It was always a crowd pleaser and was very much a foretaste of next year's revue when professional director, Cal McCrystal, was brought in. Now president and vice president respectively, Ayoade and Oliver wanted to try something different and were fans of McCrystal having seen some of his Edinburgh fringe shows; McCrystal later worked with *The Mighty Boosh.* 'His thing was very much a kind of modern clowning style of comedy,' says cast member Matt Green. 'He was probably one of the early pioneers of it on the Fringe. It was quite a lot of physical comedy. Not so much audience interaction but very much playing on what the audience is responding to, not having quite really set dialogue or really set scripts. It's about having fun with the audience and seeing what works and what doesn't. And that was quite a big change.'[21]

One of the conditions of McCrystal directing was that he wanted to hold open auditions and personally select the cast without any committee interference; Ayoade and Oliver were guaranteed to be in it. Still in his first year, Matt Green decided to have a go, not expecting anything, having previously auditioned for the panto and the spring revue without success. However, he was asked to write for the spring revue, which was viewed as a consolation prize for those who didn't get in. To his amazement, McCrystal cast him, along with Richard Thomson, another first year student, making two freshers in the show, which was highly unusual. 'And I think it probably put a few noses out of joint,' claims Matt.[22] Traditionally, people didn't get to do the revue until at least their second year. And there were good reasons for that, they had more experience for a start, and it was a bit unfair for those who had worked hard in the club and done many performances not to get the chance to do that big tour show and all the opportunities that came with it.

Growing up, Matt often heard his parents talking about their student days and going off to the Edinburgh Fringe, where one year they caught *The Cellar Tapes* and subsequently watched as the cast became famous. Matt loved watching sitcoms as a kid, Fry and Laurie, and *Blackadder*, before becoming a fan of the Chris Morris, Armando Iannucci-style of comedy. He enjoyed performing and writing at school, and his drama teacher encouraged him to put on a comedy play in his final year. Applying for university, Cambridge was top of his list. 'I guess partly because I had this thinking in my head, there's a comedy pedigree there and that might be a fun thing.'[23]

Studying English at Christ's, there was an induction day and John Oliver came to give a talk about the course and other things, and mentioned Footlights, saying that if anyone was interested in getting involved there was a thing called 'the virgin smoker'. In that first week Matt also got friendly with someone at his college who shared the same kind of humour, and they decided to write a sketch together and performed it at the virgin smoker.

The revue of 1998 was called *Between a Rock and a Hard Place* and was very different from what had come before. 'It wasn't wordy,' says Matt. 'Not a lot of one-liners. It was very much devised and built from improvisation rather than built from writing. We were all basically playing characters who sort of remained the same throughout the show, because they were our clowns.'[24] Because he looked the youngest, Matt was cast as a kind of work experience boy who had snuck into the show and was given all the rubbish jobs. In one sketch he was thrown around as a dead acrobat. The idea was that a member of an acrobatics team had died just before they are about to go on stage and they decide to carry on with the show. This was indicative of the kind of physical comedy that was a feature of the show, rather than a lot of witty banter. There was also a lot of music. In a fashion show parody, the cast paraded around in ridiculous costumes.

There was only one woman in the cast, Alex Bonham, who, in essence, was the presenter of the show and did a few monologues. There was a moment when the show suddenly stopped and Richard Ayoade came on to do a sorry-something's-gone-wrong spiel for five minutes. During the interval, John Oliver chatted to the audience, in a way that was not totally removed from his future stand-up style. There was a loose concept that knitted all these bits together, with the show presenting its own TV station and each sketch being a different channel. They also enacted a series of film trailers, using lots of props and costumes changes. The show ended with a Titanic joke and Matt's character drowning. At his funeral the cast let off fireworks made from tennis balls which were thrown across the stage at each other. 'The idea was that it was silly and joyful and a bit mad,' says Matt. 'And that was I think very unusual for Footlights. It was not what people expected. And that's partly why it got a good reaction. And because John and

Richard were very funny. They were obviously stars.'[25] For example, they were already chasing agents at Edinburgh. For Matt, being around all that made him think, for the first time, maybe I can do this as a career. 'It boosted my confidence. And that is what being in the Footlights does.'[26]

Cal McCrystal returned as director for the following year's revue, *This Way Up*, and again held open auditions. 'Again, I think that did definitely put a few noses out of joint,' claims Matt. 'Because there were some people who weren't massive fans of his style, who were more fans of the more written, witty sketch style, so they ended up doing their own show in Edinburgh that year.'[27]

McCrystal wanted Matt and Richard Thomson to return and once again cast a first-year student in Naomi Kerbel. 'And there was resentment, understandable resentment, that a first year was going in,' says Naomi.[28] Studying Anglo Saxon Norse and Celtic, Naomi had won a choral scholarship to Magdalene College and had no problems being the only girl in the cast. 'I found it an equal environment.'[29] If anything, she felt more disadvantaged by her lack of writing experience, which is the reason why she hardly did any smokers, finding them very exposing. 'That really catered to the writers. But in the show Cal never made me feel like it was necessary to write because I had stuff that the other cast members didn't have, I had the pedigree of the West End, I could read music, and I could sing really well.'[30]

From the age of six, Naomi was a child actor, appearing in the West End cast of *Les Misérables*, the National Theatre and on children's television. Her mother had been a student at Cambridge and Naomi got to know about the Footlights because one of her childhood idols, Emma Thompson, went there. 'And so, my ambition always was to be in the Footlights.'[31]

According to Matt, *This Way Up* was less of a success than its predecessor, mainly due to scheduling. McCrystal was busy on other projects this time and so wasn't always around, leaving assistants to sometimes handle the work, meaning there was less time to prepare and put the whole show together. Nevertheless, Naomi enjoyed rehearsals and working with the director. 'Such fun, such joy in the rehearsal room. Everything had to be fast, Cal doesn't have a very long attention span, so everything moved on very quickly. Really good fun.'[32] And the cast worked well together. Matt and Robin French were very much their own team. 'They were Footlights aficionados,' says Naomi, who found herself gravitating more towards Finnian O'Neill. 'He was more of a serious actor who could be funny and silly.'[33]

Curiously, Robin French had never heard of the Footlights until he arrived in Fresher's Week, 'though obviously I had heard of a lot of its alumni. I was a comedy fan. I'd already dipped my toe in comedy writing at school in Birmingham, writing silly articles for the school newspaper – so Footlights seemed like something I could have a bash at.'[34] That school newspaper stuff was written with friend Kieron Quirke, with whom Robin later wrote the BBC sitcom *Cuckoo*. 'Our articles were shameless rip-offs of

The Day Today – we were in love with Chris Morris's mangled, surreal idiom.'[35] Morris's influence over factions of the Footlights was undeniable, and Robin sensed on arriving at the club that there was an unacknowledged ideological battle between a sort of traditional 'Radio 4 comedy' voice and those more aligned with say Chris Morris or Newman and Baddiel's comedy as the new rock 'n' roll, where there was an attempt to be hip in the kind of funny material being put out. 'I suppose that was partly about pushing the envelope. I tried to do that sometimes, but looking back, so much stuff was extremely derivative. I suppose that is what happens when you're starting out at something.'[36]

At an early smoker, Robin watched Richard Ayoade and John Oliver performing, 'in their student pomp', and remembers thinking, oh brilliant, you just do three years of Footlights and you end up as funny as those guys. Not necessarily, as it happens. Robin already had a strong intuition that writing was something he wanted to explore, as for performing, he had no reason to believe he would be any good at it, and so was pleasantly surprised when he did well in his first smoker. 'It was thrilling to have written something very quickly, then for it to work with an audience.'[37] Even so, the more he performed the more he noticed those select few performers who just had that hard-to-describe extra something others just lacked, and so ultimately he stuck with writing.

Robin was studying Italian literature at Selwyn College and thought, back then, how similar Footlights was to a Renaissance Italian court. 'The ambition, the factionalism and political skulduggery, but most of all the highly creative mix of collaboration and competition. We were all co-evolving in our style – being inspired by each other, by older students, by the Edinburgh Festival, by new TV comedy. It all felt so alive and fertile – it had such a charge. I have never found it surprising that Footlights created so many successful comedians and writers.'[38]

Diversity, however, was still an issue. Richard Ayoade was vice president in Robin's first year, but there was a distinct lack of representation from people of colour. 'Although it didn't feel wildly different from the wider Cambridge student population,' confirms Robin, 'that is, very little diversity. Footlights felt very male dominated. A particular kind of male funniness was seen as the default setting – though that was definitely much discussed, and there were a lot of great female Footlights comedians in every year.'[39] Robin was friends with Beth Morrey and Lydia Aers who were both vice president during his time.

The emphasis with *This Way Up* was once again clowning and physical comedy. 'This was the second year that Cal McCrystal directed the revue,' states Robin. 'His was rather a daring proposition, to do Footlights shows eschewing clever wordplay or clever concepts, and to try to find laughs in more clown-inspired ways. It was a really fascinating upside-down way to think about what we did, because most Footlights people were all about brainy laughs.'[40] Each cast member was given a certain clown type to play.

'I was told that my comic persona was to be impish and mischievous,' recalls Robin, 'which was maybe code for "annoying."'[41]

The setting was a cruise ship with the cast playing members of staff. In one sketch Naomi is a masseuse offering Richard Thomson a massage. 'But I relax him so much in the chair with the kind of preamble that he falls asleep. I feel like I should complete the massage, only he's like this lifeless dummy and I'm trying to get him on the table and get into these ridiculous physical positions. The whole show was very silly, very good fun, nothing heavy or hard.'[42] There was a Lara Croft parody, and a sketch where the cast took on the role of the Spice Girls. One sequence took place underwater with the stage in a black out and the cast wearing fluorescent costumes as underwater creatures like octopi doing a crazy dance.

The show was heavily music orientated. This being 1999, the idea was to perform a pastiche of a song from every decade of the 20th century. 'Some of them were quite fun,' says Matt, 'but I think the show itself slightly sagged under the weight of its own structure. There were slightly too many things trying to happen within it and we weren't quite sure how to make it all work. It was OK, but it didn't do as well in Edinburgh, and we got a couple of nasty reviews.'[43] Robin is of the opinion that the show, probably inevitably, 'wound up being in the shadow of the previous year, which had had the Ayoade/Oliver double act.'[44]

At the time a news crew from Channel 4 was following the cast around the Festival and wanted to film their reaction to the bad notices. They found a newsagent and Matt went in, coming out with a paper, and being a fairly serious and matter-of-fact type of guy, said, 'Fair enough, it's fine.' Channel 4, however, wanted a much more emotional reaction, an 'Oh my god, it's a disaster' type thing, and asked him to do it again.

In his first two years, Matt had been very involved with Footlights but still managed to do well on his course. Going into his third year, his director of studies informed him, 'All this Footlights stuff you're doing is all well and good, but remember the third year is the one that really counts. You've got to make sure you do well in that.' Matt recalls distinctly having the thought, umm, no. I'm not going to. 'Because, actually, what I was doing in Footlights was more important for my career.'[45] Indeed, he had already secured an agent and was occasionally travelling to London for auditions. 'And that gave me a real feeling of, I'm already kind of in this world and let's see where I can go with it.'[46] Of course, observes Matt, this varied depending on the person. 'Some people were very into Footlights and then suddenly when exam term came, they disappeared and they were just totally doing exams. Everyone understood that.'[47]

Elected president in his final year, Matt's most far-reaching decision was to get rid of the club room. Over the last few years, it had fallen into disrepair. 'It was a fucking mess,' declares Matthew Holness. 'By the time we got there it just became a bin, essentially. It was disgusting with spilt beer and rubbish.'[48] One novel feature, however, was a disused fridge full of discarded scripts that went back several years. The club room was no longer being used very much. The virgin smoker was held there, along with auditions, but for the most part the ADC Theatre had taken over as the place where most of the activity happened. Certainly no one met at the club room socially anymore, much preferring to go to a pub or the ADC bar. When Matt began to investigate the club room, he learnt there was some kind of rent issue. 'Essentially the club room was costing money and since it wasn't really being used, we gave it back to the Union, who wanted to develop it into a space anyway. It was a sad moment in many ways because it felt like giving up a place with some history. But it would have cost a lot of money to revamp it into something that was worth keeping. And Footlights just didn't have that money.'[49] Instead, a deal was made with Corpus Christi to allow the club put on their smokers at the playroom, which was a medium-sized space that was Cambridge's primary Fringe space, showcasing a variety of productions.

Another decision Matt made as president was not to appear in that year's tour show, which went by the name of *Sensible Haircut*, and instead direct it. 'I wanted to reintroduce the idea of getting students to direct it again because it felt like we'd had a few years of getting somebody else to do it.'[50] It was also to have a narrative structure, 'like a romantic comedy type film with five main characters', says Matt,[51] with lots of elements that tied up at the end. It began with a crazy nonsensical scene and then ended with that same scene only now it made sense after seeing the whole show. And it was written, rather than devised out of the rehearsal process, as had been the case with the two previous shows. Two of the cast, Kevin Baker and John Finnemore, were in a comedy act together and very much into the more traditional style of Footlights sketches. Matt also wanted two women in the cast this time and brought in Marianne Levy and Victoria Morris. The final cast member was a fresher, Ed Weeks, who had played Sherlock Holmes opposite Matt's Watson in the panto.

The Holmes panto was written by John Finnemore and Owen Powell and managed to be an amusing Holmesian parody while remaining true to certain pantomime tropes, such as having a dame, which, incidentally, was played by a woman (Tamsin Hewett), and instead of a pantomime cow there was a panto hound of the Baskervilles. John enjoyed writing it but had a problem with the technicians who always latched onto one thing they found technically interesting and spent most of the money and their time on that. The previous year, on *Sinbad*, which John wrote with Kevin Baker and Robin French, it was a roast pig that fired sweets out into the audience when you turned the handle. In Holmes, Moriarty's lair was inside Big Ben. 'It was only in two scenes,' recalls John, 'but the techies got very excited about being able to do all the clockwork mechanisms and spent all their time on that to the extent that the flat that was flown in every now and again depicting 221b Baker Street was unfinished on the first night.'[52]

John Finnemore grew up watching Fry and Laurie, Victoria Wood and *The Day Today* on TV and wanted to do Footlights at Cambridge if he could, targeting the virgin smoker first. 'This was in the days when they used to pin the cast lists up on the notice board outside the ADC Theatre. I was at Peterhouse, at the other end of town, and I remember cycling up and my delight to see that I was going to be in the virgin smoker.'[53] Then later, when he was on the committee, everyone was wracking their brains how to get more people to audition for the virgin smoker, as it was a fallow year. 'And I realized, anyone who turned up and who wasn't mad got in.'[54] It was at that virgin smoker that John and Kevin Baker first met; Baker had planned to come along with someone else and when that person ditched at the last minute improvised a new routine on the spot.

When John first arrived, Chris Morris was still a big influence around Footlights, as was, interestingly, a voice from the past, that of Stephen Fry. 'People were either doing their edgy stuff in a Chris Morris voice or their cosy stuff in a Stephen Fry voice.'[55] This mirrored the era when people sided either with the silly, surreal humour of Python, or the witty word play of Fry and Laurie. In some years, the two camps were quite distinctive, with each almost looking down their noses at the other, with the highbrow witty camp saying, what a bunch of silliness with their big silly voices, and then the big silly voices saying, highbrow group take themselves far too seriously.

Others preferred not to do their comedy with Footlights at all, such as a comedy troupe called the Hollow Men who met as students at Cambridge but didn't go down the Footlights route, similarly Fat Fat Pope. 'We did feel unfashionable while I was there,' admits John. 'But I don't think that particularly bothered us.'[56]

The fact that Footlights was heavily writer-centric suited John, who had always written and hoped to make a career from it, but he also got to enjoy performing, too. 'What I loved best about Footlights was the smoker system where you're forced to do a new thing every fortnight, and then you get to perform it, and you get to see other people and what they're doing and what works for them and what doesn't and what works for you and what doesn't, then go away and try again. And that was great for me in making me churn through all the bad writing you must do before you start getting good.'[57]

By his second term, John had been asked on the committee, and by his second year was secretary, taking minutes at all the meetings, 'and trying to put jokes in them.'[58] When Matt became president, John was his vice president. Despite all this activity, including involvement in two spring revues, John had tried in vain to get into both previous tour shows. Director Cal McCrystal's desire for a more physical type of comedian ruled him out. *Sensible Haircut* suited John's more traditional style, although its narrative structure was an issue for him. 'It was a decent show, my regret is that we slightly fell between two stools, between going for a story, or stick to our tradition, our strength, and do sketch blackout sketch blackout. We tried to do a story but we didn't fully commit and so when there was a good bit from someone's act or a good sketch that had come up in the writing process, we'd just crowbar it in, which is always a mistake because it makes people enjoy the good sketch less and enjoy the story less.'[59]

Something John always looked forward to during the tour was arriving in a new town and reading the local papers in the morning with Kevin Baker and picking out something funny or interesting to bring up in the show. 'And it went down well because people could tell that it had been written that day and was just for them and we could never do it again.'[60] One performance took place at an air force base near Cambridge, it was their annual ball and the audience were pretty pissed by the time they went on. 'We were crashing and burning,' recalls John, 'but earlier we'd got hold of their base newsletter and Kevin and I did some stuff out of it and they loved it.'[61]

During his three years at Cambridge, thanks to meeting other like-minded people who seemed to think a career in comedy was a reasonable ambition to attempt after university, John's desire to do comedy turned into a belief. He had enough experience now and sufficient sketches to put on his own show at the Edinburgh Fringe, or send off stuff he'd written. Just to try something and see what happens. The classic and familiar route that had worked for so many past Footlights, of walking into a job at the BBC especially, thanks to the old boys' network, had evaporated long ago. And it was no longer the case that producers turned up at revue shows anymore. 'I think if anything we were a bit out of fashion in 2000,' admits John. 'I sent my scripts off to all the sketch shows I could think of, but I never said, you'll know me from such things as Cambridge Footlights, because I don't think that was the selling point.'[62]

17

Far Too Happy

It had been twenty years since *The Cellar Tapes* won the inaugural Perrier comedy award at the Edinburgh Festival. No one expected them to win it then, and certainly no Footlights revue team going up to the Fringe in the interim years expected much either. 'It felt then like there really wasn't a chance,' says Spencer Brown from 1997's revue.[1] On the positive side, at least the anti-Oxbridge rancour had mostly subsided. 'It was still there a bit,' claims Matt Green. 'There was still a bit of, well, just because you came from Cambridge don't think you can get a gig. And you had to prove yourself. But it wasn't quite – fuck you, you went to Cambridge.'[2]

The team behind the 2001 revue, *Far Too Happy*, travelled to Edinburgh without too much hope, either, except that they knew they had a pretty good show. 'I think we had the sense that people were quite surprised and thrilled by it,' recalls cast member Sophie Winkleman. 'We did a trial run in London and it was such a good energy from the audience, we thought we had a chance. I think we did feel very confident.'[3]

Sophie never expected to be in the show in the first place. She had worked before with Phil Breen, co-director with Owen Powell, in her second year in a play at Queens' College and attended the auditions. 'And then you have that moment when you go up to the ADC notice board with a ball of anticipation and dread in your stomach and I saw my name and I was just utterly thrilled. It was the apex of everything I wanted to do at Cambridge.'[4]

As a teenager Sophie was in the National Youth Theatre which gave her the desire to carry on acting when she went to university. 'I chose Cambridge because of the Footlights. All my heroes and heroines had been in the Footlights, particularly Emma Thompson.'[5] When she arrived, Sophie involved herself in plays at the ADC, but in her first term she performed stand-up at a Footlights smoker. 'It was a very good experience because I was terrified.'[6] For her it was a personal challenge, thinking it was the hardest thing a performer could do. 'I had it in my daft, studenty, bold, silly mind that I had to just try stand-up. If you get a few laughs, you're alright, you just think, OK, I've done it, and I didn't put myself through it again.'[7]

In *Far Too Happy*, Sophie joined a cast of five men, Ed Jaspers, Tim Key, Day Macaskill, James Morris and Mark Watson. She wasn't bothered or enraged about being the only woman. As far as she was concerned, Footlights should be a meritocracy, with the best being chosen regardless of sex. 'I'd had such a horrible time at girls' school, I was so thrilled to be in a long tour with a group of boys. I think I was deeply unfeminist about it and thrilled that there were no other chicks in it.'[8] And she very much became one of the lads. 'Which was so fun, all of them were very adorably, it's such a boring word, but respectful and unpervy, they were like a gang of brothers.'[9]

Far Too Happy had a theme, of a kind, or at least a link, and that was loneliness. All the main characters were faint oddballs, disconnected and malfunctioning. 'And Phil managed to string it all together to make it funny,' says Sophie.[10] Early in rehearsals, Mark Watson came up with the idea of having a Welsh Grim Reaper. Everyone liked it so much that Death became a character throughout the show. Striding onto the stage at the beginning in a dark hood, with menacing music playing and thunder and lightning, all quite bleak and horror film, and then the lights came up and Watson took his hood off and said, in his lilting Welsh, 'Hello.'

There were other linking characters, too. In a series of monologues Tim Key played a lonely loser trying unsuccessfully to fit in, while Ed Jaspers was a taxi driver on his own, quite isolated in his taxi. 'Phil was quite a visionary,' asserts Sophie, 'and it wasn't as cosy and sketchy as it usually is. And we had brilliant music throughout.'[11] This wasn't in the form of the usual Footlight ditties, but a familiar soundtrack. The show kicked off with Iggy Pop's 'The Passenger'. 'A lot of it was quite cinematic,' recalls Sophie. 'It was all quite graphic and quite unusual. It wasn't the usual sweet middle-class thing. It was quite arresting.'[12]

Sophie involved herself very much in the writing process. For her, rehearsals and the actual creation of the show was the most fun. 'It was a mass of productivity in the beginning, we were all like just bubbling volcanoes full of material. It was so exciting.'[13] Sophie and Day Macaskill appeared in one sketch together about a sarcastic married couple. 'It sounds very obvious and clichéd now, but they were very delightful, very middle class, very polite and utterly vile to each other, in a very polite, lovely way. And that always went down incredibly well.'[14]

At most places on tour the reception was good and before Edinburgh the cut version was given a trial run at the Canal Theatre in Maida Vale, for family and friends. For Sophie, it was one of the best performances of the tour. Unexpectedly, at Edinburgh, they ended up nominated for Best Newcomer at the Perrier comedy awards. This was the first time in twenty years that the troupe had received any kind of recognition at the Festival. As a result, they played one night at the Fortune theatre in London.

The success of *Far Too Happy*, for Sophie, had much to do with the fact it was a very inclusive show. Both directors, for example, came from state schools, as did Tim Key; Mark Watson was a grammar school boy. 'And the main characters throughout the show weren't an elitist bunch of knobs at all. It was quite an authentically inclusive play from authentically diverse performers, and I think people could feel the integrity of that and the realism of it. So, it wasn't the usual posh Cambridge twats who people would associate with the Footlights.'[15]

Far Too Happy's solid run at Edinburgh lent a modicum of prestige to the following year's revue, *Today of All Days*, but not enough, it appears, to halt a steady decline. 'The appetite for some Cambridge students doing their revue in Edinburgh was slightly fading,' claims cast member Tom Bell. 'And costs for everything were mounting. We still did a big tour, but it was becoming harder and harder for whoever was booking it. It wasn't as easy to play fifty dates with a student sketch show. We had a great time but it was on the wane.'[16]

It did seem that this was a period of change, the fact that the club room had not been replaced for example. 'There was a sense that the club was homeless,' says Tom. 'And there was a sort of counter-culture movement where Footlights was deemed to be not very cool, and that the pantos were lame. There was a sketch group called Fat Fat Pope which were like the anti-Footlights.'[17] This group consisted of members intent on rebelling from within, while at the same time remaining broadly on side. 'It felt like there were two gangs who got on perfectly well,' observes Tom,[18] who did a spring revue with them. Their humour was never really that edgy, although in that spring revue there was a desire for weirder and off the wall humour. 'The most controversial thing they did,' Tom recalls, 'was a sketch at a urinal and they were going, we should just actually piss on the stage, right. And the rest of us were like, er no.'[19] At the time, a television crew from Japan was making a documentary and following some of the members of the revue around, including Tom and Alex Horne, later creator of the TV series *Taskmaster*. The Japanese couldn't get their heads around why these bright young people were at one of the most prestigious universities in the world and being ludicrously silly.

The prevailing attitude in Footlights regarding comedy remained more or less traditional, and that certainly suited Tom, who had grown up listening to his father's collection of comedy records, like The Goons and Peter Cook, before gravitating to watching *Blackadder* and Fry and Laurie, which got him interested in wanting to do comedy. He went on a day trip to Cambridge organized by his comprehensive school in Nottinghamshire with the six other students who had Oxbridge ambitions. 'I couldn't believe it really, that a place like this existed. My history teacher said, "If you want to get into comedy, this is where you should go." '[20] Tom began to join the dots between some of his favourite comedians and Footlights and was eager to join. 'Everybody thinks Footlights is this closed off, elitist thing, but it's not at all, everything is open auditions and the very first thing you do is the virgin smoker. So, I popped along to that and got hooked. It was genuinely a no fail. You'd bump into a lot of like-minded people there and it's like, I'm not the only weirdo who listens to old comedy tapes and can quote all of *Not Only … But Also*.'[21] At the start of term, the previous year's tour show would return to the ADC for several performances. 'And you're thinking, this is where I could be in three years.'[22]

The smokers at which Tom began to perform regularly saw monologues, sketches and some stand-up from the likes of Alex Horne and Mark Watson. In his second year, Tom was asked to be junior archivist which put him in direct contact with Harry Porter, who still wanted production posters sent to him, along with the programme, flyers and press clippings. Like many before him, Tom enjoyed looking through the archive and recalls coming across a poster signed by Mike Myers. The Canadian comic had performed years before at the club room with Neil Mullarkey. 'And he had written a recipe on the back of the poster on how to make the best Canadian popcorn.'[23]

At the time, Tom had struck up a double act with Ed Weeks, and was vice president to his president. As well as keeping a steady rudder on matters, they came up with the idea of creating a website to keep members up to date with news and featuring archive material. Attempts were also made to find a new club room. 'In the end we realized it wasn't the end of the world not having a club room.'[24] The ADC remained the place for members to gather and shows were regularly put on there, as well as the playroom at Corpus Christi. And there was a desire to get more women involved in Footlights. 'Women were very welcome,' stresses Tom, 'it was just hard to convince them to have a go. More men wanted to do it than girls. So, we were always, like, a funny woman, thank God!'[25] One woman determined to try was Ruth Pickett, although her immediate reaction to the suggestion by her sixth form teachers that she apply to Cambridge was – no way. 'I'd never been there but my perception was a load of poshos poncing about, don't want to go there. Then I went to look round Cambridge and was just completely bowled over by how beautiful it was.'[26] She got into Emmanuel reading English. Ruth had always written stuff as a child, then at her school in Ilkley she did satirical sketches for assemblies. A friend also happened to be the younger brother of Matt Green and mentioned he was in this comedy thing called the Footlights. 'And I think that influenced why I wanted to go, oh that sounds cool.'[27]

When she arrived, Ruth discovered there were only a handful of women taking an active role in the club and even fewer performing or appearing at smokers. Many had simply concluded that it wasn't for them because there was very little female representation. That didn't stop Ruth trying out for a smoker. 'It came down to my personality. I've always been a bit singular, and an only child, and always did my own thing regardless of whether anyone else was doing it. So, it didn't faze me that there weren't any girls. And my friends in sixth form had been mostly boys, and so at the time I felt like I could be one of them. I don't think I missed a smoker for two years.'[28]

Directing that year's tour show was Paul King, who had graduated from St Catharine's College in 1999 and directed the Perrier award winning Garth Marenghi show at the 2001 Edinburgh Festival. He later worked on the subsequent TV transfer and *The Mighty Boosh*, so he was something of a catch and added some kudos. Still in her first year, Ruth auditioned for King and won a place in the cast of *Today of All Days*, as did another fresher by the name of Dan Stevens. Like Ruth, Stevens had done lots of smokers and it was obvious to the whole cast he was going to do well in the industry. 'He was already a very good actor,' declares Ruth.[29]

It was always assumed that third years got preferential treatment over first and second year students when it came to the tour show, and so Ruth was surprised to be given the nod. 'Also, at that time, it was not even an unspoken rule, it was a spoken rule, that only one woman would get in. It was always, who's going to be that one girl?'[30] Much more egalitarian was the open writing sessions. 'Anybody who wanted to come down and write sketches, great,' confirms Tom. 'You'd come down and throw some ideas around, go to the pub with some people, write and come back.'[31] *Today of All Days* took place in a pub. The roads are closed and it's a blustery night. Various people arrive as a guest to the bar and tell their story, with the other cast members as characters in the tale. Ed Weeks, as the barman, was the narrative thread throughout the show. There were lots of visual jokes and elements of surrealism. One skit Tom wrote and performed was a drama teacher trying to get his pupils to really feel the emotion of *Romeo and Juliet* to the extent that ultimately, he kills one of them.

In Edinburgh, they once again resided at the Pleasance, going on before the evening headliner, Noel Fielding, and picked up the usual mixed notices. 'There was definitely an anti-Footlights attitude,' Ruth recalls. 'People were saying, I don't want to come and see you lot, you're all posh kids, and feeling a bit down because, I'm not.'[32] Afterwards, Tom and Ed Weeks tried to set up an American tour but with no luck. One positive thing did come out of it for Ruth when she managed to secure an agent on the back of her Edinburgh appearance. It capped off a wonderful first year. Her next two years were less enjoyable. Tom and Ed were gone and she experienced what she describes as a, 'toxic' atmosphere. 'It felt like it was still acceptable to be sexist then, and to say sexist things. I distinctly remember we were talking about whether Sarah Solemani should be on the committee and this person said, well, women aren't usually funny, but she's quite funny so I suppose we should let her on.'[33] There was also a hard competitive edge to everything, and for Ruth a lot of unnecessary pressure heaped on people. 'If you weren't funny, you may as well be dead. If everything that you do and say is not the funniest funny thing then not only do we not like your comedy, but we also hate you. And the way that some people were spoken about, who came to audition and who they didn't think were funny enough, it was very snidey.'[34]

Even when Ruth got on the committee in her final year, one of the very few women who did, she faced the ordeal of having to try out a sketch in front of a line of the guys, and to their stony-faced reaction seeing whether they thought it was funny enough to be in a smoker. 'It felt very uninclusive.'[35] She did write that year's panto, a modern take on *Alice in Wonderland*, with Alice working in the Co-op. As her boss, Ruth cast Simon Bird (of *The Inbetweeners* fame) in his first role in a Footlights production. She was also involved in organizing a tribute evening for Harry Porter, which was put on at the Arts Theatre in honour of the former archivist who had died in December 2003. Former alumni such as David Mitchell, Richard Ayoade, Robert Webb, Matthew Holness and Tony Slattery showed up to perform old sketches, and messages were read out from those unable to attend. The vast Footlights archive that Harry kept in his house was removed and taken to the University Library, where it remains.

The current generation of Footlights also performed, and someone suggested that they put on an old song called 'No More Women,' the lyrics of which are seared on Ruth's memory: 'There are no more women in the footlights club, there are no more women here./They were all very pleasant little girls to know, so we tried them out last year./Last year they were a flop, so we thought we'd better stop, so there are no more women here.' And it was performed in the traditional *Cheer-Oh Cambridge!*-style, as though it was all wonderfully ironic.

Another of the organizers of that show was Stefan Golaszewski, who appeared in the 2003 revue. Golaszewski was also involved in the setting up of an award in memory of Harry Porter. The panto, the spring revue and the tour show stood as the main yearly Footlight productions, but there was nothing that represented actual narrative writing. And so, the Harry Porter Prize for a one-hour comic play came into being and it continues to this day. People submit their play, a judge picks the winner and then that play is performed at the ADC. The first year there were just three entrants but since then it has become well established. 'The competition forces people to understand and play with narrative,' contests Stefan.[36] If somebody is especially good at writing comic narrative, previously there hadn't been much use for it in Footlights, since writing monologues or sketches is a very different skill set. 'And because nobody puts on sketch shows anymore,' says Stefan, 'really the competition is quite useful experience and training for people long term if that's what they want to do.'[37]

Stefan didn't necessarily think he'd end up in comedy but was interested in doing plays and acting and knew anecdotally that there was a lot of creative opportunity at Cambridge and that the Footlights was a big part of that. But Stefan found going to Cambridge quite a complicated matter, essentially from a class perspective. 'I was from a lower middle-class family, working class background, immigrant background. My father was the first one to go to university from our wider family, and there was nobody from my family in the creative industries. And so going to Cambridge, I felt quite different to some of the other people there. It was all new to me. And I approached Footlights with a kind of fuck you, poshos, attitude.'[38] In the end he was to find that Footlights was far from elitist. 'But that was my childish assumption.'[39]

It was with that attitude that Stefan approached the virgin smoker determined to annoy as many people as possible. He did this by performing the most offensive monologue he could come up with. 'I remember that it started with my saying, "I'm Stefan and I'm a mother fucker. I've been fucking my own mother now for thirteen years."'[40] It carried on it that vein culminating in the revelation that his mother was dead. 'It was literally me thinking of how many taboos I could break just to see what would happen, as an experiment for myself. I wasn't interested in doing comedy. I was interested in pissing everybody off. And amazingly they all laughed, which I really wasn't ready for.'[41] That got him thinking – this is actually quite fun and interesting – and so he decided to take it a bit more seriously and do more smokers, but continuing to experiment with dark and weird humour that didn't find favour with some people, all the time seeing himself very much as an outsider.

It was James Morris, then president, and a fan of what Stefan was doing, who made the decision to put him on the committee, 'Because if I don't,' said Morris, 'then they're going to stop you doing smokers.' Ironically, Stefan ended up organizing them. 'And by doing that I was able to slowly change the direction of Footlights away from some of the more traditional stuff that had been going on towards what I considered a more contemporary form of comedy based on the sort of stuff that we were all watching on telly, things like *The Office* and *The Royle Family*. Before then I still felt it was sort of stuck in the Monty Python/Goodies kind of comedy. And I did notice as the club moved in that direction the audience figures really went up.'[42] Stefan's impression when he first arrived was that audience figures were quite low, both on the tour and within Cambridge itself; the general feeling was: Don't bother going to see the Footlights, it's shit. 'By the time I left it was really picking up and then after us, with guys like Jonny Sweet, Nick Mohammed and Simon Bird, it was through the roof.'[43]

When Stefan became president in his final year he took charge of the tour show. *Non-Sexual Kissing* was set in a large house divided into flats and was essentially a series of playlets. Stefan, for example, played a man whose wife had dumped him for his identical twin and was trying to process it with a kind of fury. Coming in as joint directors were Tim Key and Mark Watson. Key lived in Cambridge and Watson was still around because his girlfriend at the time was at the university. 'And we all knew each other and got on,' says Stefan,[44] who appeared with Tom Basden, Lloyd Thomas and Jot Davies.

As usual, there was just the one woman in the cast, Emily Howes. When people heard that Emily intended to study at Cambridge the first thing anybody asked her about was the Footlights. 'It seemed unbearably cool, which I obviously wanted to be.'[45] The fastest way in was still the virgin smoker, where Emily showed up to perform something a friend helped her write. 'It was excruciating hearing people die through the wall of the playroom, waiting in the corridor in a state of pure, clammy horror. I wonder, looking back, if there could have been a gentler way to allow curious teenagers to start writing comedy. Perhaps this is why the Footlights retains its reputation, though, in part. It was a lions' den.'[46]

Emily remembers her friend saying at the time that women didn't get up and do the virgin smoker, and that she should go for it for that reason. 'There were a couple of women there, but it's true that the feeling was very male, both in terms of the people running it, but also the atmosphere. It wasn't the most welcoming atmosphere to arrive into. I think that changed even during my three years there, but the kind of confidence you need to stand up and try to make people laugh was, then, not so easy for women.'[47] Women did audition for the panto and the tour shows, perhaps, as Emily reasons, because it felt safer in that kind of group work. Otherwise, she found the club, 'brilliantly democratic because you had to put yourself out there and live or die by your material, and nothing else mattered. Not, in theory, your gender or your background. There wasn't a class snobbery in Footlights that I recall. No one in Footlights cared who your parents were.'[48]

Emily respected her male colleagues in the revue, although she would have liked to have had another woman in the cast, just to dilute a little of what was an overwhelmingly male environment, given the fact both directors were also men. 'Overall, I'd say there was definitely, among the crowd attracted to Footlights, a large quota of edgily ambition-fuelled men, but there was also space for the quirky, the shy and the thoughtful. Most of the men were lovely. But it was a male space, and you knew it.'[49]

It was very much a group of writer-performers. Interestingly, given that Emily went on to become a novelist, she felt too intimidated to do a lot of writing herself. This had always been an issue; one everyone was conscious of. 'I don't know how much of it was unconscious sexism or conscious sexism,' argues William Sutcliffe, 'I think the men took over the writing a lot. I think it took extra mental strength for a woman to fight to the front of what was a bit of a boys' club.'[50] It was only when Emily left university that she began to gain enough confidence to really write on her own and find, as she terms it, a 'strong' voice. 'If I hadn't been in Footlights, though, and tried right from the very beginning to face my fears in that world, I might not have thought to write at all.'[51]

Given the somewhat darker nature of *Non-Sexual Kissing*, and its narrative structure, Stefan was pleasantly surprised and heartened that most audiences took to it. 'I seem to remember it going down better on tour than it did in Edinburgh, because in Edinburgh there was a kind of, oh God, here's the Footlights. They're not as good as they used to be. All of that. While on tour people were just a bit readier to give us the benefit of the doubt.'[52]

The following year's revue followed very much the same thematic direction as *Non-Sexual Kissing* and was almost a piece of theatre rather than a sketch show. *Beyond a Joke* was set in and around a remote snowbound community and featured a gallery of assorted grotesques and social misfits. The cast included Nick Mohammed, Sarah Solemani and Jonny Sweet. The tour of 2005's show, *Under the Blue, Blue Moon*, featuring

FIGURE 17.1 *The 2005 Footlights tour performing at the Edinburgh Fringe.* ©
John Linford.

Simon Bird and Nadia Kamil, had a distinctly surreal tone revolving around a coma patient who flits between real life and a dream-like state.

Having in recent years weaved their ideas into some sort of narrative, the 2006 revue, *Niceties*, offered a back-to-basics approach of just random sketches. Helen Cripps was in her second year at Homerton on an English and drama course when she auditioned, convinced that she wouldn't get in. 'Because I was like, well they only ever have one girl in these shows, don't they.'[53] And that girl, everyone assumed, including Helen, would be Tiani Ghosh, then in her third year, so it was her last chance to do it. There was much surprise when both got in. 'And I was like – two women!' says Helen. 'How strange. Now I'm like, obviously it should be at least two, if not three if you're having five people in the cast.'[54]

Helen grew up watching Monty Python because her parents had all the videos. 'And I watched *Fawlty Towers* on repeat.'[55] When she learnt a lot of the Pythons came from Footlights that became her main motivation for wanting to go to Cambridge, even though there was really no history of students from her state school going to Oxbridge. Her first term passed by in a bit of a blur. 'By the second term I realized what was going on. I think that's the case with a lot of people who start university, if there's no one that you can talk to at the college that you go to, or if you don't know anyone that's been, it takes you a term to figure out what's going on.'[56]

Helen arrived with a clear idea that she wanted to be an actor. 'But I don't think I realized until I got to uni that comedy was the route I was going to go down.'[57] She also never realized what an opportunity there was at Cambridge to put on your own shows. On her course she met Anna O'Grady, also in Footlights, and they formed a comedy partnership that is still going today. At first Helen tried to get into the smokers but found the whole process a bit cliquey. It seemed to her that it was basically the committee members doing most of the performing, with a few spots open for everyone else. 'I didn't realize it at the time but it's a microcosm of the whole industry basically. You've still got to be good, but it is a lot of who you know.'[58] It also came as a revelation that Footlights was all about new writing. 'I think I just assumed they put on funny plays written by other people. And that's what's so amazing about Footlights, it forces you to write your own stuff. And I hadn't really done any comedy writing before.'[59] So, Helen started out by acting in other people's sketches, then she got into the panto and was cast in the Harry Porter Prize winning play. 'From then on I felt like I was granted access to the mystical world of the clique because I'd become friends with these people and it was like, you're good, you learn your lines, you turn up for rehearsal on time.'[60]

The main influence on Footlights comedy during this period was undoubtedly *The Office*. It seemed to permeate everything. 'All of our

FIGURE 17.2 *The 2005 pantomime,* Spartacus. © *John Linford.*

comedy started becoming defined by *The Office*,' claims Helen. 'If you did an audition for a smoker sometimes the feedback was, it's a bit too Officey. And it would be, hang on a minute, all these other sketches in the smoker are basically *The Office*. Even when we were on tour with *Niceties*, wherever we were staying we would watch *The Office* in the evening on DVD.'[61]

Because this was her first revue Helen was delighted just to be there and didn't really write very much, feeling a bit inexperienced to fully contribute in that way. 'But I felt like that didn't matter. I think they wanted me in it as an actor. So, in some ways I didn't feel as much pressure as maybe some of the others to get their sketches in.'[62] The show opened with the bizarre sight of the whole cast pretending to be quintuplets in a womb fighting amongst each other as to who was going to get out first.

In Edinburgh, Helen found the critics particularly harsh, with statements along the lines of, well I don't think we've got the new John Cleese amongst these guys. This had been a bat with which to wallop the Footlights almost since the days of Peter Cook, trotting out the usual, not as good as last year line. 'They're always comparing you to whoever came five years before,' argues Matt Green.[63] Stephen Fry once said that the first thing any fresher arriving at Cambridge will be told is that, 'apparently the Footlights are crap this year'. On the positive side, Helen hadn't appreciated the audience that Footlights still pulled in, 'because, of course, it's the brand.'[64] However, on tour they played a 400-seat theatre and only twelve people showed up. After the interval the cast discovered that even some of those had left. 'That was a bit of a low point. But I do think we just found it funny.'[65]

Helen appeared in the following year's revue, too, *Wham Bam*, and was much more involved in the writing this time. 'We all sat down one day and brainstormed funny ideas for sketches. And it was, I like the sound of that one, I'll do that. Then we went off individually and wrote them, it was all very separate.'[66] After a break of a few weeks there was a full read through and sketches were chosen to either be in the full tour show or the one-hour Edinburgh version. During the run changes were being made all the time, stuff taken out, new bits put in that might appeal to audiences at specific venues. 'But the main show was geared towards the student crowd, which was the same show as the Edinburgh show.'[67]

Because some of the cast could play instruments, *Wham Bam* featured a lot of music: Helen was a mean drummer, Henry Eliot played the accordion and Will Sharpe the guitar and so they formed a small band and played songs on stage. Indeed, the critic for the Edinburgh Festival's Fringe magazine commented, 'Should they fail to make it professionally in comedy, they could still have a career as a serviceable indie band.' A few of the songs harked back to Footlights past and were written and performed by Henry Eliot. There was a musical number extolling the virtues of Mr Kipling's cakes and as a waiter in a pasta restaurant Henry performed a patter song going through all the types of pasta. 'I feel like my sense of humour was probably a bit more old fashioned going into that revue,' he says, 'because

I'd been brought up on old radio comedies like *Round the Horne* and *I'm Sorry, I'll Read That Again*, which always had songs.'⁶⁸

Both Henry's parents had been at Cambridge so it was something he had grown up with, but it was also the reason why he didn't want to go and initially applied elsewhere. When he didn't get into his favoured choice, Henry took a year out and then applied to Cambridge and was given a place. He took part in a couple of smokers but mainly did theatre, appearing in a play with Helen, and writing his own college musical. He had been at school with Will Sharpe, then president, and began to make friends with a few Footlights members. 'There are so many worlds at Cambridge that you can get involved in, that it's partly who do you want to hang out with. I'm not sure I would have been drawn to get involved in Footlights particularly if it hadn't been that I liked those people and wanted to do more stuff with them.'⁶⁹

But his calling card, as it were, was when he won the Harry Porter Prize. A Footlights alumnus was always asked to judge and when Henry heard it was to be Michael Frayn he included a small part for his voice; Frayn later told Henry he admired his chutzpah. When the play went into production, Henry obviously had to go and record Frayn's voice. 'So, I had this incredible moment as a second-year undergraduate of being invited down to Richmond in London to have lunch with Michael Frayn and Claire Tomalin, his wife. And he said, before I came down, "We've invited another couple to lunch, I hope you don't mind." And that turned out to be Bamber Gascoigne and his wife, who was also at Magdalene College where I was. It was a very memorable lunch for me.'⁷⁰

Put on the committee, Henry next wrote and directed the panto with Will Sharpe, and John-Luke Roberts, who came up with the idea of doing *Faust*, simply because he wanted to call the dame Mrs Topheles. 'Before the interval we got through the main plot, so Faust got sent down to hell. And then after the interval it was a completely invented story of rescuing him from hell.'⁷¹ What was particularly impressive was the set design based on German expressionist cinema. 'It looked incredible,' recalls Henry. 'The first half was set in a library and then everything swivelled and became hell. And the whole thing was narrated by a huge papier-mâché mouth of hell on the side of the stage which Will Sharpe voiced every night.'⁷² The pantomime horse was Cerberus. 'It was probably the thing I was proudest of that I did at Cambridge because it felt like such a huge operation and being involved in the writing and the directing it was a feat to pull it off.'⁷³

The cast of *Wham Bam* was mostly made up of third years, which led, as Henry recalls, to a little bit of friction. 'Because, having graduated, most of us were looking ahead to what was next and wanting to get different things out of the show. But mostly it was pretty positive.'⁷⁴ It followed *Niceties* in being very much a sketch show, although a lot more varied in style. One sketch parodied a sit-com with a very loud and intrusive laughter track. 'There was definitely no desire to be controversial,' states Helen. 'Both shows were very different but there was just an emphasis on it being very silly. There was this very strange sketch called 'Man Farmer' that Will Sharpe wrote and it was about cloning babies. It was very surreal.'[75] Henry defines *Wham Bam* has having been generally light humour, but there were some darker moments. 'Someone was laid out on an operating table and then two of us came in dressed as clowns and to music we did this pantomime surgery on this figure. It was quite different to the rest of the show.'[76]

Henry's warmest memory of the tour was the fun of packing up this big van and driving all together around the country to different venues. Although it was a very slimmed down tour schedule, which had been the trend of late, there was the occasional break between gigs. At one point Henry had the van with everything in it at his parents' house in Dorset before everyone reconvened for a performance in North London. 'I set off in very good time, but the traffic was horrendous, there was just a series of crashes. And I remember a terrifying series of phone calls and watching the time tick down, and thinking I've literally got all the stuff everyone needs. I did just make it in the end, but it was a close thing.'[77]

As for Edinburgh, Henry recalls that reviews were not great. 'It was a little bit disheartening and the feeling we had was that people came expecting to see Stephen Fry or *Beyond the Fringe*. And the fact was they knew them from their later careers and TV shows. I feel like that expectation is always going to be higher than reality.'[78]

18

Devils

Amy Hoggart only applied to Cambridge because her father had been and told her that doing the interview process was like trying to get into the army. It was a test that was so rigorous that you should do it as a life experience. So, Amy and all her cousins applied with that sort of attitude. 'And I was surprised to get in, and reluctant to go, because I didn't think it would be very fun, my experience is that it actually was.'[1]

In her first term Amy picked up a flyer from the Freshers' Fair. Obviously, she knew about the Footlights, but a friend's humiliating story about her failed audition to get into the panto put Amy off and so she concentrated on other things like theatre and radio. 'And because of the Footlights name it does seem really intimidating.'[2] She still harboured acting ambitions but wasn't at all confident about it. 'I'd always get a funny part in a play and enjoy it, but I had imposter syndrome. I never thought that I would be good enough for Footlights and so I didn't have anything to do with it, or even go and see any productions.'[3]

It was during her third year and while at a friend's house watching a documentary on television about Fry and Laurie that something clicked. 'I thought, God, I'm at this university and I haven't done any of this, and I'm about to graduate.'[4] Hearing that auditions were being held for the tour show, Amy decided to try her luck, even though she hadn't even gone to a smoker, let alone performed in one. She decided to write a monologue where she played the role of a woman at an audition that's deeply disconcerting and socially awkward; not too far away from the kind of characters she went on to play on television.

The auditions were taking place over two days. Amy woke up the first day and couldn't face it. 'I'd slept badly because I was stressed about it.'[5] Her friend Dan, who went on to be a criminal barrister, was auditioning, too, and told her, 'I'm going to make you do it tomorrow.' And he did, they both ended up going together. There were two directors, Tom Williams, who had been in *Wham Bam*, and Ed Gamble, who had just graduated from Durham University. 'And he has the most generous laugh,' says Amy. 'But he uses it as a tool to make people feel comfortable, so I could hear this loud laugh at all the auditions. And I thought, I can do this, I'm never going to know if it's shit, because this really sweet man is just laughing at everything.'[6]

As usual, the tour cast ended up as four blokes and one woman. 'And they always pluck people from the committee,' states Amy. 'It's very political.'[7] There was just the one woman on the committee, and it was expected that she would be given the nod, as such she didn't bother trying too hard. As she later told Amy, 'I was a shoo-in.' The spanner in the works was Ed Gamble. Not being in the Footlights, he didn't care about the committee, or how many times someone may have done smokers, he was auditioning on merit. 'So, he put me in,' says Amy, 'which didn't help because I had imposter syndrome. I didn't know why I was there. And I do think that I ruffled feathers. And I felt badly about that.'[8]

Amy carried the offbeat character she played at her audition into most of the sketches she wrote and performed in the 2008 show, entitled *Devils*. It was a pure sketch show, 'quite old fashioned, really,' declares Amy,[9] with elements of physical comedy, music and songs. There was a sketch brutally mocking improv groups and Pete Riley, an academic who never pursued a comedy career, played the world's worst croupier. For Amy, sat with the rest of the cast around a table bombarded by flying cards, it was very hard not to laugh. 'I remember Tom and Ed the directors having to train us not to laugh. And that's still with me, when I need to control my laughter at work, I always come back to that.'[10]

Despite 2008 marking the 125th anniversary of the Footlights, there wasn't much of a fanfare made of it during the tour show. One former alumnus did make a visit and bought out an entire performance at the ADC for his friends. He met the cast, managing to tell them how successful he had been with the club, and even performing an old routine. 'He did not find our show funny,' laments Amy.[11]

That year's tour visited places like Dartmouth Naval College and it seemed too many boarding schools. 'It was quite a lacklustre tour,' according to Amy.[12] In Edinburgh, though, audiences still turned out in force. 'That was the best Edinburgh anyone could have,' says Amy. 'The bits that make it hard just didn't apply to Footlights, like not selling, we sold out every night, having to flyer, we never had to flyer. I didn't have to arrange anything. I didn't have to pay for anything. Everything is taken care of, you turned up and it was just done.'[13] It did wonders for Amy personally, too. Ed Gamble had written a sketch in which Amy played a historical interpreter in a museum dressed as a Victorian cockney prostitute and speaking utter filth and shocking a visiting school party. A TV producer saw her and that led to work in television.

Amy was reading English at King's, one of the few colleges at Cambridge trying to recruit from some of the poorer areas around the country and from state schools. As a result, King's had a little bit more diversity than the rest of the university. As for the Footlights, Amy noticed a propensity of people from public school. 'There was no diversity. No one thought about that. Diversity was putting one woman in the tour show, maybe. It's an entitlement thing, I think. There were the odd few people of colour, Nick Mohamed, Keith Akushie. I don't think it was discrimination. I just think, with comedy you need confidence and confidence often comes from privilege, and so however you cut it, if you're looking at gender or race or class or whatever, the most confident people are most likely to get there.'[14]

When she got involved in Footlights, Amy worried that with her finals coming up, she was taking on too much extracurricular stuff. One of the directors of *Devils* had graduated in English and seeing how anxious Amy was, reassured her that he could get her a good mark. 'He sat me down and he gave me "the talk" and "the talk" was how you get a really good English degree while doing Footlights. He said there was a document that someone in Footlights a few years before had written, that had everything you needed because a lot of them do English. And it was literally, how you get a first at Cambridge, only for Footlights people. And that's how I did well.'[15] In essence this document, which was emailed to her, offered tips and short cuts, emphasizing how to work smart, not hard. It came with a proviso, not to share it with anyone. Amy ignored that and passed it around her circle of friends, only nobody took advantage. 'And when people say, you went to Cambridge so you must have worked really hard, I say, yeah, I did work really hard, but I never did well. And then I did Footlights and I stopped working hard and I was fine.'[16]

When Abi Tedder began to find her place in the Footlights, things were slowly getting a bit better in relation to the representation of women. Yes, it remained tradition that only one woman got into the tour show, but at least

FIGURE 18.1 *Visiting the ADC Theatre, Stephen Fry was introduced to the current Footlights president, Abi Tedder. 'He called me "Madam President" the whole time and I was delighted,' says Abi. © John Linford.*

there were now three women on the committee and in 2010 Abi was elected president, the first woman in the post for twelve years. 'The system that we had, as flawed as it was, and as much as white public-school boys did get elected, it was very much a meritocracy, or at least I felt it was. If you were funny and you worked hard and you did lots of stuff, you would get into the committee. The committee would vote based on the funniest writers, the funniest performers and commitment to the Footlights.'[17] At that time, presidential candidates were interviewed by the committee and asked to give a presentation about what they would bring to the role. Abi was surprised to get the nod and still feels great pride in having been president, but there was a lot of pressure involved. 'Looking back now, I wish I'd worried less about proving myself to them and more time putting things in place to make more women get into the Footlights.'[18]

Abi grew up very much the class clown at her school, with everyone saying she should do comedy. When someone mentioned Footlights, she realized that was the place to go. She studied ancient history at Girton. 'But I did so much Footlights I didn't take any notice of the Greeks or the Romans.'[19] This was largely the attitude of most of Abi's colleagues. 'We never discussed our studies; it was never important. Because those people were so hyper focused on the Footlights, the academic side of things was sort of irrelevant to our journey together.'[20] This kind of attitude did create a 'brutally competitive'[21] atmosphere, Amy recalls, especially on the tour show. 'It was so competitive because you knew what Footlights could do for you. There were a lot of people thinking about the TV producers they're going to meet, they're thinking about the agents who are going to come to the show.'[22] The irony was that many of Abi's contemporaries, who went on to enjoy a career in comedy, either hid or kept quiet about their involvement in Footlights for many years.

Like many before her, Abi's first start was the virgin smoker, and she was encouraged to do more. 'We'd rock up and you'd have somebody that's got a piece of paper, and they're like, I've written a sketch, you've got twenty minutes, do you want to learn it? And you'd be like, oh OK, and it was, you're playing Tatiana, the evil Russian ballerina or whatever, you'd read the thing and then you'd go and perform it ten minutes later.'[23] And sometimes those sketches would go over well and that was a fantastic feeling, and sometimes they'd go down the pan, but it never seemed to matter. 'And that's why I think Footlights people still continue to do well, partially because they're intelligent people, but also because they get three years of safe practice space and that's incredibly lucky and powerful to get.'[24]

Along with appearing in the Harry Porter prize-winning play, which was written for her by Mark Fiddaman and Lucien Young, Abi's fondest memories of Footlights are the pantos. In her first she played a cockney minotaur in a papier-mâché head made with chicken wire. At one point her character came into the audience to perform a rap, handing over the microphone to a child to join in. 'And this one child looked at me, frozen in fear. OK, they're scared. I went to the next one, same thing. So, I thought I'd better go to an adult, and he looked a bit alarmed, too, and that's when I felt blood. The chicken wire was cutting my head and I was bleeding into my eyes. Imagine the sight for a child of a massive woman dressed as a minotaur bleeding into her eyes shouting in cockney in their face.'[25] In *The Pied Piper* Abi played the dame, Frau Fabergé, in a costume covered with sausages. Her opening line was, 'I'm Frau Fabergé, more ovaries than normal.'

Unfortunately, Abi's experience of the tour show was a negative one. 'We had the most miserable time. We put so much pressure on ourselves because you're fed all this history and hear about all these amazing people. You both want to live up to those people, but you also don't want to be those people. If we went on stage in Edinburgh and did posh Cambridgey comedy we'd be ripped to shreds by reviewers. But if we did modern edgy comedy the audiences would be like, what's this.'[26] It was a dilemma many tour shows had faced. In the end it was decided, screw the audience, we're going to do cool, edgy comedy. The result was *Wishful Thinking*. 'It stopped being fun. We were so focused on trying to be edgy, trying to do something different that we didn't do the thing that we were good at, which was writing fun sketches. And that show was not a good show. We tore ourselves apart trying to be everything for everybody, and we had people walking out in our Edinburgh show.'[27] There was a long form sketch about drug dealing and something called the fingering bench, 'That's not necessarily what Marjorie from Wiltshire wants when she goes to the theatre for an evening out.'[28]

Thrown in amongst a cast of five men, Keith Akushie, Tom Evans, Daran Johnson, Al Roberts and Liam Williams, Abi's preference for weird, dark and larger than life characters went against the grain of the naturalistic comedy of shows like *The Office* and *Peep Show* that was in favour within Footlights. 'My style didn't really line up with some of the guys in that show. They saw it as being a bit old fashioned.'[29] As for the tour, two dates stick in Abi's mind. At Dartmouth Naval College, the officers had been up since 3 am running up and down a hill finishing their physical exam and probably not in the mood for a bunch of twenty-year-olds doing sketches about drug dealers. 'I remember looking out into the audience and half of them were asleep.'[30] Then there was the 600-seat Nottingham Arts Theatre. On tour, the Footlights relied on the individual theatres to advertise the show. Some did better jobs than others. In Nottingham just five tickets had been sold. 'It was so awful. In the end we shut the curtain and put seats on the stage and did the show sideways to these five people.'[31]

Ben Ashenden must find himself in the minority of people who hadn't in some part applied to Cambridge in recent years with the Footlights in mind. He'd admired it and seen the tour show *Devils* when it played the ADC in the first week of term. 'And I was blown away. It was such an electric atmosphere. I've never been in a theatre where the audience was demographically a block, everyone was there for kind of the same reason, and they were there at the same sort of point in their life. It was like a rock concert. And I remember sitting there thinking, quite clearly, that's it, that's what I want to do.'³²

Ben was spending most of his time playing rugby and not doing much acting when someone told him how the whole acting thing works in Cambridge, that there was an emailed list of all the auditions and where they were being held. He landed a small role in a Marlowe Society production of *Romeo and Juliet* and mucked about so much the director afterwards suggested that maybe he try comedy. 'By which she was saying, stop ruining our plays.'³³ In that production, Ben got friendly with Joey Batey, who was planning with a bunch of others their own sketch show called *Good Clean Men*, convinced that they probably wouldn't get into the Footlights in their first year. Did Ben want to get involved? It sounded fun so Ben popped round to Batey's room in Robinson College to meet the cast, which was five other guys. 'One of them was lying on the bed and was way more interested than anyone else in talking about this coming show in a very grown up, considered way. He was talking about ticket prices and who we were going to get to design the poster and what do we think about sound design, and everyone else was just getting drunk and loosely talking about whether we should do this comedy show. I found this funny, so I started mocking him. And he's an old Etonian, with blonde hair, he looks like an AI generated image of Malfoy. And he seemed to find the fact that I was undermining him quite funny, and we were having our own little dialogue amidst this big conversation. And that was Alex.'³⁴

Alexander Owen arrived at Cambridge interested in theatre and acting, aware of the university's rich tradition in those areas. He wasn't much aware of the Footlights until the summer before he started. Performing in a play at the Edinburgh fringe with his school, Alex became obsessed with a show called *House of Windsor* featuring Simon Bird, Jonny Sweet and Joe Thomas. 'I went to see that show probably twelve times. And then when I found out they'd been in Footlights I was, this is perfect because I'm going there next month. Now I know what to aspire to.'³⁵

Good Clean Men went on at the Corpus playroom and put everyone on the radar of Footlights and both Ben and Alex got cast in the 2010 tour show, *Good for You*. Having already found they got on, the two men bonded further on a tour that not only took in Edinburgh, but this time went further afield to the United States. Many of the sketches revolved around faux informative lectures, stuff with teachers, a group of actors visit a school to give a presentation about sexual health, Alex played a 'business innovator' called Chad Slazenger who goes into businesses telling them how to be more efficient. In retrospect, it was obvious that the cast were exorcizing their demons of having just come out of education. 'A lot of the characters we were mocking were people who were coming in with a sense of authority,' offers Ben. 'You should listen to me about what I have to say. And they have nothing to say. Which is very cathartic when you're nineteen or twenty. I think now we probably wouldn't write that stuff, because we'd be like, well actually listen to those people, because we've got kids in nursery and we want people to listen to authority figures.'[36]

The tour continued to play in provincial towns and cities like Nottingham and Carlisle, where audiences were again thin on the ground. A common theme on tour was still having to deal with an audience assumption that Peter Cook or Stephen Fry was going to appear. At one point, the cast urged the tour producer to focus the ad campaign for Edinburgh on the likes of Tim Key, Nick Mohamed and Richard Ayoade, the supposition being that if people liked them, then they'd like this show. Another idea was to change the title to *Fuck Off*, to dissuade those with a view of Footlights that was stuck in the past. They still faced something of a backlash at Edinburgh, not the kind of visceral hatred that used to exist, but that they were all from public school. 'There was an assumption that we'd be dicks,' says Alex, 'And then we would gradually, hopefully, grind people down into finding us tolerable.'[37]

Agents hovered around the Fringe, some Radio 4 producers, some from TV, but there was no expectation of any industry favours or leg ups, as had sometimes happened years before. It was a running joke at this time that a phone had been installed that went directly to John Cleese. And there was still no club room either, just a room with a sofa in it and a microwave in the basement of the ADC Theatre. 'The glamour and the old boys' network had been truly dismantled by the time we got there,' claims Ben.'[38]

The tour was produced by Tim Checkley, who ambitiously set his sights on taking it to America, just to see if they could pull it off. They went up and down the East Coast, 'with mixed results,'[39] according to Ben, playing such varied locations as the renowned Second City comedy club in Chicago, and a hotel lobby. Ben's mum and dad came out for that gig to surprise their son on his twenty-first birthday. Only thirty elderly folk had bothered to turn up and Ben's mum knew the show wasn't going to do particularly well when, just before it started, one old dear turned to her friend and said, 'So, what instruments do they play?'

Not helping matters was the fact, unbeknown to the cast, that the blackouts were going to be complete blackouts. All the lights went out, even the fire exit signs. One five second transition between sketches required the cast to pick up a poker table, a load of poker chips and several chairs, and put them on the stage. 'We completely lost our bearings in the blackout,' recalls Ben, 'and instead dragged the poker table directly into the front row. When the lights came up me and Lucien Young were garrotting an old woman with a table.'[40]

Teddy Rose was the producer of the following year's tour show, *Pretty Little Panic*, and took up the challenge by expanding the US tour by adding the West Coast, to places like Las Vegas, San Francisco and Los Angeles. In Vegas, they played a room at the back of a sex shop. 'You had to walk past a lot of interesting things before you got to the stage,' recalls Ben. 'And the other acts performing in that space were of a more physical nature.'[41] Throughout the performance, rather disconcertingly, two guys sat in the front row discussing whether they would rather sleep with Ben or Alex. Their decision was loudly announced midway through the final sketch – the blonde. 'That was the fun thing about the American leg,' says Alex. 'On the UK tour you really knew what to expect, the Footlights had been doing these venues for years and years, where America was, ten people in a sex shop on the Tuesday, and on the Wednesday 800 people in Pittsburgh going absolutely crazy.'[42]

The most contentious aspect of *Pretty Little Panic* was the fact that it was a totally male cast; Ben and Alex were joined by Mark Fiddaman and Adam Lawrence. It was an unusually small cast, too. 'Every tour is a bit of a reaction to the one that went before it,' relates Alex. 'Like a band talking about how they're going in a new direction with their next album, they'd be rumblings around Michaelmas term that the next tour should be completely different.'[43] The idea was to do something a bit more pared down. They had no props, for example. It was very bare bones. And there were no blackouts or music breaks, each sketch flowed into the next one. It was very much in the style of a show that Ben and Alex did in their third year that they called *The Pin*.

When Ben and Alex arrived in the Footlights the influence of *The Office* was still around, especially in a naturalistic approach to comedy. Like Ben, Alex went to see the tour show in his first term. 'I always thought sketch comedy meant basically big, wacky characters, that's what I'd been brought up on in the 1990s and noughties was a lot of that sort of style, which had never really appealed to me. But then I was introduced to this idea that sketches and the concepts, ideas and the characterization could be much more natural. That was very much the prevailing style in Footlights.'[44] Alex and Ben, who had formed a double act by now which continues to this day, were also highly influenced by a comedy troupe called Cowards, comprising Tom Basden, Stefan Golaszewski, Tim Key and Lloyd Woolf, who all met in Footlights. 'The *Little Britain* period of sketch show, being like, these are wacky characters put into normal circumstances,' says Ben, 'Cowards kind of flipped it and had very wacky situations played out very normally.'[45]

This idea of sketches that are generally scenes from the everyday with a surreal element thrown in for good measure was adopted for the 2012 revue, *Perfect Strangers*. It was directed by a returning Abi Tedder who was determined to learn from the mistakes of *Wishful Thinking*. 'I tried my best to try and cast people who seemed complementary or were friends.'[46] The cast featured Jason Forbes, Pierre Novellie, George Potts, Emma Powell and Phil Wang. 'And I really tried, along with my co-director Jonny Lennard, to facilitate a healthy and happy atmosphere, telling them, please don't try to be cool, or to be as neurotic as they would want to be about every little detail, if you think it's funny, that'll do. And that show was much better and got much better reviews.'[47]

At Edinburgh, the show marked fifty years of the Footlights at the Fringe; David Mitchell was spotted in the audience for one of the performances.

Edinburgh had always sold well enough to pay for the UK tour. But Abi planned to take *Perfect Strangers* across to America. Since the two previous US tours had put a huge financial strain on the club, this idea was received with deep scepticism. That was until Abi put together a proposal of how to make the budget work. 'We did go to America in the end,' she points out, 'but we had to fight hard to be allowed to go.'[48] They played an arts festival in Philadelphia, a comedy club in New York, there was a return visit to Chicago's Second City and appearances at university comedy clubs in Yale and Harvard. 'It's funny,' comments Abi, 'because quite a lot of comedy clubs set up are based on Footlights, they've taken some inspiration from that, and it was interesting to see what it had become in America. I remember when we went to Yale, a lot of the buildings are replicas of Cambridge buildings. It was like being in Disneyland Cambridge.'[49]

The following year's tour show, *Canada*, also played the US, so by the time the 2014 revue, *Real Feelings*, hit the States the whole thing was a well-oiled and professional enterprise. 'I heard about tours that had happened previously that took on myth status the amount of money that had been spent,' says cast member Alex MacKeith.[50] Certainly, by now lessons of the pitfalls to avoid and the best venues to play had been passed down by previous producers. Audiences for *Real Feelings* were mostly appreciative, especially at Meltdown, a comedy club in Los Angeles, and at the Philadelphia Improv Theatre, where they responded to several improvisational elements in the show. Mostly, though, it was made up of sketches, there was a very physical skit on motion capture with somebody dressed in a morph suit and a pastiche of *The Great British Bake Off* that represented Mary Berry as some high gothic grotesque straight out of *The League of Gentlemen*.

In marked contrast to *Canada*, which featured three women in its cast of four, *Real Feelings* consisted of five men, all of whom were committee members. In Alex's first year there had been just two women sitting on a committee of eight, and that number was reduced to one the following year. 'And that gender divide didn't reflect the number of women who were performing great comedy at the time.'[51] Despite the fact both tour managers were women, the general feeling afterwards, in terms of gender representation, was that it had been wrong for the make-up of the show to have been all-male. 'And the answer obviously wasn't tokenism,' stresses Alex. 'The answer was greater representation and more channels for access.'[52]

Alex's route into the Footlights, like so many before him, was the smokers, which he loved doing; by his second year he asked to be put in charge of them. 'They could be unbridled, anarchic and rammed. It was amazing to see people who were more established and then people who'd been selected by the committee that week to perform and suddenly you'd have a completely different voice on stage and a completely different style.'[53] The emphasis, as always, was on writing one's own material; indeed, a mass email would be sent out for the virgin smoker emphasizing this fact. 'You kind of had to say it three times, this is self-written material,' confirms Alex.[54]

Applications to join the committee opened at the halfway point of a student's second year. An applicant would send an email stating their case, basically a CV and a covering letter combined. Once on the committee, audition material for any of the smokers was no longer required. 'And that opens up the remit of experimentation,' says Alex.[55] In the last couple of years, the Footlights had radically shifted its rules regarding membership. The outgoing committee chose the incoming committee, including the president, and it was made up of between eight or ten people, all of them in their third year. It was this select group that officially performed, and were known, as the Footlights.

Becoming a Footlight member became very much a rite of passage. It was for those who had shown a commitment to comedy throughout their time at Cambridge. There were pros and cons to the new scheme, the biggest negative being that it restricted those who could take up membership. What it did mean was that members had more responsibilities, and being in the same circles for three years had got to know each other well. It was almost about creating an internal company, that was the ethos behind the idea originally.

This change, with something like thirty people vying for so few places, inevitably led to a highly competitive environment as groups and allegiances began forming and rivalries built up. 'A lot of that was not particularly healthy,' recalls Archie Henderson. 'There was lots of unspoken jealousy and spikiness, and the occasional backstab.'[56]

Archie Henderson remembers going up to the Edinburgh Fringe in his final year at school and wanting to see the Footlights because he was going up to Cambridge, only it was sold out. Disappointed, he checked out another comedy show the club had organized. 'It was great, and I thought, how the hell am I ever going to do that.'[57] Archie had grown up loving comedy, and performing, but hadn't given much thought to doing it as a career. He was reading Classics at King's, which was still very much at the vanguard of bringing in students from state school backgrounds, rather than private schools, disproportionally compared to the rest of the university. 'It was a very left leaning college,' says Archie, 'and wore that badge with pride.'[58] Compared to King's, Archie saw Footlights as much less inclusive, and still heavily male dominated, although there were some good talented women on the committee. By his third year, however, the committee was almost exclusively white male. 'After that point we were slightly starting to think, it's probably time to put an end to this. We were well intentioned and trying to do accessy and outreachy things, but when you're then writing shows and doing other things they all end up falling by the wayside. It was all good intentions, well-meaning, but maybe not very well executed.'[59]

It took a while for Archie to make his mark on the club, doing endless auditions without any success in getting into a smoker in his first year. 'I knew I was bad but I persevered. Either I was oblivious or just blinded by desire to make it work.'[60] He went away that summer and wrote a pile of material, including a comedy song which he performed as Severus Snape, morosely singing about all the horror he'd gone through in his life. It went down a storm at the first smoker of the new term.

This song fell into a long tradition of comedy songs in Footlights that had thinned over the years to barely a trickle. Archie's parents loved old variety acts like Flanders and Swann and he had listened to those growing up. Then, as a teenager, he became obsessed with Tim Minchin. At Footlights, Archie continued performing songs and began a writing association with Adrian Gray to put on their own shows, as well as regularly featuring in smokers. 'The great thing about Footlights is there's not really any time to bring your head up to take a breath of air and see where you are because as soon as you're finished, you're already thinking about what the next thing is. You're forced to just churn out so much material and less than half of it survives, but I think there's something so valuable in that, just churning through relentless things.'[61]

Archie and Adrian also took advantage of a new scheme that was called Footlights Presents. This had only been running a couple of years and was a chance for those in their first or second years to craft an hour's-worth of material that reflected their comic sensibilities. A stand-up performer or a comedy troupe could pitch their idea for a show and the committee would decide whether it warranted sponsorship. Archie and Adrian's production ended up running over five nights at the ADC.

The money to cover this and other enterprises came from a large sum that had been left to the club by Harry Porter upon his death. Porter intended the money to go towards the acquisition of another club room, but it was decided by the committee, along with senior members of university staff who were in control of where the fund was allocated, that the Footlights didn't require their own club room since they had been a resident company at the ADC Theatre for many years now. Instead, the best way to use the money was to sponsor students and members to undertake comedy projects they wouldn't be able to afford to put on otherwise.

The exact amount of money at the club's disposal was revealed to Archie when he became a committee member in his third year. 'I remember our first meeting and we said, "Right, who's the treasurer." Someone said, "I'm the treasurer." We said, "How much money do we have." He said, "Well, it looks like there's a quarter of a million pounds in the bank account." And there's eight students thinking, what shall we do with all that money. There was a senior treasurer who you would hope kept things in check. But just the idea that we were just these kids contemplating what to do with all that money.'[62]

Archie and Adrian made the cast of that year's tour show, which went by the title of *Love Handles*. It had a very loose concept in that it was set in a town that was about to be hit by a meteor and the characters in the sketches were in some way responding to the oncoming catastrophe. Archie loved high concept, silly sketches. One had the bizarre setup of a woman in a restaurant who has had her arms surgically replaced, only to retain a memory of the donor. Enter Archie as this blustery ancient colonel who has lost his arms and it's clear that they've been transferred to this woman. As they both try to have a normal dinner conversation the colonel's gesturing is making the woman's limbs manically swing about.

The long UK tours of the past had now given way to a few sparse dates, mostly private schools, where the Footlights performed workshops that paid handsome fees into the club's coffers. They did, however, get to play one date at London's famous Comedy Store. Footlights continued to be a fixture at Edinburgh, where they regularly sold out while still being regarded as coming from a place of privilege. 'I don't think that will ever die,' argues Archie. 'And it probably shouldn't. It's good to keep them level-headed.' The American tour went ahead much as before, although according to Archie, 'it was a bit of a car crash.'[63] Some venues barely sold, such as New Orleans where only four people attended. Another venue, in Las Vegas, cancelled on them at short notice and then, turning up for a gig at Second City in Chicago, it was discovered the offices had burnt down the day before and it was temporarily closed. There were highpoints, of course, playing to a huge crowd of students at Princeton, and appearing at improv clubs in New York and Sacramento. 'I remember feeling so in disbelief of what we were experiencing and trying to experience it properly,' says Archie. 'It's so insane to be going on tour to America when you're that age. It was so exciting.'[64]

The following year's American tour also looked like being something of a disaster. The mood was optimistic to start with as the cast prepared for the first gig at a trendy bar in San Francisco, only barely anyone showed up. 'We were all thinking, oh God, this is going to be a long run if it's going to be like this,' recalls cast member Jordan Mitchell.[65] It also transpired that some of the sketches weren't translating well, so after the show the cast asked a few in the audience to help with altering portions of dialogue to suit an American idiom. Things picked up on the second night in Sacramento where they received a great reception in a packed comedy club. After that the tour continued in good spirits. They played Second City in Chicago. 'That was great,' recalls Jordan, 'going in the dressing room and seeing photographs of Bill Murray on the wall.'[66] And they played Harvard. 'People would always want to invite you to their frat parties afterwards and ask you questions about what it was like living in England.'[67]

Going to Cambridge had never been a long-term goal for Jordan until his English tutor, who had studied there, encouraged him to go. Growing up Jordan had been a fan of Mitchell and Webb and Garth Marenghi. 'Watching these people on TV and then learning that they all seemed to be part of this kind of secret society and thinking, how does that all work, was something that I was really intrigued by.'[68] In his first week, Jordan went to see the returning tour show perform. 'And I just remember being absolutely blown away. These people weren't that much older than me, but when you're that young they seem like grown-ups, and I felt like a school kid. It was really inspiring.'[69] Then, auditioning for a smoker, he found one of the cast members on the panel, which made it seem even more daunting. He didn't get in.

Fortuitously, back on his first day Jordan met up with three like-minded students at his college, Fitzwilliam, and they started putting on their own sketch shows. These were very much Python-inspired, something university reviewers picked up on. 'If you do something that's vaguely silly or surreal that's the label you get,' claims Jordan. 'And if you do something a bit witty then you're considered Fry and Laurie.'[70] Many students brought their influences with them, which over time fade as they develop their own comic voice and style. 'But once you're there, the main influences really are the people around you or in the years above you,' says Jordan. 'The biggest influence was whoever was in Footlights that year, whatever they were doing, that's kind of to some degree what people were emulating, and you would see that in the smokers. It felt like a very alive culture, that people were really responding to each other, and that's what was exciting about it.'[71]

In his third year, Jordan was made vice president; he and his friends made up half of that year's Footlights committee. As usual there was fevered competition to get in, and much anger and disappointment for those who lost out. Anyone could still audition for the panto and the tour show; indeed, the only production that was reserved for committee members was now the spring revue, which was essentially the best of the sketches from that year's smokers, plus some new material. In a bid to make the Footlights more accessible, the committee instigated a comedy social evening, which took place a week ahead of the virgin smoker. 'We put on this night at the Maypole,' recalls Jordan, 'where anyone that was interested in comedy would come to the pub near the ADC and we'd put a bit of money behind the bar.'[72] The funding for that came yet again courtesy of the late Harry Porter. 'That money allowed a lot of creative things to happen,' states Jordan.[73]

While the auditions for the tour show remained open to anybody, generally the cast was made up from the eight or ten members. 'It was a bit of a corrupt system,' explains Jordan, 'where whoever was on the committee that year would appoint the director and then the director would choose the cast. So, I think there was often a fair amount of, we'll appoint you, you appoint us. But usually, those people who were on the committee were the most experienced, probably the most confident, and therefore won a part in the show on their own terms.'[74] In the case of 2016's production, *Lagoon*, four out of the five cast members sat on the committee, including Jordan. And only one of those was a woman. When Jordan first arrived, the majority of those doing comedy within Footlights were men. Before leaving, Jordan and his fellow committee members made sure to choose an incoming committee that was 50/50 both sexes, the first ever mixed gender committee. 'And we were able to do that because it happened to be that in the year below us there was loads of girls who were really good.'[75] It was one way of trying to make a difference, to combat the stigma that Footlights was a predominantly white male dominated space. There had always been a lot of talk about how things could be made better, always difficult when Cambridge itself wasn't exactly the most diverse of environments. And as students there was so much other stuff going on. Many people seemed to have the same experience as Jordan. 'First of all, you arrive and wonder if you can do it. Then you're doing some stuff and think, maybe I can get on the committee. Then you get on the committee and you're like, we're going to do it really differently and make it really amazing, and then you realise it's really hard, and you just oil the machine to keep it going and not mess things up.'[76]

Not to mention there was one's studies, too. Jordan was doing anthropology, but really treated comedy as his proper degree. Unfairly, the bulk of grades were decided on the final exam. 'So, there's a lot riding on them. And my first exam was the day after our opening night of the tour show, so we were so stressed because we were trying to get this show on its feet and preparing for our finals. That affected everyone in the cast.'[77]

One of Jordan's favourite sketches, which didn't feature in *Lagoon* but in another Footlight show, had him playing a lab rat. The gag was that this lab rat overhears two other lab rats saying mean things about him, 'I can hear what you're saying,' and he turns round and has a giant ear on his back. This prop ear was bought for something like £200. 'As a consequence, we ended up in possession of a niche prop that had cost you so much money that you would try and work it into other sketches down the line. You would be trying to figure out something for a smoker the night before and you'd be, can we use the giant ear, maybe.'[78]

In the following year's tour show, another memorable prop appeared, a giant cat costume. The stage was dark and voice was heard, 'Well, well, Mr Bond. I've been expecting you.' The lights came up, and there was a giant cat stroking a man. The costume cost hundreds of pounds, only to end up in landfill. 'That sketch was a favourite one of mine,' recalls John Tothill, 'because it was so stupid.'[79]

Growing up, John loved Fry and Laurie and wanted to do sketch comedy. 'I read Stephen Fry's autobiography when I was about thirteen and he talked about doing Footlights. And I became quite unhealthily obsessed with the whole thing. As a result, I was very sure that I wanted to go to Cambridge and spent the next four or five years doggedly pursuing that in a way that was quite unattractive. And I was very clear that once I got there, I really wanted to do Footlights.'[80]

The thing was, John didn't really have much experience of writing comedy. Auditioning for the tour show in his first year, during the second round of auditions he was paired with Ralph Wakefield, who was on the Footlights committee, to write material together. 'He arrived in my room, and it felt like meeting a celebrity,' admits John. 'There was actually a Footlight in my room.'[81] Out of that grew a writing partnership. 'I was so lucky to be paired with Ralph because he showed me what he had learned across those three years, the whole process of writing comedy, which is a painstaking process. That set me free a little bit. That there was no secret to good writing. It's just hard work.'[82]

Over time, John's sketches became more character driven and he showed a desire to become an actor by joining the Marlowe Society. There was so much creativity going on around the university that looking back at his diary after graduation John realized that he was on stage somewhere every other day throughout his time at Cambridge. 'In many ways that isn't surprising. You get a group of really excitable, very keen nineteen- and twenty-year-olds who are meeting at a subsidized bar every night and were routinely neglecting their studies, because most of us did arts and most of us were there to do Footlights.'[83]

What changed his drama aspirations was playing the dame in the panto. 'There were a few jokes written for me but most of it was ad-libbed. I just found that so exciting.'[84] It led to a decision to do stand-up, and even today John's routines are heavily improvised and fourth wall breaking. 'And sometimes I still feel like I'm back at the ADC.'[85]

In his third year, John made it onto the committee, which because it was a committee of writers and performers at that time did no administrative work. The president did most of it, such as booking the room to hold auditions for the smoker. Responsibility for the bigger projects was more diffuse; the panto was organized by directors and producers appointed by the committee, and stage managers took charge of the tour show. All those weird titles like falconer were long gone. There was still a role for an archivist, however, and John was the obvious candidate. 'I had a reputation at the time for being a Footlights history nerd. I think it was the source of embarrassment for most people, and a source of embarrassing pride for me.'[86] There was very little to do except hand in the script for the panto and tour show at the university library. 'And there ended my archivist duties.'[87] One thing the library did not accept was reel to reel recordings, and so a box of these had been passed amongst the Footlights for years. By John's time these tapes had become so delicate they could no longer be played and so nobody knew what was on them.

It remained the case that the committee was the performing troupe, and no applicants were eligible until their third year. 'And to get in you had to be good and you had to be prolific,' says John.[88] Competition for places remained high; there was something like fifty applicants in the year John graduated. 'By the time I got there, the Cambridge Footlights was such an institution, and such a corporation that I can see why you would want to limit who could actually call themselves a Footlight.'[89] Views on this differed amongst the committee and there were constant pushes to return to the days when Footlights was a club with a much larger general membership. John numbered amongst those who wanted it to remain as exclusive as possible. 'Because I remember thinking, I've worked really hard to do this. I've sacrificed getting a good mark in my degree [he was reading music]. I know I want to be a comedian and I want to be able to go into productions as a graduate and say I was a Footlight and for that to mean something. How wrong I was that to be a Footlight is a toxic thing that I would never put on my CV for a second because you'd lose every job ever.'[90] Isn't it interesting, how this attitude still persisted well into the 2000s?

The 2017 tour show, *Dream Sequence*, again played America, mostly comedy clubs. 'It was the best month ever,' John declares. 'You felt like a rock star. We arrived in Las Vegas and stayed in the Luxor Hotel. We went to Sacramento, Chicago, New York. What a once in a lifetime opportunity.'⁹¹ The much-shortened UK leg of the tour paid a second visit to the Comedy Store in London. Sitting in the dressing room, John recalls being 'star struck' by the photographs on the walls of the famous comedians who had played there. And the whole thing finished off with a return visit to the ADC. There was always something special about coming back and putting the show on one last time at the place where it had all started. Most of the cast would have graduated by that stage, and so it was the final show they ever did at Cambridge. For some, it was also the first show they saw as eager freshers. Many people had that same bookending experience of seeing the previous tour show, and ending up performing in it themselves, before heading off into the world. It was always an emotional experience.

19

Are We There Yet?

When Robert Webb was asked on an episode of *Celebrity Mastermind* what advice he might give to a young aspiring comedian he gave a rather long-winded answer about the Footlights. At the end, host John Humphrys said, 'So, basically what you're saying is go to Cambridge?' Webb laughed and said, 'Yeah.' Watching at home was a young Hasan Al-Habib. Born to Iraqi parents who moved to Birmingham, after deciding Baghdad wasn't dangerous enough, their son liked to joke, Hasan was always interested in making people laugh. At school, whenever he had to do a presentation in front of class, he made it funny. 'I realize now looking back I was basically doing stand-up.'[1] He'd watch programmes like *Have I Got News for You* and *Goodness Gracious Me*, but the first time he heard about the Footlights was from that episode of *Mastermind*. 'I had always kind of dreamed about going to Cambridge anyway, but when I heard that I was, right, I must go. That's the only route I can see, because I don't know anything about how you would do comedy otherwise.'[2]

When Hasan failed to get into Cambridge as an undergraduate, he decided to take a gap year and re-apply, despite good offers from other universities. He didn't get in the second time, either, having failed to put enough stamps on his interview letter and it never arrived. Instead, Hasan went to Imperial College, London, studying biochemistry for three years before doing his Master's at Oxford. He wanted to do his PhD at Cambridge and got an offer, as well as an offer to stay on at Oxford. 'When I told my supervisor that I was going to go to Cambridge she was like, I don't understand, we have this great lab, you're already here, everyone gets on, I don't understand why you're leaving. I said, oh I just fancy a change. I was too embarrassed to say, it's because I want to join the Footlights.'[3]

On his first day, Hasan turned up at the Freshers' Fair, seeing all the stalls for the different university societies. 'And I remember seeing the Footlights stall and having to find a quiet corner, because I just started crying. It had been so long, this path, ten years since watching that *Mastermind* episode, and after so many failed attempts, I was there.'[4]

The real drama, though, had only just begun.

Due to the sheer number of people applying, the virgin smoker now took place at two venues, as normal at the ADC, and at the playroom at Corpus

Christi. Everyone who auditioned was guaranteed a place, the only decision to be made was whether you were at the ADC or in the much smaller show at Corpus. While at Imperial College, Hasan had performed some stand-up in London clubs, which put him at a distinct advantage. He was also a few years older than most and much of his comedy revolved around him being Muslim, an Arab and from Birmingham, 'which you were not hearing from anybody else at the Footlights.'[5] Hasan's appearance at the virgin smoker went well, and he was further encouraged by his performance at a smoker for ethnic minority students, a recently instigated event, which like the virgin smoker everyone was guaranteed to get in.

When it came to auditioning for a regular smoker Hasan made two failed attempts. It was galling to think, I'm just as good as they are, but having to stand there and be told, no, you're not good enough. The third time he walked in, saw the auditioning panel facing him, began his routine and got plenty of laughs. 'And then I did a joke about Isis, the dog from *Downton Abbey*, and literally as soon as that word was said, just silence for the rest of the set. They never said this to me, but it really felt like, you can't talk about this on stage. And when that happened, I was just like, OK, they're telling me this is not for me.'[6] Disappointed and frustrated, it looked like Hasan's Footlights career was dead in the water before it even had a chance to begin. So, instead, he took advantage of the multiple other opportunities to do comedy around Cambridge.

Hasan was not alone in feeling marginalized. The suspicion was that the lack of cultural diversity in Footlights had created an unconscious bias against certain kinds of material. Old-fashioned sketch comedy, in the style of Monty Python or Peter Cook, also things like Fry and Laurie, had a very specifically English sensibility. By adhering too much to those old sensibilities, those who didn't embody them, or grew up with other comedy influences, tended to feel shut out.

The campaign for greater female representation had, it seemed, finally been won. During John Tothill's time on the committee it was gender balanced, five men and five women. But it was *all* white. This was not at all representative of the university population. Looking at the university's equality and diversity report for the year 2017–18, students from a BAME background made up 29.2 per cent of all undergraduates who disclosed their ethnicity. This was not reflected in the Footlights committee. The lack of diversity was glaring, and when it was called out, the committee, as twenty-year-olds, with liberal mindsets for the most part, had to say, yes, you're right, no defending it.

While recent club presidents had included Richard Ayoade, the son of a Nigerian father, and Phil Wang, who was British-Malaysian, diversity in the club was an issue. Having done a year at Oxford, Hasan did feel that Cambridge was a bit more diverse. And to be fair, over the past year the committee had continued with termly smokers for ethnic minority students, as well as launching open mic nights for women.

But it was all about to kick off.

In February 2018, the Red Brick Café Bar, a student venue at Robinson College, was booked for an evening of music and comedy from a lineup of black and ethnic minority Cambridge students. Hasan had been asked to perform. As soon as he walked in, he knew it was going to be a disaster. The place was packed with noisy revellers enjoying a beer festival that had been running all day. 'There were some people sat waiting for the gig to start, but there was all this background noise so I could tell it was going to be a really tough gig.'[7] As the audience struggled to hear the opening acts over the noise, Hasan took to the stage. During the interval, one of the organizers was seen in tears. Someone had complained at the bar that some of Hasan's jokes were racist to white people. 'To this day I still don't know what joke they were referring to or if the person was being serious, but they kicked us out.'[8] The gig moved into a room inside Robinson College and continued in an air of defiance and solidarity. Even so, the experience left a bitter taste in the mouth of everybody involved. The night had been created as a space for ethnic minority students to be heard, and in a blogpost written by the organizers the following morning, the claim was that its cancellation sent out a clear message: White comfort is more important than BAME voices.

While the event at the Red Brick Café had no connection with the Footlights, as the biggest comedy voice in Cambridge, with huge influence, one would have thought a showcase for ethnic minority voices being kicked out of an establishment might have warranted a word of condemnation. They were silent on the matter.

A month later, the university hosted one of its best-known comedy nights, the Wolfson Howler, where students perform alongside professional comics. This year the date happened to fall on International Women's Day. Unfortunately, not a single female performer featured in the line-up. The organizer apologized, saying this was due to a last-minute drop-out. This time, Footlights did not remain silent. The next day, the club's president, Ruby Keane, issued a statement on the Footlights Facebook page criticizing the lack of female representation. This elicited a response from the organizer, stating that it was rich of Footlights to criticize the diversity of one line-up when their committee was made up of ten white people.

Like a moth to a flame, Hasan was drawn into this war of words and posted his own thoughts about going to auditions and only seeing white faces on the panel, along with pointing out the fact that the club's largest show of the year, the spring revue, had had an all-white lineup. Ruby Keane ended up deleting her post, but another member of the committee claimed Hasan's accusations could discourage ethnic minority students from auditioning. 'So, I was now being blamed for their own lack of diversity.'[9]

Something needed to be done. The committee decided to host an open meeting in the Maypole pub where ethnic minority performers could air their grievances and discuss potential solutions. The room was rammed, with over sixty people showing up. Ken Cheng, a former Footlight and

British-born Chinese, invited members of the audience to stand up and speak. And there was no shortage of volunteers. It was obvious that there had been very many very frustrated people too scared to say anything before because they didn't want to ruin their chances of getting in the Footlights. And a lot of them were saying the same things, that they didn't feel represented or had no sense of belonging, mainly because of the propensity of privately educated people. Most of them came from state schools and probably hadn't been on a stage before and didn't feel that the club was as accessible as it could be. 'It was really cathartic,' says Hasan who attended and spoke at the event. 'And most of the members had the foresight to just be quiet and listen. And that was the beginning of, there's going to be big change.'[10]

Another issue raised at the meeting was the unfairness of the current Footlight system, that ten all powerful people voted for the next ten all powerful people. This had always struck Hasan as a bit strange. While at Imperial College he had been on the comedy committee where everyone was democratically voted in. 'I really felt that this nepotistic way of picking the committee was making the Footlights worse. Instead of the objective to be funny and be seen by people on stage, and people think, oh yeah, I'll vote for that guy, you were having this thing of what determined if you got in or not was how good friends you were with the previous committee.'[11] This had been a long-standing accusation about the system, that outgoing members often chose friends or those with whom they went to school.

One of the outcomes of the meeting was to initiate a much more open voting system. The new committee would no longer be hand-picked by the outgoing members. 'And that felt like a really big move,' declares Hasan.[12] It was agreed that anyone performing comedy in Cambridge should be able to sign up to vote. The aim was to be more like all the other university societies where the committee does the actual organizing, the admin, and stood quite separate from the performing members. In future years, there was to be some overlap, even though essentially applying for membership and applying for committee became two separate processes.

In his third year, Hasan made it on to the committee. He also co-directed the Footlights first stand-up showcase. This was an attempt to place stand-up as close as possible in terms of equal status to sketch comedy. The event, which ran across four days, proved a big success and continues to this day as a showcase of the best stand-up talent. Along with two fellow Cambridge students, Danny Baalbaki and Patrick Sylla, Hasan also formed the first BAME-only troupe of Footlights performers. Hasan came up with the ironic name, FootDarks. They performed at the Edinburgh Fringe across the road from where the main Footlights show was on.

With Footlights in the throes of change, the best entry point remained auditioning for smokers or trying for the panto. That's what Ash Weir did. And only because she loved pantos. 'I didn't realize it was such a big thing.'[13] It was the first show she did at Cambridge. The panto was *Robin Hood* and as usual it was music heavy. 'The score was amazing.'[14] The composer was Toby Marlow, best known for co-creating the hit musical *Six* with Lucy Moss; both worked on the project while in their final year at Cambridge. 'My solo was a ballad called Against the Grain,' Ash recalls, 'which was a 'Let-It-Go'-esque anthem absolutely packed with bread puns. It was such an amazing introduction to the Cambridge comedy and theatre scene. I think doing that show was what solidified me wanting to do more with the Footlights, and ultimately probably to pursue a career in performing.'[15]

Ash didn't go to Cambridge with the intention of joining the Footlights, but it was definitely on her radar. 'Mainly because when I told people I'd got into Cambridge, which coming from a state school in Rotherham wasn't exactly a well-trodden path, they'd reel off a list of very impressive names of its former members and raise their eyebrows at me.'[16] She wrote a lot with John Tothill, they'd perform comedy songs at May Balls and smokers and in other people's sketch shows. She also followed John onto the Footlights committee, and made the 2018 tour show, *Pillow Talk*. 'That taught me so much about tailoring material and performance to international audiences. The way to sell sketches in Cambridge and Edinburgh was drastically different to what went down well in Sacramento, or Vancouver or New York.'[17]

Probably the most memorable sketch in *Pillow Talk* was 'Horse Dad'. During the show's writing process, the cast was always put into different pairs so no one ended up writing with the same people. Meg Coslett was paired with Will Bicknell for this one session, and they were very different comics. Meg was very much of the Victoria Wood, French and Saunders, Caroline Aherne school of character comedy, whereas Will was a bit Mighty Boosh-y, more off the wall and absurdist, so it was a very odd clashing of styles. 'They both wanted to write a sketch about a girl bringing her new boyfriend home to meet her dad for the first time,' Ash recalls, 'but Meg wanted the dad to be obsessed with horses – like a sort of zany dressage nut – whereas Will wanted him to actually be a horse. It ended up being somewhere in the middle, and after feeding him sugar lumps and winning his trust, at the end of the sketch the boyfriend rode off into the sunset on the dad's back.'[18] Nobody could ever really work out if the sketch was any good or not. 'It was the kind of thing where audiences would either say it was the best sketch in the show or the worst thing they'd ever seen,' jokes Ash.[19]

The tour show kicked off as usual in Cambridge but because the ADC was undergoing refurbishment at the time, the run took place at the Cambridge Union instead. In the US, the group played at the Upright Citizens Brigade Theatre in New York and Second City in Chicago. Travel-wise, the cast was split into a pair of big cars, with two drivers in each. Ash was one of the designated drivers. 'One of my abiding memories is running out of petrol halfway through Yosemite National Park, which was terrifying and hilarious and entirely my fault.'[20] Other highlights included going to a student party in Pittsburgh after performing at Carnegie Mellon University, and watching the Chicago Philharmonic in Millennium Park with deep dish pizzas and Prosecco. Another favourite show was at the Fallout Theatre in Austin. 'They let us raid their props box, it was carnage. It's wild that aged twenty-one we took an hour of original comedy writing on an all-expenses paid road trip across America.'[21]

Pillow Talk had a cast of three men and two women, a situation that was reversed for the 2019 tour show, *Look Alive*. Angela Channell, an English student at St John's College, didn't know if she had a chance of getting in but was desperate to give it her best shot. The audition process resembled something like a boot camp. For the initial audition the candidate brought along their own material to perform, either a sketch or a bit of stand-up. At the second audition, they performed material that was given to them. At the final stage they were paired with another person to write a sketch together and perform it, to see how they worked and got on together. Angela thinks she was chosen because she was a strong writer, others were good at ad-libbing, someone else might have this alt comedy persona. A great deal of thought went into creating a good mix.

Angela came from state school in Manchester and found everything at Cambridge completely alien; many people already seemed to know each other, having arrived from the same private schools. It was so overwhelming, and Angela felt so homesick in her first week she wanted to get out. The students in the year above organized an activity to bring all the freshers together, a trip to see that year's returning tour show. 'I'd grown up with sketch comedy on TV, but I'd never seen live sketch comedy,' admits Angela. 'And I realized as I was watching it, I was laughing so much, it was the first time that whole week that I'd stopped thinking, I hate it here, I'm stressed, I'm scared.'[22] Something else left an impression, seeing women on stage being funny. And even though Angela was of the frame of mind that she could never do that herself, she was intrigued enough to visit the Freshers' Fair the next day and approached the Footlights stall. Encouraged to attend the freshers' workshop, Anna was to perform her own sketch in front of a crowd of 250 people. 'And I just didn't look back after that.'[23]

The Footlights stall that year was manned entirely by female committee members. Angela isn't sure that if it had been all men she would have gone over. This was a deliberate decision to encourage more women like Angela to get involved. Committee members Ruby Keane and Ania Magliano-Wright had also recently set up Stockings, a comedy collective for women and non-binary comedians to try out material in a relaxed, supportive environment. This included open mic nights where there were no auditions, so everyone was guaranteed a spot.

The comedy vibe in Footlights when Angela arrived was still sketch heavy, but with a zeal for experimentation. 'Tim Key and American alt comedy was a huge influence on our set of people coming through.'[24] There was very little political humour going on or anything that was especially edgy or heavy. The edginess, especially in smokers, came from playing around with form, or with jokes that weren't really jokes, anti-humour. There was certainly a lot more thought and consideration taken about how their comedy might affect people in the audience. 'We didn't want to punch down,' says Angela. 'And there was much more awareness, which is part of learning comedy. OK, if you are going to make a joke that is a bit close to the line, who is the actual person that you're making fun of? I wouldn't describe it as a fear of cancel culture, it was more like people just being a bit more open minded and empathetic.'[25]

Angela recalls something like 100 sketches being written for *Look Alive* during the writing week that was whittled down to a core number that were interchangeable. 'Normally, you're performing to other students who need something that's like, not just a twist, it's a twist upon a twist. But we were very aware that we were writing for people who were buying tickets because they loved the Footlights that got onto the TV in the 1980s and 1990s. So, the style of comedy was very much classic sketches, bits of parody, silly exaggeration sketches, and some topical bits, we had an Elon Musk sketch and an *X Factor* parody, things like that.'[26]

The interesting premise had the cast of six as an earth exhibit coming alive in the future to represent what life was like on this planet. There was a big opening number showing the history of mankind from Jesus to Shania Twain, all done to a techno remix of *2001: A Space Odyssey*. One sketch had the cast 'babysitting' the audience, which included a lot of interaction. At one point, Angela had to run around the auditorium throwing lettuce around. During a performance at Edinburgh, she locked eyes with a stone-faced Hugh Laurie who was sitting in the back row with Stephen Fry. 'OK, I thought, they're not liking it. And you just have to carry on.'[27]

Look Alive turned out to be the last tour show for two years. The casting process had gone ahead as per normal, everyone was ready, but the writer's week that was due to start in March kept being delayed, until finally it was called off. It was in that final week of the Lent term that Covid hit. News of the virus first began to spread around the university in January. 'I was doing a solo stand-up show and I'd seen the news,' recalls Angela. 'I'm quite a hypochondriac and I had a bit of a sore throat and thought, it could be that. And I remember my mum being like, no Angela, it's not even in this country yet.'[28]

Increasingly, Covid began to be referenced in jokes and at smokers. Then, with the spring revue out of the way, focus turned to a show Footlights put on every year at the ADC, where it hosted some of the best student comedy troupes from around the country across two consecutive Sunday evenings. Angela was involved and recalls that the first show had gone down well, but this was the week when Covid really got serious and everything was beginning to shut down. By the end of the week, all the colleges sent out messages to their students saying that unless there was a specific reason why they couldn't go home, they should leave the university and go home – immediately. The hope was that this was just for a few weeks. But Angela and the rest of the cast still had a show to put on that Sunday. Everyone expressed concern that it wasn't safe to put the show on, with some members of the cast beginning to feel ill. 'The Arts was a 700-capacity theatre,' says Angela, 'and we knew that some of the audience were elderly and vulnerable. But the theatre was saying, you must perform, you are contractually obliged. There was a lot of toing and froing, and in the end, we did get faculty involved because we were saying, look, we're stuck in the middle here, we are still only students, and we're being told that we can't stay at the university but also that we have to perform this show with half the cast struck down.'[29] Most likely this was a case of end of term colds rather than Covid, but at the time no one knew what was going on.

In the end, the show was cancelled and theatre staff sent out alerts on social media and personally phoned every ticket holder to apologize. There was hardly one complaint, it was seen as the most sensible thing to do. The official lockdown followed soon after and Angela left the university on the Saturday night. 'I packed a suitcase with a bunch of stuff thinking I wouldn't be away for too long. Those of us who were left had a final breakfast, and we were all distributing any random perishables we had and saying, see you in a few weeks. I didn't get back to clean out my room until after I graduated in July. It all stopped. Completely.'[30]

Angela ended up graduating in absentia. 'Normally, there's a grad smoker which is quite emotional because it's the very last show that everyone does before they graduate, and we couldn't do that so we did a virtual grad smoker.'[31] After that she was told to book a date and a time slot to pick up her belongings and clear out her rooms. It was the first time she'd been back since having to leave those months before and the university was like a ghost town, with posters still up advertising shows that never happened. 'I went back on the day my college's May Ball would have been held, so I was just wandering around in the grounds thinking, this is what they had started planning. And my room was untouched, there was even an orange that I'd left on the side that had gone completely petrified.'[32]

The hope was that at least the tour show would go on that summer. Auditions had already taken place, and a cast assembled, but when it became clear that lockdown was going to last for a considerable time the committee made the only decision that it could, to postpone the show for a year and go ahead instead in 2021. Everyone involved was gutted. It was especially galling since the new production highlighted the successful work of the outreach programmes that had been put in place. 'I know it's horrible to talk in tick boxes,' says assistant director Jade Franks, 'but it demonstrated how much the Footlights had changed in just a short period.'[33] Plans had also been put in place to visit comprehensive schools and give workshops, rather than the previous lucrative practice of going to private schools.

While everyone shared a sense of disappointment, at least there was the prospect of the show going ahead next year and writing sessions for it continued, on Zoom. With everyone back home, efforts were made to form some kind of community online. It was very much a case of figuring out how to navigate the online world. It was a whole learning process. 'We had to be really imaginative,' declares Jade.[34] Ultimately, a whole host of events took place, like improv shows, livestreams, committee meetings went ahead online and smokers went on Zoom. People also took it upon themselves to put things on TikTok and YouTube. It was all an effort to keep the comedy scene alive. 'Definitely making videos kept me sane,' says Angela, 'because it was just something to do that still felt like being in Footlights. Honestly, I think I spent more time doing digital sketches than I did doing my work.'[35] But it was no substitute for the real thing.

Jade was president at this difficult time and felt a huge responsibility to keep the momentum going because everyone was so deflated. 'My whole manifesto was built on the idea of welcoming people who didn't think that comedy would be for them, or didn't think they'd even fit in in that world.'[36] Covid dashed all that, and doing things remotely was difficult. Jade had attended a comprehensive school in Merseyside, 'where maybe one person had been to Cambridge.'[37] Although interested in comedy, hanging around the comedy circuit in Liverpool, Jade had wanted to be an actress and auditioned for drama school in London. Accepted by Mountview and RADA, she couldn't attend because of the expense involved. Instead, she travelled around for a bit before getting a job in a call centre in Liverpool. There, she found herself at something of a crossroads, should she go to university, where she had the grades, or apply for drama school again? There was a course at Cambridge that appealed, a BA in Education, with English and theatre, and she got in. 'I knew about the Footlights but I don't think I fully understood what it meant. And so, I felt a little bit on the backfoot to everyone else who seemed to know each other or went to the same schools.'[38] Auditioning for smokers, Jade felt like a bit of a dark horse, 'because a lot of my material was observations about being working class in Cambridge, and how alien it was for me.'[39] After doing well at the smokers, Jade felt more accepted, and in her second year got a place on the committee where she became outreach officer, her job to bring in more people from working class and diverse backgrounds.

In her third year, besides getting onto the tour show, Jade was asked to co-write the panto with Joe Venable. It was *Sleeping Beauty*. 'The premise was,' recalls Jade, 'the prince came to kiss her when she was sleeping and she's like, you can't kiss me when I haven't even consented. That was the start of it. It was very left-wing, borderline Communist. There was a lot of political stuff going on at the time that we could make jokes about.'[40] Jade and Joe were both at St Edmond's College and regularly attended protests, marches and demos, 'as you do when you're a student'.[41] They were also influenced by the previous year's panto, *Robin Hood*. 'All the Merry Men had a sickle and hammer as their emblem. That was kind of the vibe.'[42] Traditionally, Footlights didn't stray into politics. For Jade, though, she

FIGURE 19.1 *Jade Franks and Adedamola Laoye (president after Jade) on stage in 2020 during the Covid-19 pandemic.* © *Jade Franks.*

never even considered that the Footlights weren't political during her time there. 'A lot of my comedy was rooted in discussions of classism, government corruption, Thatcher.'[43]

The panto was for the most part written remotely, thinking that everyone would be back at least by the end of the year. All the auditions were done on Zoom. When lockdown looked likely to continue, the decision was made to do the panto live online. The musicians recorded their parts separately at home, and it was all put together by the musical director. The cast also pre-recorded their singing. When it went live everyone joined the Zoom call and waited in the wings, as it were, to be brought into the call for their scenes, with the actors in full costume. Jade watched the production in her flat with ten friends she'd invited. 'It was lockdown and it was the rule of six, but we thought, so much has been taken away from us, so we did a test and then sat and watched it and that was one of my favourite moments.'[44]

As for the delayed tour show, everyone waited and hoped. If the Edinburgh Fringe was going ahead, the signs were good, but when that was postponed for the second year running the tour producers followed suit. It was a tough decision, all the flights had been paid for the US leg, so a lot of money was lost. For the students, the news was devastating. 'For everyone in their Cambridge journey,' says Jade, 'that is the pinnacle of what you can do as part of the Footlights, to go on this incredible tour, and to be embedded in history. There's definitely something to say about being a part of this archive and what it means to have been a comedian at Cambridge.'[45] Professionally, too, it had an effect. There has always been the possibility of being spotted and signed up by any number of the agents who regularly turn up at the Edinburgh Fringe. This was never to happen for them, and consequently, many of Jade's contemporaries decided not to pursue comedy careers.

When everyone was finally allowed to return to Cambridge, it was a hybrid time. For smokers participants could be in the ADC again and stand on the stage, but there was no audience, only a camera placed in the fifth row, and the event was live streamed. 'That was a weird time,' admits Jade. 'We were kind of back and kind of not back.'[46]

So many people missed out on the opportunities Footlights brought because of the pandemic. Two tour shows were scrapped and when things began to open up again so much momentum and training had been lost. It was especially bad for those that had applied to be members, got in, and met just the once in person before Covid hit. 'One of the things that makes the Footlights so strong is that there is a big connection between a lot of the

FIGURE 19.2 *The ADC Theatre, Cambridge, home of the Footlights. Jeffrey Blackler/Alamy Stock Photo.*

members which allows them to write sketches and do comedy together,' states Adam Al-janabi. 'They've got an intimate relationship which our year didn't particularly have because of Covid.'[47]

Adam had always wanted to go to Cambridge, but coming from Newcastle his parents discouraged him from applying to anywhere down south because of the costs. Instead, he went to York University. Interested in comedy, while at York he read a book called *Comedy Rules* by Jonathan Lynn, which went into detail about his time in Footlights. Adam was fascinated. 'I started looking up all the other Footlights and thought, wow, OK, if you want to do comedy this seems like the place to go.'[48] So, he did his Master's in chemistry at Cambridge and took advantage of the numerous shows and smokers that took place at all the colleges. 'I would be doing stand-up, doing improv, performing in sketches with other people. Every single moment that I wasn't studying I was out talking to other comedians and performing.'[49]

When the pandemic struck Adam wasn't living at uni but in private accommodation so didn't have to go home. 'But there was no one in Cambridge, it was completely dead.'[50] Coming from York University, Adam was in awe of the Footlights. At York, the performance space they used for comedy was a lecture hall, 'and we used to hang torches up to make the stage lights.'[51] And then coming to Cambridge, the facilities and opportunities were worlds apart. In Adam's year as a member there turned out to be more women than men, but the club still struggled when it came to diversity and the fact that it was predominantly white. 'I remember feeling intimidated as an Arab,' admits Adam. 'Am I going to get in?'[52] In the year above there was Hasan Al-Habib. And while Adam struggled to get into smokers when he first arrived, he did appear at the BAME smoker, held at the ADC. 'And I was so nervous. It was the biggest stage I'd ever performed on. And to this day it's one of my favourite gigs. It went so well. And when I got off stage afterwards Hasan said, "Finally we've got another Arab in the Footlights." And him saying that was enough for me to think, you know what, I can do this.'[53]

Adam's preference was for stand-up, which in the last couple of years had begun to take over. 'The majority of Footlight members were stand-ups.'[54] Adam performed in the first Footlights stand-up showcase, where audiences were a bit rough, with cruel heckles and boos for some of the less experienced or just plain bad performers. Adam went on to host the event.

In 2022, the spring revue and tour show were back, and stuck reverentially to the sketch format, even though in the year Adam got in, only two out of a cast of five had written sketches before and were primarily stand-up comics. Adam had always been interested in writing sketches and so enjoyed the challenge, although as usual it was stressful coming up with an entire show during the exam period. He wrote one sketch that revolved around the fact that many birds have dirty names, like blue tit, great tit etc. At a meeting to come up with names for birds, accompanied by a big PowerPoint presentation on birds, Adam played a lecherous old man making the most vulgar suggestions – 'Let's call it the great shag.'

The theme of 2022's revue show, *Are We There Yet?*, was travel, hence the title, only the cast soon found the concept limiting and instead just focused on what they considered the funniest sketches. There was an opening dance number revolving around flight safety rules being read out – your exits are here, here and here. At the opening night at the ADC, an elderly man, in his nineties, came along and wanted to speak to the cast afterwards. It transpired that he had seen every revue show at Cambridge going back to the 1940s. 'We were so impressed,' recalls Adam. 'But he was so old that when he sat down next to us, he shat himself, immediately. And we were all like, what do we do. But he was lovely. Bless him.'[55]

In Edinburgh, the show went well but some critical judgement remained jaundiced. 'We got a bunch of reviews complaining we were just a bunch of private school twats,' says Adam. 'The director said to me, "As you're the only one not from a public school, at the end say thank you for coming to the audience in the most Geordie of accents that you can do just to prove to people that it's not all private school twats." Which we did for the rest of the run and we stopped getting the private school twat allegations.'[56]

The biggest reception of all awaited the production in America. 'They were so happy to see us back,' Adam recalls. 'The one venue that really struck a chord for me was in Sacramento. It was this tiny little theatre and when we got there it was packed and they were so enthusiastic. We stayed behind for maybe four hours because all the audience just wanted to stay and talk with us.'[57] Again, they played Second City in Chicago, the Peoples Improv Theater, also known as the PIT, a comedy theatre and training centre in New York, and a couple of shows in LA. And there was another trip to the Harvard Lampoon and an invitation to the club house. 'Which is this giant castle,' says Adam. 'And you're only allowed in if you're a Lampoon or a celebrity guest. Or a Footlight. It's a crazy space.'[58]

As with previous tour shows to the States, the cast found that some of the sketches didn't translate or were too subtle. For example, Adam wrote a sketch with fellow cast member Jonathan Neary in which he played a father sitting down with his son. 'There comes a point in every son's life where he has to teach his father about sex.' Jonathan, as the son, announces, 'No, no, you've got it the wrong way round.' Adam replies, 'No, I don't know how it works.' The joke is that the father is Joseph and his son is Jesus. Joseph doesn't know the mechanics of sex because Mary's pregnancy was an immaculate conception. 'In Britain you just had to do a little hint of who they really were and that was enough, they got it,' Adam explains. 'In America, no, you had to spell it out.'[59]

Following the US tour for *Are We There Yet?*, there was much debate about whether playing a few club gigs in New York and Los Angeles really justified the enormous financial outlay. The US tour did go ahead in 2023 but with a reduced number of dates, and there was no tour in 2024. 'I feel so lucky that I got to do that US tour in 2023,' declares Izzie H-P.[60] Studying Anglo-Saxon, Norse and Celtic, Izzie was someone else who was affected by Covid. Like Adam, Izzie had been doing numerous shows, building momentum, when Covid shut everything down. 'And then coming into my second year it was very hard to keep the comedy going because there just wasn't the infrastructure to support it, so it was really hard to get anything off the ground.'[61] When the lockdown laws began to ease, smokers returned but there was a reluctance to attend. 'Covid had really disrupted the legacy of the smokers,' insists Izzie. 'When I first started, they were super exciting, they were selling out, and then after Covid people didn't really know what they were because they just hadn't seen them and they weren't buying tickets.'[62]

Another problem was getting anyone to sign up and perform. The resources that usually get passed down between years, to the second years and freshers, simply didn't exist. Covid had destroyed all those important channels of communication. Those coming in also had no time to make friends or put on shows, they had no time to make what are vital connections. And it was a knock to their confidence. Instead, there was a gravitation towards online comedy, which continued post-Covid, with performers filming their own material and putting it on YouTube and TikTok. In the social media age maybe this was viewed as a better way to get seen than inviting people to shows.

Izzie made it onto the committee and was given the role of social secretary, organizing events, doing outreach and helping with workshops. The committee remained open to candidates at any point, while you could still only be a writing/performing Footlight member in your final year. Becoming a member for Izzie required a written application that asked the candidate to talk about what they liked to do comedy-wise, why they were so passionate about it, and what they thought they could bring to membership. Lastly, they were asked to provide links to videos or clips of them doing comedy online. There was no face-to-face interview or audition.

The danger for Izzie, having wanted to do Footlights from being a teenager, was that it might prove a disappointment. Instead, it surpassed all expectations, and getting into the 2023 tour show was massive. 'It was the most exciting summer. Everyone got on so well.'[63] Entitled *The Search Continues*, the framing of the show was that the cast of five were searching for their sixth member, which by the end of the evening turned out to be someone from the audience. All five cast members had quite different comedy styles which during the writing process produced some interesting sketches. 'I think there was a bit of something for everyone,' says Izzie. 'We were relatively self-aware about what people expected from us. We did a sketch set on a submarine which was our Monty Python sketch. It was very silly and we said, this is for the people who think we're Monty Python. We're going to give them this, they're going to be happy, then let's move on and do something weird and different afterwards.'[64] There wasn't anything too dark or experimental. 'That would be too far from what was expected of us. Because going into a tour we have a knowledge that we need to make some money so they can do this tour next year. None of us wanted to ruin it for the following year.'[65]

The UK tour, according to Izzie, was, 'absolutely miniscule,'[66] just Bristol, London and Newcastle, along with the one school workshop. At Edinburgh, they played the Pleasance, 'and I was so excited to be there, but it was terrifying and completely exhausting.'[67] One interesting aspect of the production was that the cast was made up of four women and one man, Daniel Patten. 'We made a lot of jokes in the show about Dan being our token man,' says Izzie.[68] The casting hadn't been intentional, it just turned out that way. However, during the casting process for whatever production it may be, everyone always made sure that all demographics were being represented. 'Because there are enough talented people to make that work,' confirms Izzie.[69]

When Margaret Saunderson arrived in Cambridge from Liverpool in 2022, there was an even split of male and female club members. Her issue was the distinct lack of people from the north who were visible in any of the shows. 'And then I was very lucky in my second year that the president was also northern, and she was very encouraging of me. So, that representation is something that we really push for.'[70] A realization exists still that some people might be intimidated to join the Footlights, perhaps because you must both write and perform your own material, or its very name and reputation. A lot of freshers say, 'You've got all these famous alumni; I don't think I'm good enough,' only to be reassured, 'No, you are! We want to help make you that famous alumni.'

Ultimately, it's a matter of trying to implement accessible opportunities. The club continues to put on a large programme of shows every year, scope enough for groups which have traditionally been underrepresented in comedy. For example, 'Second Generation' is a sketch show that is put on once a year that has an entirely BAME cast and crew. There is a smoker for disabled students, which also includes neurodiverse people. And the women-only smoker, which Jade Franks always enjoyed better than a normal smoker. 'I just loved the positivity and the celebration that was happening in those spaces.'[71] There's something called, 'A Comprehensive Understanding,' which is a sketch show made up of performers who all went to a state school. In recent years, Footlights had begun to make visits to state schools to host workshops for less-advantaged pupils. And Footlights Presents continues to give people with less comedy experience the chance to get involved. Margaret directed the show one year and found that most of the cast hadn't done sketches before or any kind of group performance.

And there are the smokers of course. Margaret is one of those who never experienced how the smokers used to be before Covid. When she hosted one in 2023, only about twenty people showed up. Afterwards, the manager of the ADC told her how when he was a student there were long queues outside the door. 'I thought that was an absolutely ridiculous notion.'[72] The following year, Margaret instituted a big push to win audiences back, including setting up social media accounts just for smokers, and they started selling out again. 'We were turning people away at the door.'[73]

Margaret had always been interested in the theatre and writing, and knew about the Footlights and was drawn to Cambridge because of its thriving drama scene. She wasn't disappointed and was able to put on her own comedy show under the umbrella of the club. 'And that's such a crazy opportunity to have as a student doing her own stand-up hour completely funded and with an entire technical team behind you. I'm aware that's such an incredible opportunity and one that you don't want to take lightly.'[74]

In 2024, Margaret took over the presidency of a club that after the trials and tribulations of Covid was returning to something like its old rude health. The 2024 tour show, *This Time We Have a Dog*, was once again a success, and even though there was no US trip it played to strong audiences at Edinburgh, proving the name Footlights is still a draw. However, there has been recent talk of changing the tour show to keep up with current comedy trends. 'People who come to see the revue show,' says Margaret, 'are still expecting to go and see the Footlights and see something very similar to what you would have got in the 1970s in terms of the sketch. But that doesn't resonate with young people, which is what we are.'[75] The 2024 tour show opened with the entire cast standing on stage declaring: We're not the people you saw in the 1960s, we're something different now.

Thoughts have turned to the spring revue, too, and whether it necessarily needs to be a sketch show. Sketch as a concept is something that no longer dominates the comedy scene, so should it dominate within the club? Certainly, in the last few years stand-up has taken over from sketch comedy as the form most members prefer. No doubt because stand-up is more recognizable for young people today, with very few sketch shows featuring on TV anymore, certainly not in the same way they used to.

As the newest president, Margaret sees the Footlights as a club that is there to nurture talent. And not necessarily a talent that may want to go on in the business, but a student who just wants to do it as an activity while studying. Not everybody who gets involved wants to be Stephen Fry. And there is always the desire to make Footlights as welcoming an environment as possible. Outside perceptions still exist, the idea that the club is a prep school for comedy, an enclave of privilege. 'But admissions to the club have changed, as admissions to the university has changed,' states Margaret. 'It used to be that people coming out of Footlights were white upper-class men, and I don't think that is the case anymore.'[76]

A new and somewhat controversial change is the introduction of a 'sensitivity reading' service to ensure, in the words of a press release from the club, that 'all student comedy' is as 'inclusive and welcoming as possible'. This doesn't extend to all Footlight shows, and is an 'optional request'. However, there is a sensitivity reader for the panto. Back in 2021, Izzie co-wrote the panto, *Rapunzel*. It was a queer retelling of the fairy story and due to elements of homophobia, and the theme of kidnap (in the story Rapunzel gets kidnapped), there were some content warnings. Although this followed ADC theatre policy, the show was criticized by the *Daily Mail*, which Izzie found rather cool and something of a badge of honour. All this was before the sensitivity reader service was created. In her year group, if there was going to be an issue Izzie would seek advice from fellow writers. 'Because as a comedian you must be aware of the stuff you're joking about. I think it would be very odd if something slipped through the net and then got picked up by a sensitivity reader. When I was doing workshops there was so much emphasis on comedy training about punching up rather than punching down.'[77]

It was the same for Jade Franks. 'There was a tension around that if you were going to do a more edgy joke, I think you'd speak to your closer people first of all and be like, what do you think about this? Is this too close to the bone? Is this going to offend anyone? I think that's a positive thing. If comedians are thinking about, OK I'm going to do this joke, is it funny, or is it punching down? We spoke so much about punching up and punching down.'[78] There was still comedy being performed that Jade felt was inherently sexist, or classist, such as the use of accents to portray a certain character. Why, for example, had somebody chosen for a sketch to use a Scouse accent for a thief? It was lazy comedy. 'I would never cancel anyone, but there was more of an open conversation around people's backgrounds and people's communities, and what is potentially punching down.'[79]

Whatever the merits, good or bad, of a sensitivity reader, by introducing such a policy, Footlights is simply mirroring what is already happening in the wider comedy and entertainment industries. 'We aren't here to censor people from telling an authentic truth or anything,' claims Margaret, 'but as a club that wants to nurture, it's about protection of people as well. If you say something on stage which is offensive it could follow you, which we don't want for anyone. We're not here to say, we don't want anything risky or edgy, it's about having people identify what is the difference between something that is actually authentically funny and then something that is just said for shock value.'[80]

20

Gone with the Clappers

For most of the people interviewed for this book, Footlights was a wholly positive experience. 'The friendships that I have from Footlights have lasted me most of my life,' declares James Bachman. 'It was one of the most important things that happened to me. It's affected everything that I've done since.'[1] Graeme Garden feels much the same. 'I owe it a lot really. But I don't feel I owe the Footlights so much as I owe the people that I was there with, and then went on working with for most my life.'[2]

Just being in a place where there were so many other people with the same interests and obsessions must have been invigorating. These were people who loved comedy and wanted to spend more time doing that than they did their academics. 'It taught me so much about making comedy,' says Izzie H-P. 'Not necessarily through some central institution that is teaching you how to write jokes, but through the people you meet who bring out different parts of your comedic voice. And that's how you find it, you can't do that in a vacuum, you have to meet other people who also do comedy and work with them. And that's what the Footlights did for me.'[3]

Many perhaps didn't appreciate at the time what an amazing training ground Footlights was in terms of honing one's performance skills and writing. According to Jan Ravens, 'It gave me the opportunity to, I wouldn't say hone my craft because it wasn't really at a honing stage, it was at a kind of knocking great lumps out of things stage, but it gave me the chance to practice my craft.'[4]

The advantages were many. It bestowed enormous confidence. And in the Footlights, you got confidence from two things. First from doing lots of shows: smokers, the tour etc. This regular performing experience was so invaluable. 'At smokers,' says Robin French, 'just being able to write some nonsense, and immediately being able to get the feedback from a full ADC to know whether it worked or not. It's hard to imagine a better training – we were all very lucky.'[5] The advantages of this were obvious to Mark Evans when he moved to London after graduating and performed at a very small fringe show. 'On the first night this lovely older comedian said, "This is a big night for you, remember this night." And we were playing a fifty-seater, and I just bit my lip because I wanted to go, the last three summers on the tour show I've spent playing to 400-seaters.'[6]

The other big confidence builder was that Footlights made a creative career seem possible. A huge factor was its continuing connection to students who had already graduated and making their way in the profession. Mitchell and Webb and Matthew Holness, for example, would return as graduates to test out their shows at the ADC. 'I think for a lot of people the idea of working in comedy feels mad,' argues Matt Green. 'But if you know a few people who have already started doing it then it feels like, oh, maybe that's possible.'[7]

It toughened you up as well. Footlights was a place where you could go and fall flat on your face, where you could learn from your mistakes in front of a reasonably friendly and encouraging student audience. 'It was a safe place to try stuff,' says John Tothill, 'as opposed to say starting out on the club circuit to hecklers and boos. Footlights was the opposite of that. It was to mollycoddle you for three years until you're able to write a joke.'[8] One buzz word that was around a lot during Jade Franks's time was, permission to fail. 'In different fringe theatres in London and across the UK, artists are less and less being given the chance to just try something out without any stakes and financial repercussions. Just try something out and if it's shit, it's shit, you'll learn and do better next time. Cambridge was that place. It was a place to play, it was a place to try stuff out.'[9]

Being in Footlights afforded other opportunities, too, such as interpersonal skills, just being forced to work with others in a tense environment. 'And experience this kind of burst of creative excitement of working with people and cooperating and collaborating on something,' states Archie Henderson. 'And also, the bubble being burst, oh actually this person can be really annoying and we're now in a working relationship and we have to get this done in the next two months because there's a lot at stake. I felt already it was like my job for that reason, the fallouts that you have, being a bit stuck together with people and navigating that.'[10]

These lessons are as relevant today as they ever were, especially because the Footlights remain just as focused on original writing, as well as performing, than they ever did in the past. 'And I think that's a good thing,' argues Margaret Saunderson, 'because to put them hand in hand you are forced to become very good at both, and it lends itself to making you a bit of an all-rounder and a better understander of what you want to represent as a performer on stage. And I think that's so important because in comedy people laugh when they see something that's reflected in truth, and if you're trying to figure out your own truths, especially at such a young age, it's very important to look inward and then be brave enough to show that of yourself.'[11]

Looking back, many felt immense pride to be in the Footlights, keenly aware of the sense of heritage and history, and duty bound to maintain its place in the culture and not jeopardize its future. 'Each intake inherits this thing that has this history, this reputation, that everyone knows,' says Katie Breathwick. 'You have all of this expectation, but it comes with a weight as well, that you are the generation that fucks it up.'[12]

David Mitchell recalls just how proud he was of the Footlights tradition when he was there, feeling that he was part of something that had fed into British comedy. 'Now I'm older and the world has changed you look at it differently and you reflect on that, and obviously there is a great deal of privilege underlying people who were at Cambridge, academic privilege or in earlier decades class or financial privilege. Footlights people were in a position to be able to invest hope and expectation in the life of just writing the performing joke, which sort of takes away from any sense that there was something in the Cam water that makes you funny.'[13]

For people like David, Footlights was a world around which their ambition to do comedy or to perform professionally could coalesce. 'Its existence as an institution sort of justified that ambition for people who were nervous of taking that risk who in most cases, if they're at Cambridge, have been quite academically strong at school, so will have gone to university feeling they had good options in terms of proper, stable professions and the word Footlights was almost like a life buoy that allowed you to bob away from the ship. The fact that other people have had a go at comedy as a job from here, so why shouldn't we, at a point where you really have no idea how you're going to turn it into a job, or whether the things you find funny anyone else will find funny, was tremendously reassuring. And I hope it provides that for people still.'[14]

NOTES

Chapter 1: Beyond the Fringe

1 Roger Wilmut (ed.), *The Complete Beyond the Fringe* (London: Methuen, 1987).
2 Ibid.
3 Michael Frayn, author interview.
4 Ibid.
5 Ibid.
6 Bill Oddie, author interview.
7 Michael Romain, *A Profile of Jonathan Miller* (Cambridge: Cambridge University Press, 1992).
8 *Parkinson*, BBC1, 1972.

Chapter 2: Cheer-Oh Cambridge

1 Jack Hulbert, *The Little Woman's Always Right* (London: W. H. Allen, 1975).
2 Eric Maschwitz, *No Chip on My Shoulder* (London: Herbert Jenkins Ltd, 1957).
3 Ibid.
4 Cecil Beaton, *The Unexpurgated Beaton Diaries* (London: Phoenix, 2003).
5 Robert Hewison, *Footlights! A Hundred Years of Cambridge Comedy* (London: Methuen, 1983).
6 Ibid.
7 *Homes and Garden*, Vol. 38, 1957.
8 Hewison, *Footlights! A Hundred Years of Cambridge Comedy*.
9 Ronald Millar, *A View from the Wings* (London: Orion, 1993).
10 Ibid.
11 Jimmy Edwards, *Six of the Best* (London: Robson Books, 2002).
12 Frederic Raphael, author interview.

Chapter 3: Cabbages and Kings

1 Peter Firth, author interview.
2 Ibid.
3 Ibid.
4 Ibid.
5 Ibid.
6 Ibid.
7 Ibid.
8 Ibid.
9 Ibid.
10 Ibid.
11 Ibid.
12 Frederic Raphael, author interview.
13 Ibid.
14 Ibid.
15 Peter Firth, author interview.
16 Frederic Raphael, author interview.
17 Peter Firth, author interview.
18 Ibid.
19 Ibid.
20 Frederic Raphael, author interview.
21 Ibid.
22 Ibid.
23 Peter Firth, author interview.
24 Frederic Raphael, author interview.
25 Ibid.
26 Ibid.
27 Ibid.
28 Ibid.
29 Ibid.
30 Ibid.
31 Leslie Bricusse, *Pure Imagination: The Life and Good Times of a Songwriter – A Sorta-biography* (London: Faber Music, 2015).
32 John Drummond, *Tainted by Experience* (London: Faber & Faber, 2001).
33 Michael Frayn, author interview.
34 Frederic Raphael, author interview.
35 Ibid.
36 Ibid.

37 Ibid.
38 Ibid.
39 Geoffrey Strachan, author interview.
40 Ibid.
41 Ibid.
42 Ibid.
43 Michael Frayn, author interview.
44 Ibid.
45 Ibid.
46 Ibid.
47 Ibid.
48 Ibid.
49 Ibid.
50 Ibid.
51 Ibid.
52 Ibid.
53 Ibid.
54 Geoffrey Strachan, author interview.
55 Ibid.
56 Ibid.

Chapter 4: The Last Laugh

1 Roger Wilmut, *From Fringe to Flying Circus: Celebrating a Unique Generation of Comedy 1960–1980* (London: Metheun, 1982).
2 Lin Cook (ed.), *Peter Cook Remembered* (London: Arrow, 1997).
3 David Frost, *David Frost: An Autobiography* (London: HarperCollins, 1994).
4 Ibid.
5 David Gooderson, author interview.
6 Bill Oddie, author interview.
7 Pete Atkin, author interview.
8 Harry Thompson, *Peter Cook: A Biography* (London: Hodder & Stoughton, 1997).

Chapter 5: I Thought I saw it Move

1 Bill Oddie, author interview.
2 Christopher Stuart-Clark, author interview.

3 John Cleese, *So, Anyway* (London: Random House, 2014).
4 Bill Oddie, author interview.
5 Andy Mayer, author interview.
6 Cleese, *So, Anyway*.
7 Ibid.
8 *London Review of Books*, 1 September 1983.
9 Graham Chapman, *Calcium Made Interesting: Sketches, Letters, Essays & Gondolas* (London: Sidgwick & Jackson, 2005).
10 Christopher Stuart-Clark, author interview.
11 Graeme Garden, author interview.
12 Wendy E. Cook, *Peter Cook, So Farewell Then: The Biography of Peter Cook* (London: HarperCollins, 2006).
13 Robert Hewison, *Footlights! A Hundred Years of Cambridge Comedy* (London: Methuen, 1983).
14 Lin Cook (ed.), *Peter Cook Remembered* (London: Arrow, 1997).
15 Robert Ross, *The Goodies Rule OK* (London: Carlton Books, 2006).
16 Ibid.
17 Bill Oddie, author interview.
18 Ibid.
19 Ibid.
20 Ibid.
21 Ibid.
22 Cleese, *So, Anyway*.
23 Sue Heber-Percy, author interview.
24 Miriam Margolyes, *This Much Is True* (London: John Murray, 2021).
25 Tony Hendra, *Father Joe: The Man Who Saved My Soul* (London: Random House, 2004).
26 Cleese, *So, Anyway*.

Chapter 6: A Clump of Plinths

1 Bill Oddie, author interview.
2 David Gooderson, author interview.
3 Ibid.
4 Bill Oddie, author interview.
5 Ibid.
6 Ibid.
7 David Gooderson, author interview.
8 Christopher Stuart-Clark, author interview.

9   Bill Oddie, author interview.
10 Anthony Hayward, obituary, *Guardian*, 3 February 2022.
11 Christopher Stuart-Clark, author interview.
12 John Cleese, *So, Anyway* (London: Random House, 2014).
13 Christopher Stuart-Clark, author interview.
14 David Gooderson, author interview.
15 Christopher Stuart-Clark, author interview.
16 Graeme Garden, author interview.
17 Christopher Stuart-Clark, author interview.
18 Cleese, *So, Anyway*.
19 Michael White, *Empty Seats* (London: Hamish Hamilton, 1984).
20 Richard Crane, author interview.
21 Christopher Stuart-Clark, author interview.
22 White, *Empty Seats*.
23 Christopher Stuart-Clark, author interview.
24 Ibid.
25 Ibid.
26 Bill Oddie, author interview.
27 Ibid.
28 Ibid.
29 Ibid.
30 Ibid.

Chapter 7: Stuff What Dreams Are Made Of

1   Graeme Garden, author interview.
2   Ibid.
3   Ibid.
4   Ibid.
5   Ibid.
6   Bill Oddie, author interview.
7   David Gooderson, author interview.
8   Ibid.
9   Graeme Garden, author interview.
10 David Gooderson, author interview.
11 Ibid.
12 Ibid.
13 Ibid.

14 Ibid.
15 Ibid.
16 Ibid.
17 Ibid.
18 Ibid.
19 Bill Oddie, author interview.
20 Graeme Garden, author interview.
21 David Gooderson, author interview.
22 Graeme Garden, author interview.
23 Christopher Stuart-Clark, author interview.
24 Graeme Garden, author interview.
25 Ibid.
26 Brian Gascoigne, author interview.
27 Graeme Garden, author interview.
28 Ibid.
29 Ibid.
30 Ibid.
31 David Gooderson, author interview.
32 Ibid.
33 Ibid.
34 John Cameron, author interview.
35 Andy Mayer, author interview.
36 John Cameron, author interview.
37 Ibid.
38 Ibid.
39 Ibid.
40 Ibid.
41 Sue Heber-Percy, author interview.
42 Ibid.
43 Ibid.
44 Ibid.
45 Ibid.
46 Ibid.
47 Graeme Garden, author interview.
48 Ibid.
49 Ibid.
50 Ibid.
51 Ibid.
52 John Cameron, author interview.

53 Ibid.
54 David Gooderson, author interview.
55 Graeme Garden, author interview.
56 Ibid.
57 Sue Heber-Percy, author interview.
58 Graeme Garden, author interview.
59 David Gooderson, author interview.
60 Richard Crane, author interview.
61 Bill Oddie, author interview.
62 Robert Hewison, *Footlights! A Hundred Years of Cambridge Comedy* (London: Methuen, 1983).
63 John Cameron, author interview.
64 Ibid.
65 Clive James, *May Week Was in June* (London: Picador, 2008).
66 Ibid.
67 Andy Mayer, author interview.
68 Ibid.
69 John Cameron, author interview.
70 Ibid.
71 Ibid.
72 Ibid.
73 Ibid.
74 Ibid.
75 Ibid.
76 Ibid.
77 Richard Syms, author interview.
78 Ibid.
79 Ibid.
80 Ibid.
81 Ibid.
82 Richard Crane, author interview.
83 Ibid.
84 Ibid.
85 Andy Mayer, author interview.
86 Ibid.
87 Ibid.
88 Richard Crane, author interview.
89 Ibid.
90 Ibid.

91 Ibid.
92 Andy Mayer, author interview.
93 Richard Syms, author interview.
94 Nick Hancock, author interview.
95 Andy Mayer, author interview.
96 John Cameron, author interview.
97 Richard Crane, author interview.
98 Richard Syms, author interview.
99 Andy Mayer, author interview.
100 Richard Syms, author interview.
101 Richard Crane, author interview.

Chapter 8: Supernatural Gas

1 Richard Syms, author interview.
2 Richard Crane, author interview.
3 Barry Brown, author interview.
4 Richard Syms, author interview.
5 Andy Mayer, author interview.
6 Richard Syms, author interview.
7 Adrian Edwards, author interview.
8 Ibid.
9 Pete Atkin, author interview.
10 Robert Hewison, *Footlights! A Hundred Years of Cambridge Comedy* (London: Methuen, 1983).
11 Barry Brown, author interview.
12 Ibid.
13 Pete Atkin, author interview.
14 Ibid.
15 Ibid.
16 Ibid.
17 Ibid.
18 Ibid.
19 Barry Brown, author interview.
20 Adrian Edwards, author interview.
21 Pete Atkin, author interview.
22 Ibid.
23 Ibid.

24 Ibid.
25 Ibid.
26 Ibid.
27 Ibid.
28 David Hare, author interview.
29 Ibid.
30 Barry Brown, author interview.
31 Pete Atkin, author interview.
32 Barry Brown, author interview.
33 Ibid.
34 Adrian Edwards, author interview.
35 Barry Brown, author interview.
36 Ibid.
37 Pete Atkin, author interview.
38 Ibid.
39 Ibid.
40 Adrian Edwards, author interview.
41 Pete Atkin, author interview.
42 Ibid.
43 Clive James, *The Revolt of the Pendulum* (London: Picador, 2009).
44 Pete Atkin, author interview.
45 Barry Brown, author interview.
46 Ibid.
47 Ibid.
48 Ibid.
49 Ibid.
50 Adrian Edwards, author interview.
51 Ibid.
52 Ibid.
53 Ibid.
54 Ibid.
55 Ibid.
56 Ibid.
57 Ibid.
58 Ibid.
59 Mark Wing-Davey, author interview.
60 Ibid.
61 Ibid.
62 Ibid.

63 Ibid.
64 Ibid.
65 Ibid.
66 Simon Jones, author interview.
67 Mark Wing-Davey, author interview.
68 Simon Jones, author interview.
69 Hewison, *Footlights! A Hundred Years of Cambridge.*
70 Simon Jones, author interview.
71 Ibid.
72 Ibid.
73 Ibid.
74 Barry Brown, author interview.
75 Mark Wing-Davey, author interview.
76 Simon Jones, author interview.
77 Ibid.
78 Robert Rowe, author interview.
79 Ibid.
80 Ibid.
81 Ibid.
82 Simon Jones, author interview.
83 Adrian Edwards, author interview.
84 Robert Rowe, author interview.
85 Ibid.
86 Sarah Dunant, author interview.
87 Ibid.
88 Ibid.
89 Ibid.
90 Ibid.
91 Ibid.

Chapter 9: Norman Ruins

1 Simon Jones, author interview.
2 Ibid.
3 M. J. Simpson, *Hitchhiker, A Biography of Douglas Adams* (London: Justin Charles & Co., 2003).
4 Simon Jones, author interview.

5 Barry Brown, author interview.
6 Simon Jones, author interview.
7 Ibid.
8 Barry Brown, author interview.
9 Ibid.
10 Ibid.
11 Ibid.
12 Ibid.
13 Simon Jones, author interview.
14 Barry Brown, author interview.
15 Sarah Dunant, author interview.
16 Ibid.
17 Simon Jones, author interview.
18 Sarah Dunant, author interview.
19 Simon Jones, author interview.
20 Ibid.
21 Sarah Dunant, author interview.
22 Simon Jones, author interview.
23 Ibid.
24 Stephen Wyatt, author interview.
25 Ibid.
26 Ibid.
27 Ibid.
28 Simon Jones, author interview.
29 Stephen Wyatt, author interview.
30 Jon Canter, author interview.
31 Ibid.
32 Ibid.
33 Ibid.
34 Ibid.
35 Ibid.
36 Mary Allen, author interview.
37 Ibid.
38 Ibid.
39 Jon Canter, author interview.
40 Mary Allen, author interview.
41 Ibid.
42 John Lloyd, author interview.

43 Ibid.
44 Ibid.
45 Ibid.
46 Ibid.
47 Ibid.
48 Ibid.
49 Ibid.
50 Ibid.
51 Ibid.
52 Ibid.
53 Ibid.
54 Stephen Wyatt, author interview.
55 John Lloyd, author interview.
56 Ibid.
57 Jon Canter, author interview.
58 Mary Allen, author interview.
59 Ibid.
60 Jon Canter, author interview.
61 Ibid.
62 Ibid.
63 Ibid.
64 Graeme Garden, author interview.
65 John Lloyd, author interview.
66 Clive Anderson, author interview.
67 Ibid.
68 Ibid.
69 Clive Anderson, author interview.
70 Jon Canter, author interview.
71 Ibid.
72 Clive Anderson, author interview.
73 Jon Canter, author interview.
74 Clive Anderson, author interview.
75 Ibid.
76 Ibid.
77 Jon Canter, author interview.
78 Clive Anderson, author interview.
79 Jon Canter, author interview.

Chapter 10: A Kick in the Stalls

1. Clive Anderson, author interview.
2. Ibid.
3. Ibid.
4. Ibid.
5. Ibid.
6. Ibid.
7. Ibid.
8. John Lloyd, author interview.
9. Clive Anderson, author interview.
10. John Lloyd, author interview.
11. Chris Keightley, author interview.
12. Ibid.
13. Ibid.
14. Ibid.
15. Ibid.
16. Jimmy Mulville, author interview.
17. Ibid.
18. Ibid.
19. Ibid.
20. Ibid.
21. Jon Canter, author interview.
22. Jimmy Mulville, author interview.
23. Ibid.
24. Chris Keightley, author interview.
25. Ibid.
26. Ibid.
27. Neil Gaiman, *Don't Panic: Douglas Adams and The Hitchhiker's Guide to the Galaxy* (London: Titan Books, 2003).
28. Chris Keightley, author interview.
29. Jimmy Mulville, author interview.
30. Jon Canter, author interview.
31. Chris Keightley, author interview.
32. Ibid.
33. Ibid.
34. Jimmy Mulville, author interview.
35. Chris Keightley, author interview.

36 Jimmy Mulville, author interview.
37 Ibid.
38 Chris Keightley, author interview.
39 Ibid.
40 Jimmy Mulville, author interview.
41 Ibid.
42 Ibid.
43 Ibid.
44 Ibid.
45 Ibid.
46 Ibid.
47 Martin Bergman, author interview.
48 Jimmy Mulville, author interview.
49 Martin Bergman, author interview.
50 Ibid.
51 Ibid.
52 Chris Keightley, author interview.
53 Martin Bergman, author interview.
54 Jan Ravens, author interview.
55 Paul Shearer, author interview.
56 Jimmy Mulville, author interview.
57 Martin Bergman, author interview.
58 Ibid.
59 Ibid.
60 Ibid.

Chapter 11: The Cellar Tapes

1 Clive Anderson, author interview.
2 Ibid.
3 Ibid.
4 Ibid.
5 Ibid.
6 Jan Ravens, author interview.
7 Ibid.
8 Ibid.
9 Ibid.
10 Ibid.

11 Clive Anderson, author interview.
12 Jan Ravens, author interview.
13 Ibid.
14 Ibid.
15 Ibid.
16 Ibid.
17 Martin Bergman, author interview.
18 *Fry and Laurie Reunited*, [TV programme] Gold, 24 November 2010.
19 Martin Bergman, author interview.
20 Ibid.
21 Ibid.
22 Jan Ravens, author interview.
23 Ibid.
24 Ibid.
25 Ibid.
26 Ibid.
27 Ibid.
28 Ibid.
29 Ibid.
30 Ibid.
31 Ibid.
32 Ibid.
33 Ibid.
34 Ibid.
35 Paul Shearer, author interview.
36 Ibid.
37 Ibid.
38 Ibid.
39 Ibid.
40 Ibid.
41 Ibid.
42 Ibid.
43 Jan Ravens, author interview.
44 Ibid.
45 Ibid.
46 Paul Shearer, author interview.
47 Jan Ravens, author interview.
48 Ibid.

49 Paul Shearer, author interview.
50 Ibid.
51 Ibid.
52 Ibid.
53 Jan Ravens, author interview.
54 Paul Shearer, author interview.
55 Jan Ravens, author interview.
56 Paul Shearer, author interview.
57 Ibid.

Chapter 12: Hawaiian Cheese Party

1 Peter Bradshaw, author interview.
2 Neil Mullarkey, author interview.
3 Ibid.
4 Ibid.
5 Chris England, author interview.
6 Ibid.
7 Ibid.
8 Steve Punt, author interview.
9 Ibid.
10 Ibid.
11 Ibid.
12 Ibid.
13 Ibid.
14 Neil Mullarkey, author interview.
15 Ibid.
16 Ibid.
17 Ibid.
18 Nick Hancock, author interview.
19 Ibid.
20 Steve Punt, author interview.
21 Neil Mullarkey, author interview.
22 Ibid.
23 Ibid.
24 Ibid.
25 Nick Hancock, author interview.
26 Ibid.

27 Steve Punt, author interview.
28 Neil Mullarkey, author interview.
29 Chris England, author interview.
30 Ibid.
31 Ibid.
32 Ibid.
33 Steve Punt, author interview.
34 Nick Hancock, author interview.
35 Steve Punt, author interview.
36 Nick Hancock, author interview.
37 Ibid.
38 Steve Punt, author interview.
39 Christopher Luscombe, author interview.
40 Lucy Montgomery, author interview.
41 Nick Hancock, author interview.
42 Ibid.
43 Christopher Luscombe, author interview.
44 Ibid.
45 Ibid.
46 Ibid.
47 Ibid.
48 Ibid.
49 Ibid.
50 Ibid.
51 Ibid.
52 Ibid.
53 Ibid.
54 Nick Hancock, author interview.
55 Martin Knelman, *Mike's World: The Life of Mike Myers* (Firefly Books, 2003).
56 Steve Punt, author interview.
57 Christopher Luscombe, author interview.
58 Ibid.
59 Ibid.
60 Ibid.
61 Ibid.
62 Ibid.
63 Ibid.
64 Ibid.

65 Ibid.
66 Ibid.
67 Ibid.

Chapter 13: Another Fine Mess

1 David Baddiel, author interview.
2 Ibid.
3 Ibid.
4 Nick Hancock, author interview.
5 Peter Bradshaw, author interview.
6 David Baddiel, author interview.
7 Michael Marshall Smith, author interview.
8 David Baddiel, author interview.
9 Ibid.
10 Ibid.
11 Ibid.
12 Chris England, author interview.
13 Ibid.
14 Ibid.
15 Ibid.
16 Steve Punt, author interview.
17 Peter Bradshaw, author interview.
18 David Baddiel, author interview.
19 Christopher Luscombe, author interview.
20 Ibid.
21 Ibid.
22 Ibid.
23 Peter Bradshaw, author interview.
24 David Baddiel, author interview.
25 Ibid.
26 Ibid.
27 Christopher Luscombe, author interview.
28 Chris England, author interview.
29 David Baddiel, author interview.
30 Neil Mullarkey, author interview.
31 David Baddiel, author interview.
32 Ibid.

33 Ibid.
34 Ibid.
35 Ibid.
36 Peter Bradshaw, author interview.
37 Ibid.
38 Ibid.
39 Ibid.
40 Ibid.
41 Ibid.
42 Ibid.
43 Ibid.
44 Ibid.
45 Ibid.
46 Ibid.
47 Ibid.
48 Ibid.
49 Ibid.
50 Ibid.
51 David Baddiel, author interview.
52 Ibid.
53 Chris England, author interview.
54 Ibid.
55 Ibid.
56 Ibid.
57 Ibid.
58 David Baddiel, author interview.
59 Ibid.
60 Ibid.
61 Michael Marshall Smith, author interview.
62 Ibid.
63 Ibid.
64 Peter Bradshaw, author interview.
65 Michael Marshall Smith, author interview.
66 Ibid.
67 Ibid.
68 Peter Bradshaw, author interview.
69 Ibid.
70 Ibid.

71 Michael Marshall Smith, author interview.
72 Ibid.
73 Ibid.
74 Ibid.
75 Ibid.
76 Ibid.
77 Peter Bradshaw, author interview.
78 Ibid.
79 Ibid.
80 Ibid.
81 Ibid.
82 Ibid.
83 Ibid.
84 Simon Munnery, author interview.
85 Ibid.
86 Ibid.
87 Ibid.
88 Ibid.
89 Ibid.
90 Chris England, author interview.
91 Richard Crane, author interview.
92 Simon Munnery, author interview.
93 Ibid.
94 Ibid.
95 Ibid.
96 Ibid.
97 Ibid.
98 Ibid.
99 Jon Canter, author interview.

Chapter 14: Back and Beyond

1 Joel Jeske, author interview.
2 Ibid.
3 Ibid.
4 Henry Naylor, author interview.
5 Ibid.
6 Ibid.

7   Ibid.
8   Joel Jeske, author interview.
9   Ibid.
10 Ibid.
11 Ibid.
12 Ibid.
13 Anna Cottis, author interview.
14 Ibid.
15 Ibid.
16 Ibid.
17 Ibid.
18 Ibid.
19 Ibid.
20 Ibid.
21 Ibid.
22 Joel Jeske, author interview.
23 Ibid.
24 Ibid.
25 Ibid.
26 Ibid.
27 Ibid.
28 Ibid.
29 Ibid.
30 Ibid.
31 Ibid.
32 Henry Naylor, author interview.
33 Ibid.
34 Anna Cottis, author interview.
35 Ibid.
36 Henry Naylor, author interview.
37 Ibid.
38 Ibid.
39 Ibid.
40 Nicola Walker, author interview.
41 Ibid.
42 Ibid.
43 Ibid.
44 Ibid.

45 Ibid.
46 Ibid.
47 Ibid.
48 Ibid.
49 Ibid.
50 Henry Naylor, author interview.
51 Nicola Walker, author interview.
52 Ibid.
53 Henry Naylor, author interview.
54 Ibid.
55 Nicola Walker, author interview.
56 Ibid.
57 Henry Naylor, author interview.
58 Ibid.
59 Nicola Walker, author interview.
60 Ibid.
61 Ibid.
62 Ibid.
63 Ibid.
64 Ibid.
65 Mark Evans, author interview.
66 Ibid.
67 Ibid.
68 Ibid.
69 Ibid.
70 Ibid.
71 Ibid.
72 Ibid.
73 Ibid.
74 Ibid.
75 Ibid.
76 William Sutcliffe, author interview.
77 Ibid.
78 Ibid.
79 Ibid.
80 Ibid.
81 Ibid.
82 Ibid.
83 Ibid.

84 Mark Evans, author interview.
85 Ibid.
86 William Sutcliffe, author interview.

Chapter 15: Barracuda Jazz Option

1 Katie Breathwick, author interview.
2 Ibid.
3 Ibid.
4 Ibid.
5 Ibid.
6 Ibid.
7 Ibid.
8 Ibid.
9 Ibid.
10 James Bachman, author interview.
11 Ibid.
12 Ibid.
13 Ibid.
14 Ibid.
15 Ibid.
16 Katie Breathwick, author interview.
17 Ibid.
18 William Sutcliffe, author interview.
19 Katie Breathwick, author interview.
20 Ibid.
21 Ibid.
22 Ibid.
23 Ibid.
24 Ibid.
25 Ibid.
26 Ibid.
27 Ibid.
28 Ibid.
29 Ibid.
30 Lucy Montgomery, author interview.
31 Mark Evans, author interview.
32 Ibid.

33 Ibid.
34 James Bachman, author interview.
35 Lucy Montgomery, author interview.
36 James Bachman, author interview.
37 Ibid.
38 Katie Breathwick, author interview.
39 Ibid.
40 James Bachman, author interview.
41 Ibid.
42 Ibid.
43 Ibid.
44 David Mitchell, author interview.
45 Ibid.
46 Ibid.
47 Ibid.
48 Mark Evans, author interview.
49 James Bachman, author interview.
50 Ibid.
51 Ibid.
52 David Mitchell, author interview.
53 Matthew Holness, author interview.
54 Ibid.
55 Ibid.
56 Ibid.
57 Ibid.
58 Ibid.
59 Ibid.
60 David Mitchell, author interview.
61 James Bachman, author interview.
62 Ibid.
63 Matthew Holness, author interview.
64 Ibid.
65 Ibid.
66 Ibid.
67 Ibid.
68 David Mitchell, author interview.
69 Ibid.
70 Ibid.
71 Ibid.

72 Matthew Holness, author interview.
73 Ibid.
74 Ibid.
75 Ibid.
76 David Mitchell, author interview.
77 Ibid.
78 Ibid.
79 Ibid.
80 Matthew Holness, author interview.
81 Lucy Montgomery, author interview.
82 Ibid.
83 Ibid.
84 Ibid.
85 Ibid.
86 Ibid.
87 Ibid.
88 Matthew Holness, author interview.
89 Ibid.
90 Ibid.
91 Ibid.
92 David Mitchell, author interview.
93 Ibid.
94 Lucy Montgomery, author interview.
95 Ibid.
96 Ibid.
97 Ibid.
98 Matt Green, author interview.
99 Matthew Holness, author interview.

Chapter 16: Emotional Baggage

1 Matthew Holness, author interview.
2 Ibid.
3 Ibid.
4 Ibid.
5 Ibid.
6 Ibid.
7 Ibid.

8 Ibid.
9 Spencer Brown, author interview.
10 Ibid.
11 Ibid.
12 Ibid.
13 Ibid.
14 Ibid.
15 Ibid.
16 Ibid.
17 Ibid.
18 Ibid.
19 Barry Brown, author interview.
20 Spencer Brown, author interview.
21 Matt Green, author interview.
22 Ibid.
23 Ibid.
24 Ibid.
25 Ibid.
26 Ibid.
27 Ibid.
28 Naomi Kerbel, author interview.
29 Ibid.
30 Ibid.
31 Ibid.
32 Ibid.
33 Ibid.
34 Robin French, author interview.
35 Ibid.
36 Ibid.
37 Ibid.
38 Ibid.
39 Ibid.
40 Ibid.
41 Ibid.
42 Naomi Kerbel, author interview.
43 Matt Green, author interview.
44 Robin French, author interview.
45 Matt Green, author interview.
46 Ibid.

47 Ibid.
48 Matthew Holness, author interview.
49 Matt Green, author interview.
50 Ibid.
51 Ibid.
52 John Finnemore, author interview.
53 Ibid.
54 Ibid.
55 Ibid.
56 Ibid.
57 Ibid.
58 Ibid.
59 Ibid.
60 Ibid.
61 Ibid.
62 Ibid.

Chapter 17: Far Too Happy

1 Spencer Brown, author interview.
2 Matt Green, author interview.
3 Sophie Winkleman, author interview.
4 Ibid.
5 Ibid.
6 Ibid.
7 Ibid.
8 Ibid.
9 Ibid.
10 Ibid.
11 Ibid.
12 Ibid.
13 Ibid.
14 Ibid.
15 Ibid.
16 Tom Bell, author interview.
17 Ibid.
18 Ibid.
19 Ibid.

20 Ibid.
21 Ibid.
22 Ibid.
23 Ibid.
24 Ibid.
25 Ibid.
26 Ruth Pickett, author interview.
27 Ibid.
28 Ibid.
29 Ibid.
30 Ibid.
31 Tom Bell, author interview.
32 Ruth Pickett, author interview.
33 Ibid.
34 Ibid.
35 Ibid.
36 Stefan Golaszewski, author interview.
37 Ibid.
38 Ibid.
39 Ibid.
40 Ibid.
41 Ibid.
42 Ibid.
43 Ibid.
44 Ibid.
45 Emily Howes, author interview.
46 Ibid.
47 Ibid.
48 Ibid.
49 Ibid.
50 William Sutcliffe, author interview.
51 Emily Howes, author interview.
52 Stefan Golaszewski, author interview.
53 Helen Cripps, author interview.
54 Ibid.
55 Ibid.
56 Ibid.
57 Ibid.
58 Ibid.

59 Ibid.
60 Ibid.
61 Ibid.
62 Ibid.
63 Matt Green, author interview.
64 Helen Cripps, author interview.
65 Ibid.
66 Ibid.
67 Ibid.
68 Henry Eliot, author interview.
69 Ibid.
70 Ibid.
71 Ibid.
72 Ibid.
73 Ibid.
74 Ibid.
75 Helen Cripps, author interview.
76 Henry Eliot, author interview.
77 Ibid.
78 Ibid.

Chapter 18: Devils

1 Amy Hoggart, author interview.
2 Ibid.
3 Ibid.
4 Ibid.
5 Ibid.
6 Ibid.
7 Ibid.
8 Ibid.
9 Ibid.
10 Ibid.
11 Ibid.
12 Ibid.
13 Ibid.
14 Ibid.
15 Ibid.

16 Ibid.
17 Abi Tedder, author interview.
18 Ibid.
19 Ibid.
20 Ibid.
21 Ibid.
22 Ibid.
23 Ibid.
24 Ibid.
25 Ibid.
26 Ibid.
27 Ibid.
28 Ibid.
29 Ibid.
30 Ibid.
31 Ibid.
32 Ben Ashenden, author interview.
33 Ibid.
34 Ibid.
35 Alexander Owen, author interview.
36 Ben Ashenden, author interview.
37 Alexander Owen, author interview.
38 Ben Ashenden, author interview.
39 Ibid.
40 Ibid.
41 Ibid.
42 Alexander Owen, author interview.
43 Ibid.
44 Ibid.
45 Ben Ashenden, author interview.
46 Abi Tedder, author interview.
47 Ibid.
48 Ibid.
49 Ibid.
50 Alex MacKeith, author interview.
51 Ibid.
52 Ibid.
53 Ibid.

54 Ibid.
55 Ibid.
56 Archie Henderson, author interview.
57 Ibid.
58 Ibid.
59 Ibid.
60 Ibid.
61 Ibid.
62 Ibid.
63 Ibid.
64 Ibid.
65 Jordan Mitchell, author interview.
66 Ibid.
67 Ibid.
68 Ibid.
69 Ibid.
70 Ibid.
71 Ibid.
72 Ibid.
73 Ibid.
74 Ibid.
75 Ibid.
76 Ibid.
77 Ibid.
78 Ibid.
79 John Tothill, author interview.
80 Ibid.
81 Ibid.
82 Ibid.
83 Ibid.
84 Ibid.
85 Ibid.
86 Ibid.
87 Ibid.
88 Ibid.
89 Ibid.
90 Ibid.
91 Ibid.

Chapter 19: Are We There Yet?

1 Hasan Al-Habib, author interview.
2 Ibid.
3 Ibid.
4 Ibid.
5 Ibid.
6 Ibid.
7 Ibid.
8 Ibid.
9 Ibid.
10 Ibid.
11 Ibid.
12 Ibid.
13 Ash Weir, author interview.
14 Ibid.
15 Ibid.
16 Ibid.
17 Ibid.
18 Ibid.
19 Ibid.
20 Ibid.
21 Ibid.
22 Angela Channell, author interview.
23 Ibid.
24 Ibid.
25 Ibid.
26 Ibid.
27 Ibid.
28 Ibid.
29 Ibid.
30 Ibid.
31 Ibid.
32 Ibid.
33 Jade Franks, author interview.
34 Ibid.
35 Angela Channell, author interview.
36 Jade Franks, author interview.
37 Ibid.

38. Ibid.
39. Ibid.
40. Ibid.
41. Ibid.
42. Ibid.
43. Ibid.
44. Ibid.
45. Ibid.
46. Ibid.
47. Adam Al-janabi, author interview.
48. Ibid.
49. Ibid.
50. Ibid.
51. Ibid.
52. Ibid.
53. Ibid.
54. Ibid.
55. Ibid.
56. Ibid.
57. Ibid.
58. Ibid.
59. Ibid.
60. Izzie H-P, author interview.
61. Ibid.
62. Ibid.
63. Ibid.
64. Ibid.
65. Ibid.
66. Ibid.
67. Ibid.
68. Ibid.
69. Ibid.
70. Margaret Saunderson, author interview.
71. Jade Franks, author interview.
72. Margaret Saunderson, author interview.
73. Ibid.
74. Ibid.
75. Ibid.
76. Ibid.

77 Izzie H-P, author interview.
78 Jade Franks, author interview.
79 Ibid.
80 Margaret Saunderson, author interview.

Chapter 20: Gone with the Clappers

1 James Bachman, author interview.
2 Graeme Garden, author interview.
3 Ibid.
4 Jan Ravens, author interview.
5 Robin French, author interview.
6 Mark Evans, author interview.
7 Matt Green, author interview.
8 John Tothill, author interview.
9 Jade Franks, author interview.
10 Archie Henderson, author interview.
11 Margaret Saunderson, author interview.
12 Katie Breathwick, author interview.
13 David Mitchell, author interview.
14 Ibid.

BIBLIOGRAPHY

Cook, Lin (ed.). *Peter Cook Remembered*. London: Arrow, 1997.
Drummond, John. *Tainted by Experience*. London: Faber & Faber, 2001.
Frischauer, Willi. *Will You Welcome Now . . . David Frost*. New York: Hawthorn Books, 1971.
Frost, David. *An Autobiography, Part One: From Congregations to Audiences Pt 1*. London: HarperCollins, 1993.
Hewison, Robert. *Footlights! A Hundred Years of Cambridge Comedy*. London: Methuen, 1983.
James, Clive. *May Week Was in June*. London: Random House, 1990.
Oddie, Bill. *One Flew into the Cuckoo's Egg: My Autobiography*. London: Hodder & Stoughton, 2008
Paskin, Barbra. *Dudley Moore: The Authorised Biography*. London: Sidgwick & Jackson, 1997.
Simpson, M. J. *Hitchhiker: A Biography of Douglas Adams*. London: Hodder & Stoughton, 2003.
Vickers, Hugo. *Cecil Beaton: The Authorised Biography*. London: Phoenix Press, 2002.
White, Michael. *Empty Seats*. London: Hamish Hamilton, 1984.
Wilmut, Roger (ed.). *The Complete Beyond the Fringe*. London: Methuen, 1987.

INDEX

Adams, Douglas, 1, 79, 80, 83, 87, 89, 95, 96, 101
Aers, Lydia, 177
Adams, Will, 79, 87, 89
Akushie, Keith, 198, 201
Al-Habib, Hasan, 213, 214, 215, 216, 224
Al-Janabi, Adam, 224, 225
Allen, Mary, 84, 85, 86, 87
Amazons (revue), 149
Anderson, Clive, 85, 88–89, 90, 91–92, 93, 94, 95, 98, 101, 102
Armstrong, Alexander, 1
Ashenden, Ben, 201–202, 203, 204
Atkin, Pete, 34, 66, 67–68, 69, 70, 71, 75, 99
Atkins, Robert, 41
Atkinson, Rowan, 50, 98, 109
Ayoade, Richard, 1, 172, 173, 174, 175, 177, 188, 214

Baalbaki, Danny, 216
Bachman, James, 156–157, 160, 161–162, 163, 165, 231
Baddiel, David, 125, 126, 127, 128, 129, 130, 131, 132, 134, 138, 139, 153
Baker, Kevin, 179, 180, 181
Baker, Richard, 18
Nick Ball, 149, 151
Banks, Morwenna, 111, 114
Barclay, Humphrey, 40, 41, 42, 45, 47, 50, 51, 52, 53, 55, 57
Basden, Tom, 189, 204
Bassett, John, 3
Batey, Joey, 202
Bathurst, Robert, 94, 101, 103, 110
Beach, Jim, 56
Beaton, Cecil, 13

Beaumont, Geoffrey, 19
Beaumont, Robin, 23
Beecher, Tony, 24
Bell, Tom, 185, 186, 187
Bellwood, Peter, 32, 33, 34, 39
Bengo, Anna, 170
Bennett, Alan, 3, 4, 6
Benton, Robert, 83, 86
Bergman, Martin, 97, 99, 101, 103, 104, 109, 110, 116, 117
Bevan, Georgie, 156, 157, 158
Beyond the Fringe, 1, 4, 5, 6, 24, 25, 26, 33, 35, 41, 43, 47, 48, 49, 50, 93, 122, 141
Bicknell, Will, 217
Bird, John, 31, 32, 33, 39, 40
Birdsall, Timothy, 32
Bird, Simon, 186, 188, 191, 202
Blackwood, Commander, 88, 96, 174
Bonham, Alex, 175
Booker, Christopher, 35
Bourne, James, 113
Bradshaw, Peter, 111, 126, 128, 129, 130–131, 135–136, 137, 138
Branch, Tony, 39
Breathwick, Katie, 155–156, 157, 158–159, 160–161, 232
Breen, Phil, 183, 184
Brenman, Owen, 98
Bricusse, Leslie, 23, 24, 25, 26
Brierley, Michael, 155
Bron, Eleanor, 33, 35, 40, 59
Brooke-Taylor, Tim, 6, 41, 42, 45, 46, 47, 48, 50, 51, 52, 57, 60
Brown, Barry, 65, 66, 69, 70, 71–72, 73, 75, 79–80, 174
Brown, Spencer, 172, 173, 174, 183
Browning, Oscar, 9
Buckley, Geoffrey, 142, 143

INDEX

Buckman, Robert, 72, 99
Buffery, Anthony, 47, 48, 50
Buhr, Sheila, 58
Burgess, Nigel, 16
Burnaby, Dave, 10
Burridge, Richard, 85

Cambridge: colleges,
  Caius, 11, 23
  Christ's, 7, 27, 94, 153, 172, 175
  Churchill, 84
  Clare, 23, 84
  Corpus Christi, 7, 16, 179, 186, 213
  Downing, 28, 37, 41, 142
  Emmanuel, 21, 22, 27, 38, 50, 94, 98, 99, 154, 156, 186
  Fitzwilliam, 209
  Girton, 28, 42, 56, 200
  Homerton, 66, 102, 114, 160, 191
  Jesus, 18, 56, 61, 62, 92, 120
  King's, 9, 10, 19, 31, 39, 84, 135, 143, 198, 206
  Magdalene, 12, 26, 27, 75, 176, 194
  Newnham, 33, 42, 60, 78, 103, 149, 155
  New Hall (Murray Edwards college), 107, 147, 148, 151
  Pembroke, 31, 37, 41, 42, 47, 52, 111, 112, 123, 131
  Peterhouse, 103, 164, 180
  Queens', 27, 52, 183
  Robinson, 111, 203, 215
  St Catharine's, 26, 27, 32, 52, 112, 149, 172, 186
  St Edmund's, 221
  St John's, 17, 22, 27, 66, 72, 79, 87, 218
  Selwyn, 88, 98, 101, 106, 177
  Trinity, 9, 19, 27, 28, 65, 72, 82, 84, 85, 97, 138
  Trinity Hall, 75
Cambridge Footlight Pantomimes:
  Aladdin, 7, 8, 75, 103, 126
  Alice In Wonderland, 187
  Babes In the Wood, 91
  Cinderella, 76, 87, 91, 104, 160, 168
  Faust, 194
  Peter Pan, 160

  Pied Piper, The, 201
  Rapunzel, 228
  Robin Hood, 126, 134, 216, 221
  Robinson Crusoe, 94
  Sherlock Holmes, 179
  Sinbad, 179
  Sleeping Beauty, 221
  Snow White, 94, 167, 168
  Three Musketeers, The, 134
Cambridge: Periodicals
  Cambridge Review, 7, 8, 9, 13, 14, 24, 29
  Cambridge Evening News, 13, 80, 102
  Granta, 8, 13, 15, 28, 32, 53
  Varsity, 16, 21, 28, 32, 94
Cambridge Footlight premises and venues:
  Bridge Street, 9
  Corn Exchange Street, 9, 10, 11
  Dorothy café, 18, 32
  Falcon Yard, 34, 38, 40, 53, 59, 60, 67, 75, 81, 82, 99, 151, 168
  Sidney Street, 8
  Student Union, Round Church Street, 99, 141, 168, 173, 178, 179
Cambridge Footlight revues:
  Absurd Persons Plural, 149, 150, 151
  All The Vogue, 13
  Alma Mater, 8
  Always In June, 19
  And Don't Come Back, 153
  Another Fine Mess, 128, 129, 130, 132, 133
  Anything May, 27, 28
  Are We There Yet?, 224, 225
  Back And Beyond, 142, 146
  Backwards Into the Limelight, 136
  Barracuda Jazz Option, 160, 161, 162, 163
  Between a Rock and a Hard Place, 175
  Between The Lines, 26, 38
  Beyond A Joke, 190
  Bombastes Furioso, 7, 8
  Bumps, 13
  Cabbages And Kings, 22

INDEX

Cambridge Underground, 151, 152, 155
Canada, 205
Cellar Tapes, The, 105, 107, 108, 109, 117, 118, 121, 134, 175, 183
Cheer-Oh-Cambridge, 11, 42, 60, 83
Chox, 87, 88, 89, 90, 92
Clump of Plinths, A (also Cambridge Circus), 6, 45, 46, 47, 48, 49, 51, 55, 56, 62, 63, 69, 77, 105, 121, 141
Devils, 198, 199, 201
Double Take, 41, 42, 43
Dream Sequence, 211
Electric Voodoo, 104
Emotional Baggage, 172, 173, 174
Every Packet Carries a Government Health Warning, 82, 83, 84, 85, 86, 87, 89
Fall From Grace, 163, 165, 166, 169
Far Too Happy, 183, 184, 185
Flash in the Cam, A, 21
Fools Rush In, 72, 73
Footlights Comic Annual, 73, 74, 82
Freshman, The, 10
Full Swing, 17
Gone With the Clappers, 75, 76, 77
Good For You, 202
Hawaiian Cheese Party, 114, 115, 116, 117, 118, 121, 133
His Little Trip, 11
I Thought I Saw It Move, 39
Kick In the Stalls, A, 95, 96
La Vie Cambridgienne, 18
Lagoon, 209, 210
Last Laugh, The, 32, 33, 128
Laughing At Love, 14, 15
Look Alive, 218, 219
Love Handles, 207
May Fever, 13
Mixture Remixed, The, 9
My Girl Herbert, 59
New Dean, The, 10
Niceties. 191, 193, 194
Nightcap, 103, 104

No More Women, 15
Non-Sexual Kissing, 189, 190
Norman Ruins, 80, 81, 82
Oriental Trip, The, 10
Out of the Blue, 24, 25, 27
Paradise Mislaid, 92, 95
Perfect Strangers, 204, 205
Pillow Talk, 217, 218
Please Tell Others, 14
Pop Goes Mrs Jessop, 35, 39, 52
Premises Premises, 111, 112, 113, 118
Pretty Little Panic, 203, 204
Rainbow Stranglers, 167, 169, 174
Real Feelings, 205
Search Continues, The, 226
Sensible Haircut, 179, 180
Sham Duke, The, 9
Sheep Go Bare, 139, 140
Some Wood and a Pie, 156, 157, 158
Springs To Mind, 29
Stage Fright, 101, 102
Story So Far, The, 118, 120, 121, 127
Stuff What Dreams Are Made Of, 53, 55, 56, 57
Supernatural Gas, 66, 67, 69
Tag, 97, 98
This Time We Have a Dog, 228
This Way Out, 60, 61, 62, 63, 64
This Way Up, 176, 177
Today Of All Days, 185, 187
Topical Heatwave, 122, 127
Turn Over a New Leaf, 16
Turns Of the Century, 69, 70, 71, 74, 82, 83
Uncle Joe at Cambridge, 8
Under The Blue, Blue Moon, 190
Varsity BC, The, 10
Wham Bam, 193, 194, 195, 197
Wishful Thinking, 201, 204
Zounds, 28, 29, 33
Cambridge: Societies
    ADC (Amateur Dramatic club), 13, 21, 23, 47, 52, 73, 75, 81, 90, 94, 111, 183

INDEX

CULES (Cambridge University Light Entertainment Society) 51, 56, 79, 106, 113, 119, 129
Marlowe Society, 13, 18, 41, 61, 62, 73, 88, 102, 148, 202, 210
Pitt Club, 29
Union Society, 9
Cambridge: Theatres
  ADC Theatre, 99, 102, 105, 121, 137, 138, 142, 149, 166, 179, 185, 186, 188, 198, 201, 203, 207, 212, 213, 219, 225, 227, 229
  Arts Theatre, 4, 16, 17, 33, 34, 38, 68, 70, 75, 82, 87, 88, 89, 97, 104, 111, 115, 123, 150, 166, 174, 179, 188, 220
  St Andrews' Hall, 7
  Theatre Royal, 8
Cameron, John, 53, 55, 56, 57, 58–59, 60, 63
Canter, Jon, 83–84, 85, 86, 87, 88, 89, 90, 94, 95, 140
Chalmers, Ali, 168
Channell, Angela, 218, 219, 220, 221
Chapman, Graham, 1, 6, 38, 39, 41, 43, 48, 57, 60, 89, 95
Checkley, Tim, 203
Cheeke, Stephen, 138, 140
Cheng, Ken, 215
Churney, Russell, 128
Clarke, Gina, 149
Cleese, John, 1, 6, 37, 38, 39, 40, 41, 42, 43, 45, 46, 47, 48, 50, 52, 53, 60, 70, 79, 87, 98, 101, 117, 128, 130, 134, 193, 203
Codron, Michael, 27, 33
Cohen, Sacha Baron, 153, 162
Colman, Olivia, 160
Comedy Store, 207, 212
Cook, Peter, 1, 3, 4, 5, 6, 31, 32, 33, 34, 35, 39, 40, 41, 45, 69, 77, 83, 98, 101, 104, 112, 113, 117, 119, 125, 127, 134, 141, 164, 193
Cook, Wendy, 40
Cooke, Alistair, 33
Coslett, Meg, 217
Cottis, Anna, 143, 144–145, 146

Cotton, Morten Henry, 7, 8
Courtneidge, Cicely, 11, 72
Courtneidge, Robert, 11
Covington, Julie, 66, 67, 69, 70, 75
Crane, Richard, 48, 58, 61, 62–63, 64, 65, 139
Cranks (revue), 27, 28
Crew, Kathryn, 121
Cripps, Helen, 191, 192–193, 194–195

Daughters of England (revue), 148
Davies, Jot, 189
Davies, Russell, 72
Day Today, The, 171, 177, 179
Dennis, Hugh, 121, 127
Dickinson, David, 113
Donaldson, William, 33
Drummond, John, 25, 63
Duchene, Kate, 111
Duguid, Hilary, 105
Dunant, Sarah, 77, 78, 80, 81
Dwyer, Penny, 106, 109

Eade, Peter, 17
Eady, David, 18
Edinburgh Festival, 1, 3, 4, 43, 51, 52, 63, 67, 68, 69, 70, 72, 73, 77, 81, 85, 86, 90, 96, 97, 99, 103, 104, 109, 113, 116, 117, 122, 127, 130, 132, 133, 134, 136, 137, 140, 145, 146, 151, 152, 154, 158, 162, 164, 167, 170, 174, 175, 176, 177, 178, 181, 183, 184, 185, 186, 187, 190, 193, 195, 198, 201, 202, 203, 204, 205, 206, 208, 216, 217, 219, 223, 225, 227, 228
Edwards, Adrian, 65–66, 67, 69, 70, 72, 73, 76
Edwards, Jimmy, 17, 18
Eliot, Henry, 193–194, 195
Elizabeth II, 129
Elton, Ben, 69, 108, 125, 132
England, Chris, 112, 114, 117, 127, 128, 129, 133, 134, 138
Establishment Club, 40, 143
Evans, Mark, 151, 152, 153, 154, 156, 159, 160, 162, 163, 231
Evans, Tom, 201

INDEX

Ewins, Rory, 156
Eyre, Richard, 52

Fellowes, Julian, 75
Fiddaman, Mark, 200, 204
Finnemore, John, 179, 180–181
Firth, Peter, 21, 22, 23
Firth, Tim, 135, 136
Forbes, Jason, 204
Fortune, John, 39, 40, 47
Foster, Michael, 140
Franks, Jade, 220, 221, 222, 223, 227, 229, 232
Frayn, Michael, 4–5, 25, 27, 28–29, 39, 194
French, Robin, 176–177, 178, 179, 231
Frith, Fred, 74
Frost, David, 32, 34, 35, 38, 39, 40, 45, 47, 50
Fry, Stephen, 1, 35, 105, 106, 107, 108, 110, 111, 112, 130, 180, 193, 199, 210, 219
Furshpan, Katy, 128

Gamble, Ed, 197, 198
Garden, Graeme, 40, 48, 51–52, 53, 55, 56, 57, 58, 62, 88, 119, 231
Gascoigne, Bamber, 27, 33, 55, 194
Gaster, Dan, 154, 155
Ghosh, Tiani, 191
Giedroyc, Mel, 1, 139
Gilliam, Terry, 50
Golaszewski, Stefan, 188–189, 190, 204
Gold, Sarah, 147, 149
Golson, Nick, 125, 126, 127, 129, 130, 132
Gooderson, David, 32, 45, 47, 48, 52–53, 55, 57, 58
The Goodies, 1, 6, 41, 51, 111, 141, 151, 156
Goodman, Lizbeth, 148, 149
Gowers, Patrick, 32, 33
Gray, Adrian, 207
Gray, Emily, 149
Green, Matt, 170, 174, 175–176, 178, 179, 180, 183, 186, 193, 232
Grigor, Sarah, 149

Greer, Germaine, 58, 59, 60, 62, 65, 82, 113, 159
Grenfell, Joyce, 59, 71
Gutteridge, Bill, 72, 73
Gutteridge, Tom, 117

Hackett, Leila, 168
Hall, Peter, 23, 26
Hamer, Robert, 16
Hancock, Nick, 63, 114, 115, 116, 117–118, 119, 120, 121, 125, 127
Hare, David, 69
Harley, Robert, 111, 114
Hartill, Charlie, 158
Hartnell, Norman, 12, 13, 18
Hatch, David, 47, 86, 92, 113
Heber-Percy, Sue, 42, 56, 57, 58
Helpmann, Robert, 16
Henderson, Archie, 206, 207, 208, 232
Hendra, Tony, 43
Hewett, Tamsin, 179
Hewison, Robert, 117, 173
Hickin, Henry Arthur, 7, 8
Hickish, James, 149, 151
Hill, Ronald, 14
Hitch-Hiker's Guide to the Galaxy, 74, 79, 83, 87, 92, 134
Hoggart, Amy, 197, 198–199
Hollander, Tom, 139, 140
Holness, Matthew, 163, 164, 165, 166, 167, 168, 169, 170, 171–172, 173, 178, 188, 232
Horne, Alex, 185, 186
Hough, Felicity, 56, 57, 58
Howell, David, 32
Howes, Emily, 189, 190
Hulbert, Claude, 11, 18
Hulbert, Jack, 11, 72, 127
Hurok, Sol, 49–50
Hurran, Liz, 160
Hytner, Nicholas, 76, 97
Hytner, Richard, 106

Idle, Eric, 1, 5, 41, 50, 52, 55, 56, 57, 58, 60, 61, 62, 66, 172
I'm Sorry I'll Read That Again, 48, 50, 57, 77, 85, 194
Izzie H-P, 225, 226–227, 228, 229, 231

James, Clive, 38, 59, 61, 65, 66, 67, 68, 69, 70, 71, 72, 73, 74, 83, 99
James-Moore, Jonathan, 67, 73
Jaspers, Ed, 183, 184
Jeffrey, Peter, 19
Jenkins, Dai, 142
Jeske, Joel, 141, 142, 143, 145–146
Johnson, Daran, 201
Jones, Ann, 28
Jones, Griff Rhys, 83, 88, 91, 92, 95, 96, 97, 98, 99, 101, 102, 128, 145, 163
Jones, Simon, 74, 75, 76, 79, 80, 81, 82, 83
Joseph, Stephen, 18

Kakkar, Saurabh, 148
Kamil, Nadia, 191
Keane, Ruby, 215, 218
Keightley, Chris, 92, 93, 94, 95–96, 99
Kendall, Jo, 47
Kenyon, Roland, 142, 146
Kerbel, Naomi, 176, 178,
Key, Tim, 183, 184, 189, 204, 218
Lord Killanin, 16
King, Paul, 186

Langdon, Donald, 31
Laoye, Adedamola, 222
Latimer, Hugh, 16
Laurie, Hugh, 1, 103, 104, 105, 106, 107–108, 109, 110, 111, 112, 219
Lawrence, Adam, 204
Lawrence, Gertrude, 11
Lee, Anna, 15
Lennard, Jonny, 204
Levene, Simon, 91
Levin, Bernard, 4, 26, 49
Levy, Marianne, 179
Lillie, Beatrice, 11, 25
Limb, Sue, 81
Liston, Ben, 128, 130
Lloyd, John, 84, 85–86, 88, 92, 101
Lord Chamberlain, 29, 40, 63
Lowry, Malcolm, 15
Luard, Nicholas, 40

Luscombe, Christopher, 118, 119, 120, 121, 122, 123, 128–129
Lynn, Jonathan, 49, 53, 57, 99, 224

MacAskill, Day, 183, 184
Macdonald, Graeme, 28
MacKeith, Alex, 205, 206
McBurney, Simon, 103, 104
McCloud, Kevin, 107
McCrystal, Cal, 174, 176, 177, 180
McEwen, Rory, 26
McGivern, Geoffrey, 88, 92
McGrath, Rory, 94, 98, 99, 101, 104, 108
Magliano, Ania, 218
Marber, Brian, 26
Margolyes, Miriam, 42, 47, 56, 59
Marlow, Toby, 217
Maschwitz, Eric, 12
Massey, Daniel, 27
Mayer, Andy, 38, 56, 59, 62, 63, 64, 65
Mazer, Dan, 156, 157, 160, 162
Melia, Joe, 28, 29, 33
Millar, Ronald, 17
Miller, Ben, 149, 150, 151, 152
Miller, Jonathan, 1, 3, 4, 6, 25, 26, 27, 38, 45, 101
Mitchell, David, 1, 162–163, 164–165, 166, 167, 168, 169–170, 171, 173, 188, 204, 232, 233
Jordan Mitchell, 208, 209, 210
Mohammed, Nick, 189, 190, 198
Monro, Harold, 10
Montgomery, Lucy, 118, 159, 160, 168, 169, 170, 171
Monty Python, 1, 6, 41, 77, 83, 93, 97, 108, 111, 117, 141, 151, 156, 164, 180, 191, 226
Moore, Dudley, 1, 3, 4, 6, 40, 67
Morahan, Rebecca, 172
Morris, Chris, 172, 173, 175, 177, 180
Morris, James, 183, 189
Morris, Victoria, 179
Morrey, Beth, 177
Moss, Lucy, 217
Mulcahy, Dorothy, 28
Mullarkey, Neil, 111, 113, 114, 115, 116–117, 120, 121, 130, 159, 186

INDEX

Mulville, Jimmy, 93, 94, 95, 96, 97–98, 99, 102, 108
Munnery, Simon, 138, 139–140
Murdoch, Richard, 13, 128
Murphy, Maeve, 144
Myers, Mike, 120, 121, 186

Naylor, Henry, 141, 142, 143, 144, 146, 147, 148–149, 150, 151, 159
Nicholson, Brynsley, 11
Nobbs, David, 29
Novellie, Pierre, 204
Nunn, Trevor, 41, 42, 52

Oddie, Bill, 5, 6, 34, 37, 38, 41, 42, 45, 46–47, 48, 49–50, 51, 52, 53, 55, 57, 58, 60
The Office, 189, 192, 193, 201, 204
O'Grady, Anna, 192
Oliver, John, 172, 173, 174, 175, 177
O'Neill, Finnian, 176
Orders, D'Arcy, 18
Osborne, Will, 111
Outram, Lance, 8
Owen, Alexander, 202, 203, 204

Palmer, Sarah, 102, 103
Parker, Charles, 18
Parnaby, Bert, 76
Parsons, Andy, 141, 142, 146, 149, 150
Patten, Daniel, 227
Pattie, Geoffrey, 32, 33
Pattinson, Charlie, 121
Peart, Kirsty, 147
Perkins, Sue, 1, 147, 148, 150, 151, 155
Perkins, Geoffrey, 88, 90
Perrier Award, 109, 183, 184
Sarah, Phelps, 151
Phipps, Simon, 18, 19
Pickett, Ruth, 186, 187, 188
Pollitt, Herbert Charles, 8, 9, 12
Ponsonby, Robert, 3
Porter, Harry, 55, 58, 66, 72, 95, 98, 99, 101, 117, 120, 127, 128, 147, 159, 161, 168, 172, 186, 188, 207, 209
Portillo, Michael, 85

Potts, George, 204
Powell, Emma, 204
Powell, Owen, 179, 183
Prince Charles, 65, 66, 81
Prince Edward, 120, 128, 129
Princess Margaret, 19, 26, 129
Private Eye, 32, 35, 40
Punt, Steve, 112–113, 115, 116, 117, 118, 121, 127, 128

Raphael, Frederic, 19, 22, 23, 24, 25, 26
Ravens, Jan, 99, 102, 103, 104, 105, 106, 107, 108, 109, 121, 155, 231
Rawlinson, Peter, 17
Rhodes, William Barnes, 7
Riley, Pete, 198
Roberts, Al, 201
Roberts, John Luke, 194
Robinson, Albert, 15
Rose, Teddy, 203
Rottenburg, Henry, 10, 11, 16
Rowe, Robert, 76–77
Rubens, Paul, 10
Rylands, George, 16

Saunderson, Margaret, 227, 228, 229, 232
Sayle, Alexei, 108, 125, 127, 130
Scobie, Pam, 84
Scott, Maggie, 66, 70
Scott, Tim, 135
Searle, Ronald, 25
Second City Comedy Club, 203, 205, 208, 217, 225
Seghatchian, Tanya, 136, 147
Shaffer, Peter, 19
Share My Lettuce (revue), 27
Sharpe, Will, 193, 194, 195
Shearer, Paul, 99, 106, 107, 108–109, 110
Shepherd, Vicky, 172
Sherrin, Ned, 39
Slade, Adrian, 31, 32
Slade, Julian, 19, 40
Slattery, Tony, 106, 109, 111, 112, 188
Smith, Ali, 149

Smith, Jerome, 172, 173
Smith, Martin, 79, 87, 89
Smith, Mel, 86, 90
Smith, Michael Marshall, 126–127, 134, 137
Smith, Mike, 135
Solemani, Sarah, 187, 190
Stanley, Tamsin, 155, 156
Stevens, Dan, 187
Strachan, Geoffrey, 26–27, 29
Stuart-Clark, Chris, 37–38, 39, 47, 48, 49, 53
Sutcliffe, William, 153, 154, 157, 158, 190
Sweet, Jonny, 189, 190, 202
Swinton, Tilda, 106
Sylla, Patrick, 216
Symons, Neil, 114
Syms, Richard, 60, 61, 63, 64, 65

Tedder, Abi, 199, 200–201, 204, 205
That Was the Week That Was, 32, 39, 40, 42, 47
Thomas, Crispin, 90, 104
Thomas, Huw, 159
Thomas, Lloyd, 189
Thomas, Richard, 135
Thompson, Emma, 1, 98, 103, 104, 105, 106, 107, 108, 110, 112, 147, 155, 160, 176, 183
Thomson, Richard, 174, 176, 178
Thorn, Steve, 77
Thorogood, Robert, 155, 156, 163
Toksvig, Sandi, 104, 105
Tomalin, Claire, 194
Tonge, Jane, 149
Tothill, John, 210, 211–212, 214, 217, 232
Tranchell, Peter, 19
Turner, Richard, 111
Tynan, Kenneth, 4, 25, 29

Ullett, Nick, 43

Vandyck, William, 135, 136
Venable, Joe, 221

Wakefield, Ralph, 210
Walker, Nicola, 147, 148, 149–150, 151
Wang, Phil, 204, 214
Warman, Mark, 114
Warrender, Harold, 13
Waters, Naomi, 15
Watson, Hilary, 58
Watson, Mark, 183, 184, 186, 189
Webb, Robert, 1, 6, 160, 161, 162, 164, 168, 169, 188, 213, 232
Weeks, Ed, 179, 186, 187
Weir, Ash, 216, 217, 218
Wellings, Bob, 28
Wells, H. G., 13
Westmore, Michael, 18
White, Michael, 48, 49, 63, 89
Wickham, Chris, 142, 143
Wilde, Oscar, 8
Williams, Liam, 201
Williams, Raymond, 64
Williams, Tom, 197
Wilson, Dennis Main, 89, 109
Wing-Davey, Mark, 73, 74, 75
Winkleman, Sophie, 183, 184–185
Wolfson, Paul, 77, 81
Wolstencroft, David, 153, 154
Woman's Hour (revue), 104–105
Wood, Nick, 142
Wood, Sarah, 149
Wood, Victoria, 99, 179
Woodthorpe, Peter, 26
Wyatt, Stephen, 76, 82, 83, 85, 86

The Young Ones, 108, 118, 134, 141
Young, Lucien, 200, 203
Young, Terence, 16